MEGA-PROJECTS

MEGA-PROJECTS

The Changing Politics of Urban Public Investment

Alan Altshuler
David Luberoff

BROOKINGS INSTITUTION PRESS
Washington, D.C.

LINCOLN INSTITUTE OF LAND POLICY
Cambridge, Massachusetts

Library of Congress Cataloging-in-Publication data
Altshuler, Alan A., 1936–
  Mega-projects : the changing politics of urban public investment /
Alan A. Altshuler and David E. Luberoff.
      p.   cm.
Includes bibliographical references and index.
  ISBN 0-8157-0128-4 (cloth) — ISBN 0-8157-0129-2 (paper)
  1. Community development, Urban—United States. 2. Community
development, Urban—United States—Case studies. 3. Urban
policy—United States. 4. Urban policy—United States—Case studies.
I. Luberoff, David. II. Title.
HN90.C6 A668 2003
307.1'416'0973—dc21   2002152773

9 8 7 6 5 4 3 2 1

The paper used in this publication meets minimum requirements of the
American National Standard for Information Sciences—Permanence of Paper
for Printed Library Materials: ANSI Z39.48-1992.

Typeset in Sabon

Composition by OSP
Arlington, Virginia

Printed by R. R. Donnelley
Harrisonburg, Virginia

Contents

Preface

During the 1980s there was much talk of a national infrastructure crisis. Federal data indicated that, whereas the per capita net stock of state and local fixed capital had risen by an average of more than 4 percent annually during the middle and late 1960s, its rate of growth had plummeted to zero from the late 1970s through the mid-1980s.[1] Toward the end of this period, as the nation's most prominent pending highway project was cancelled (because of environmental restrictions and an interstate development conflict), Senator Daniel Patrick Moynihan (D-N.Y.) observed: "There is a kind of stasis that is beginning to settle into our public life. We cannot reach decisions. Central Park could not conceivably be built today as it was when there was enough power in Tammany Hall to make the decision."[2]

Just a few years later, however, striking changes were occurring. There was a modest increase in capital infrastructure investment nationwide, suf-

1. See Altshuler and Gómez-Ibáñez (1993, table 2-2).
2. Cited by Alan Finder, "Westway: A Road That Was Paved with Mixed Intentions, Losing Confidence and Opportunities," *New York Times*, September 22, 1985, sec. 4, p. 6. One of the present authors, Altshuler, had expressed similar pessimism in a 1975 article coauthored with Robert Curry, concluding that while the new constraints on development had been beneficial in many respects, "a significant danger remains, however, and its name is paralysis. The points of potential veto are proliferating at a remarkable rate . . . and threaten nearly all projects that arouse any significant controversy with endless delay, if not with definitive rejection. Our system of shared power, in short, threatens to become a system of shared impotence." See Altshuler and Curry (1975, p. 40); and see also Popper (1991).

ficient in magnitude to be captured in national statistics. The per capita rate of growth in state and local fixed capital increased from zero in 1980–84 to 0.9 percent and rising in 1985–89.[3] Vastly expensive urban projects were moving forward—including a new airport in Denver, a new subway in Los Angeles, light rail lines in Los Angeles and numerous other cities, the depression and decking over of Boston's elevated Central Artery in concert with the construction of a new expressway and tunnel to Logan Airport, the multibillion-dollar (court-ordered) cleanup of Boston Harbor and its tributary waterways, and the development of sports facilities and convention centers in cities across the United States.

It gradually dawned on us that no other scholars had yet focused on the (limited) revival of public capital spending in urban areas or on its implications for a deeper understanding of urban and intergovernmental politics. Indeed, theorists of urban politics—while emphasizing its profound thrust toward economic growth and development—were devoting scarcely any attention to public capital investment as either a development instrument or source of intense conflict in local affairs.

While pondering this theme, most notably in connection with our teaching, we launched a study in the early 1990s of the political history of one such undertaking, Boston's Central Artery/Tunnel project.[4] Learning in depth about the remarkable trajectory of this project—probably the largest and most complex ever undertaken within a single urban core—we became increasingly interested in the extent to which it reflected broader patterns, and we began to conceive the present study. As our work progressed, its scope vastly expanded—to encompass 50 years and more of history, a wide range of project types (though still concentrated in transportation), a focus on intergovernmental as well as local politics, and a serious effort to integrate our work with more general recent efforts to theorize about urban and intergovernmental politics.

This work has been a collaboration in the truest sense of the word. Each of us was centrally engaged in the research and writing of every chapter, and the book's central ideas are all products of this joint effort. Amid our multiple responsibilities, however, the completion of this effort has proven to be the work of half a decade, and along the way we have accumulated debts to many others as well. We are most grateful for financial support at critical moments from the Lincoln Institute of Land Policy, the U.S. Department of Transportation's University Transportation Center Program, the Taub-

3. Altshuler and Gómez-Ibáñez (1993, table 2-2).
4. See Luberoff and Altshuler (1996).

man Center for State and Local Government of Harvard's John F. Kennedy School of Government, and the Massachusetts Executive Office of Transportation (through two gubernatorial administrations that had little else in common and under the leadership of three state secretaries of transportation: Fred Salvucci, Richard Taylor, and James Kerasiotis).

For advice and feedback, we are especially grateful to the following: Steve Adams, Joachim Blatter, H. James Brown, Nancy Rutledge Connery, Joseph Coughlin, Richard DeNeufville, Joseph DiMento, Jameson Doig, Steven Erie, Charles Euchner, John Fischer, Kathryn Foster, Emil Frankel, Bernard Frieden, Barbara Goldoftas, José Gómez-Ibáñez, Mary Graham, Arnold Howitt, Elizabeth Humphrey, Robert Levers, James Levitt, Peggy Levitt, Judith Grant Long, Charles Magraw, Bill Manning, Steve Miller, Eric Nass, Ken Orski, Bill Parent, David Perry, Paul E. Peterson, Alan Pisarski, Jonathan Richmond, Lynne Sagalyn, Heywood Sanders, Eric Segal, Jefferey Sellers, Joe Sussman, Brian Taylor, Jay Walder, Allan Wallis, Melvin Webber, Jack Wofford, and Paul Zigman.

We benefited as well from the contributions of a group of superb research assistants: Mary Dunn, David Landau, David Greenberg, Melissa Chan, Julia Koster, Tamar Shapiro, Meredith Rubin, James Ebenhoh, and Stephanie Glazerman. We are also most grateful to Susan Bailey of the Kennedy School Library, who was both ingenious and tireless in assisting us to track down many fugitive sources and facts, and to Claire Brigandi, Sandra Garron, Siobhan McLaughlin, Deborah Voutselas, Julie Zanotti, Julie Farris, and Ryan Almstead, who all provided important logistical support.

Our greatest debts of all, of course, are to our long-suffering families—both to the youngest among them, who coped with our distraction and arcane preoccupations for years, and to their elders, who encouraged and supported us throughout. This book is dedicated by David to Jody, to their daughters Rebecca and Anna, and to Ben and Neil Luberoff, who both would have been proud. By Alan it is dedicated to Julie, their children (by both birth and marriage), Jenny, David, Barry, and Jill, and their adored grandchildren, Jacob, Ben, Evan, Zachary, and Jason.

CHAPTER ONE

Introduction

Viewed internationally, American cities are unique—extraordinarily self-reliant in relation to higher level governments, but also extraordinarily dependent on private sector investment decisions. Providing a wide array of essential services and exercising most land use authority within their boundaries, they finance their activities mainly with revenue that they raise themselves. When they do seek assistance from higher levels of government, they engage vigorously as well in political mobilization. Their physical and economic development has been driven overwhelmingly, however, by private for-profit investment. In many respects, as a result, local politics has always been an aspect of business—a way of bringing government power to bear in support of private investment opportunities. American cities are conspicuous for the emphasis they place on growth and in the intensity with which they compete with one another for it. Higher-level governments have rarely sought to curb this feature of the system, doubtless because it greatly enhances investor influence and business leaders passionately support it. These have been the fundamental attributes of city politics throughout American history.

Within this framework, however, the system of urban governance has continually adapted to changes in the broader society, economy, and national polity of which it is a part. The focus of this book is on a series of profound changes that occurred during the second half of the twentieth century involving the politics of large-scale government investments in

1

physical capital facilities—*mega-projects,* we label them—to revitalize cities and stimulate their economic growth.[1]

This was a period, particularly during the third quarter of the century, of kaleidoscopic change, as governments first took on a substantially more active role in promoting development and then pulled back in the face of massive public backlash. It was also a period in which higher-level governments became far more engaged in assisting localities to realize their development ambitions, and in which—during the late 1960s and early 1970s—ordinary citizens and ideologically driven associations were empowered as never before to constrain development where it threatened to disrupt valued elements of the existing urban fabric. Local governments and their private constituencies for growth did not retreat—at least not in general or for long—from their thoroughgoing commitment to economic development, but they did adjust their tactics profoundly. Most notably, they shifted tactics in seeking to lure major investors, relying more on fiscal and regulatory inducements, less on public infrastructure development; and within the arena of public development they shifted tactics as well, striving to reduce disruption and minimize citizen resistance.

The original research presented in this book focuses on transportation mega-projects: highways, airports, and mass transit systems. More broadly, however, drawing on the work of other scholars as well, we endeavor to answer the following questions:

—Why did American governments undertake such ambitious, highly disruptive activities as urban renewal and intraurban expressway con-

---

1. The term *mega-project* as employed in this book denotes initiatives that are physical, very expensive, and public. More specifically, mega-projects involve the creation of structures, equipment, prepared development sites, or some combination thereof. They cost at least $250 million in inflation-adjusted year 2002 dollars. (This is an approximate rather than a hard-and-fast threshold, but most of the projects discussed in this book exceeded it by a very comfortable margin.) Mega-projects are fundamentally an expression of public authority. The clearest indicator of their public nature since about 1920 has been public financing, wholly or in large part. Other indicators, some of which were even more significant during the nineteenth and early twentieth centuries, include government-granted monopoly franchises, land grants, delegations of eminent domain authority, loan guarantees, and access to the benefits of public debt financing (for example, via the issuance of privately guaranteed public revenue bonds).

The prefix *mega* to indicate "very large" became common in science and engineering during the late nineteenth century. (See *Chambers Dictionary of Etymology*, 3d ed, s.v. "mega.") The term *mega-project* itself dates to the late 1970s, when the Canadian government and the Bechtel Corporation more or less simultaneously adopted it, the former to describe massive energy development projects to which it had recently committed, the latter to describe its general portfolio of very large-scale projects. (See Jeff Sallott, "Oil Sands Alberta's Wildcard in Pricing Battle with Ottawa," *Globe and Mail*, November 7, 1979, p. P9; and Thomas Lueck, "Bechtel and Its Link to Reagan," *New York Times*, December 5, 1980, p. D1.)

struction during the 1950s and 1960s? Why did public investments of such magnitude, involving large-scale displacement of current residents and enterprises, become feasible for the first and only time during this period?

—What changed during the late 1960s and early 1970s, delaying or derailing most urban mega-projects then in the pipeline and sowing widespread doubt that their like would often prove feasible again?

—How, and to what extent, did the political impulses that generated mega-projects in the 1950s and 1960s find expression in the remaining three decades of the century? How did the strategies and tactics required to carry out mega-projects change after 1970, and at what cost? Did these new requirements entail a shift as well in the dominant mega-project types?

—Are the political forces that have generated urban mega-projects over the past half century so irrepressible and adaptive that a continuing flow of such investments in the decades ahead may be anticipated? Or have the constraints on such development become so burdensome, and so expensive to overcome, that urban mega-projects are likely to be very rare in future?

Interjurisdictional Competition

What competition means for American local governments, above all, is striving to make themselves attractive to private investors. In bedroom suburbs, the investors of primary concern are homebuyers.[2] In major employment centers, though, competitive efforts focus mainly on business investors—because the largest among them control very large sums indeed, because they bargain hard, and because local companies that stand to profit from growth tend to be better funded, better organized, and more highly motivated than anyone else to engage in politics on an ongoing basis.

This is not to say that the dominance of local growth interests is invariant across local policy arenas, over time, or across jurisdictions. Growth elites care most about such issues as downtown revitalization and improving regional infrastructure. Other groups typically have other priorities— for example, improving neighborhood services and schools, police-community relations, or conditions of public employment. In certain periods, moreover, groups critical of growth initiatives become far more active and better mobilized than usual, forcing growth elites to retreat or at least to adapt their plans in significant ways. Such eruptions of antigrowth sentiment eventually run out of steam, but they may leave enduring legacies. Finally, the balance among local interests varies from one jurisdiction to

2. See Fischel (2001, pp. 14–16, 242–44); and Schneider (1989, pp. 39–40, 125–46).

another. While growth coalitions appear dominant in most cities, at least when it comes to their highest priority issues, there are also conspicuous exceptions: cities like San Francisco, California, and Cambridge, Massachusetts, in which groups emphasizing the need to constrain investors have dominated for considerable periods. Such jurisdictions are invariably prosperous nonetheless, because they are endowed with such assets as favorable climate, historic character, or anchor employers with very little capacity to move (for example, universities and medical centers), which ensure strong investment demand almost regardless of what they do.[3]

The instruments available to cities in pursuing their growth objectives fall into two broad categories: inducements to private investors and direct public investments. The former include zoning concessions, tax abatements, low-interest loans, and the use of eminent domain to assemble and prepare large parcels of land, often overlaid on a general pattern of low taxation and minimal business regulation. The latter are most commonly for purposes that large segments of the business community view as vital to local competitiveness, but from which it is generally impossible to extract profits directly. Mass transit and convention center investments, for example, tend to be intrinsically unprofitable. Airports and highways could in theory be profitable but regulatory uncertainties, federal aid rules, and the ubiquity of publicly owned, underpriced alternatives render them, with rare exceptions, unduly risky for private investors. The inducement-investment distinction frequently blurs in specific cases—as when governments build stadiums to attract sports franchises or undertake road improvements to clinch deals with private factory and office developers—but it is clear and significant in many others.

We have chosen to focus on public investment strategies primarily for two reasons. First, efforts to realize large-scale investment projects often provide an unusually revealing window on patterns of influence in urban development politics. Such projects involve huge commitments of public resources and often entail significant threats to some interests and values even as they promise great benefits to others. Because the stakes are so high, the struggles over project authorization, planning, and implementation often draw in powerful actors whose activities are normally camouflaged or who stay out of lesser political disputes, confident that others will adequately protect their interests.

---

3. P. E. Peterson (1995, pp. 28–29). Clarence Stone emphasizes, on the other hand, that cities blessed with very strong investor demand often choose nonetheless to impose few restrictions. Stone (1993, pp. 19–20).

Second, while political scientists concerned with urban politics have recently been preoccupied with business influence and economic development policy, they have devoted remarkably little attention to the politics of direct public investment. The most obvious explanation, noted above, is that during the final three decades of the twentieth century cities shifted notably away from public investment toward monetary and regulatory inducements in their efforts to attract investors. It is less obvious, though, why this shift occurred. One possibility is that cities were simply responding to economic and technical changes. A service economy may require less public infrastructure for each unit of output, for example, than its industrial predecessor. Another possibility is that certain forms of large-scale public investment became vastly more expensive, time consuming, and politically difficult after about 1970. We argue mainly in this book for the latter, political, explanation. The reductions in new urban highway and airport construction, for example, were both abrupt and long lasting, despite burgeoning motor vehicle and air travel demand. Even as governments turned away from these project types, moreover, they turned toward others much easier to site in the new political environment but with far weaker economic rationales: for example, rail transit systems, convention centers, and stadiums for professional sports franchises.[4]

One might reasonably conclude, on reviewing the most influential recent works on American urban politics, that both competitive strategies and the distribution of influence in urban politics have been fundamentally constant over the past half century—though with slight adjustments to reflect such factors as the declining economic value of new highways (Paul Peterson), the growing minority share of the central-city electorate (Clarence Stone), and the increasing importance of amenity as a competitive asset (John R. Logan and Harvey Molotch).[5]

We concur in part with this view. There certainly has been continuity on two dimensions: the central role of business-led growth coalitions in urban development politics and the disposition of cities to compete proactively for investment rather than merely encourage it by holding down their tax rates and minimizing their regulatory demands.

---

4. Similar changes occurred within the highway and airport sectors—toward the improvement of existing highways rather than the construction of new ones, and improvements to airport terminals rather than runways. We do not argue, however, that these shifts entailed any worsening of typical project benefit-cost ratios.

5. P. E. Peterson (1981, p. 135); Stone (1989, pp. 79–82); and Logan and Molotch (1987, pp. 76–81, 290–91).

But we develop three collateral arguments in this book as well: (1) the capacity of local growth coalitions to impose disruption on other local interests sharply—and durably—declined in the late 1960s and early 1970s; (2) the new constraints imposed in this period stimulated changes in the types of projects undertaken, required major alterations in design and mitigation strategies, and greatly drove up project costs; and (3) these changes merit recognition as significant alterations in the overall character of urban politics.

From the standpoint of local business and political leaders, the primary effect of the changes noted above has been to require tactical adjustments—they have by and large found new ways to pursue their traditional objectives of growth and economic competitiveness. From the standpoint of ordinary citizens, however, particularly in the categories most commonly victimized by mega-projects in the 1950s and 1960s (low-income and minority residents of older neighborhoods), their significance has been fundamental. The capacity to defend one's home and immediate environment, and the power to influence decisions about how to distribute the costs and benefits of government activities bearing on them, are not everything one might desire as a citizen. But they are, for most urban residents, the most important stakes of urban politics—and thus merit a prominent place in theories about it.

Plan of the Book

A generic problem in studies of this type is to find the right balance between depth and breadth. To keep the focus sharp, we concentrate on three interrelated mega-project types: highways, airports, and rail transit systems, the largest categories of public mega-project spending in and around cities during the second half of the twentieth century. We opt for breadth, however, on four other dimensions. First, we integrate our findings with leading theories of urban politics and with the empirical research of others on urban renewal and its successors, particularly the recent investment booms in downtown festival malls, sports facilities, and convention centers. Second, we address national patterns. Though we make substantial use of case narratives, they are drawn from multiple cities, chosen to illustrate broad themes, and interspersed with examinations of national developments. Third, our focus is intergovernmental. Most urban mega-projects during the latter half of the twentieth century were undertaken within contours of opportunity defined by federal programs and with substantial, often predominant, federal financing. They were frequently carried out, moreover, by state agencies and regional authorities, leaving just a minor role in the formal sense for local governments. We delineate the multilevel dynamics of these cases while highlighting as well the key roles that local actors invariably performed. Finally, whereas most in-depth studies of urban politics focus on relatively brief time periods and portray apparently stable patterns of influence, we examine developments over half a century, long enough for considerable evolution to have occurred.

This is, for most of its length, a work of empirical narrative and analysis, intended for readers with a serious interest in urban politics and public policy but not necessarily in urban political theory. Even its most empirical chapters are driven, though, by concerns arising from political science theory, and we bring these concerns to the fore in two chapters, 3 and 8. In these we ask:

—What light can leading contemporary theories of urban and American politics shed on the politics of large-scale public investment and its place within the broader framework of urban governance?

—How well does each theory explain the observed facts? The significance of this question, of course, is that general theories must inevitably be tested against particular observations. No single failure is fatal, but the path to theory appraisal (and perhaps refinement) must consist of an accumulation of specific tests.

Readers who wish can skip chapters 3 and 8 without missing any portion of our empirical argument. It is these chapters, however, that most explicitly address the place of mega-project politics within the overall context of urban and American governance and examine broad controversies about the forces that have shaped urban development policy over the past half century, so we hope that most will be drawn in.

Chapter 2 provides an overview of urban mega-project politics through the second half of the twentieth century. Chapter 3 examines leading theories in search of propositions—hypotheses, from our standpoint—that seem pertinent to our investigation. Chapters 4, 5, and 6 focus on highway, airport, and rail transit mega-projects, respectively. Chapter 7 draws out common themes from these mode-specific narratives. Chapter 8 revisits the formal theories discussed in chapter 2, asking which accord best with our empirical findings. Finally, in chapter 9 we review developments since the turn of the twenty-first century—including the terrorist attacks of September 11, 2001, and their early aftermath—and speculate on the future of urban mega-projects.

CHAPTER TWO

Overview: Four Political Eras

We identify four stages in the history of urban public investment over the past century:

—The pre-1950 era: Localities received little aid from higher levels of government, had limited resources, were generally reactive in their capital investment strategies, and almost never imposed significant disruption on existing built-up precincts.

—The "great mega-project era" (1950–late 1960s): With unprecedented infusions of federal aid, cities and states undertook massive investment programs—designed above all to retrofit cities for the technologies and corporate preferences of the mid-twentieth century.

—The era of transition (mid-1960s–early 1970s): Community and environmental impacts of these programs provoked intense citizen protests, leading governments to adopt rules greatly constraining disruptive public investment.

—The era of "do no harm" (mid-1970s–present): Public investment in mega-projects remains substantial if more limited than during the great mega-project era, and quite central to the development strategies of many cities. The dominant project types and implementation strategies are quite different, however, because it is now essential to avoid or fully mitigate any significant disruption.

The Pre-1950 Era

From the earliest days of the Republic, civic boosters have prodded governments to participate in the development of large-scale physical facilities—from canals and railroads in the nineteenth century to airports and convention centers today—deemed essential by private investors but beyond their own unaided capacity. And they have frequently succeeded. Until the middle of the twentieth century, though, such projects rarely involved significant disruption of the existing urban fabric, and they typically proceeded within a broader framework of minimalist government— that is, one in which services were extremely limited by modern standards. Governments appealed to investors primarily by offering low taxes and negligible regulation.[1]

Until the final years of the nineteenth century, large infrastructure improvements were undertaken far more commonly by private than public entities. The role of government was to provide exclusive franchises, authorizations to take property by eminent domain, grants of land, and, more rarely, loan guarantees or direct equity (stock) investments. During the first half of the nineteenth century, when urbanization was still in its infancy, state governments played a leading role in such efforts, often with federal assistance in the form of land grants.[2] State and federal involvement diminished subsequently, but cities, which were growing rapidly and acquiring far greater institutional capacity, became increasingly active.[3] For political machines, at their zenith in this period, capital projects offered uniquely attractive opportunities for profit and patronage as well as for the cultivation of key constituencies.[4] Machines did not require public ownership to reap the political benefits of capital spending, however; it was sufficient to grant the franchises and maintain some ongoing regulatory presence. An additional advantage of private development was that it took the issue of

1. Works that have been helpful in considering the pre-1950 era include: Aldrich (1980, pp. 32–48, 77–99); Goodrich (1965); Sbragia (1996, pp. 44–79, 102–34); Teaford (1984, pp. 217–306); Perry (1995, pp. 202–36); Melosi (2000, pp. 117–74); and Tarr (1984, pp. 21–43).

2. State aid contracted sharply after the depressions of 1837 and 1857. By the beginning of the Civil War, local aid for infrastructure was roughly equal to that provided by the states. Tarr (1984, p. 8).

3. The first census of local and state governments was conducted in 1902. By that time localities were responsible for more than 80 percent of all public capital spending. Authors' calculations from Bureau of the Census, *Historical Statistics of the United States: Colonial Times to 1970* (1975, series F 1–5, series Y 783–95).

4. See Shefter (1976); and Merton (1973).

taxation off the table. Investors were expected to draw their revenues from customer payments, and consumers who felt aggrieved were expected to address their complaints to the private operators. Thus as major new infrastructure technologies emerged in the late nineteenth and early twentieth centuries—rail transit, the telephone, and electric power, in particular—cities brought them on-line primarily by franchising companies rather than investing directly.[5] Over time, as these entities grew far beyond local boundaries, the regulatory function was increasingly taken over by higher levels of government, but telecommunications and electric power remain almost completely private to the present day.

Cities did not rely entirely on franchising, however, to address their growing infrastructure needs. It was difficult or impossible, given the metering technologies then available, for private operators to recoup the costs of certain types of infrastructure that nonetheless came to be viewed as essential to public health and economic growth. The debates about whether to undertake such improvements were typically intense and often inconclusive until crises (such as epidemics) forced action, but they were increasingly resolved in the affirmative.[6]

Most direct public investment during the late nineteenth and early twentieth centuries was concentrated in four areas: education, water and sewage, street improvements, and urban beautification. The school-building boom was fueled by explosive urban population growth and substantial increases in the percentage of school-age children who attended school.[7] Water and sewage investments were driven by growing public health knowledge, continually reinforced by outbreaks of fatal disease that ravaged rich as well as poor (though not, to be sure, in equal measure, as the rich were less densely packed and could often escape the city in periods of epidemic). Spending on streets and roads, already the second largest item in most municipal budgets by the late nineteenth century (trailing only education), increased sharply during the 1910s and 1920s in response to surging motor vehicle usage. Most investment in this domain consisted of paving existing streets, though many cities also widened major streets within and on the approaches to downtown and at times, if land were available, built landscaped boule-

5. See Fogelson (1967, pp. 86–92); Bottles (1987, pp. 28–33); Barrett (1983, p. 12); and Warner (1978, p. 60).

6. For a vivid account of the years of controversy (amid repeated devastating plagues) that preceded Chicago's decision in the 1890s to incur the cost of reliably separating its sewage and water systems, see D. L. Miller (1996, pp. 423–32).

7. Aldrich (1980, pp. 37–38).

vards.[8] During the same period, finally, many cities invested heavily in public buildings, often of a monumental character, and parks, particularly with the aim of enhancing the attractiveness of their downtowns.

These efforts were generally promoted by leading local businessmen, and indeed this was a period of unprecedented growth in formal business organizations. While their vision of the proper role of government remained narrow by later standards, they had arrived at the view that key attributes of a competitive city included a better-educated (and Americanized) work force, freedom from waterborne plagues, modern streets, and a beautified central area.[9] It is impossible to gauge the precise magnitude of these efforts before 1902, when the Bureau of the Census began keeping track. From 1902 to 1927, however, local capital expenditures nearly quintupled in real terms and rose from 0.7 percent to 1.5 percent of gross domestic product.[10] By and large, the revenue base for core water and sewage investments, arterial road improvements, and downtown projects was the local property tax. On the other hand, water and sewage connections to specific neighborhoods and properties and street paving projects in residential areas were often financed by special assessments after petition from the owners involved. This fee-for-service approach led, of course, to sharp disparities in service between more and less affluent areas.[11]

The results of these spending and taxing policies were dramatic. To illustrate, while only 310,000 people had access to treated water in 1890, more than 45 million did by 1930.[12] Similarly, while total road and street mileage increased only 3 percent between 1914 and 1929, paved mileage increased by 157 percent.[13]

The Great Depression brought an abrupt end to this local investment boom, and indeed numerous local governments defaulted on bonds that

8. By the late 1920s limited-access parkways were under construction in a few localities, and many major urban areas were developing plans for even more downtown-oriented high-speed roads. Seely (1987, pp. 149–54); and McShane (1994, pp. 203–28).

9. Tarr (1984, pp. 26–29); Teaford (1984, pp. 187–214); and Boyer (1983, pp. 63–70). More broadly, this was an era marked by business-backed efforts to assert more control over local government and, as Robert Putnam has noted, a particularly vibrant time for the formation of all types of voluntary associations. Putnam (2000, pp. 383–401).

10. Authors' calculations from Bureau of the Census, *Historical Statistics of the United States: Colonial Times to 1970* (1975, series F 1–5, series Y 783–95).

11. Sbragia (1996, pp. 75–76).

12. Tarr (1984, p. 24); and Dupuy and Tarr (1982, p. 337), as cited by Sbragia (1996, p. 70).

13. Rae (1971, p. 354).

they (or special districts they had set up) had issued in the booming 1920s.[14] Local spending cuts were partially offset by federal aid, which became an important factor for the first time since the early nineteenth century, but the principal aim of such aid was to create jobs, not facilitate the realization of ambitious local visions. So New Deal programs typically spread their resources over very large numbers of projects—small, simple to design, and labor intensive. The largest single source of funding, for example, the federal Works Progress Administration, had an official dollar ceiling of $25,000 a project—though larger projects were frequently subdivided into several $25,000 components. As of June 1938 the program had helped finance the construction or repair of more than 34,000 schools, 280,000 miles of streets and roads, 2,700 new parks and playgrounds, 153 new airports, 280 miles of new airport runway, and 250 docks, as well as the planting of 24 million trees.[15]

Federal jobs programs were curtailed in the late 1930s and ended during World War II.[16] The federal government undertook numerous projects, most notably airport improvements, during the war that later proved suitable for civilian use, but local capital spending plummeted—to a level, by 1944, lower than at any time since the Census Bureau had begun keeping track in 1902.[17] Nonetheless, during the latter years of the war many cities, in cooperation with their leading business groups, developed ambitious revitalization plans—calling for new expressways and airports, downtown beautification projects, and (in many locales) programs to replace slums with new commercial facilities and market-rate housing.[18]

For the time being, these remained statements of aspiration rather than serious action plans. In the absence of aid from higher-level governments, very few cities were in a position to undertake major new projects. But they did respond with sharp increases in capital spending to improve their existing infrastructure which, after a decade and a half of neglect, was typically in an advanced state of decay.[19] In aggregate, local capital expenditures rose sevenfold in real terms from 1944 to 1950—finally reaching their pre-

14. Sbragia (1996, pp. 128–29).

15. Couch and Shughart (1998, pp. 113–18).

16. See Gelfand (1975, pp. 45–46, 63–65, 82–98); and D. K. Goodwin (1994, pp. 481–83).

17. Authors' calculations from Bureau of the Census, *Historical Statistics of the United States: Colonial Times to 1970*, (1975, series F 1–5, series Y 783–95).

18. Teaford (1990, pp. 83–121).

19. Teaford (1990, pp. 76–79).

Depression level in the latter year.[20] The politics of local capital budgeting, however, particularly where local legislatures were ward-based or bond issues required direct voter approval, strongly favored the diffusion rather than concentration of resources—that is, small projects spread widely across the city.[21] During this period new limited-access roads were built in several cities (including Los Angeles, Boston, New York, and Detroit), most commonly under state auspices.[22] By and large, however, local mega-project plans gathered dust.

The Great Mega-Project Era

As the nation emerged from World War II, there was great concern that the economy would slide back into depression, and the idea—a New Deal legacy—that government could stimulate a weak economy by financing public works enjoyed broad support. This was a period, furthermore, in which public confidence in government was unusually high. The private economy had failed in the 1930s, forcing vast numbers of people to turn to government for employment or relief. Large sectors of business as well had turned to government for subsidies, contracts, and regulatory protection (against price-cutters and new entrants). Then, in the pressure cooker of world war, tens of millions of people had served in the military or worked for military contractors. The outcomes had been total victory abroad and full employment at home.

Against this backdrop a variety of national, business-led coalitions assembled to spur ambitious peacetime investment programs, largely financed by the federal government. Though unswerving in their commitment to capitalist organization of the economy, these groups now favored vigorous government action to further growth as well—and not merely during emergencies like war and depression, but on a regular basis. Their path was by no means easy, because pressures for tax cuts and a return to prewar patterns of governance remained very strong. But several of these coalitions did bring about major new programs in the decade or so following World War II, most notably in support of housing, highway, and airport development.

20. As of 1950 the local share of total capital spending was 50 percent, down from 70 percent just before the Great Depression. See Bureau of the Census, *Historical Statistics of the United States: Colonial Times to 1970* (1975, series F 1–5, series Y 783–95).
21. See Sanders (1992a, 1992b); and Teaford (1990 pp. 67–81).
22. See Taylor (2000).

The housing and motor vehicle industries—together with their suppliers, distributors, franchisees, contractors, and collateral service businesses— were already among the nation's largest, while the commercial aviation industry, though still in its infancy, was among the most rapidly growing. Each of these coalitions credibly claimed to represent surging popular demand as expressed in the marketplace, and each was a formidable presence in nearly every congressional district.

These were years of growth and prosperity nationally, but not in older central cities, which were experiencing a severe loss of both residents and employers to the suburbs. Their handicaps in competing with newly developing areas were legion, from their physical layout and decay to their large numbers of low-income and minority residents. And even the advantage of centrality itself appeared to be a rapidly diminishing asset. Whereas virtually all transit lines radiated out from downtown, urban area residents were now abandoning mass transit for cars at an astonishing rate. And cars worked least well in cities, with their high-density, often narrow streets and very limited space for parking.

Thus central-city leaders experienced a growing sense of desperation. In order to head off a death spiral, they came to believe, nothing short of radical surgery would do—to clear away slums, to assemble and write down the cost of large development sites, to build expressways from the suburbs and regional airports into downtown, and more generally to retrofit "obsolete" elements of the urban fabric for the dominant technologies and corporate space demands of the second half of the twentieth century. The cities were already under severe fiscal strain, however, and had never financed projects of such magnitude. Nor were the states likely to provide the lead. The national coalitions for new federal programs represented an alluring opportunity, however. If central-city interests could gain inclusion in these coalitions and share in their victories, perhaps the federal government could be enlisted as a partner in revitalizing central-city economies.

In the event, these national coalitions proved open to their central-city petitioners—even, on occasion, where this required stretching their core rationales considerably. Consider the campaign for urban renewal, which had to overcome two objections to its inclusion as a housing coalition priority. First, it was by no means obviously a housing program. Its aim was to stimulate for-profit, mainly commercial, investment in central cities— particularly in central business districts, where its principal advocates were most heavily invested. Proponents were eager to clear away slums, but certainly not to redevelop the cleared areas with new housing for the poor. The ingenious solution was to define slum clearance as itself a housing program, whether or not the housing destroyed was replaced.[23] Second, urban renewal was to involve compulsory land taking from private property owners, most frequently for resale at subsidized prices to other private owners. Many people found this extremely hard to swallow, and some were sure the courts would find it unconstitutional. A few years earlier, this would doubtless have been the case. Now, however, with broad support from the private business community, it passed constitutional as well as congressional muster—on the grounds that both slum clearance and urban revitalization were legitimate aims of public action.[24]

In seeking to join the highway coalition, city interests faced two other hurdles. First, federal highway aid (excluding some New Deal work relief projects) had hitherto been reserved exclusively for the improvement of rural roads. Second, the core argument for a new federal program to finance a network of expressways connecting the nation's major urban areas did not suggest any rationale for aiding expressway construction *within* cities. Urban representatives countered that whereas motor vehicles had first become critically important in rural areas, they now were so in urban areas as well; that the scale of the proposed new program would be unprecedented, so the history of federal highway aid should not be decisive; and that urban motorists would be paying most of the fuel and other motor vehicle

---

23. The 1949 Housing Act specified that all urban renewal projects had to be "predominantly residential" as thus generously defined. After localities complained that this was too constraining, Congress in 1954 allowed 10 percent of grants to be used for nonresidential projects. In subsequent acts it expanded this exception, ultimately (in 1965) to 35 percent. See Foard and Fefferman (1966, pp. 104–13); and Frieden and Sagalyn (1989, pp. 23–24). It bears emphasis that the housing coalition also included groups committed to federal aid for the production of low- and moderate-income housing. They too obtained provisions in the 1949 Housing Act responsive to their demands, but the act did not connect its affordable housing and urban renewal components. In practice, moreover, federal credit agencies refused to lend in neighborhoods with significant numbers of multifamily housing units or nonwhite residents, and local resistance to the siting of public housing projects was generally fierce. As a result, low-cost housing production lagged far behind government-financed slum clearance throughout the life of the urban renewal program. See Von Hoffman (2000); B. Frieden and Sagalyn (1989, pp. 22–37); Weiss (1985, pp. 153–276); Foard and Fefferman (1966); and Gelfand (1975, pp. 136–56).

24. Courts in at least three states—Florida, Georgia, and South Carolina—did hold that redevelopment was unconstitutional because the end product was commercial rather than public. The great majority of state courts, however, accepted the argument that slum clearance was a valid public purpose quite apart from the question of how the acquired sites were subsequently redeveloped. See Sogg and Wertheimer (1966, pp. 132, 147–48).

excise taxes expected to finance the interstate system.[25] These arguments had strong appeal in the suburbs as well as in the central cities, and to the major industry groups in the highway coalition. The automobile and oil industries, for example, earned most of their domestic revenue in urban areas, and if traffic congestion was a threat to future sales, it was so primarily in urban settings. Truckers and major shippers were as eager to improve travel times within urban areas as between them. And highway construction interests were eager to build wherever they could.[26]

The advocates of federal aid for urban airports also faced two critical challenges. In collaboration with rural jurisdictions and corporate aviation interests, they had first to overcome resistance to any federal aid for airports at all. And then they had to struggle for a share of such aid consonant with their share of the national air travel market. Since the 1920s the federal government had exercised broad responsibility for air traffic control, and it had promoted airline industry development by subsidizing airmail services, but it had also chosen explicitly not to become involved in civilian airport development. The armed forces invested heavily in domestic airports during World War II, however, and turned over many new or improved facilities to civilian authorities in the early postwar years. Further, with wartime production over, the airplane manufacturers were desperate to expand the civilian market for their products, while the airlines and local boosters everywhere maintained that improved airports were indispensable to future prosperity. In this early glow of postwar enthusiasm, Congress enacted the Federal Airport Act of 1946. It proved to be a hollow victory, though, for champions of a major federal role in peacetime airport development. Appropriations to implement the act proved meager for many years, while its distribution formulas powerfully favored general aviation and small-city airports over the nation's major commercial airports. The aviation industry continued to grow apace, however, and local business coalitions were eager to accommodate it. Consequently, airport operators in most major cities were able to finance ambitious projects without large-scale federal aid—drawing initially on the authority of local governments to issue tax-exempt

25. The federal Bureau of Public Roads first proposed amending the federal highway program to include urban roads in its landmark 1939 report, *Toll Roads and Free Roads*, wherein it observed that most traffic and most traffic problems were located in and near urban areas. Public Roads Administration (1939, pp. 89–114); and Seely (1987, pp. 166–77). The program was subsequently amended, in 1944, to make urban roads eligible for federal aid and also to authorize establishment of an interstate highway system. Significant new funding, however, with specific earmarking for the interstate system, did not follow until 1956.

26. For additional details and documentation on the highway program, see chapter 4.

bonds and provide modest direct subsidies but increasingly as well on revenues from landing fees, terminal rentals, and concessions.[27]

Public spending for mass transit capital improvements first became significant in the latter half of the 1960s, following a campaign that had begun in several of the nation's largest cities at the end of the 1950s. Transit had developed originally as a privately owned, though publicly regulated, industry. Four of the nation's five rapid transit systems—in New York, Philadelphia, Chicago, and Boston—fell into public ownership or receivership between the two world wars, but nearly all the rest of the industry remained private until the mid-1960s. Transit ridership fell precipitously in the decades following World War II, however, resulting in massive service cutbacks, neglected maintenance and capital stock replacement, frequent fare increases, and the disappearance of service in many areas.

During the late 1950s this downward spiral generated a significant political reaction for the first time, largely provoked by two developments at the federal level. The immediate trigger was a 1958 federal statute authorizing the Interstate Commerce Commission to overrule state regulatory bodies in cases where railroads proposed to terminate passenger service. For many years the nation's railroads with significant passenger (including commuter rail) services had been complaining of the massive deficits they were required to incur by state regulators—who in turn were acutely sensitive to the political agitation that invariably accompanied passenger fare increases and service cutbacks. So long as the railroads could cross-subsidize passenger services from freight profits, they were generally unable to obtain relief. By the late 1950s, however, railroad profits were anemic overall (in the face of intense competition from the trucking industry), and those railroads with the largest passenger commitments were on the verge of bankruptcy. Only five urban areas had commuter rail service, but they were among the nation's largest, and the railroads affected were among the nation's most important. Within months after the 1958 law took effect, these railroads sought permission to abandon most of their commuter rail service. Local officials of the areas most affected, led by their central-city mayors, went to their state and national capitals in search of fiscal assistance, and the transit lobby was born.

The other new development of this period, of course, was the dramatic expansion of federal highway assistance—which both threatened mass transit and provided its advocates with an opportunity. The threat was obvious: improved highways were likely to accelerate the shift toward private vehi-

---

27. For additional details and documentation on the airport program, see chapter 5.

cles in urban travel. The opportunity was to argue for greater "balance" in public spending. If governments were going to invest heavily in urban transportation, why shouldn't mass transit receive a healthy share?

The limited victories of transit advocates through the early 1960s were mainly at the state level, involving subsidies to maintain existing service rather than aid for new investment. In 1964, though, following years of defeat at the national level, they finally secured enactment of a small federal grant program authorizing $375 million for transit capital projects over three years. The two great obstacles they faced in their quest for more "balanced" federal funding were the lack of a user tax base comparable to that which fueled the Highway Trust Fund and the very limited number of congressional districts in which mass transit was a significant issue. Gradually, however, the transit lobby extended its base to include those advocating for new rail transit systems in such cities as Atlanta, Los Angeles, and Seattle; bus systems nationally (including private operators hoping to be acquired by local governments); and transit suppliers. During the later 1960s, moreover, as a backlash against urban expressway construction gathered momentum, increasing numbers of politicians and even highway user groups found it convenient to argue that they favored transit as well as highway aid. But large-scale increases in federal transit assistance were not to occur until the 1970s.[28]

It was during the great mega-project era as well that cities began to invest in tourist facilities: that is, physical spaces for activities deemed likely to attract large numbers of nonresidents with a high propensity to spend money while in the city. Such projects became increasingly central to local growth strategies in subsequent decades.[29] This represented a historic departure. As Peter Eisinger observes, while cities have always competed to attract investment, they had traditionally directed their services—including such recreational services as parks and civic auditoriums—toward local residents and businesses. Today, by contrast, they are engaged in "the construction of expensive entertainment amenities, often in partnership with private investors, designed to appeal primarily to out-of-town visitors, including the suburban middle classes. This is true even in the nation's poorest, most decrepit cities, such as Detroit and Newark. . . . Increasingly, the urban civic arena is preoccupied by a politics of bread and circuses."[30]

28. For additional details and documentation on the transit program, see chapter 6.
29. Fainstein and Judd (1999, pp. 261–72).
30. Eisinger (2000, p. 317). The best general overviews of the tourist phenomenon are Fainstein and Judd (1999); Eisinger (2000); and Frieden and Sagalyn (1989).

Bernard Frieden and Lynne Sagalyn observe that the full set of tourist facilities, as it emerged by the late 1980s, included convention centers, stadiums and arenas for professional sports teams, festival retail malls, redeveloped waterfront areas, casinos, performing arts centers, museums, and aquariums.[31] We confine our attention here, though, to convention centers, sports facilities, and (in a later section, since the first were built in the 1970s) festival malls.

Cities had long invested in civic centers and auditoriums, but these had been tiny facilities by comparison with those to come, conceived mainly as amenities and symbols of civic greatness rather than as direct instruments to lure dollars from afar. Before World War II, their primary function was to accommodate such events as visits by renowned performing artists, amateur sporting events, and local trade fairs. After the war, however, with prosperity and the rapid growth of air travel, large business meetings came into fashion, often drawing attendees from great distances, and local business groups pressed for the construction of facilities to accommodate them. But convention centers were never profitable in and of themselves, the convention business was still young, and the cities were fiscally strapped.[32] So even though the number of large cities with convention facilities almost doubled in the 1950s and then doubled again in the 1960s, the largest centers built in this period were very modest by comparison with what was to come (see table 2-1). When Chicago's McCormick Place opened in 1960, for example, it was the nation's largest convention center, offering 320,000 square feet of exhibition space. Its expanded version of the late 1990s offered 2.2 million square feet. Atlanta, which proudly opened its new convention center in 1967 with 70,000 square feet of exhibition space, three decades later had 950,000 square feet in an entirely new facility, 100,000 in a domed football stadium next door, and 700,000 more planned.[33]

As of 1950 no locality had constructed a stadium for a professional sports team, though one major league baseball team and several football teams were playing in public stadiums that had been built in connection with bids for the Olympic games. Basketball and hockey teams more commonly played in public arenas, but these tended to be modest facilities that also housed a wide variety of amateur sports events. Overall, the four main

31. See Frieden and Sagalyn (1989, pp. 259–85).
32. Another complication in some cities was opposition from the owners of private exhibition facilities. See Banfield (1961, pp. 193, 197, 225). There are still, it bears mention, many private exhibition halls, though they are not among the largest such facilities. E. S. Mills (1991, p. 3).
33. Sanders (1998, pp. 58–59; 1992b).

Table 2-1. New Convention Centers, pre-1950–1990s

Number of centers

Period	Cities > 100,000 people	Cities < 100,000 people	Total
Pre-1950	26	7	33
1950s	17	8	25
1960s	45	17	62
1970s	54	42	96
1980s	64	40	104
1990s	42	47	89
Total	248	161	409

Source: Laslo (1998, table 1).

professional sports leagues played in just 30 stadiums and arenas, 21 of which were entirely private (in both their ownership and in having been developed without public financial participation).[34] During the 1950s, however, in the new environment of local development activism, cities began to compete for teams—primarily by offering them new, publicly financed venues in which to play. This was a particularly attractive offer, as many teams were playing in facilities built before World War I (and nearly all football teams were playing in stadiums configured for baseball), yet many teams were struggling financially and there was little prospect that new facilities would be profitable in and of themselves. Only six new stadiums and arenas were built in the 1950s, all publicly funded and publicly owned, but the pace accelerated thereafter. Twenty-five new facilities opened in the 1960s (a decade in which more teams moved than ever before, the major baseball and basketball leagues significantly expanded, and a new football league came into being), of which 17 were publicly funded and owned. Over the entire 20-year period 1950–70, the number of major league stadiums and arenas increased from 32 to 52, and the proportion owned publicly rose from 28 to 60 percent.[35]

Only a few of these new facilities were located in or near downtown areas. For reasons similar to those of shopping center developers, professional sports team owners, particularly in baseball and football, strongly pressed for outlying locations, close to major highways and with plenty of land for parking. Governments, eager both to accommodate them and also to economize, generally went along. In consequence, 61 percent of the new stadiums and arenas built between 1950 and 1979 were located in subur-

34. J. G. Long (2002, table 2-2, appendixes A, B).

35. J. G. Long (2002, table 2-2); and supplemental data calculated by Long at the request of the present authors.

ban locations.[36] The days of big television revenue and multimillion-dollar player salaries were yet to come, however; the leagues had not yet perfected their techniques for intensifying local competition for teams; and localities were still constrained in most cases by the need to secure voter approval for general obligation bonds. So most of the facilities built were not lavish by later standards. The new stadiums, for example, were generally intended for dual baseball and football use, and no stadium had either luxury boxes or a dome until 1965, when Houston's Astrodome opened with both.[37]

What is most striking in retrospect is the rapidity and lack of controversy with which an activity viewed as mainly private through the first half of the twentieth century—the construction of facilities for professional sports— became mainly public during the 1950s and 1960s.[38] There were, to be sure, precedents for this in the history of urban infrastructure. Most early water-works, mass transit systems, and airports were private, for example, and subsequently became public. The professional sports teams did not become public, however. Quite the contrary: while on the verge of their greatest growth and prosperity as private business enterprises, they succeeded in shifting an important element of their cost structure to the public sector.[39]

The Era of Transition

Through the 1950s and early 1960s urban renewal, highway construction, and airport development appeared politically unassailable. All enjoyed near-consensual business, labor, and media support in most cities—due in no small part to the fact that, while generating much economic activity, they absorbed little or no general tax revenue. Major highway projects were funded entirely by higher levels of government; the local contributions to urban renewal were mainly in kind; airport investments were financed primarily by user fees along with small amounts of federal aid. Virtually no one

36. Data calculated by Judith Grant Long at the request of the present authors.

37. Danielson (1997, pp. 178–81,188–94, 222–27, 238–40).

38. The most conspicuous exception during this period—and indeed the only baseball stadium built privately between 1950 and the late 1990s—was Los Angeles Dodger Stadium, which opened in 1960. The team was given a 300-acre site valued at $18 million in the late 1950s, however, as well as nearly $5 million in publicly financed infrastructure improvements and sole ownership of the ballpark. Danielson (1997, p. 249).

39. One might say the same about airlines and airports, and indeed there are important similarities, but there are also two important differences. Few airlines ever developed or owned airports, and airports are open to multiple users, whereas stadiums and arenas are built for one or at most two prime tenants.

seemed to realize, or perhaps care about, the devastation such projects might cause in older, densely settled, mainly low-income urban neighborhoods. The dominant assumptions, rather, were that the projects were required for the greater good and that the residents of such neighborhoods would in most cases be better off for their demolition.[40] There were controversies, to be sure, but mainly within the business sector itself—about whether, in some cities, to accept the urban renewal program's expanded rationale for public takings of private property, about specific fiscal choices (such as taking on long-term local debt and levying user fees to finance airport expansion), and about precisely where to site specific projects.

The programs operated, moreover, in relative secrecy, so that those affected often learned of projects just before the bulldozers rolled. In the early years there were no organized interest groups monitoring or learning from these experiences, much less providing potential victims with tactical assistance. Since their cause seemed hopeless, even those most adversely affected generally gave in without a fight. This tendency was accentuated by the fact that the victims were disproportionately poor and black. Slum clearance, after all, was an explicit objective of the urban renewal program, while highway planners were attracted to low-income corridors as both relatively cheap and particularly defenseless. In some cases, moreover, highway planners sited new highways with slum clearance as an explicit objective.[41]

The dominance of program advocates began to erode in the mid-1960s, however, and within half a decade it was no more. How was such an abrupt shift possible? Multiple factors appear to have contributed, some broadly societal, some program-specific. The 1960s were a decade of citizen activism combined with spreading awareness of the disruption associated with urban mega-projects. This activism found many outlets, but three are of particular significance in the present context: the movements for civil rights, citizen participation, and (toward the end of the decade), environmental protection. The civil rights movement mobilized African Americans against "institutional" as well as personal discrimination: that is, patterns of discrimination built into ostensibly race-neutral policies and norms, such as the idea that the best way to deal with low-income neighborhoods (slums) is to clear them. The movement for citizen participation was organized, above all, around the premise that citizens had a right to be consulted in timely fashion, and with access to all pertinent evidence, about government deliberations that might profoundly affect them. The environmental movement took off

40. Caro (1974, pp. 854–55).
41. Mohl (1993); Keating (2001, pp. 91–95); and Altshuler (1965, pp. 49–51).

Boston's West End in the mid-1950s, a few years after city officials declared the neighborhood—home to about 7,000 people—a slum that should be torn down. (From a booklet put together by West End residents as part of their unsuccessful efforts to stop the clearance plan.)

from the premise that human beings are biological organisms, to whom nothing means more than the preservation of a healthy ecology. It seemed to follow that a central responsibility of government was to avoid damaging the environment with its own programs. Renewal, highway, and airport development activities were each vulnerable to these new forces in somewhat different ways, but we focus here primarily on renewal since the highway and airport programs are treated at length in subsequent chapters.

At the beginning of the 1960s several well-researched critiques of urban renewal, from opposite ends of the political spectrum, attracted widespread attention. Martin Anderson attacked the program as an example of profligate, bungling big government, emphasizing that many cleared renewal sites had been sitting vacant for half a decade or more with no redevelopment in prospect, and that even where redevelopment was occurring it was typically with very high ratios of public to private investment.[42] Herbert Gans documented the last days of Boston's West End, a working-class neighborhood of extended families and other highly valued social networks. Its demise, Gans argued, had nothing to do with the supposed social pathology of

42. See Anderson (1964).

Boston's West End in the early 1960s, about two years after the city began clearing the neighborhood. As a result of intense lobbying by preservationists, city officials spared the Old West Church (left), constructed in 1806. The buildings on the right are part of Massachusetts General Hospital, which supported the West End clearance project. Credit: Irene Shwachman/Boston Athenaeum.

slums. Rather, this was a simple case of low-income people happening to occupy a site attractive to developers.[43] Once the floodgates were opened, academic critiques of the urban renewal program poured forth over the next several years.[44]

In combination, these intellectual attacks and growing neighborhood resistance to clearance stimulated incremental reform at the national level—most notably, improved relocation assistance—and tactical adaptations in some cities (including Boston, the focus of Gans's critique) away from wholesale clearance. Dramatic national change, though, awaited the urban riots of 1965–67. Some of the poster cities of the urban renewal program, such as Newark and Detroit, were among the hardest hit. Study commissions appointed to explain what had caused the riots, moreover, commonly found government clearance activities to be among the most intense sources of ghetto resident grievance.[45]

43. Gans (1962, esp. pp. 305–28).
44. J. Q. Wilson (1966).
45. See Kerner Commission (1968); New Jersey Governor's Select Commission on Civil Disorder (1972, esp. pp. 9, 55, 60); Frieden and Sagalyn (1989, p. 52); and Button (1978, esp. p. 73).

Boston's West End in 1962, now renamed Charles River Park, about six months after completion of the first two new luxury apartment buildings on the site. Credit: Courtesy Boston Herald.

More generally, the riots were a signal that Americans could no longer take social peace for granted. This was a shock in and of itself, provoking calls for bold action. Liberals urged redistributive initiatives and neighborhood empowerment, while conservatives argued for stronger law enforcement. There was little disagreement, however, about the propositions that riots were frightening, bad for business, and politically dangerous for officials on whose watch they occurred. Further, while the actual riots had been unplanned, chaotic, and mainly confined within ghetto boundaries, many feared that the nation could be in for worse.

One immediate result was a near-total abandonment of slum clearance activities. Some renewal officials, of course, wanted to proceed with their plans, but virtually no one else cared to risk provoking riots. And among the risk-averse were federal urban renewal officials, so the issue was moot.[46] Over the next several years responsible officials scrambled to create a kinder, gentler version of urban renewal, omitting the slum clearance component. Whereas the primary focus of renewal before the riots had been downtown

46. Danielson and Doig (1982, pp. 306–09).

revival, moreover, many agencies now turned toward the neighborhoods—seeking to work with existing residents, encourage the rehabilitation of existing structures, and use clearance very selectively if at all.

Unfortunately, such activity was extremely time consuming, the investments stimulated were small, and constituency support was weak. The old core renewal constituency, downtown business, had little enthusiasm for this new mission. And the neighborhoods themselves were, in general, neither united nor well mobilized politically.[47] So urban renewal became a policy backwater, fraught with far more local controversy than (to most political leaders) it seemed worth. Years of controversy ensued about how, if at all, it might be further adapted, until in 1974 it was terminated as a distinct program. (To be more precise, it was consolidated along with 10 other programs into the Community Development Block Grant Program.)[48]

The Interstate Highway Program proved more robust. It was, after all, a truly national program, with most of its mileage in rural and exurban areas. Its most expensive and disruptive segments, however, were in densely settled cities and inner suburbs, and most of those still incomplete encountered severe resistance in the late 1960s and early 1970s. Though the highway story differs in major respects from that of urban renewal, it is parallel in at least two: (1) as the massive displacement effects of both programs became widely understood, neighborhood resistance sharply intensified; and (2) in each case a program that had enjoyed near-consensual support for a dozen or so years after enactment suddenly became intensely controversial, spurring major modifications, including the abandonment of many long-planned projects.

Growing opposition to airport expansion reflected the introduction of jet aircraft in the late 1950s (in combination with the broad societal factors noted above). The new planes were extremely noisy, required substantially longer runways, and attracted large amounts of additional patronage—all of which intensified conflicts with nearby residential neighborhoods. Some localities responded with efforts to construct new airports away from residential concentrations, but such facilities generally required sites of 10,000 acres or more; such large parcels of land could be assembled only at distances from the urban core that most airlines and local business groups deemed unacceptable. On those rare occasions when sites both adequate in scale and acceptable to business *were* identified, moreover, it was often impossible to overcome environmental objections—as witness the failure of

---

47. Keyes (1969); and Sanders (1980, pp. 103–26).
48. Conlon (1988, pp. 44–63); and Frieden and Sagalyn (1989, pp. 49–53).

proposals for a new Miami airport adjacent to the Florida Everglades, a fourth airport for the New York region in New Jersey's Great Swamp, and a major expansion of John F. Kennedy Airport into New York City's Jamaica Bay.

This was also a period, finally, in which the movement for mass transit support came of age. The most critical reason appears to have been the growth of antihighway sentiment. Finding it valuable to have a positive program of their own, those fighting new highways hammered home the argument that urban mobility needs could be met more effectively and equitably by improving mass transit. Emboldened by this new support, the coalition of local officials, transit operators and labor unions, transit suppliers, and downtown business groups that had been seeking increased aid for transit throughout the 1960s intensified its campaign.

This campaign began to bear fruit in the final years of the decade and gathered much stronger momentum in the early 1970s as the national transit coalition found increasing numbers of allies in the highway camp. For highway interests, the central issue was the growing vulnerability of their own program. After rising sharply from the late 1950s through the mid-1960s, federal highway aid declined by roughly a quarter in real terms from 1968 to 1973. Increasingly controversial, it had become a tempting program for the president to cut, and a more difficult one for which to muster veto-proof congressional majorities. The solution, urged by transit lobbyists, was a highway-transit alliance. The resulting surface transportation coalition survives to the present day. The most notable of its early achievements were a tenfold increase in federal transit aid in real terms from 1968 to 1980, the abatement of controversy surrounding the federal highway program after about 1973, and a reversal of the downward trend in federal highway expenditures in the mid-1970s.

The Era of "Do No Harm"

U.S. infrastructure investment declined sharply, in aggregate, through the 1970s and early 1980s,[49] and doubtless more so in major cities, where siting disputes were most intense, than elsewhere. Local impulses toward

---

49. The net stock of fixed assets owned by U.S. state and local governments rose at an annual rate of 4.5 percent from 1947 to 1973, but only 2.3 percent from 1973 to 1998. During the first half of the 1980s, the absolute trough, it rose less than 1 percent a year absolutely, and the stock actually declined slightly (.13 percent a year) in per capita terms. See Herman (2000, p. 17); and Altshuler and Gómez-Ibáñez (1993, table 2-2, p. 28).

economic development activism by no means withered away, however. Facing new constraints—stagflation, a shift in federal spending toward Social Security and health programs, and intensified citizen resistance to both new taxes and disruptive projects—local growth coalitions were required to adapt. And adapt they did, with extraordinary success. In part they did so by shifting toward greater reliance on inducement strategies (see chapter 1). In part as well, however, their mode of adaptation was to identify new investment strategies more suitable for an era in which large projects were certain to be highly controversial and in which opponents were armed with a variety of legal weapons unknown in the great mega-project era.

The most significant new criterion that mega-project advocates now had to satisfy was avoidance of disruptive side effects—on neighborhoods, parks, natural species, historic sites, and a panoply of other valued community assets. This is not to say that every project was entirely nondisruptive. Particularly where localities were competing to attract large—or, as in the case of major league sports teams, symbolically important—private corporations and intense competitive pressure was perceived, significant amounts of dislocation still occurred at times. Detroit, for example, in two separate episodes during the 1980s, displaced more than 1,800 households and 200 small businesses to clear sites for automobile assembly plants (one for General Motors, the other for Chrysler).[50] And more than 1,000 Chicago residents were displaced in 1989 to make way for the new Chicago White Sox baseball stadium.[51] Such disruption was unheard of, though, where projects were entirely public, and was far less common than it had been even when localities were striving to accommodate private investors. Futhermore, localities were under increasing pressure to avoid reliance on general tax revenues.

Striving to realize their aims within the framework of these constraints, growth advocates shifted focus toward different types of projects, accepted amenity-enhancing features that they would previously have found outrageously expensive, and devised ingenious financing schemes that did not appear to burden local taxpayers. Clearance-based urban renewal, the construction of new urban expressways, and the development of new airports (or even new runways at old ones) became rare. Direct public investment in rapid transit, festival retail markets, convention centers, sports facilities, and airport terminals, on the other hand—all far easier to site and build

50. Jones and Bachelor (1993, chs. 6, 10); and Bachelor (1994, pp. 596–616).

51. The implementing agency in this case, recently established at the city's instigation by the state of Illinois, was an authority rather than the city itself. Euchner (1993, pp. 150–56).

without substantial neighborhood or environmental disruption—ratcheted up. These shifts, moreover, with the exception of that toward rapid transit, were not significantly driven by federal aid policy.[52] Indeed, the great majority of retail, convention center, and sports facility projects occurred without any direct federal aid (though most benefited from the ability of localities to issue tax-exempt bonds). And even after federal highway and airport grants increased (in real terms) during the mid-1980s and early 1990s, very few recipient governments sought to build new facilities in areas already developed at urban densities. Chapters 4, 5, and 6 consider post-1970 highway, airport, and rapid transit development in depth. Thus we focus here on retail, sports facility, and convention center development.

The thrust toward publicly sponsored retail development got under way in the early 1970s, though its heyday—chronicled most notably by Bernard Frieden and Lynne Sagalyn—was the 1980s.[53] Whereas traditional urban renewal had focused on the development of high-end offices, hotels, and housing, the view was now gaining favor that if downtowns were to thrive, they also needed to be exciting retail environments. In practice, however, virtually all new retail development since World War II had occurred in the suburbs. And there was no reason to believe that this pattern would change if left simply to the marketplace, given the high cost of land in downtown areas, the difficulty of assembling large parcels, regulatory hurdles more complex and unpredictable than in most suburbs, security concerns, and traffic congestion. Finally, there was no recent experience of successful downtown retail development from which prudent investors and lenders could extrapolate.

Once several of the nation's leading shopping center developers led the way, however, mayors, often spurred by local business groups, were eager to work with them. When a few developments were in place and apparently thriving, scores of cities and many other developers rushed in. The pattern of action required to bring this about took off from the urban renewal model, but with several critical differences.

It resembled urban renewal in that governments assembled the sites and subsidized the projects, while leaving most elements with profit potential to the private sector. Examining 39 projects in detail, Frieden and Sagalyn calculated that the median public share of gross investment was 32 percent. As in the case of renewal, moreover, the local shares were invariably well cam-

52. Even in the case of transit, moreover, investment continued to rise after federal aid stabilized in the 1980s.
53. Frieden and Sagalyn (1989).

ouflaged, enabling mayors to proclaim that these projects were essentially free from the standpoint of local taxpayers.[54] The availability of federal aid was considerably less than during the great mega-project era, but several of the earliest projects did benefit from urban renewal assistance while many of those built later drew upon federal Urban Development Action Grants (until their termination in 1988).[55] The primary sources of public revenue were local, however, both traditional (such as allocations from existing public works budgets) and new (such as tax-increment financing, public construction of collateral projects, tax abatements, low-interest loans to private developers, and new excise taxes—on hotel and restaurant bills, for example—crafted to draw most of their revenue from visitors to the city rather than residents).

To illustrate, during the mid-1970s, years before its downtown festival mall (Horton Plaza) went into construction, San Diego placed its site within a much larger tax-increment district, one in which large amounts of private, fully taxpaying development were already scheduled. It also successfully lobbied the federal government to lease its new federal courthouse within the district from a private developer, who would pay full taxes. Within just three years these projects were yielding tax increments in excess of $1 million a year—none of which was attributable to the festival mall project and all of which would otherwise have been available to support general city services. The city turned over the festival mall site, which had cost it $18 million, to the developer for $1 million. And it pledged to the developer that it would build or otherwise assure the construction of a new convention center in the immediate vicinity, several thousand parking spaces, 4,000 units of housing, street improvements, and a new downtown marina.[56]

The most striking differences between traditional urban renewal and the new downtown retail initiatives, however, were in the realms of siting, urban design, and business-government relations. The sites were nonresidential and, by mega-project standards, extremely small. The median project in a sample of 71 analyzed by Frieden and Sagalyn occupied just 5.7 acres. These were mainly areas of local embarrassment, moreover—a skid

54. Frieden and Sagalyn (1989, ch. 8).

55. Frieden and Sagalyn (1989, pp. 215–18, 308–09). See also Jacobs and Roistacher (1980); and Gist (1980).

56. Frieden and Sagalyn (1989, pp. 138–39, 146–47, 161–62). After the original agreement, Proposition 13 severely reduced the city's fiscal capacity while also contributing to an increase in property values and a reduction in the prospective taxes for which the developer would be liable. In this context, the developer assumed responsibility for the parking component of the project.

Baltimore's Inner Harbor in 2002. Like many other cities, Baltimore focused its renewal efforts in the 1970s on draw-ing people to the core—in this case, a revitalized waterfront—for shopping and other recreational purposes. Credit: Bill Swartwout/www.SouthBaltimore.com.

row/pornography district in San Diego, a long-cleared renewal site in St. Paul that had never attracted a developer, historic but derelict market struc-tures in Boston and Seattle. So there was little controversy about their suitability for redevelopment. Additionally, the projects were low-rise—never more than four or five stories—and designed to lure the public in rather than (as typically in urban renewal) to wall it out.[57]

Finally, whereas the urban renewal model had been one of detailed pub-lic planning without developer input (so as to avoid potential favoritism) and binding developer competitions on the model of those for public works contracts, the new model was one of public-private partnership from a very early stage.[58] Frieden and Sagalyn emphasize that the initial agreements between cities and developers tended to be highly unstable, not as a result of carelessness or bad faith but due to inevitably changing circumstances. As a result, the real agreement in every successful case they examine was to con-tinually work the problem and rework the deal. Often, moreover, the deals provided for governments, in partial return for their investments, to share in mall revenues or to build collateral revenue-generating facilities (such as

57. Frieden and Sagalyn (1989, pp. 107, 115, 119, 123 [in reference to Boston, Seattle, St. Paul, and San Diego, respectively], p. 134 [in reference to average parcel size], pp. 199–203 [in reference to mall design]).

58. The old model had almost never worked and was generally considered responsible in later years for the vast number of failed urban renewal projects. The renewal agencies that achieved greatest success, at least by the measures of attracting large amounts of federal aid and private investment, all seem to have worked closely with developers in selecting sites as well as developing plans for them. See Danielson and Doig (1982, pp. 291–315); H. Kaplan (1963, pp. 15–38); Caro (1974, pp. 979–83, 1005–23); and Frieden and Sagalyn (1989, pp. 43–44).

Table 2-2. New Major League Stadiums and Arenas, 1940–2005[a]

Facility	1940–49	1950–59	1960–69	1970–79	1980–89	1990–99	2000–05
All facilities							
Total number built	0	6	25	28	14	52	20
Average cost (millions of dollars)	0	51	126	132	157	226	314
Reported public share (percent)	0	100	78	89	66	57	67
Reported public subsidy (millons of dollars)	0	51	99	117	104	129	211
Stadiums							
Total number built	0	4	11	16	4	22	15
Average cost (millions of dollars)	0	50	153	171	261	261	354
Reported public share (percent)	0	100	86	88	50	79	68
Reported public subsidy (millons of dollars)	0	50	132	150	131	206	240
Arenas							
Total number built	0	2	14	12	10	30	5
Average cost	0	51	85	79	111	201	197
Reported public share (percent)	0	100	71	91	72	42	63
Average reported public subsidy (millions of dollars)	0	51	60	72	80	84	124

Source: J. G. Long (2002, tables 2-1, 2-2).

a. Dollar figures are millions of 2001 constant dollars based on the construction cost index for structures and the consumer price index for the land component.

parking garages). The variety of possible adjustments enabled cities, as new obstacles arose, to assure developers, lenders, and retailers that strong returns were still in prospect and to satisfy local critics that their government was acting in businesslike fashion.

The model of public-private partnership came into vogue as well in the realm of stadium and arena development, though not until the 1980s. Through the 1970s, as during the prior two decades, nearly all such investment continued to be 100 percent public (see table 2-2).[59] This pattern was transformed after 1980, however.

With vastly increased television revenues and franchise expansion into many new cities, the major sports leagues had achieved much higher profiles than formerly as symbols of "big league" cities. They were also attracting more sophisticated capital and had become highly adept at stoking competition among localities, both to secure new teams and retain the ones they already had.

The most distinctive feature of this competition was the insistence of all four major sports leagues—baseball, football, basketball, and hockey—on

59. J. G. Long (2002, table 2-1).

better, more heavily subsidized facilities in which to perform. Baseball and football teams were now insisting on separate stadiums, though purpose-built stadiums for professional football teams, which play just eight regular season home games a year, were unheard of till the 1970s. All of the leagues now had size, design, amenity, and luxury box standards driving costs far higher than they had been in prior decades. They increasingly made clear, moreover, that cities wishing to attract teams, or even retain those they already had, would do well to satisfy these demands. Thus St. Petersburg and St. Louis each invested hundreds of millions of dollars in a new stadium without having a team—just to improve their chances of attracting one. And even the largest cities had learned that their teams might depart—either to suburban locations (in football, for example, the New York Giants to the New Jersey Meadowlands and the Los Angeles Rams to Anaheim) or other urban areas entirely (the Rams, for example, in a second move, to St. Louis, and the Raiders, first from Oakland to Los Angeles in the 1980s, then back to Oakland in the 1990s).

It was virtually impossible to find an independent economist who viewed sports facility subsidies as good investments in local economic growth.[60] The chief executives of most large American cities, however, urged on by local business groups and the media, took this competition as one in which it was urgent to succeed. It provided a highly visible indicator of mayoral success or failure. The local support base included highly motivated fans as well as the usual array of business and labor supporters for development projects. The media, with their large commitments to sports coverage, were intensely interested. And doubtless many public officials believed as well the consultant reports—commissioned by teams—that promised large spin-off economic benefits.

The advocates of sports facility investment faced a serious problem, though. Even as the costs of accommodating new league and team demands were sharply escalating, local voters were communicating far greater resis-

---

60. John Siegfried and Andrew Zimbalist note: "Few fields of empirical economic research offer virtual unanimity of findings. Yet independent work on the economic impact of stadiums and arenas has uniformly found that there is no statistically significant positive correlation between sports facility construction and economic development." In support of this view, they cite work by 10 different economists published in eight different pieces, most of them peer reviewed. In a similar vein, Alan B. Krueger, an economist at Princeton University who edits the *Journal of Economic Perspectives*, has contended: "Experience suggests that subsidies for stadiums yield negligible economic benefits and expand the gap between the superrich and everyone else." See Siegfried and Zimbalist (2000, esp. p. 103); and Alan B. Krueger. "Take Me Out to the Ballgame but Don't Make Taxpayers Pay for the Park," *New York Times*, January 10, 2002, p. C2.

tance to property tax increases than a few years earlier, and also objecting to public subsidies for private teams. Michael Danielson reports, for example, that local electorates, when given a chance to express their views directly, rejected 13 of 15 sports facility proposals during the 1970s and 1980s (versus only two of nine in the prior two decades) and that "poll after poll underscores hostility to public financing of sports facilities."[61] Such resistance may help explain why the pace of development actually slowed in the 1980s, when only 14 new facilities (of which 10 were publicly owned) were built (see table 2-2).[62]

Sports facility coalitions reversed this negative trend in the 1990s, however, with a series of tactical adjustments.

—They turned to different sources of public revenue, less likely to trigger voter ire or referendum requirements than broad-based taxes on host city residents. The favored alternatives at the local level were visitor and "sin" taxes (most commonly, on hotel, restaurant, bar, and auto rental services) and regional sales taxes (which generated substantial revenues at very low add-on rates). These sources financed just 8 percent of public expenditures for new stadiums and arenas constructed before 1990, but 37 percent from 1990 through 2005 (projected).[63]

—Additionally, they were far more successful in eliciting contributions from state and county governments—particularly for new stadiums. States provided only 9 percent of funding for stadiums built before 1990 but 19 percent thereafter, while the county share rose from 30 to 45 percent. Meanwhile, the average local share declined from 28 to 13 percent.[64] State involvement also enabled stadium and arena advocates in many cases to tap new sources of revenue without referendum approval and to bypass normal procedural constraints. The Maryland Stadium Authority, for example, was empowered to select a stadium site, condemn property without negotiation, and finance most of its activities by operating sports lotteries.[65]

—Particularly where referendum approval was required, they secured much larger participation in the capital costs of facility development by the teams and other private investors. Whereas teams bore just 11 percent of

61. Danielson (1997, pp. 269–74; the quotation is from p. 269); and Fort (1997, pp. 168–70).

62. J. G. Long (2002, table 2-2).

63. J. G. Long (2002, table 4-30).

64. J. G. Long (2002, table 4-27). The pre-1990 figures are for facilities still in use as of 2001. On state involvement more generally, see Danielson (1997, pp. 130–32); and Eisinger (2000, pp. 324–25).

65. Euchner (1993, p. 121).

such costs in the 1970s, they contributed 34 percent in the 1980s and 43 percent in the 1990s (see table 2-2).[66] In several cases, particularly where referendums were required, teams eventually assumed the entire direct cost of facility construction itself. The voters of San Francisco, for example, rejected stadium proposals for the baseball Giants on four occasions during the late 1980s and early 1990s but finally approved a fifth in 1996, providing that the stadium would be built with no public funding at all.[67]

In order to obtain these up-front, highly media-worthy commitments from the teams, public authorities granted them compensating (and less visible) concessions: sweeter lease terms, long-term maintenance commitments, land contributions, collateral infrastructure investments, and property tax exemptions.[68] (The Giants received substantial public contributions in the latter three of these categories.)[69] After adjusting for these factors, Long concludes, the actual trend in public subsidization was opposite to that reported publicly. Whereas the reported public sector share of new stadium and arena costs dropped from 66 percent before 1990 to 57 percent thereafter, the "real" public sector share rose from 69 percent to 80 percent.[70]

With these changes in place, most projects were able to go forward without referendums, and when there were referendums, voters proved generally more receptive. To illustrate, less than a quarter of the 57 stadiums and arenas built between 1990 and 2001 were approved in referendums.[71] Whereas only 13 percent of major league sports facility ballot propositions were approved in the 1970s and 1980s, however, 71 percent were approved between 1990 and 1996.[72] It also bears mention that whereas referendum approvals tended to be final, defeats were generally way stations, either to

66. The public share of arena costs has consistently been lower than that for stadiums, and it dropped sharply in the 1990s. The reason is that arenas tend to be used far more intensively than stadiums. The most economic ones house both a hockey and a basketball team and are often used for other events such as rock concerts when the teams are not playing. The private investment share of new arena costs, in consequence, rose from 19 percent before 1990 (for facilities still in use as of 2001) to 58 percent thereafter. See J. G. Long (2002, table 4-27).

67. Agostini, Quigley, and Smolensky (1997, pp. 385–426).

68. J. G. Long (2002, ch. 4); see also Danielson (1997, pp. 227–33).

69. Specifically, the city leased the land to the team for less than market value, exempted both the land and stadium from property taxation, and committed to improving transit access. See J. G. Long (2002, appendix C, table 2-1).

70. J. G. Long (2002, table 4-1[a]).

71. Data calculated by Judith Grant Long at the request of the present authors.

72. Danielson (1965, p. 271); and Fort (1997, p. 161).

revised ballot propositions (as in the San Francisco Giants case) or to new arrangements eliminating the need for voter approval.[73] In 1995, for example, electorates (local in one case, statewide in the other) turned down proposals for publicly funded baseball stadiums in both Seattle and Milwaukee. In the wake of these defeats, local officials and the teams quickly obtained legislative approval for funding packages similar to those rejected by the voters.[74]

The net result of these developments, in combination, has been a tremendous stadium and arena building boom, with 52 new facilities opening in the 1990s and another 20 scheduled to come on-line between 2000 and 2005. If all of the latter are in fact completed by 2005, more than seven of every 10 major league stadiums and arenas will have opened since 1990. This is all the more striking in that the new facilities are also far more expensive than their predecessors. In constant 2001 dollars, the average cost of new facilities rose from $51 million in the 1950s to $132 million in the 1970s to $226 million in the 1990s; and those scheduled to open between 2000 and 2005 are estimated to cost, on average, $314 million (see table 2-2). Whereas fully two-thirds of stadiums built in the 1950s were for joint baseball and football use, moreover, this was so of fewer than 10 percent in the 1990s, and no more joint stadiums are anticipated. Cities wanting football and baseball teams are now expected to finance, in whole or major part, a stadium for each.[75]

The escalation in new sports facility costs was, it bears emphasis, not solely attributable to new luxury features demanded by the teams. It also reflected a shift toward in-town, more expensive locations. For reasons similar to those of shopping center developers, professional sports team owners, particularly in baseball and football, had strongly pressed for outlying locations during the period 1950–80, close to major highways and with plenty of land for parking. Governments, eager to accommodate team preferences and also to economize, had generally gone along. This pattern altered markedly in the 1980s, however. Central cities, having identified recreation as central to their downtown growth strategies, were now determined to host these facilities.[76]

73. Danielson (1997, p. 274); and Fort (1997, pp. 163–70).

74. Fort (1997, pp. 168–70). (This source incorrectly states that the Milwaukee referendum occurred in 1994.)

75. J. G. Long (2002, table 2-1 and, more generally, ch. 2); and Siegfried and Zimbalist (2000, tables 1, 2, pp. 96, 97). Arena costs have risen at a roughly comparable rate, from $82 million on average during the period 1960–79 to approximately $200 million since 1990.

76. Danielson (1997, pp. 283–84).

Los Angeles' Dodger Stadium in the mid-1960s. Like most stadiums built between the 1960s and 1980s, it had good highway access and plenty of parking. Credit: Security Pacific Collection/Los Angeles Public Library.

Reflecting the predominant post-1990 pattern, San Francisco's Pac-Bell stadium, which opened in 2000, was built close to the downtown office district. Credit: AP/Wide World Photos.

In accounting for the enthusiasm of top elected officials, it bears emphasis that stadiums and arenas were relatively easy to site in urban areas.
Mayors and governors were eager for visible successes in the competition for
professional teams but not for battles with neighborhoods, environmentalists, and historic preservationists.[77] Exclusive of parking, stadiums and arenas
have relatively small footprints, though—typically 15 to 25 acres for a central-city stadium, four to six for an arena.[78] And unlike festival markets,
which depend significantly on impulse visits from nearby office workers and
residents, sports facilities can be located successfully on the edges of downtown, in older commercial or industrial districts. Virtually all cities have
suitable locations available, unlikely to generate substantial resistance but easily accessible from the heart of downtown (and by transit as well as car).

Finally, most baseball, basketball, and hockey teams had also become far
more receptive to downtown locations: in part because they had discovered
that downtown employers constituted the core market for their premium
seats, a source of revenue on which they were increasingly focused, and
doubtless in part as well because the shift was occurring in a context of
sharply rising public subsidies.[79] The upshot, Long reports, was that 79
percent of the new facilities constructed between 1990 and 2001 were sited
in central cities (generally in or very close to downtown), by comparison
with just 39 percent during the previous three decades.[80]

The public-private partnership model has never proven feasible, even
cosmetically, for convention center development because convention centers
lack prime tenants and long-term lease agreements. Rather, they host an

77. Urban sites also were appealing because in comparison to projects proposed for suburban sites, their opponents tended to represent a smaller share of their jurisdiction's overall
electorate and therefore had less political leverage than their suburban counterparts. To illustrate: local opposition stymied the Chicago White Sox's plan to build a new stadium in the
Chicago suburb of Addison, while local opponents of a subsequent plan to build a new stadium on Chicago's South Side, near the existing stadium, were unable to stop that project. They
were able, however, to secure particularly generous compensation for those displaced by the
new stadium. See Danielson (1997, pp. 262–66, 280–84).
78. Where space is available, however, teams often seek and obtain considerably larger sites
in order to accommodate thousands of spaces of surface parking. See J. G. Long (2002, ch. 4,
p. 7); and D. C. Peterson (1996, pp. 134–75, 222–70).
79. Professional football was different. Because most of its games occur on Sunday after-
noons and because large numbers of fans are enthusiasts for "tailgating" (eating, drinking, and
socializing from the backs of motor vehicles) in parking lots before and after games, team owners still strongly prefer large suburban sites with plenty of room for surface parking. With only
eight or 10 events a year, moreover, football stadiums surrounded by vast parking lots are less
attractive to central cities than arenas and baseball stadiums.
80. Data calculated by Judith Grant Long at the request of the present authors.

unending series of one-shot events. The competition for such bookings, particularly of the most prized—national trade shows with many thousands of attendees—is fierce, with the result that no convention center generates enough revenue to cover its debt service and few even cover their operating costs alone.[81]

Not surprisingly, therefore, private investors have never built full-fledged convention centers (though many hotels have less ample meeting facilities and there are even a few private exhibition halls, which cater mainly to local trade shows). Led by downtown property owners, developers, and tourist industry groups, though, local business groups have long made public investment in convention center development a high priority, portraying it as an important component of local infrastructure. One might think that this would be a very hard sell, in that convention centers are corporate meeting venues with little to excite voters as potential users. In practice, moreover, when put to the voters, convention center proposals have generally proven less popular than most other types of public works.[82]

Nonetheless, the number of cities with convention centers more than tripled from the late 1960s to the late 1990s (120 to 409; see table 2-1), the total amount of available exhibition space nearly tripled (24 to 65 million square feet), and an additional 15 million square feet are scheduled to come on-line between 2000 and 2005.[83] While national data are lacking, it also seems clear that most of the space in use during the 1960s has since been replaced or dramatically upgraded.[84]

Heywood Sanders, who has most closely analyzed this history, and on whose work this section is based, reports that the business advocates of convention center investment, bolstered by standard-issue consultant studies, routinely made the following claims: (1) new convention center development was essential to keep up with improvements in other cities; (2) it would spark large amounts of collateral development; and (3) it would more than pay its way when economic multiplier effects were taken into account. Except in a handful of the most successful cities, however, both collateral

81. General Accounting Office, "Convention Centers' Economic Benefits" (1998); and Sanders (1997, pp. 13–18; 1998, pp. 63–68).

82. See G. E. Peterson (1990); and George E. Peterson, "Infrastructure Investment: Are We Misleading the Voters?" *Governing*, July 1992, pp. 78–80.

83. Authors' calculations from data presented in Laslo (1998, pp. 6–8); and Sanders (2001, pp. 3–4).

84. Maria Lenhart, "Expand and Deliver: Cities Build More or Expand Existing Convention Facilities," *Meetings and Conventions*, December 1, 1999, p. 79; and David Dunlap, "Built but Not Destined to Last: A Robert Moses Legacy, Coliseum Is Coming Down," *New York Times*, February 20, 2000, sec. 1, p. 39.

development and multiplier benefits have been extremely weak.[85] Since there are no long-term contract tenants, moreover, cities are unable to hedge the risk that convention centers will be underused. Many projects have generated substantially less business than originally projected, and this problem became more common in the 1990s as feverish expansion coincided with a slowdown in the rate of convention attendance growth.[86]

While advocates portrayed their recurrent expansion plans as needed to lure high-spending visitors from great distances, meetings of this type accounted for only a small, indeed often negligible, proportion of the business that most convention centers were able to attract. In 1996, for example, 55 percent of the nation's largest 200 trade shows occurred in just five cities (Las Vegas, Chicago, Atlanta, New York, and Dallas).[87] Consequently, while consultants routinely projected that the average meeting attendee would rent a hotel room for three or four nights, patronize restaurants, and shop, the actual mean was almost invariably in the range of one night or less. And this held true even for some of the most successful centers. Sanders reports, for example, that despite the large number of national trade shows New York City's Javits Center attracted, their attendees were mainly local—with the result that, as of 1995, the convention center generated fewer than 0.2 hotel nights per attendee. [88]

Studies of attendees, moreover, ignore the question of whether in periods of high demand others might rent the rooms in question if conventioneers had not booked them (usually at discounted rates) in advance. Striving to capture this effect, Sanders examined hotel demand in Boston during and after its Hynes Center closed for a three-year expansion and renovation during the late 1980s. In the event, local hotel room use continued to rise, topping out just before the center reopened. Then, with the center back in business, hotel demand was flat for six years. These trends were basically reflective of local economic conditions, but Sanders could find no evidence that the center's closing reduced hotel occupancies or that its reopening increased them.[89]

85. Sanders (1998, p. 59; 1997, p. 8; 2001, p. 3).

86. Sanders (2001, pp. 4–5); and Laslo (1998, table 12, p. 20).

87. Sanders (1999, p. 5).

88. Sanders (1999, p. 12). It also bears mention that convention centers are generally viewed as uncompetitive unless adjacent to high-quality hotels. Few are such reliable generators of hotel business, however, that hotel development accompanies their construction automatically. As a result, many cities have ended up subsidizing nearby private hotels as well as their convention centers. See Sanders (1997, p. 17).

89. Sanders (1997a, pp. 22–23, fig. 7). In a similar analysis involving stadiums, John Zipp found no discernible impacts of the seven-week major league baseball strike of 1994 on the economies of the affected cities. See Zipp (1996).

What, then, drove the surge in convention center investment after 1970? Three factors stand out, all familiar to observers of the festival mall and sports facility booms. First, convention centers are relatively easy to site. That is, they are discrete structures with relatively modest acreage requirements, and while advocates might prefer locations in the heart of downtown, the centers are quite viable (with adjacent hotels, often subsidized as well) in downtown edge locations.[90] Second, local growth coalitions successfully insulated most of their convention center initiatives from direct voter review beginning in the 1970s. By 1990, Sanders reports, city governments were directly issuing only one quarter of convention center bond issues. Nearly three-fifths were being issued by special authorities that states had recently authorized and exempted from referendum requirements.[91] Third, the advocates adapted successfully to growing voter tax resistance by shifting to a mix of state aid, local taxes aimed primarily at visitors, and off-budget arrangements.

For example, the city of Denver built its first convention center (as opposed to civic auditorium) in the 1960s, using a mix of existing sales tax revenues and urban renewal assistance. Little more than a decade after its 1969 completion, local business leaders began campaigning for a tripling of its size. Though they and the mayor were eager to avoid a referendum, one plan was placed before the voters at the city council's insistence in 1985, only to meet rejection by a vote of nearly two to one. Two years later the state of Colorado agreed to contribute $36 million (roughly 30 percent) toward the project's cost, while the city adopted a revenue package for its share consisting of hotel, prepared food and beverage, and auto rental taxes. On this basis, and without a further referendum, the project went forward.[92]

San Diego had been averse to urban renewal, and had never been able to secure voter approval for a convention center, but it had managed to build a small one in the 1960s (41,000 square feet) nonetheless. In order to avoid direct local borrowing, and with it the need for voter approval, it had arranged for its own employee pension system to issue the necessary bonds,

---

90. As centers have grown, though, they have needed much larger sites. For example, Boston's Hynes Convention Center occupies 5.5 acres, while its new center will occupy a 60-acre site. In general, most of the large convention centers are on 40- to 60-acre sites, but some of the largest—in Orlando, Atlanta, New Orleans, and Chicago, for example—occupy more than 100 acres. At the other extreme, New York's Javits Center occupies just 22 acres. D. C. Peterson (1996, pp. 176–221).

91. Sanders (1992b, pp. 154–55). It bears emphasis that this reflected a far more general pattern. Localities have cut back sharply on their issuance of general obligation debt since the 1970s in favor of revenue bonds issued by special authorities. See G. E. Peterson (1978, p. 59); and Sanders (1995, pp. 191–96).

92. Sanders (1992b, pp. 148–52).

secured by a long-term city lease. Beginning in the late 1970s, the city's redevelopment agency and main downtown business group mounted a campaign for a vastly larger facility. Put before the voters in 1981, this proposal received just 43 percent voter approval. The advocates persisted, however, and prevailed two years later when the San Diego Unified Port District stepped in. The district, an appointive body with responsibility for the San Diego airport, seaport, and harbor tidelands, had sufficient resources in hand to finance the project (at 760,000 square feet, nearly 19 times the scale of that built two decades earlier) without issuing any debt and had substantial land on the downtown fringe that it had been eager to develop for some time.[93]

When Chicago sought a $1-billion expansion of its McCormick Place convention center in the early 1990s, the most critical approvals that it needed were from the state of Illinois. Though the state was not a financial participant and the project was to be carried out by a special authority, state authorization was required for the financial package—new taxes on hotel, restaurant, auto rental, and airport taxi bills. The required legislation was approved in 1991, though only after Chicago legislators agreed to support a relaxation of air pollution rules sought by downstate legislators to protect high-sulfur coal mining in southern Illinois. This highlights a broader point, Sanders observes. Whereas downtown project advocates in the referendum era had to package their initiatives with neighborhood-based investments (and keep them relatively modest), so as to attract broad voter support, their post-1970 focus has increasingly been on potential allies outside the framework of local democracy, in particular state and special district officials.[94]

Looking Ahead

At the turn of the twenty-first century, the trajectory of urban mega-project investment was upward, and "do no harm" constraints were fraying at the edges. But the pace of change—at least by comparison with the early postwar years and the period around 1970—seemed gradual. States and localities were investing unprecedented sums of their own money in airport and rail transit improvements as well as in new stadiums, arenas, and con-

---

93. See Sanders (1992b, pp. 144–48). The port district, established by the state of California in 1962, is governed by a seven-member board—three appointed by the San Diego City Council, one each by the councils of four other localities bordering San Diego Bay.

94. Sanders (1992b, pp. 156–57).

vention centers. And broad-based coalitions had recently secured large increases in federal aid for all three transportation modes on which this book focuses (highways and mass transit in 1998, airports in 2000). In essence, though, the idea that mega-projects should proceed only if their negative side effects were negligible, or at least fully mitigated, appeared to be solidly entrenched.

The most notable recent trend generally in American politics, one that appeared to be sharply reinforced by the presidential election of 2000, was the ascendancy of organized business at all levels of American government. As it related to the subject matter of this book, the consequence was growing pressure to relax or eliminate many of the barriers to physical development put in place over the previous three decades. The new Bush administration was aggressively committed to this agenda, and the courts as well were fading as an obstacle to controversial projects. Reflecting a wave of conservative appointments during the Nixon, Reagan, and first Bush administrations (plus the barriers to counterbalancing liberal appointments posed by Republican Senate control through most of the Clinton administration), a series of judicial rulings since the late 1980s had sharply narrowed the grounds on which aggrieved groups could challenge official decisions or even achieve standing to litigate them.[95] Thus, for example, federal and state courts rejected all but three challenges to airport expansion brought before them in the 1990s. The exceptions, moreover, were relatively trivial: two upholding the authority of adjacent communities to regulate land use in their own jurisdictions, and one ordering a more thorough environmental review.[96]

On the other side of the coin, however, environmental organizations remained potent politically at all levels of government, as did neighborhood, historic preservationist, and other grassroots groups in most localities. The former, in particular, had stymied efforts by the new Republican majority in Congress during the mid-1990s to weaken environmental statutes,[97] and they now frustrated several of the new Bush administration's high-profile early proposals. In response to their protests, for example, Congress balked at the administration's recommendation to authorize oil exploration in the Arctic National Wildlife Refuge, while the administration itself

95. McSpadden (2000, pp. 145–64, esp. 147–51, 158–60). For a more sympathetic treatment of this trend, see Greve (1996, esp. pp. 42–63).

96. The land-use rulings involved Dallas/Fort Worth International Airport and Cleveland's Hopkins International Airport, while the EIS ruling involved Oakland's airport.

97. Kraft (2000); and Bosso (2000).

withdrew a proposal to roll back standards (recently promulgated by the outgoing Clinton administration) limiting the amount of arsenic permissible in drinking water. Locally, meanwhile, though more projects involving residential displacement were going forward than at any time since the 1960s, the scale of disruption remained very minor in comparison with the great mega-project era, and that which did occur was almost invariably accompanied by generous compensation and mitigation programs.

So matters stood at dawn on September 11, 2001. The horrific assaults of that day instantly refocused the nation's agenda, however, even as they intensified an economic downturn that was already under way. There is no precedent for the global struggle against nonstate terrorism in which the nation is now engaged or for the sense of vulnerability that Americans now feel at home. So projections of their effects on domestic priorities beyond the next two or three years are mere guesses. At least a couple of things seem clear, however. In the short term, resources will be scarcer for such pre–September 11 priorities as airport and highway capacity expansion. But—if prior experiences of war and recession are any guide—those projects for which resources can be found are likely to encounter fewer restrictions. Notably, moreover, even in the mega-project category most obviously affected by September 11—the expansion of airport runway capacity—no major projects have been cancelled as of late-2002. Most advocates and managers of major infrastructure systems still anticipate, it appears, that the current interruption of their momentum will prove temporary, a source of numerous project deferrals but very modest change when viewed from the perspective of a decade or so hence. Whether they are correct in this appraisal seems most likely to hinge on the nation's success in preventing future terrorist incidents. A glance at the early deliberations on redevelopment of the World Trade Center site, however—with the prospect of billions of dollars of mass transit, street, park, and memorial investment—suggests that even in the wake of terrorist horror mega-projects loom prominently on the urban public agenda.[98]

98. We examine post–September 11 developments in greater detail in chapter 9.

CHAPTER THREE

Mega-Projects and Urban Theory

One cannot, of course, construct or fully appraise a theory of urban politics on the basis of any single-sector study. Theories of the whole must stand or fall, though, on their capacity to explain a wide variety of specific observations. Thus theoretically guided, in-depth studies are essential contributors to general theory construction and refinement. This study is such a contribution.

The present chapter reviews leading theories of urban and American politics in search of hypotheses and orientation. What do the theories have to say about the place of large-scale public investment in urban politics? How do they account for, and interpret, the major changes that have occurred over the past half century? In particular, to what do they attribute the great surge of urban mega-project investment that occurred in the 1950s and 1960s? How do they explain the fairly abrupt end of this period, here labeled the great mega-project era, during the late 1960s and 1970s? What, if anything, do they have to say about the politics of large-scale public investment since the mid-1970s? Finally, where the theories are silent, can we reasonably infer why?

Initially we had planned to limit this review to theories of urban politics. We soon realized, however, that these were conspicuously weak on two topics central to the present study: federal aid policymaking and the ways in which inherited legal and institutional patterns shape current choices. So we consider here as well two more general theories of American politics:

public choice theory and historical-institutional theory. We return to these theories in chapter 8, asking how well they correspond to and explain the facts as we have come to understand them.

Explaining a Void

Theorists of urban politics have paid scarce attention to mega-projects. There are exceptions, to be sure, but even these focus mainly on a single program: urban renewal as it functioned during the 1950s and 1960s. At first this pattern appears surprising, for two reasons. First, the chief themes of contemporary urban theory are business domination and the primacy of economic development as a local policy objective. Second, in their efforts to promote development, both before and since the 1970s, business leaders have routinely championed public mega-project investments. Given this record, one might think that cases of mega-project decisionmaking would stand out as a rich source of theoretically pertinent evidence. That they have not occupied this role in the literature is, we judge, attributable to the following:

—First, whereas students of urban politics have focused on power relations within local jurisdictions, mega-projects are usually constructed by regional or state agencies—with some combination of federal, state, regional, and user financing. Urban renewal was the great exception. Renewal projects were planned and administered by local governments, even though the public money was mainly federal and the aim was private redevelopment.

This does highlight an important definitional issue. Should the field of "urban" politics be circumscribed by local government boundaries? Or should it be defined to include activities at all levels of government insofar as they are elements of the governance of urban places? We embrace the latter view, for the obvious reason that U.S. local governments are far from having exclusive jurisdiction over their territories, and even the powers that they do exercise are subject to the laws and regulations of higher-level governments.

A central part of local governance, moreover, is lobbying to affect the actions of higher-level governments. This is particularly apparent with reference to the topic of this book. The public investments that have most profoundly shaped urban places in the past half century have occurred within the frames of federal and state programs. Local interests have routinely been active members of the support coalitions for these programs, and then played central roles in advancing specific projects. Other local interests, wishing to block or modify such projects, have learned to play intergovernmental cards as well, from filing environmental lawsuits to lobbying their representatives in Congress. Practitioners, at least, recognize that such activity is a standard feature of politicking to shape the local built environment.

Why would scholars define urban politics more narrowly? Most probably, because trade-offs are inevitable in defining manageable topics for research and theorizing. The present study itself, seeking breadth on the dimensions of time and federalism, is confined to a slice of policy. So it is not difficult to understand why scholars striving to portray urban politics more generally have tended to slight the intergovernmental dimension. To understand is not to endorse this constrained vision of the field, however. It seems clear that an adequate theory of urban politics must encompass government actions at all levels that profoundly affect and deeply engage local actors.

—Second, political scientists, like journalists, are drawn to controversy. When elites are united, they typically contrive to present issues as technical, which is to say nonpolitical. This may involve the creation of semiautonomous authorities and self-perpetuating revenue streams (precluding the need for legislative appropriations) or simply the establishment of strong norms against political intervention (as in the awarding of most peer-reviewed grants for research in the natural sciences). In the realm of urban politics, the most frequent beneficiaries of these strategies have been economic development and infrastructure agencies. Political scientists recognize, in general, that the achievement of such insulation from day-to-day politics invariably reflects an extraordinary massing of political influence.[1] They tend to gravitate in their research, however, toward arenas of overt controversy.

From the late 1940s through the early 1960s, elite consensus regarding urban renewal, highway, and airport investment was extraordinarily solid. What controversies did occur were mainly fiscal and at higher levels of government.[2] The agencies entrusted with program and project execution were

1. There is disagreement, however, about the sources of this influence. Scholars who emphasize interest group and class conflict in local politics attribute it mainly to the power of pro-growth business interests. Others view it as evidence of local consensus on the centrality of development as a local government objective. See Piven and Friedland (1984, pp. 390–420); Foster (1997, pp. 49–50); and P. E. Peterson (1981, pp. 133–36).

2. Some localities, particularly in the South and Southwest, chose not to participate in urban renewal during its heyday. Though hostile to government activism for purposes of inner-city revitalization, it should be added, they were generally supportive of highway and airport development programs. See Thomas and Murray (1991, pp. 285–86); and Smith and Keller (1983, pp. 126–66, esp. 132).

usually semiautonomous, and they invariably took the position that their decisions were technical. They were in fact highly adept at nurturing support, often by blatantly political means (in awarding jobs and contracts, for example).[3] But the unity and influence of their supporters, reinforcing the myth that their decisions were technical, enabled them to prevail in nearly all cases where their decisions were challenged. And not only to prevail but to keep specific complaints from escalating into broader controversies—successfully framing disputes, for example, as pitting the narrow self-interest of a few (for example, residents to be displaced) against the public interest of the city or region as a whole.[4]

This quiet period was followed, to be sure, by one of furious controversy—most conspicuously about urban renewal in the mid-1960s and shortly thereafter about highways and airports. Political science urbanists did pay close attention to the former, though much less to the latter (which generally involved implementation by higher-level governments); and theorists continue to highlight the renewal experience in their accounts of recent history.

By the mid-1970s, controversy had again abated, urban renewal had disappeared as a distinct federal program (having been folded, in 1974, into the new Community Development Block Grant Program), and the sense that mega-projects were a dying breed may have further deterred political scientists from paying them much attention. In fact, however, numerous transit mega-projects were in construction or on the drawing board, many highway projects were still moving forward, and cities were groping toward new public investment strategies for downtown revitalization.

In the years since, all these activities have retained or increased their momentum, but controversy has remained muted. The years since 1990 have witnessed a flood of investment in convention centers and sports facilities, significant increases in highway spending, and major programs of expansion and modernization at leading airports. But public investment planners have taken great care to minimize community and environmental disruption, with the result that controversies have rarely stirred broad protest, or (with rare exceptions) otherwise shaken the government-business-labor coalitions determined to advance such projects.

3. See Caro (1974, chs. 33, 43); and H. Kaplan (1963, pp. 30–32, 41–43, 57).
4. See Altshuler (1965); and Danielson and Doig (1982, pp. 336–37).

Five Theories

The remainder of this chapter examines leading theories of urban and American politics—portraying their distinctive visions of urban politics but asking as well what, if anything, each has to say about mega-project politics. Several are virtually silent on mega-projects but are included because their silence itself is significant and because they suggest patterns of influence that, if valid, should apply in the mega-project arena. This review is, of necessity, selective. It does, however, touch upon all the schools that have dominated the field of urban politics at one time or another since the 1950s, along with two others prominent in the broader field of American political studies. In order to highlight family resemblances, the theories under review are grouped into five categories—listed below in rough order of their emergence historically.

—Elite-Reputational: Argues, primarily on the basis of survey research, that corporate elites dominate local politics.

—Pluralist: Argues, primarily on the basis of case observations, that influence in local politics is very widely distributed. (Because of space considerations, this review omits theories of hyperpluralism and the consequent ungovernability of cities, which enjoyed a brief vogue in the 1970s.)[5]

—Public Choice: Argues, from a mix of observational data and deductive models, that politics is best understood as the expression of rational choice by actors within frameworks of incentives. We label the most pertinent variants of public choice theory "hard" and "soft." Hard public choice theory is the mainstream version in political science. It portrays a world in which narrowly self-interested individuals, acting quite rationally from their own perspectives, tend to produce collectively irrational outcomes. Soft public choice theory, by contrast, perceives the actors as more enlightened in their self-interest and generally able to arrive at collectively rational outcomes.

—Elite-Structural: Argues, from a mix of historic and observational evidence, that corporate elites tend to dominate, and that their ability to do so is largely a function of the broader structures within which local politics occurs—for example, of capitalism, state and national governance, and culture. Neo-Marxist and regime (including growth machine) theories are included in this category.

—Historical-Institutional: Argues, primarily on the basis of historical evidence, that collective choices are strongly influenced by institutional

5. See Yates (1977); Lowi (1968, pp. v–xviii); and Savitch and Thomas (1991, pp. 10–11, 235–50).

arrangements, which in turn largely reflect long-past decisions. The implication is that analyses of policy based on current interest configurations and incentives are, in general, very incomplete.

Elite-Reputational

The behavioral revolution in political science reached its urban subfield about a decade later than the field of American politics more generally. By the time it did, in the mid-1950s, the discipline's pluralist interpretation of American politics was well established.[6]

Before this time, most research and theorizing about urban politics had been legalistic in focus and normative in orientation. That is, most studies examined the formal structures and legal arrangements of local governance and concluded with recommendations for reform.[7] The late 1950s and early 1960s witnessed a flowering of research on local political behavior, however. The theoretical impact of this work was to reinforce the pluralist vision of American politics already in vogue at the national level. The immediate stimulus to undertake it, however, was a provocation that arose in sociology—most specifically, Floyd Hunter's research purporting to demonstrate elite domination of local politics. Sociologists had long studied urban communities, but they had rarely, if ever, placed political power at the center of their work. In a book entitled *Community Power Structure* (published in 1953), though, Hunter did exactly that, in effect challenging the primacy of political science on its home ground.[8] When the dust eventually settled, roughly a dozen years later, it was clear to close observers that the debate between pluralists and elite theorists had deep roots in the disciplines of sociology and political science.

Among the standard categories that social scientists use in analyzing populations—class, status, power—the one that sociologists had traditionally "owned" was status. Status, as it happens, is purely a matter of perception, so the obvious way to map it is to ask people whom they view as having it in particularly high or low measure; Hunter's contribution was to extend this method to the study of power relationships. It turns out, however, that to ask this question is largely to answer it. That is, if you ask people to rank one another, they will do so. And if you employ "snowball" sampling, asking those ranked high in one round to identify whom they would rank high in

6. See Key (1942); Truman (1951); Latham (1952); Schattschneider (1960); and Zeigler (1964).

7. See Herson (1957).

8. Hunter (1953). Its national counterpart, theoretically if not methodologically, was C. W. Mills (1956), which became a crossover best-seller.

the next, you will eventually generate a rank-ordered pyramid. There is no doubt that people do perceive gradations. So Hunter was able to identify a clear pyramid of power in Atlanta.[9] At the top was a small group of leading businessmen. Even the highest public officials ranked a category below. Hunter avoided Marxist language, but his message was unmistakable. The capitalists were in charge, and local government was their servant.[10]

Pluralist

If status is perceptual, power is behavioral: A induces B to act differently from the way that B would have acted otherwise. The decisive test, in short, is whether B's actions are altered, not B's opinion. In practice, of course, an observer confronts enormous difficulties. It is often less than obvious what A did to influence B and whether B's behavior was altered. The actors themselves may not be sure, and some of those who are may prefer concealment. Power is often reciprocal, moreover: I follow your lead in some domains, you follow mine in others. Political scientists acknowledged these difficulties, but they were insistent that valid generalizations must rest on the evidence of observed behavior. Quite a few were attracted to the study of localities, moreover, as governments that were general purpose yet small enough to observe holistically.

The result was an outpouring of scholarship on local politics, the best of which appeared at the very beginning of the 1960s.[11] Without exception these studies found that the power of elites had been vastly overrated, that in truth local influence was very widely distributed. In contrast to nearly all succeeding schools, the pluralists had no strong preconceptions about which local government activities were most revealing of the fundamental distribution of influence. Their tendency, rather, was to focus on those activities that most absorbed local officials, activists, and journalists during the period of their research. Thus, in particular, they varied widely in the extent to

9. To be fair, he did not rely exclusively on reputational surveys. He also provided numerous illustrations of business power in action. These too were drawn from his survey responses, however, supplemented in some cases by journalistic accounts. For all the limitations of Hunter's methodology, it does seem probable that Atlanta in the 1950s was among the most elite-dominated cities in the United States. For a similar portrayal of Dallas—another young, growth-obsessed, southern city—in this period, arrived at by very different means, see Elkin (1987, ch. 4).

10. Hunter (1953, chs. 4, 6, 7).

11. Major pluralist works of this period included Dahl (1961); Greer (1963); Banfield (1961); Wildavsky (1964); Wood (1961); Sayre and Kaufman (1960); Long (1958); and Lowi (1964). For an overview of the elitist-pluralist community power debate, see Polsby ([1960]1980).

which they examined business-government relations and economic development strategies. One of the most widely acclaimed pluralist studies, for example, Sayre and Kaufman's *Governing New York City,* scarcely mentioned business influence at all and contained just two brief mentions of urban renewal.[12] Edward Banfield examined two business-oriented projects in his acclaimed study of Chicago, but these were just two of his six key cases.[13] In the first of these two, involving an urban renewal proposal, business groups stalemated among themselves and with other affected interests. In the other, a proposal for a new exhibition hall, success was achieved, but mainly because one corporation, the *Chicago Tribune,* made a crusade of it. The rest of the business community was, according to Banfield, divided or disengaged.

We focus here on Robert Dahl's study of New Haven—the most influential work in this genre, arguably the best, and the one that paid most attention to a mega-project program (urban renewal).[14] Dahl chose three arenas of political activity on which to focus in New Haven: (1) urban redevelopment, because it was the most salient local issue at the time of his research; (2) education, because it was the largest item in the city's budget; and (3) political nominations, because the need to secure nomination is clearly of major importance in determining the priorities of elective officeholders. While leadership in each arena was relatively concentrated, he found, there was little overlap among these elites in different sectors. More generally, Dahl concluded, political influence was widely dispersed, and imbalances of power from one arena to another were noncumulative. Wealth was a valuable resource, he acknowledged, but just one among many. And the others—such as skill, numbers, and activist intensity—were by no means routinely dominated by the power of money. Nor was political influence a private sector monopoly. Public officeholders, particularly the mayor, were extremely significant players, both shaping issues and prodding potential supporters to mobilize.

Dahl acknowledged that only a small proportion of New Haven residents engaged in political activity. Apathy and indifference were the norm rather

12. Sayre and Kaufman (1960). The references to business make clear that it is just one interest group among many (pp. 77, 160, 496–97, 502–15). There is no hint of business dominance. The cursory references to urban renewal are on pp. 56–57 and 589.

13. Banfield (1961, chs. 5, 7). His other four cases involved development of a branch of the county (public) hospital, a proposed merger of the city and county welfare departments, transit subsidies, and development of the University of Illinois Chicago campus.

14. Dahl was also unique among the pluralists in devoting considerable attention to history, with a focus on how patterns of influence had changed over the previous 175 years. See Dahl (1961, book 1, esp. ch. 7).

than the exception. How to reconcile this with the idea that New Haven was a hotbed of democratic pluralism? The answer: apathy in New Haven was a reflection of broad public agreement.[15] Political activism requires a great deal of time and effort. Why bother if one is generally satisfied? Groups of normally inactive citizens, however, can quickly mobilize if aroused and thereby become influential.[16] Elected officials, Dahl judged, are both acutely sensitive to this potential and deeply imbued with the American "democratic creed." Consequently, they are quite sensitive to "the real or imagined preferences of constituents . . . in deciding what policies to adopt or reject."[17]

At the very zenith of pluralist dominance two critiques appeared, neither with an urban focus initially, but each with obvious implications for thought about urban politics. Each stressed the need to place direct observations of political behavior within a more general framework. Their lenses were quite different, however—one emphasizing microincentives, individual rationality, and fine-grained conflicts within a basically pluralist framework, the other highlighting such macrofactors as capitalist organization of the economy and providing a much more frontal challenge to pluralism. The former, rooted in neoclassical economics, was gradually to achieve dominance in American political science as the public (also known as the rational) choice approach. The latter, here labeled elite-structural theory, embodied common features of subsequent neo-Marxist, growth machine, and regime theories of urban politics. Let us consider each in turn.

Public Choice

Public choice analyses of politics, mainly by economists, date to the late 1950s, and several of the earliest had an urban focus.[18] They were not cast as theories of urban politics, however, nor did they touch on the subject of mega-projects, so they are not discussed here. The seminal public choice critique of pluralism is Mancur Olson's 1965 book, *The Logic of Collective Action*. Olson's focus was the problem of "collective action" in public life: under what circumstances do individuals join together effectively in the pursuit of common goals, and why do people organize far better for some

15. See Dahl (1961, p. 198).

16. No other pluralist scholar left comparable room in his theory to accommodate future social movements. This is not to say, of course, that Dahl had any idea the quiet politics of the 1950s might shortly give way to a politics of turmoil.

17. Dahl (1961, pp. 164, 3, 316).

18. See Tiebout (1956); and Ostrom, Tiebout, and Warren (1961). Tiebout was an economist; Ostrom and Warren were (and are) political scientists. Other early landmarks of public choice theory, both by economists, are Downs (1957); and Buchanan (1962).

purposes than for others? The facts, he argued, belie the standard pluralist views that the capacity of like-minded voters to mobilize is quite evenly distributed (even if most, when satisfied, do not bother), that government officials are well aware of this fact, and that government decisions, in consequence, tend to reflect the major concerns of all substantial groups. Quite the contrary, Olson maintained. Governments greatly favor the well mobilized, who in turn differ systematically from other groups. Further, knowing just a few of a group's attributes, one can reliably estimate its mobilization potential. The reason: such attributes add up to a structure of incentives, within which individuals make rational choices about whether, and how intensely, to mobilize.[19]

Where groups, for example, cannot deny benefits to nonmembers, actual and potential beneficiaries have a strong incentive to "free ride"—that is, let others do the work. This is particularly a problem for large groups and for groups whose individual members can anticipate only small gains. If the group is large, one can often shirk, or even slip away entirely, without being noticed. In contrast, the members of small groups are much better able to monitor and bring pressure to bear on one another. Similarly, groups differ in the gains that individual members can reasonably anticipate from mobilization; members with the largest stakes tend to be the most highly motivated. So politics tends to be dominated by small groups, each of whose members has a great deal at stake: producers, employers, and subsidy recipients, for example, by comparison with consumers, employees, and taxpayers.[20]

Olson's analysis points directly toward the version of public choice theory that we label "hard" and that has reigned supreme in the field of American politics for the past couple of decades. Above all, this version has influenced (and been influenced by) research on Congress, with particular attention to our own topic, public works decisionmaking. Key propositions emerging from this body of work are:

19. Rational actor analyses of collective action problems in the public sphere, it bears mention, were first elaborated by game-theoretic analysts of international relations in the late 1950s. See Morton Kaplan (1957); Wohlstetter (1959); and Schelling (1960). Olson imported and adapted this approach to the analysis of political relations between individuals and domestic interest groups.

20. Olson does note in passing that groups differ in organizational resources, but his overwhelming focus is on incentives and disincentives to mobilize. Olson (1965, chs. 1, 6). His focus is almost entirely on economic organizations and incentives. The landmark work extending his line of argument to include political organizations and noneconomic incentives is J. Q. Wilson (1973). See esp. ch. 2 and pp. vii–viii of the introduction to the 1995 paperback reissue of the same book. J. Q. Wilson (1995).

—The central fact about each decision to allocate divisible benefits is that small numbers of beneficiaries reap large gains, while costs are widely diffused.[21] The greater the number of districts, the more this is the case—because the share of total project cost borne by the district in which it is located correspondingly declines.

—Members of Congress value such projects as means to solidify their political bases rather than as efficient economic investments. Indeed, they value them so highly that at times they transform programs that appear on the surface to be of an entirely different character into divisible benefit programs. National defense and redistributive programs, for example, are often structured so that members of Congress can claim credit for district-specific benefits—weapons procurement contracts, for example, or empowerment zone designations.

—Political entrepreneurs perform essential functions in project development: perceiving opportunities, mobilizing advocates, and providing strategic leadership. Kenneth Shepsle and Mark Bonchek put it thus: "A political entrepreneur is someone who sees a prospective cooperation dividend that is currently not being enjoyed. . . . For a price, whether in votes . . . or a percentage of the dividend, or the nonmaterial glory and other perks enjoyed by leaders, the entrepreneur bears the costs of organizing, expends efforts to monitor individuals for slacker behavior, and sometimes even imposes punishment on slackers."[22]

—Projects tend to originate locally—promoted by "rent-seekers" who aspire to reap private gains at public expense.[23] Members of Congress are particularly attentive to such claimants because they are major sources of

21. Wilson framed this argument in terms of a two-by-two matrix (benefits and costs, concentrated or distributed). J. Q. Wilson (1973, pp. 332–37). See also Jonas and Wilson (1999).

22. Shepsle and Bonchek (1997, p. 245). This book is a superb general exposition of the public choice literature. Shepsle and Bonchek attribute the term *political entrepreneur* to Richard Wagner who, in a 1966 review of Olson, asserted the need for such a role to explain the organization of labor unions, environmental organizations, senior citizen associations, and the like. For the work that first brought this term to the attention of large numbers of political scientists, see J. Q. Wilson (1973, ch. 10, esp. pp. 196–98). A useful recent treatment, which both reviews the literature on public entrepreneurship and seeks to examine it in a sample of U.S. suburbs, is Schneider and Teske (1995). This volume's literature review and analysis are excellent, but its empirical component—based on survey responses by a sample of town clerks and attributing entrepreneurship to anyone the clerks identified as having taken positions that "represented a dynamic change from existing procedures" (p. 89)—is at most suggestive.

23. The origin of the label "rent-seeking" to describe this phenomenon is Krueger (1974).

campaign contributions, they are dangerous adversaries as well as valuable allies, and they are exceptionally clear about what they want.[24]

—Other voters and organized interests pay little attention unless projects directly threaten them with significant harm, because the fiscal costs are so widely diffused. Some groups do commonly mobilize to oppose projects, however, and members of Congress are wary of finding themselves in the midst of local battles. Consequently, they structure elaborate bureaucratic processes to ascertain whether locally promoted projects are in fact controversial and generally press for legislative action only when persuaded that they are not.[25]

—Congress is also aware of its limited capacity for direct oversight of the vast bureaucracies charged with implementing its mandates. Increasingly, therefore, it has empowered private parties to initiate remedial action when they believe that bureaucracies are violating their statutory responsibilities—by gathering information, for example, under the Freedom of Information Act, by launching citizen or class action suits, or by complaining to investigators (such as agency inspectors general) whom Congress has well insulated from executive branch control.[26]

—Since the only actors who seriously care about benefit-cost analysis are some professional bureaucrats, such analyses are mainly window dressing. They are routinely structured, moreover, to overestimate benefits and underestimate costs—in effect, to provide a technical veneer for politically selected projects. This is not to deny, however, that they are used at times to help filter out unusually egregious projects.[27]

—The average legislator has no point of leverage from which to think about changing the system. It is feasible only to seek benefits for one's own district. For those in key positions, such as the senior members of pertinent authorizing and appropriations committees, there is even less incentive to change the system—because they are able to command a disproportionate share of the national benefit pie.

24. See Ferejohn (1974, pp. 58–61).

25. Ferejohn observes in his study of rivers and harbors legislation, for example, that upstream landowners routinely objected to dams that would flood them out, that railroads objected to navigation projects, and that private electric companies objected to hydropower projects until the government began distributing such power through them. Ferejohn (1974, pp. 52–58).

26. See McCubbins and Schwartz (1984); and Shepsle and Bonchek (1997, pp. 368–70, 375–77).

27. See Ferejohn (1974, ch. 2).

—Public works bills in Congress tend to distribute benefits very widely and to pass almost unanimously.[28] Members of Congress find it rational to pursue agreement to near-unanimity even though they might in theory reap greater benefits by organizing bare majority (minimum winning) coalitions, because the risk of being left out is far less. In a highly partisan legislature, one might find the universalism rule confined to the majority party. In Congress, however, while being in the majority confers significant advantages, benefits are distributed to minority members as well.[29]

This is "hard" public choice theory because it draws a sharp line between individual and collective rationality and views them as typically opposed. While presenting politicians, "rent-seeking" private interests, and apathetic citizens as all quite rational, it argues that their behavior, in combination, yields patterns of government action that are "inefficient" when viewed from a societal perspective.

Hard public choice theory certainly captures important elements of American politics, and it works particularly well in the domestic public works (classic pork barrel) arena. Where it is weakest is in explaining social movements organized around diffuse interests, such as environmentalism, and behavior that seems driven by public-regarding values (such as honor, compassion, and concern for future generations) rather than narrow self-interest. It can produce explanations for such behavior, in that any human action can be presented as an expression of utility, but these generally seem contrived. The great question, of course, is how large a share of political behavior the theory captures well. There are numerous examples of hard public choice analysis in the urban politics literature, arguing most notably the benefits of local government competition (versus consolidation) in metropolitan areas and the perversity of public land use regulation.[30] They do not add up to a general theory of urban politics, however, nor has the hard public choice perspective ever loomed very large in debates about such theory.

A "soft" version of public choice theory has been greatly influential in the field of urban politics, though, since the appearance of Paul Peterson's landmark book, *City Limits*, in 1981. The essence of Peterson's argument is that American local governments serve their constituents well, by and large, and that this flows directly from the rationality of their individual participants. In short, there is a basic harmony between the interests of the collectivity and

28. Ferejohn (1974, p. 247).

29. See Shepsle and Weingast (1981, pp. 96–111); and Fiorina (1981, pp. 197–221).

30. See Ostrom, Tiebout, and Warren (1961); Ostrom, Bish, and Ostrom (1988); Oakerson (1999); Dye (1990); R. H. Nelson (1977); and Denzau and Weingast (1982).

those of its individual members, from political leaders to ordinary citizens. Peterson subsequently extended this argument to the federal level and the system of intergovernmental relations.[31] Peterson's method is to begin, mainly deductively, by formulating a "rational" policy template (that is, one consistent with the overall jurisdictional interest) and then to assemble evidence on how closely the actual pattern resembles it. His characteristic finding: the ideal and actual patterns are surprisingly well (though imperfectly) aligned at both the local and federal levels.

How can we know a city's overall interest? The answer, at least for central cities: it is essentially the same everywhere. (Bedroom suburbs, Peterson acknowledges, are different. Their residents often have the luxury of concentrating on amenity at home, while counting on other localities nearby to attract and house employers. As a theorist, however, his focus is almost exclusively on central cities.) [32] Whatever else they may desire, cities need a healthy tax base and jobs for their residents. These depend, in turn, on continual flows of new business investment and of private decisions by affluent people to live within their boundaries. It is impossible to rest on past accomplishments because investments are constantly depreciating and because some companies and residents inevitably depart each year.[33]

The methods that cities can employ in pursuing these objectives are extremely limited. They are small, open units within the nation politically and the world economically. So they cannot command businesses to invest or affluent people to move in. Nor can they protect their existing industries from competition, or keep out people they consider undesirable. A city can strive only to make itself attractive to those with resources to invest and spend.

The surface issues of local politics are rarely about such fundamentals, to be sure. Candidates for public office, local interest group leaders, and the media generally focus on issues to which the ordinary voter can more easily relate. To what extent, if at all, should minority groups receive preference in public employment? How should facilities and services be allocated among neighborhoods? Should specific schools and streets be renamed in honor of ethnic heroes? Peterson labels such issues *allocational* in *City Limits*—contrasting them with *developmental* and *redistributive* issues.[34]

31. Peterson, Rabe, and Wong (1986); and P. E. Peterson (1995).

32. P. E. Peterson (1981, pp. 30–32); and Fischel (2001, pp. 12–14).

33. P. E. Peterson (1981, pp. 22–29). So far this is a fairly simple extension of Tiebout.

34. Peterson drops the allocational category in later works, and explicitly so in *The Price of Federalism*, consolidating it with his developmental category. The reason, he explains, is that high-quality services are an important development asset. P. E. Peterson (1995, pp. 204–05).

Developmental actions serve to attract investors, while redistributive actions tend to repel them. Allocational actions are essentially neutral, in that "reasonable people can easily disagree" about their consequences for the local economy as a whole. This liberates local interests to squabble about them, and indeed allocational conflicts "consume most of the energy of urban politicians."[35] But if allocational issues are the visible, turbulent foam of local politics, developmental issues are the strong currents. Local government leaders understand that the city's highest priority must be to attract investors and affluent residents (the only kind who pay more in taxes than they absorb in services), and that this involves competing intensely for their favor. So they close ranks in the developmental arena, adopt norms of responsible behavior, and commonly insulate development agencies from day-to-day political pressures—by structuring them as independent authorities, for example, and giving them long-term revenue streams (such as tolls). They close ranks as well around redistributive issues, but with the aim in this case of keeping them off the policy agenda. Even the leaders of low-income groups understand, by and large, that redistribution at the local level is counterproductive.[36]

Business is, of course, both deeply and prominently active in local affairs. Its involvement is not narrowly self-interested, however. The benefit that businesspeople seek, most typically, is a "halo" effect—professional and personal approbation for being responsible civic leaders. The surest paths to such approbation are to serve on high-prestige nonprofit boards, such as those of the local art museum and United Way, and to join in collective business efforts on behalf of economic development.[37] For the same reason, they tend to steer clear of arenas in which they perceive a substantial risk of controversy. The outcome of such business-government collaboration, Peterson judges, is furtherance of the local public interest. It is even best for low-income residents, because efforts to run a local welfare state merely produce a downward spiral for the city's fiscal health and economy, harming worst those who are most rooted in place and dependent on public services. Political and civic leaders differ in the skills with which they pursue local

He is silent, though, on the question of how this relates to such issues as affirmative action, the allocation of services among neighborhoods, facility siting, and demands to honor ethnic heroes. Perceiving no basis for labeling these developmental, we continue to prefer his 1981 formulation.

35. P. E. Peterson (1981, p. 150).

36. Peterson is not against redistribution. He simply believes that it is necessarily a national rather than a local function. See P. E. Peterson (1981, p. 183).

37. P. E. Peterson (1981, pp. 142–43).

interests, of course. But their overwhelming propensity is to recognize the truth of these fundamental propositions and adapt effectively to their requirements.[38]

Peterson addresses the topic of large-scale public investment only once in *City Limits*—to argue that while the slowdown in urban freeway construction after 1970 was triggered in part by local protest activity, its more fundamental cause was a decline in the economic value of new expressways. Local decisionmakers understood that such projects were no longer cost-effective instruments of economic development.[39] So concessions to protesters were essentially costless. Highway investment had become an allocational rather than a developmental policy.[40]

In *The Price of Federalism* (1995), Peterson in effect ventures an explicit appraisal of hard versus soft public choice theory as applied to the American federal system ("in effect" because he prefers the terms *legislative* and *functional* theory), asking which provides a more satisfactory explanation of recent trends.[41] He commences this analysis by identifying broad points of agreement among scholars about the best ways to allocate domestic responsibilities among the levels of American government and then asks whether recent trends are in line with the recommended distribution. The scholarly consensus, he argues, is that the federal government should concentrate on redistribution, because states and localities by and large cannot (without sacrificing competitiveness). In contrast, it should leave developmental functions to the states and localities, which tend to pursue it more efficiently than the federal government—because they are more subject to market discipline and because they cannot off-load the costs of local benefits (as members of Congress often can) on taxpayers nationwide.[42] If

38. P. E. Peterson (1981, chs. 7, 9).

39. P. E. Peterson (1981, p. 135). He does not provide any evidence in support of this contention, however. As discussed in chapter 8, we find an alternative explanation more persuasive.

40. He classifies highway policy as developmental in *The Price of Federalism*, but by this time he has combined his 1981 allocational and developmental categories and he does not explicitly discuss the economic value (or lack thereof) of highway investment. See P. E. Peterson (1995, pp. 17, 64–67).

41. P. E. Peterson (1995, ch. 2).

42. Peterson was criticized for neglecting, in *City Limits*, to specify particular incentives for political leaders to adopt policies in the long-term interest of the jurisdiction. Without mentioning the criticism, he addresses this topic in *The Price of Federalism* as follows (attributing it to "functional theory"): "State and local officials who enhance the property values and economic prosperity of their constituency are more likely to be rewarded with reelection. . . . In most states and localities, however, there are few incentives to enact large-scale redistributive policies, for which the economic and political costs are likely to be very high." P. E. Peterson (1995, p. 35).

functional theory is valid, he writes, federal spending should be trending toward redistribution. If legislative theory is valid, developmental policies should be experiencing the most growth.

This is an extremely interesting way to set up the problem, but it confronts hard public choice theory from an angle rather than head-on. While hard public choice theorists have emphasized the political allure of policies that distribute geographically divisible benefits, they have not argued that only developmental policies can be structured to provide such benefits. Quite the contrary, in fact—they have emphasized that even such policies as defense and welfare can be so structured.[43] Nor have they argued that such policies are becoming more dominant over time.

Peterson concludes that while each theory captures an aspect of reality, the recent trend is clearly in the "functional" direction that scholars consider desirable.[44] From 1962 to 1990, he observes, federal spending on redistributive programs increased from 4.8 to 10.3 percent of gross national product (GNP), while spending on developmental programs rose from just 4.2 to 5.2 percent of GNP.[45] There are some problems, however, with this analysis. First, Peterson categorizes entire programs as developmental or redistributive, thereby blurring their frequently mixed character. In fact, the tilt in favor of redistributive programs is due entirely to the growth of three specific ones: Social Security, Medicare, and Medicaid. The first two are very modestly redistributive, however; indeed, their remarkable popularity is generally attributed to the fact that their beneficiaries are spread among all income classes.[46] Moreover, the latter two benefit not just patients but also medical providers, who have provided most of the lobbying thrust to keep spending controls weak. Second, the states and localities as well as the federal government tilted toward redistributive spending in the period 1962 to 1990.[47] This implies a secular shift in public priorities rather than a sorting out of functions among the levels of American government. Third, the trend lines reversed direction during the final eight years of this period, 1982–90;

43. See Stockman (1975).

44. P. E. Peterson (1995, p. 84).

45. P. E. Peterson (1995, p. 66, table 3-2).

46. Economist Jeffrey B. Liebman has recently concluded, for example, that only 5–9 percent of Social Security retirement benefit payments are redistributive across income quintiles. The inclusion of disability and survivor benefits would raise this figure, but only modestly. See Liebman (2002).

47. P. E. Peterson (1995, pp. 70–71, tables 3-3, 3-4). State redistributive expenditures rose from 1.4 to 2.5 percent of GNP, while state developmental expenditures rose from 3.6 to 5.1 percent of GNP. Local redistributive expenditures rose from 0.76 percent to 0.94 percent of GNP, while local developmental expenditures declined slightly, from 5.8 to 5.7 percent of GNP.

federal development spending actually rose in these (mainly Reagan) years while redistributive expenditures fell.[48]

Whether or not Peterson is right about a long-term trend toward sorting out responsibilities among the levels of American government, it is clear that federal spending has shifted away from physical investment in recent decades.[49] More significantly in the context of this book, state and local spending have done so as well.[50] And this move is evident even *within* the development arena—from slum clearance and highway construction, for example, to business subsidies and tax abatements. The issue here is whether these changes are best understood as adjustments to economic or to political developments—a question that is addressed in chapter 8.

Elite-Structural

As early as 1960, E. E. Schattschneider, one of the doyens of American political science, issued a caution against overreliance on the observation of overt political behavior. "All forms of political organization," he wrote, "have a bias in favor of the exploitation of some kinds of conflict and the suppression of others. Some issues are organized into politics while others are organized out."[51] The most critical task in seeking to understand widely varying polities and their component organizations, he noted, is to uncover their specific biases.

48. P. E. Peterson (1995, p. 66, table 3-2). Development expenditures rose from 4.5 to 5.2 percent of GNP in this period. Redistributive spending declined from 10.8 to 10.3 percent of GNP.

49. Of particular relevance in the present context, transportation spending declined at all three levels of government between 1962 and 1990: from 0.64 percent of GNP to 0.38 percent at the federal level, from 0.91 percent to 0.59 percent at the state level, and from 0.47 percent to 0.37 percent at the local level. P. E. Peterson (1995, tables 3-2, 3-3, and 3-4). Urban renewal does not appear in Peterson's tables as a spending category, but of course it fell to zero during this period. More recent U.S. government data indicate that, from fiscal year 1960 to fiscal year 2000, the percentage of federal grants-in-aid earmarked for physical capital programs declined from 47 to 17 percent, while the percentage earmarked for payments to individuals (including Medicaid) rose from 36 to 62 percent. These trends are projected to continue, at least through fiscal year 2006. Office of Management and Budget, "Budget of the United States Government, Fiscal Year 2003: Historical Tables" (2002, table 12-3).

50. Peterson's data indicate that from 1962 to 1990 redistributive expenditures rose more rapidly than developmental ones at both the state and local levels. Within the developmental category, moreover, the greatest increase was for a service with significant redistributive elements, education. P. E. Peterson (1995, tables 3-3, 3-4).

51. Schattschneider (1960, p. 71). Schattschneider's label for this tendency, "the mobilization of bias," became for a couple of decades one of the most commonly used in political science.

Two years later Peter Bachrach and Morton Baratz fleshed out this argument with specific reference to local politics. The findings of Dahl and other pluralists, they argued, had been "foreordained" by their focus on overt issues. What their method could not uncover was the ways in which certain issues—such as racial segregation and the distribution of wealth—had traditionally been banished entirely from local political agendas. About this "dynamics of non-decision making," the pluralists had nothing whatever to say.[52] The remedy, they argued, must be to supplement the study of controversies that do engage the body politic with research on the ways in which others are excluded.

By the mid-1960s new social movements were bursting out all over, and their demands—on behalf of formerly passive interests and invisible values—were encountering intense resistance. It seemed obvious that the widespread apathy observed by pluralist researchers just a few years earlier had reflected something other than just mass satisfaction.[53] In this context elite theory revived—but in a new guise. The common feature of the new elite theories was their emphasis on the broad political and economic contexts within which local governments function, which they viewed as establishing a strong bias toward corporate domination.

Through the 1970s this revival was cast most commonly in Marxist terms. One cannot arrive at a profound understanding of any political system, the neo-Marxists argued, merely by studying controversies and choices within it. Rather, one must place such research within broader analyses of societal structure, particularly the structure of economic class relationships.[54] The most fundamental thing to understand about local government in capitalist cities is that it expresses the needs of the dominant (capitalist) class—for expansion, for social control of the masses, for collective services, and for the reproduction of social and economic arrangements in each generation. To be sure, local governments also respond at times to the demands of urban social movements, particularly during periods of mass mobilization

52. Bachrach and Baratz (1962, pp. 949, 952; 1970). Notable rebuttals, both by former doctoral students of Dahl, are Wolfinger (1971); and Polsby ([1960]1980). Maintaining that the issues on which Dahl focused were clearly central, these critics add that the data required for empirical research on nondecisions are, in Wolfinger's language, "largely unattainable." Wolfinger (1971, p. 1079).

53. See Fainstein and others (1983, chs. 1, 7); Piven and Cloward (1977, chs. 4, 5).

54. In the words of Manuel Castells, the most influential among them, "the pluralist conception of political theory only defines empirically actors in conflict, without situating them within the structural framework of the class interests which underlie them." Castells (1978, p. 8). Two good review articles on neo-Marxist urban theory are Jaret (1983); and Pickvance (1995).

such as the late 1960s and early 1970s. The benefits provided to mass publics, though, are best understood as instruments of social control, designed to head off threats of civil disruption. And such benefits tend to be withdrawn when mass mobilization wanes—as it invariably does within a few years. Even so, the long-term trend is toward escalation in the costs of social control, producing ever more serious fiscal crises. This is a major "contradiction of capitalism."[55]

This theory seemed especially plausible at the time of New York City's near-bankruptcy in the mid-1970s. It became progressively less so in the late 1970s and the 1980s, however, as governments at all levels curtailed programs serving the poor without provoking new civil disturbances or even a revival of lower-class political activism. Particularly salient markers of this shift were New York City's emergence from fiscal crisis (which highlighted the capacity of creditors to assert control over heavily indebted states and localities), the adoption of Proposition 13 by the voters of California (which demonstrated the potential for mass mobilization around the theme of tax limitation), the election of Ronald Reagan as president in 1980 (which demonstrated the potential for organizing a national majority around themes of political and social conservatism), and the subsequent Reagan presidential record (which demonstrated the feasibility of curtailing numerous domestic programs and expressing disdain for liberal activist groups while retaining a very high level of voter popularity and civic tranquility).

The neo-Marxist school, taken as a whole, was more notable as a source of provocative ideas than rigorous scholarship: in weaker hands it tended to be formulaic, and in its general hostility to capitalism it ran strongly against the American grain. Thus even in academic circles, and even at the height of its influence, it was highly controversial. It faded rapidly, moreover, as national politics swung to the right in the 1980s, greatly diminishing the audience for Marxist rhetoric.

It was in this context that regime theory first emerged, retaining a "structural" orientation and a focus on business power but incorporating public choice and pluralist elements as well—and shorn of Marxist terminology. Regime theory argues the mutual dependence of public and private sector elites (rather than pure domination by the latter), it maps political systems in terms of rational actors and structures of incentives, and it acknowledges a wide variety of pluralistic constraints on business power. We place regime

55. J. O'Connor (1976); Castells (1978, chs. 1, 2, 9); Katznelson (1976); Gordon (1976); and Hill (1978). Important non-Marxist contributions to this line of theory are included in Friedland, Piven, and Alford (1977, esp. ch. 1).

theory in the elite category, nonetheless, because its overwhelming thrust in practice is to emphasize business dominance.

The best marker of the transition from neo-Marxist to regime analysis is a 1983 essay by Norman I. and Susan S. Fainstein—which appears, moreover, to have been the work that introduced the term *regime* (already fashionable in the field of international relations) to the study of urban politics.[56] The Fainsteins cast their analysis in a neo-Marxist conceptual and linguistic framework—which, it should be noted, they abandoned almost immediately thereafter—so it was difficult at the time to perceive its originality. In retrospect, however, it reads as a unique bridge from neo-Marxist to urban regime theory.

The Fainsteins define a regime as "the circle of powerful elected officials and top administrators" who are formally responsible for determining local policy and who are "susceptible to electoral forces."[57] Having excluded private groups from the regime definition itself, the Fainsteins nonetheless focus on government-business relationships. Fundamentally, they argue, local regimes represent dominant sectors of the local capitalist class. Regimes also mediate, however, between business and lower-class interests. (Middle- and upper-income residents have little place in this analysis.) When acting as mediators public officials never forget that their primary constituency is capital. Thus they grant significant benefits to lower-class interests only when confronted with the alternatives of protest and social disorder. Electoral representation of the lower classes is never enough to bring about such concessions. Capital mobilizes, furthermore, to resist lower-class social movements. Thus New York City's social welfare orientation in the 1960s and early 1970s led to that city's fiscal crisis and effective takeover by creditor interests.[58]

---

56. There is, it should be noted, a peculiar disconnect between international relations regime theory and urban regime theory. What is most peculiar is that these two, identically titled, versions of regime theory coexist in the same discipline and originated within a few years of each other, yet they conceive "regimes" almost entirely differently. Except for a brief mention in a 1993 article by Clarence Stone, moreover, we have never come across a work in one tradition acknowledging the existence of the other. See Stone (1993, p. 2). For urban regime theorists, as discussed below, regimes are primarily about coalitions and informal arrangements that supplement formal governance structures. In the field of international relations, by contrast, regimes are about "networks of rules, norms, and procedures that regularize behavior and control its effects," not about coalitions. The rules, norms, and procedures are often quite formal, moreover—enshrined in explicit international agreements or widely accepted precedents in international law. The quote is from Keohane and Nye (1977, p. 19). See also Krasner (1983a, 1983b).

57. Fainstein and Fainstein (1983, p. 256).

58. Fainstein and Fainstein (1983, pp. 251–52, 257–58).

So far, this is standard neo-Marxist fare. With very little Marxist over-lay, however, the Fainsteins report on studies they and colleagues had recently conducted of redevelopment politics in five cities from 1945 through 1980. In every one, they find, throughout this entire period, there had been a "symbiotic" relationship between the mayor and the business community. Each brought certain capacities to the table. The city could access federal funds, most notably, while business could make private invest-ments. When allied, moreover, they could usually count on support from the local media. In only one of the cities they studied, New Haven, had some media opposed redevelopment; and their criticism had been from the right, condemning it as a form of Big Government. There had not been any instances of left-leaning media criticism, portraying renewal as a program that victimized poor people in the service of business interests.[59]

Though local capitalists had dominated throughout, they had been under constant pressure to adapt to developments beyond their control—some representing opportunities (for example, federal funding programs), others representing risks (such as surges in lower-class mobilization). The results had been several waves of change in both business strategy and government (regime) policy.[60] Before 1949 local regimes had generally opposed inter-ventionist government, even to further local economic growth. The enactment of federal renewal legislation in that year, however, stimulated the evolution of *directive* regimes, oriented toward carrying out large-scale, federally funded redevelopment schemes. In turn, the social movements, demonstrations, and riots of the 1960s generated *concessionary* regimes, willing to incur significant costs for social peace. A decade later, as lower-class fervor waned and capitalist interests counterattacked, *conserving* regimes emerged—oriented toward the maintenance of social control at lower cost. Having been alerted, though, to the potential for lower-class mobilization in response to land acquisition and clearance programs, these regimes took care to pursue their redevelopment objectives by other (mainly fiscal rather than physical) means.[61]

Another landmark on the path to contemporary urban regime theory—though it is entirely free of regime terminology—was John R. Logan and Harvey Molotch's 1987 book, *Urban Fortunes*. Although Logan and Molotch are both sociologists, their focus in this work is squarely on politics. Their analysis is behavioral (rather than reputational), and their central

59. Fainstein and Fainstein (1983, pp. 249–50).

60. John Mollenkopf (1975) had developed a similar argument in the mid-1970s, though without the regime concept.

61. Fainstein and Fainstein (1983, pp. 258–68).

theme is that stable, business-led coalitions dominate local governance. Though Logan and Molotch are vulnerable to the criticism that their theory appears to have come first, with examples chosen to illustrate it, this is too simple an interpretation. The theory is clearly a product of long reflection on a rich, if unsystematic, body of evidence, and it has resonated powerfully with the observations of numerous other specialists in urban politics.[62]

While the visible forms of decisionmaking in American cities are democratic, Logan and Molotch maintain, the reality is plutocratic. The prevailing ideology mandates deference to private markets and private property, the central issue is economic development, and the most influential actors are "place entrepreneurs"—people who make their money by renting out real estate, developing it, or seeking to enhance its value by influencing government policies. What most distinguishes place entrepreneurs from ordinary citizens is that they value land for its "exchange value" (its capacity to generate profit) rather than its "use" value (as a locus for social interaction, the enjoyment of nature, and ecological health).[63] Their unswerving aim is growth—which, above all, means real estate development—regardless of the negative consequences it may entail for current land users, such as the ordinary residents of established neighborhoods. And they routinely seek government action to facilitate their endeavors.

To secure such action, they organize local "growth machines"—that is, alliances of those in the community who stand to profit from development. These alliances include not just place entrepreneurs themselves but also their contractors, bankers, architects, engineers, and advertising firms; the employees of such enterprises and their labor unions; local media, utilities, and retailers who think that growth will bring them more business; and politicians who recognize that growth-oriented interests are the largest contributors to local campaigns. No one else has comparable resources, or comparable motivation on a continuing basis, to influence local government decisionmaking. Citizens whose "use" values are threatened by particular development initiatives often mobilize to resist, but sporadic par-

---

62. See Jonas and Wilson (1999). Although *Urban Fortunes* was published in 1987, four years after the Fainsteins' article, Molotch had published its core argument in a 1976 article. A year earlier John Mollenkopf had coined the label "pro-growth coalitions" in another landmark article and argued their dominant role in local politics. His portrayal of these coalitions was very similar, moreover, to Molotch's of growth machines. See Molotch (1976); and Mollenkopf (1975).

63. The concepts of exchange and use value derive from Marx. See Logan and Molotch (1987, p. 1). They had not previously been applied in an urban land use context, however, or as the basis for a theory of urban politics.

ticipation of this type is no match for the continuous, well-financed involvement of the growth machine.

The growth machine even has an ideology, Logan and Molotch observe—of "value-free" development. The essence of this ideology is that, while people disagree about values, there is no serious reason to disagree about growth. Growth means prosperity, and with more money everyone in the community can pursue his or her values better. This is in fact erroneous, Logan and Molotch argue; growth has many victims and often fails even statistically to enhance per capita incomes. But it is very potent politically. Insofar as the ideology of value-free development prevails, it becomes more feasible to insulate development agencies from normal democratic controls (by organizing them as independent authorities, for example) and to portray dissenters as special-interest pleaders.

Significant as the contributions of the Fainsteins and Logan and Molotch were, the dominant path of regime analysis was set by Clarence Stone in his 1989 book, *Regime Politics: Governing Atlanta 1946–1988*.[64] Like Peterson, Stone emphasizes the limits of local authority and argues that there is little point in focusing on who has power over whom. Whereas Peterson concentrates on what is rational for jurisdictions, however, Stone's concern is the internal dynamics of governing coalitions. The central thing to understand about Atlanta politics, he argues, is how local interests, both public and private, working cooperatively and over long periods of time, have enhanced their joint capacity to cope with external pressures and realize common objectives.[65]

Despite Stone's disclaimer of interest in whether some groups have more power than others, *Regime Politics* reads in many respects like a classic power elite study. Instead of focusing on reputational power, however, it

---

64. Stone (1989). Stephen Elkin also merits note as an early regime theorist, though his regime definitions fluctuated over time and have been less influential than Stone's. See Elkin (1985; 1987, ch. 3). The former defines regimes merely as "political patterns" and stresses variations over time. The latter defines a regime as "the desired political way of life" (1987, p. 110) and focuses mainly on dominant values in the American political tradition. Elkin (1987) does focus on cities, though, in two chapters of this book, portraying three regime types a bit more precisely. Pluralist regimes, he writes, which existed in most large northeastern and midwestern cities during the 1950s and 1960s, reflected a diverse array of interests. Among these, however, land use coalitions focused on downtown revitalization were paramount. Federalist regimes were responses to the turmoil of the 1960s, seeking to reassert social control and growth-oriented politics with large infusions of federal aid. Entrepreneurial cities, most common in the Southwest, were organized to maximize business influence and a focus on growth. Elkin does not discuss specific instruments of development policy.

65. Stone (1989, pp. 8–9).

seeks to lay bare the precise means by which Atlanta's business elite domi-
nates local decisionmaking. The book provides a remarkably textured
description of this group at work over a long period of time: maintaining
internal cohesion, defining and implementing strategies, and relating to
other groups. During the 40-year period covered by his study, Stone argues,
Atlanta business and political elites alike derived great benefits from their
stable alliance; neither simply controlled the other. Their collaboration was
not merely tactical, moreover; it reflected a common vision. Both perceived
the city as in competition with other jurisdictions for investment and jobs,
and each was in a position to help the other in pursuing more narrow objectives (such as favorable tax treatment and minimal regulation on the one
hand, good press and reelection on the other).

A regime, for Stone, is an "informal" but "relatively stable" group with
"a sustained role in making government decisions." In the specific case of
Atlanta, the regime is "the informal partnership between city hall and the
downtown business elite." Operationally, it is "held together by a core
group who come together repeatedly in making important decisions."
Indeed, Stone writes, "When I refer to the governing regime in Atlanta, I
[usually] mean the core group at the center of the workings of the regime."[66]

Within this coalition, the business partners are clearly dominant. They
have strong policy preferences (for growth), great continuity, and ample
resources. What the elected officials care about, primarily, is reelection.
While their voting constituents are mainly black and low income, the business leaders control resources that they urgently need. Mayors need, for
example, to be perceived as generators of prosperity, and they need favorable media coverage. With rare exceptions, consequently, they become
enthusiastic champions of the business growth agenda. When, on occasion,
they do not, as in Maynard Jackson's first term (1973–77), they face widespread criticism, even from within their own core constituency, and
experience frustration in pursuing most of their aims.[67]

Though the business elite is much more influential than any other group
locally, its dominance is far from complete. It does not control the actions
of higher-level governments, of private sector investors, or of major social
movements (like civil rights) that can have profound impacts on local affairs.
Even its ability to mobilize its own members is extremely limited, since they
are often business competitors as well as political allies. So the regime mobilizes only around themes that are consensual in the business community.

66. Stone (1989, pp. 3, 4).
67. Stone (1989, pp. 85–94, 125, 189–92, 228, 233).

Among these, the most salient is the idea of "investor prerogative"—that is, that government restrictions on investors should be minimal.[68]

In specifying the limits of business dominance, Stone notes that the Atlanta elite, before forging its current alliance with the city's black elected leadership, sought to preserve white rule by having the city annex nearby suburbs or become part of a metropolitan government. This strategy failed.[69] More recently, the business elite has relinquished control of certain policy domains—such as public education—that were peripheral to its concerns but very important to black community leaders.[70] It has also devoted considerable energy and resources to co-opting members of the black middle class.

Stone acknowledges these developments as significant, but he also makes clear that they should not be taken as evidence of a change in regime. The main characteristics of the business elite, its internal organization, its ways of inducing cooperation, and its dominance have remained fundamentally constant.[71] The policy domains taken over by the black community were matters of relative indifference to the business leadership. And the downtown elite has managed to co-opt key members of the black middle class (professionals, businesspeople, leaders of nonprofit institutions), by and large, without sharing power. Its method, rather, has been the selective distribution of material incentives—jobs, contracts, and charitable contributions—to those who "go along." What it conspicuously has not done is invite them to participate in the meetings where important decisions are made. Indeed, Stone observes, although Atlanta has a "reform" charter and little public patronage, it is in many respects a "machine" city.[72] The regime, he writes, is "held together primarily by selective incentives; Atlanta more resembles than differs from the Daley machine in Chicago."[73] The difference is that, while the incentives are controlled by a political party in Chicago, they are controlled by private business in Atlanta.

68. Stone (1989, pp. 168–73).
69. Stone (1989, pp. 77, 163–64). As of 2000, the city of Atlanta housed only 10.1 percent of its regional population. Authors' calculations from U.S. Bureau of the Census, "U.S. Census 2000 Summary File 1 (SF1)" (www.census.gov/main/www/cen2000.html [October 2002]).
70. Stone (1989, pp. 103–06).
71. Stone (1989, pp. 9, 181).
72. Note the echo here of Molotch's growth machine terminology.
73. Stone (1989, p. 213). Stone adds that the process of distributing selective incentives rarely reaches beyond the black middle class. The black lower class, the white neighborhoods, preservationists, and others are essentially left out. Stone (1989, p. 215).

What about mega-projects? Stone observes that expressway construction and urban renewal both caused massive residential displacement in the 1950s and early 1960s, which the city offset in part with a program of subsidized housing development. The initial mobilization of the city's neighborhoods, in the late 1960s and early 1970s, was driven largely by antihighway sentiment. And the neighborhood movement in turn seems to have played an important role in electing the city's first black mayor, Maynard Jackson (1973).[74] Stone observes, moreover, that "the 1971 launching of MARTA, the mass transit system, proved to be a turning point in Atlanta politics. The issue made the white business elite realize that it must have the active support of the black middle class, and so it used the bridges it had constructed to work out new understandings—understandings that left the biracial coalition intact but with significant concessions to the black community and its increased electoral power."[75] The initial plan for MARTA failed in a 1968 referendum, due to negative pluralities in black neighborhoods of Atlanta as well as in the suburbs. The revised plan, which voters approved in 1971, included new lines serving predominantly black neighborhoods, guarantees of affirmative action in MARTA hiring and contracting, and a package of immediate bus improvements, including reduced fares and expanded service.[76]

During the subsequent administration of Andrew Young, on the other hand, at least two major highway projects opposed by black neighborhood groups went forward. As of the late 1980s, moreover, when Stone's book went to press, a MARTA spur promised to the black community in 1971 had not yet been built. These choices "signaled a basic shift in the city's politics," Stone writes, "away from responsiveness to the neighborhood movement."[77] In brief, the historic regime pattern was reasserting itself following the turmoil of the 1960s and the initial black mobilization to take over city hall.

Stone's emphasis on regime continuity is consistent with his data but driven as well by three analytic choices. First, he defines the regime in such general terms that new constraints, rising costs to mollify potential opponents, and even the end of business dominance in some major policy domains do not lead to findings of regime change. A stricter definition of the regime

74. Stone (1989, pp. 32–46, 82–84, and also pp. 110–16, 122–26, on two subsequent highway controversies).

75. Stone (1989, p. 98).

76. Stone (1989, pp. 99–100). In order to address suburban concerns the main local revenue source was also changed, from the property tax to a 1 percent regional sales tax.

77. Stone (1989, p. 116, 168).

might have produced an interpretation highlighting changes over time. Second, he takes as his central premise (in common, to be sure, with nearly all other recent theorists of urban politics) that the central issue of local governance is economic development. Had he, like Dahl, chosen to view such arenas as education and political nominations as comparably significant, he would have placed greater stress on both change and the pluralistic dimensions of Atlanta politics. Third, having noted the importance of higher-level governments at the outset of *Regime Politics*, he pretty much ignores them thereafter. Except in the arena of civil rights, a reader gets little sense that changing federal or state policies were important factors in Atlanta politics during the period studied. Yet *Regime Politics* covers mainly the same period as that examined by the Fainsteins (with also the same focuses, business-government relations and the pursuit of economic development).They perceived a great deal of local political change, it will be recalled, driven by shifts in federal policy and new social movements. With a slight shift of emphasis, we believe, Stone might have arrived at similar findings for Atlanta even if he continued to spotlight elements of regime continuity.

Regime theorists, including Stone himself, have observed that not all cities are governed by cohesive regimes, that regimes can fall apart, and that regimes vary in the degree to which business must share power with other local interests.[78] They have consistently maintained that strong business dominance is the most common American pattern, though, particularly in employment center locales (as opposed to bedroom suburbs). They have also followed the lead of *Regime Politics* in emphasizing continuity rather than change and in relegating intergovernmental relations to the far periphery. This book, in contrast, is most centrally concerned with change and with programs substantially financed by higher-level governments. On these topics the regime analysis that we find most useful is still the Fainsteins', though we are deeply indebted as well to Logan and Molotch's vivid analysis of place-based local interests and Stone's fine-grained, highly nuanced accounts of business leadership in action.

Historical-Institutional

The theories examined thus far all proceed from certain characteristic assumptions of behavioral political science: (1) individuals arrive in the political arena with their preferences already established; (2) while institu-

---

78. See Stone (1987, 1993, esp. pp. 18–23); DeLeon (1992, esp. ch. 1); Clavel and Klniewski (1990, pp. 199–234); and DiGaetano and Klemanski (1999, esp. pp. 1–29, 243–79).

tions aggregate member preferences, they neither distort nor reshape them; (3) both individuals and institutions are tactically rational; and (4) they adapt quickly to changing circumstances. Insofar as these assumptions are valid, current behavior should accurately reflect both the stable preferences and current resources of all key actors.

Suppose, however, that: (1) institutions and legal arrangements shape as well as reflect actor preferences; (2) such arrangements tend to evolve far more slowly than personal preferences or resources; (3) actor behavior in any event often reflects institutional roles and incentives more than personal values or tastes; and (4) institutional patterns of governance often lead to actions that poorly reflect member preferences. In this scenario, observed behavior may provide only a fun house mirror reflection of bedrock actor preferences.[79]

This latter set of assumptions is not antibehavioral. It stresses, however, that a deep understanding of politics must proceed from an understanding of institutional arrangements and of historic pathways that cannot be observed currently.[80] There are no general theories of urban politics with a substantial historical-institutional component, but a crucial next step for urban theory construction, we judge, is to incorporate the historical-institutional perspective, and some research already available helps point the way. To note just a few examples:

Ira Katznelson argues that the U.S. pattern of partisan organization based on ethnicity rather than class is attributable to the phasing of U.S. political and economic development in the nineteenth century. Mass suffrage preceded the industrial revolution and unionism in the United States. By the time unions came along, political parties—locally based in the American system—had already organized workers in their residential neighborhoods and were highly resistant to union competition. It made sense for unions to avoid such competition, focusing exclusively on workplace organization and generally eschewing political activity. Political parties, meanwhile, free of union pressures to stress class themes, organized around ethnicity instead.[81]

79. See March and Olsen (1984, 1989); Hall and Taylor (1996, pp. 936–57); Immergut (1998); and Thelen and Steinmo (1992, pp. 1–32).

80. The corresponding concept in contemporary economics is "path dependence." See David (1985); Arthur (1994); and Pierson (2000).

81. Katznelson (1981, chs. 2, 3). This work long predates the term *historical-institutionalism* which, according to Hall and Taylor (1996), originated in Steinmo, Thelen, and Longstreth (1992).

Of greater pertinence to the present study, recent scholars have argued that the extreme fragmentation of authority in the American system tends to dampen the effects of electoral shifts on public policy. Desmond King, for example, compares welfare-to-work reform efforts by conservative governments in the United States and the United Kingdom during the 1980s. The American tradition of federalism, combined with divided party government at the federal level, he finds, largely frustrated President Reagan's initiatives. The British traditions of unitary government and party discipline, on the other hand, enabled Margaret Thatcher to proceed with few compromises.[82]

In a similar vein, David Vogel compares environmental policy development in the United Kingdom, Japan, and the United States since World War II. During the late 1960s and early 1970s, as public concern about the environment exploded in all three countries, each political system responded with vigor. The U.S. response was distinctive, however, reflecting its wide diffusion of authority and tradition of heavy reliance on judicial oversight. Most notably, competing politicians engaged in a bidding war for the favor of environmental organizations, writing ambitious standards and deadlines (rather than general guidelines) into the statutes themselves and authorizing private citizens—even if they had no direct interests at stake—to sue government agencies they viewed as insufficiently aggressive in pursuing compliance. This policy design profoundly influenced the subsequent behavior of environmental organizations, channeling their energies toward the development of litigation staffs and strategies.

After 1980, Vogel continues, environmental influence waned in all three countries, and conservative governments sought policy rollbacks. The U.S. administration was least successful, however. Divided government prevented any weakening of the environmental laws, and the courts remained open to environmental litigants. In many instances, moreover, when frustrated at the federal level, environmentalists were able to achieve new legislative and regulatory successes in state and local jurisdictions. Vogel concludes: "Because the multiple veto points in the U.S. . . . system make it difficult to alter the statutory status quo . . . policies favoring diffuse interests are unlikely to be repealed or to fall into disuse. Policy making for diffuse interests is therefore

---

82. King (1992). For a similar analysis of tax policy, see Steinmo (1993).

more likely to be a 'ratchetlike' phenomenon (advances that are difficult to reverse) rather than the 'seesaw' (cyclical advances followed by equal declines) that often characterizes party government parliamentary systems."[83]

Stability does not mean complete rigidity, of course, and conservative judicial appointments during the Reagan and first Bush administrations produced a shift by the courts away from receptivity to environmental (and particularly citizen suit) claims during the 1990s.[84] The larger point made by historical-institutionalist scholars, however, that groups often retain policy leverage long after the circumstances in which they acquired it have changed, is highly pertinent to the present study—which has as a central concern the ways in which groups threatened by mega-projects (including but not limited to environmentalists) acquired new leverage during the late 1960s and early 1970s and then continued to exercise it even as their political strength waned in subsequent decades.

Conclusion

We make no claim to have "tested" any of the theories reviewed in this chapter. Our focus is too broad and our evidence too qualitative for that. We have structured our investigation, though, to provide fodder for disciplined reflection about how well it explains recent patterns and shifts in the single arena of urban politics with which we are here concerned. And this will be our aim when we return to these theories in chapter 8—a rigorous but qualitative appraisal, asking which seem most consistent with our findings and helpful in their interpretation.

83. Vogel (1993, p. 267). John Chubb and Terry Moe offer a similar explanation for the persistence of old mandates, often commanding little current support, in American K–12 education. Chubb and Moe (1990, pp. 41–47).

84. See McSpadden (2000, pp. 145–64, esp. 147–51, 158–60); Greve (1996, pp. 42–63); and Duke Environmental Law Symposium (2001).

CHAPTER FOUR

The New Politics of Highways

By any measure, Boston's Central Artery/Tunnel (CA/T) project is an astonishing undertaking. At a projected cost (2002) of $14.6 billion for seven miles of highway—plus several billion dollars more, off budget, to finance collateral "mitigation" agreements—it is the most expensive public works project in U.S. history. Its construction has attracted widespread attention as a dazzling feat of engineering—particularly in its downtown section, where it is being built, underground, directly beneath a still-functioning elevated highway and adjacent surface streets. It is certainly no less noteworthy, however, as a feat of politics. Its construction is occurring in the core of a region that decisively rejected new highway construction during the early 1970s. And it has survived a host of perils that might have sunk almost any other project: the determined opposition of President Reagan, the end of the Interstate Highway Program everywhere else in the country, and a bitter state political transition.

While an outlier in numerous respects, however, the CA/T is representative of post-1970 highway planning in others. Most notably, it was crafted from the outset to avoid provoking community or environmental opposition. Its cost, not coincidentally, is extraordinarily high per unit of traffic capacity added. And its implementation exemplifies what we label "bottom-up federalism," with nearly all initiative coming from the local and state levels of government but most financing from the national level. These patterns represent a significant departure from those of the late 1950s and the

1960s, when champions of new expressway construction achieved unprecedented gains and spared little concern for households, neighborhoods, ecologies, or public amenities in their path.

From what sources did the urban expressway boom emerge? Why did it prove so brief? And what are the most significant implications for future urban highway investment of the strategies that have, at least on occasion, succeeded since 1970? In demonstrating that new expressways can be constructed with minimal impact—and indeed in such a manner as to enhance surface amenities—even in very dense urban settings, do they suggest a much brighter future for such investment than might have seemed likely in the 1970s? Or, in demonstrating how much it costs to build with such exquisite sensitivity, do they suggest that in future such projects will be very rare indeed?

Run-up to the Interstate Program

Until the Great Depression, the federal government played only a minor role in highway development, providing modest aid to the states for rural highway improvements but virtually none for urban roads. States, in turn, took the lead in highway development but only, for the most part, outside of incorporated jurisdictions. Localities spent more than any other level of government on road improvements, almost entirely financing the construction and improvement of ordinary streets.[1] At least a few cities went farther, however. The nation's first limited-access highway, for example—with grade separation of cross streets, ramps for entering and exiting vehicles, and no curb cuts between ramps—was New York's Bronx River Parkway, which opened in 1923.[2] Its popularity spurred a suburban parkway boom in the later 1920s, particularly in New York's Westchester and Nassau Counties. The parkways, viewed mainly as recreational amenities, were universally hailed by urban planners and commentators.[3] By the late 1920s several cities were planning limited-access roads as well, often with the primary aim of relieving traffic congestion. In 1929, for example, Robert Whitten, one of the nation's leading traffic engineers, proposed in a plan for Boston that

1. Federal Highway Administration, "Highway Statistics Summary to 1995" (1997, table HF-210).

2. Frederick Law Olmsted had proposed a parkway along the Bronx River in 1877, even before the commercialization of motor vehicles. Its construction was not authorized, however, until 1914—and then only as part of a plan to protect the river from pollution originating in the Bronx Zoo. See McShane (1988, pp. 79–80).

3. See Benton MacKaye and Lewis Mumford, "Townless Highways for the Motorist: A Proposal for the Auto Age," *Harper's Magazine*, August 1931, pp. 347–56.

the city construct an elevated, limited-access highway (central artery) running north-south through downtown.[4] This idea was derailed by the Great Depression, but New York's Henry Hudson Parkway and West Side Highway opened in 1931, and Chicago's Lake Shore Drive opened in 1933.

Federal aid for highway improvements surged during the New Deal—from $216 million in 1932 to $805 million in 1936[5]—and for the first time some of it, justified primarily as a way of providing jobs, went to cities. With the notable exception of New York City, which used federal relief funds to build the Triborough Bridge and several other facilities, most cities used their aid for labor-intensive maintenance and repair projects. Many, however, developed plans for new roads. In 1937, for example, a regional commission in Los Angeles recommended construction of a system of elevated highways, including both radial freeways and bypass routes. In accord with this plan, the city began construction of the Arroyo Seco Freeway from Pasadena to downtown Los Angeles in 1938. The first 3.7-mile stretch opened to traffic in 1940.[6]

At the federal level as well there was growing interest in (though not yet any money for) limited-access highway construction during the late 1930s, spurred in part by the new autobahns under construction in Germany. Support gradually built for the idea that America, too, should develop a nationwide system of limited-access highways. The proponents of this idea, who included President Roosevelt, believed that such a system could be self-financed, mainly from tolls but also from the sale of land near highway interchanges. (The federal government, it was thought, could take more land than it needed and then sell off the excess as—in consequence of its investment—values rose.)[7]

In 1937 Roosevelt asked the federal Bureau of Public Roads (BPR) to examine an idea, already under discussion in Congress, for a national system of three east-west and three north-south toll roads. Reporting in 1939, the BPR concluded that few segments would generate enough toll revenue to cover their costs. It noted, moreover, that the most serious traffic problems were in cities and recommended that if the federal government proceeded it should sponsor construction within as well as between them.[8] World War II interrupted this initiative, but planning continued in the con-

4. See Green (1979); and Whitten (1930, pp. 6–14).
5. Authors' calculations from Bureau of the Census, *Historical Statistics of the United States: Colonial Times to 1970* (1975, series Y 605–37).
6. See Seely (1987, pp. 149–56).
7. See Rose (1979, p. 10).
8. Public Roads Administration (1939, p. 93).

sideration of postwar economic policy options. In 1944 Congress authorized a 40,000-mile toll-free interstate highway system, including about 4,000
miles of urban highways. (The BPR, in consultation with state officials, was
to establish the actual routes.) It deferred funding, however, because the war
was still going on.

After the war, as automobile production resumed and car ownership
boomed, many states and localities launched major highway building programs. In Boston, for example, the city's business and political leaders gave
high priority to construction of the elevated central artery, as proposed in
Whitten's 1929 plan, and a second cross-harbor tunnel. These projects were
included in the state Department of Public Works 1948 highway plan. This
plan, developed in accord with BPR guidelines for the interstate system, also
included eight radial and two circumferential freeways, one near the urban
core and the other just beyond the existing zone of suburban development.
Though federal funding had still not materialized, in 1949 state public works
commissioner William Callahan persuaded the Massachusetts legislature to
authorize bonding for a number of these facilities, including the Central
Artery and the outer circumferential (eventually designated Route 128).

To make way for the Central Artery, the Department of Public Works
(DPW) acquired and cleared about 1,000 residential and commercial structures. Though neighborhood protests were intense, state officials insisted
that their plan—including the road's precise location—was optimal from the
standpoint of motorists and downtown commerce. All of the neighborhood
groups came away empty-handed, with one exception. In 1953, very late in
the planning process, a new state administration agreed to place the artery's
southernmost segment, adjacent to Chinatown, in a tunnel.[9] This was,
apparently, the first instance anywhere in the United States of burying a
highway segment in response to community pressure.

As of 1956, there were 480 freeway miles completed or under construction in the country's 25 largest cities, of which more than half were in New
York, Los Angeles, and Chicago.[10] Virtually all of this mileage, along with
the limited-access intercity toll roads that numerous states were building,
had been financed without federal aid. Though this pace of construction was
brisk by historic standards, it was slow in relation to the growth of motor
vehicle usage—and far too slow from the standpoint of the industries (automotive, oil, construction, trucking) at the heart of the motor vehicle

9. See T. H. O'Connor (1973, pp. 82–85); Green (1979); and Geiser (1970, pp. 258–64).
10. Owen (1966, p. 47, n. 79).

The original construction of Boston's Central Artery, like many highways built in the 1950s and 1960s, required the clearance of large numbers of residential and commercial structures. Credit: Courtesy of the Boston Public Library, Print Department; photograph by Leslie Jones.

economy. In the early 1950s these industries and their labor unions, led by the motor vehicle manufacturers, mounted a massive campaign for increased federal highway aid, and their efforts received a strong boost with the 1952 election. The new president, Dwight Eisenhower, had been concerned about intercity highways since 1919, when he was a senior War Department observer on the army's first cross-country convoy, an effort that took 62 days.[11]

In 1954 Eisenhower appointed a commission chaired by General Lucius Clay, his former deputy in Europe (now a key General Motors board member), to advise on funding the interstate system that Congress had authorized in 1944. Like Roosevelt, Eisenhower was primarily interested in the intercity components of the proposed system. Some key members of the highway coalition cared most about the urban elements, however. The Clay commission report, which Eisenhower passed on to Congress with his strong endorsement, estimated that the urban sections, though only 15 percent of interstate system mileage, would carry about half its traffic and account for roughly half its construction cost (estimated to be $27 billion).[12]

The annual congress of the American Municipal Association, representing the nation's mayors, responded with an overwhelming endorsement of the interstate plan, and urban leaders testified in its support. No major group testified before Congress against the proposed system's urban components. Even transit operators, nearly all of them still private, merely sought to be exempted from federal taxes on motor fuels. Despite such support, Congress adjourned in 1955 without approving the plan because it could not agree on how to either raise or distribute the required funds.

The Interstate Era

In the wake of this defeat, supporters of the interstate system sought to develop consensus on key issues. As part of this effort the BPR, working with state (but not local) officials, prepared maps of 100 urban areas showing their approved interstate routes. Upon the release of these maps, mayors and other urban leaders stepped up their federal lobbying efforts. With such support at a peak level and with compromises having been reached on all significant points that had divided the highway coalition, in 1956 both houses of Congress voted by overwhelming margins to proceed with con-

11. For an account of the convoy, see Ann Manchester and Albert Manchester, "From D.C. to the Golden Gate: The First Transcontinental Motor Convoy," *American History* (November–December), pp. 38–69.

12. Schwartz (1976, p. 428).

Table 4-1. Total Spending on Highways, 1932–1999[a]

Billions of 2002 dollars, except as noted

Year	All levels of government	Federal government	Federal share (percent)
1932	20.2	2.5	12
1936	21.0	8.7	41
1940	23.2	8.5	37
1946	12.5	0.6	5
1950	24.4	3.1	13
1955	36.3	3.6	10
1960	46.9	14.7	31
1965	57.1	19.1	33
1970	63.4	18.7	29
1975	62.8	13.8	22
1980	65.1	18.6	29
1985	68.5	20.4	30
1990	78.8	19.1	24
1995	87.3	22.7	26
1999	98.6	24.6	25

Sources: Authors' calculations from Office of Management and Budget, "Budget of the United States Government, Fiscal Year 2003: Historical Tables" (2002, tables 9-6, 12.3); Congressional Budget Office, "Financing Small Commercial-Service Airports: Federal Policies and Options" (1999, tables 1, 2, 3, 4); Bureau of the Census, *Government Finances: 1998–1999* (2001, table 1), *Statistical Abstract of the United States: 2000* (2001, tables 495, 496), *Statistical Abstract of the United States: 1998* (1999, table 506), *Statistical Abstract of the United States: 1991* (1992, table 456; 1986, table 452), *Statistical Abstract of the United States: 1982* (1983, tables 468, 469), *Historical Statistics of the United States: Colonial Times to 1970* (1975, series Y-533–66, Y 605–37, Y-638–51, Y 682–709); and Bureau of Economic Analysis, "The National Income and Product Accounts of the United States: Statistical Tables" (2002, table 7-1) (www.bea.doc.gov/bea/pubs.htm [June 2002]).

a. Figures are for the fiscal year ending in the year shown. Constant-dollar figures are calculated using the Bureau of Economic Statistics implicit price deflator for the nation's gross domestic product. Between 1965 and 1980 the highway construction cost index rose substantially faster than the GDP price deflator. In the 1980s this pattern was reversed.

struction of the interstate highway system. More generally, the new legislation increased federal excise taxes on gasoline, diesel fuel, motor vehicles, and tires; provided for all such revenue to be deposited in the Highway Trust Fund; specified that Highway Trust Fund revenues were to be reserved exclusively for highway purposes; and made construction of the interstate system the centerpiece of the federal highway program.[13]

In consequence, federal highway expenditures more than quadrupled (in both real and nominal terms) between 1955 and 1960, and the federal share of all capital spending on highways rose from 13 to 46 percent (see tables 4-1 and 4-2). The highway program became the largest single source of federal aid to the states by 1958, a distinction it retained until Great Soci-

13. See Schwartz (1976, pp. 498–99).

Table 4-2. Capital Spending on Highways, 1932–1999

Billions of 2002 dollars, except as noted

Year[a]	All levels of government	Federal government	Federal share (percent)
1932	11.9	2.2	18
1936	14.5	3.1	21
1940	15.6	2.1	13
1946	5.3	0.6	11
1950	14.3	2.7	19
1955	24.2	3.3	13
1960	31.4	14.5	46
1965	38.8	18.8	48
1970	40.8	16.4	40
1975	37.7	12.9	34
1980	37.2	17.6	47
1985	35.9	19.1	53
1990	43.3	18.0	42
1995	48.0	21.5	45
1999	54.5	23.9	44

Sources: See table 4-1.

a. Figures are for the fiscal year ending in the year shown.

ety social programs displaced it after 1966. By 1964, 2,612 miles of expressways had been built in urban areas and another 1,600 miles were under construction.[14] Total urban highway mileage was on track to increase nearly tenfold in a decade.

The Interstate Highway Program subjected cities—particularly older, high-density cities—to major surgery, on a scale without precedent in American history.[15] Its advocates maintained that no less would enable cities to thrive in the new era of motor vehicle dominance. Sustained by this conviction and massive doses of federal aid, they had little compunction about destroying neighborhoods, parks, or other local amenities to make way for new roads. Between 1956 and 1967 more than 300,000 households were displaced to make way for federally aided highways.[16] Most of these were poor and minority, moreover, in part because state officials sought low-cost

14. Owen (1966, p. 55).

15. This was particularly true because the urban interstates, designed to satisfy federal standards drawn (with slight modifications) from rural areas, were even bigger than the highways city planners had called for in the 1930s and 1940s. See Taylor (2000).

16. Frieden and Sagalyn (1989, p. 29).

rights-of-way, in part because poor and minority residents were politically weak, and in part because local elites were often eager to use the highway program as an instrument of slum clearance and urban renewal.[17] The highway engineers gravitated toward public open space as well, since it did not have buildings that needed to be paid for and cleared—or occupants to be dealt with.

At first the interstate program encountered little criticism. Residents threatened with displacement often complained, of course, but it was easy to dismiss them as narrowly self-interested, and tempting for them (in the face of overwhelming power) to seek generous terms or minor design changes as the greatest concessions available.[18] Gradually, however, a broader critique emerged: the social costs of urban freeways were too high, they induced more driving and would consequently not provide long-term congestion relief, they were contributing to the contraction and fiscal distress of mass transit service, and they benefited white suburbanites at the expense of low-income inner-city residents.[19]

The first break in the solid phalanx of political support for interstate construction occurred in San Francisco in 1959, when city officials vetoed most further planned expressway construction in the city, including completion of the partially built Embarcadero Expressway along the city's historic waterfront.[20] But this case remained unique for a half-dozen years thereafter. When local officials in Massachusetts threatened to veto construction of the planned Inner Belt, scheduled to require the demolition of 3,800 homes and to pass through some of Boston's most valued parkland, the state (in 1965) simply eliminated their veto power.[21]

As criticism of urban freeway construction gathered force, Congress responded with a series of minor policy adjustments. In 1962 it authorized relocation assistance for displaced residents and businesses, required highway planners to consider local land use and mass transit plans, and required public hearings on planned highways.[22] In 1964 it enacted a separate grant

17. See Mohl (1993).
18. See Altshuler (1965, ch. 2).
19. For some important early critiques of the highway program, see Mumford ([1963] 1981, pp. 244–56); Jacobs (1961); and, Daniel Patrick Moynihan, "New Roads and Urban Chaos," *Reporter*, April 14, 1960, pp. 13–20.
20. The already built portions of the road remained in place until after the 1989 Bay Area earthquake, when structural damage to the road led to its demolition.
21. Federal highway officials maintained at this time that for states to authorize local vetoes was contrary to federal law, which specified that only state highway agencies could determine interstate locations. See Geiser (1970, pp. 277–78).
22. Opposition from construction interests had delayed these changes for several years. See Kahn (1982).

program for mass transit capital investment. (See chapter 6.) In 1966 it forbade the taking of parkland for federally funded transportation facilities if a feasible and prudent alternative existed. (Initially viewed as minor, this provision took on enormous significance in 1971, when the U.S. Supreme Court ruled that the option of not building at all had to be considered in each case.)[23] In 1967, responding to pleas from California—triggered by San Francisco's opposition to new state plans for the Embarcadero Expressway—Congress allowed states to replace controversial interstate segments, on a mile for mile basis, with other projects suitable for addition to the interstate system.[24] In 1968 and 1970 Congress authorized additional benefits for displaced residents and businesses, including the construction of replacement housing in some cases.[25]

During the late 1960s as well, federal highway officials (often prodded by urban members of Congress) became more inclined to approve cost increases for design features that promised to enhance community acceptance, such as depression below grade, at times with decks that could be used for development or parks.[26] In response to protests by the residents of Philadelphia's affluent Society Hill, for example, the state of Pennsylvania agreed in 1965 to alter the design of the Delaware Expressway, along the city's waterfront, from elevated to depressed and covered. (The elevated road would not merely have affected the neighborhood; it would also have cut off Independence Hall and other national historic sites from the waterfront.)[27] In the same year New York City's mayor, John Lindsay, sought to defuse a long-festering controversy about the proposed Lower Manhattan Expressway (a crosstown route in the vicinity of Canal Street) by endorsing a partially depressed, intermittently decked design. This idea only bought a little time, however. The critics, who included Jane Jacobs, continued to oppose the project, and in his 1969 campaign for reelection Lindsay agreed to kill it.[28] In 1968 federal and state highway officials agreed to consider

23. *Citizens to Preserve Overton Park, Inc. v. Volpe* 401 U.S. 402 (1971).
24. See Schwartz (1976, pp. 448–49).
25. See Kahn (1982, pp. 164–66).
26. Designs of this type first received great prominence with the report of a committee, chaired by Sir Colin Buchanan, that was examining urban roadway plans in Great Britain. See United Kingdom, Ministry of Transportation (1963).
27. Although the Federal Highway Administration agreed to fund the depression, it initially refused to pay for the landscaping on the four-block-long deck. After intense lobbying by local officials, FHWA reversed this decision in 1967. See "Modernizing U.S. Highways," *Morgan Guaranty Survey,* June 1967, pp. 3–7.
28. See Danielson and Doig (1982, pp. 266–68); Leavitt (1970, pp. 58–64); Mowbry (1969, pp. 145–49); and Caldwell, Hayes, and MacWhirter (1976, pp. 122–25).

depression of the proposed Inner Belt through Boston and Cambridge. As in New York, however, this concession proved too little and too late. In February 1970 Massachusetts governor Frank Sargent announced that he was halting work on the Inner Belt and several other controversial expressways, pending a comprehensive restudy of major highway and transit plans for Greater Boston.[29]

The growth of antihighway sentiment during the late 1960s and early 1970s was fueled in part by rising environmental consciousness. The primary legislative successes achieved by the environmental movement in the early 1970s, moreover, greatly enhanced the weaponry of antihighway activists. The National Environmental Policy Act (NEPA), most notably, which became law in January 1970, required environmental impact statements for all major federally aided projects. Although it left public officials free to decide after reviewing such statements, it required public hearings first and authorized citizen suits to ensure that all major issues had been addressed fully and candidly. As strictly interpreted by federal courts during the 1970s, these proved to be requirements of enormous significance in the hands of environmental organizations and their lawyers.[30] The Clean Air Act amendments of 1970 gave rise to numerous local controversies about whether new highways would induce so much more traffic as to vitiate their benefits, and whether continued rapid growth in motor vehicle usage was sustainable. The Clean Water Act amendments of 1972, finally, made it far more difficult to fill wetlands or build highways whose runoff might pollute water resources.

In 1972, at the conclusion of his Greater Boston restudy—which had come to be known as the Boston Transportation Planning Review (BTPR)— Governor Sargent decided to cancel nearly all of the region's proposed expressways—with two exceptions (one involving replacement of an existing facility) discussed below. In lieu of freeway building, he proposed a

29. Sargent, who was the state's lieutenant governor, became governor in 1969 when then-governor John Volpe was appointed U.S. secretary of transportation. Shortly thereafter he moved to address the region's intense highway controversies, appointing a task force of private experts to advise on what should be done. As chair of this task force he selected Alan Altshuler, then a professor at MIT and a coauthor of the present book. Early in 1970 the task force recommended the moratorium and restudy. In announcing his acceptance of these recommendations, Sargent stated that the entire rationale for the highway plans needed a comprehensive reexamination, giving no greater weight to traffic issues than to environmental protection or community preservation. He went on to win the 1970 gubernatorial election, defeating Boston mayor Kevin White, who also opposed the planned roads. See Lupo, Colcord, and Fowler (1971); and Gakenheimer (1976).

30. See Wenner (1982); and Altshuler and Curry (1975).

Antihighway and anti-airport demonstrators protest outside the Massachusetts State House in January 1969, two days after Governor Frank Sargent, shown here speaking to the crowd, took office. Though Sargent had previously served as public works commissioner, he agreed to a fresh review of the state's highway plans for Greater Boston. As this reexamination played out over the next three years, Sargent rejected nearly all of the region's proposed expressways. Credit: AP/Wide World Photos.

massive program of transit investment—to be financed in substantial part, he hoped, by a trade-in of the rejected interstate segments for equivalent mass transit funding.[31] This would require a major revision in federal highway law, which—having already rejected some proposed interstate segments—Sargent had already been pursuing (in cooperation with leading members of the Massachusetts congressional delegation) for the past year. Both houses of Congress had recently passed bills incorporating the change. These bills stalled in conference at the end of 1972, but similar legislation—with the trade-in language—became the Highway Act of 1973.

31. Altshuler, who had become state secretary of transportation in 1971, personally favored a middle option, including two of the freeways in the controversy scaled down from four to two lanes in each direction and reserved for multipassenger vehicles during peak hours. He later recalled: "Sargent confided privately that [regardless of the merits] he did not see who would support my middle-ground position. . . . The pro-highway and anti-highway forces were so polarized that he felt compelled to choose one or the other in clear-cut fashion." See Altshuler (1989, p. 160).

Where elected officials sought to press forward with planned express-ways, opponents now litigated as well as protested, increasingly emphasizing the new environmental laws. In 1972, for example, public interest lawyers in Los Angeles, representing a mix of residents and environmental groups, brought suit to halt takings of homes for the Century Freeway, a planned 17-mile expressway running mainly through poor, largely minority, neigh-borhoods.[32] About 10,000 residents had already been displaced, and 11,000 more were scheduled to be in the near future. The plaintiffs charged that the state was in violation of NEPA and the Clean Air Act. State officials responded that the former did not apply (because Century Freeway planning had preceded its enactment) and that the project complied with the latter. Federal district judge Harry Pregerson ruled that NEPA did apply, that in consequence the state would have to prepare an environmental impact state-ment (EIS), and that one of its components should be a reanalysis of the state's Clean Air Act findings.[33]

New Approaches

By the early 1970s plans for new urban expressways were fiercely contro-versial, and projects were stalled, almost everywhere. The annual rate of displacement for federally aided highway projects declined from 64,000 people in 1968–69 to 13,300 in 1975–76.[34] The obvious question was whether new urban freeways could be developed with significantly less dis-ruption. Given the need for continuous rights-of-way several hundred feet wide, for massive interchanges, and for network connectivity, most highway engineers deemed it infeasible (and certainly unaffordable) to achieve more than modest reductions in impact. But highway deliberations had by now opened up to include a variety of other players—such as politicians and their advisers, environmental and community group leaders, and urban devel-opment officials. And some of these were drawn to the challenge.

Origins of the Central Artery/Tunnel Project

At the conclusion of the BTPR in 1972, Governor Sargent carried for-ward two expressway projects. Both were very different from any of the

32. The Century Freeway had initially been planned as a highway 51 miles long. In the early 1960s the eastern 34 miles were deleted for a variety of reasons, including funding con-straints in the state highway program and a judgment by state highway officials that the eastern portion of the highway was not needed.

33. See *Keith* v. *Volpe*, 352 F. Supp. 1324 (D. Calif. 1972).

34. Federal Highway Administration, unpublished paper, as cited by Altshuler (1979, pp. 340–41).

projects halted for reexamination in 1970. The first w
purpose tunnel to Logan Airport, downsized from a foı
tunnel proposal and relocated to come up within the
than in the adjacent residential neighborhood of East B
facility would be reserved for buses, taxis, and emergo
because it would not require any significant land takings,   ᵤ it
as thoroughly consistent with the rest of his plan.

The second project was an entirely new concept that had emerged during the restudy itself. Its gist was to replace the one-and-one-half-mile
Central Artery viaduct in downtown Boston with an underground, intermittently decked road, with space in the right-of-way as well for a railroad
connection between Boston's North and South Stations, an idea that had
been discussed since the turn of the century. (It was understood that funding for the rail connection itself would have to come from some other source
than the Highway Trust Fund, but a comparable challenge had previously
been to identify a plausible right-of-way.) Originally conceived by Bill
Reynolds, who was representing highway contractors in the restudy process,
the artery depression idea quickly became a top priority for Frederick P.
Salvucci, Boston mayor Kevin White's transportation adviser. Salvucci, an
MIT-trained civil engineer, had also for some years been a leading figure in
Boston's antihighway movement.

New York's Westway

The idea of replacing an elevated with a depressed freeway was extraordinary, but a precedent did exist. In 1971 the city of New York and the New
York State Urban Development Corporation had proposed replacing the
city's aging elevated West Side Highway (a quarter-century older than
Boston's Central Artery) with a covered expressway built on piles in the
Hudson River. The financial plan was to secure 90 percent federal funding
by transferring interstate mileage from the Lower Manhattan Expressway
and two other controversial freeways rejected by Mayor Lindsay in 1969.

The detailed plan for this project, labeled Westway, emerged in 1974. It
envisioned a depressed highway covered by 200 acres of parks and commercial development, to cost $1.2 billion. To minimize impacts on existing
development, the project was to extend, on newly filled land, 600 to 900 feet
into the Hudson River, reducing the river's width by about one-sixth.[35] This

35. In contrast to the 1971 plan, which called for a highway from the southern tip of Manhattan to 72nd Street (where the Henry Hudson Parkway begins), the new plan ended at 42nd
Street, just past the Lincoln Tunnel. The stretch between 42nd Street and 72nd Street was
dropped for several reasons, most notably opposition from residents of New York's Upper
West Side neighborhood who, among other concerns, feared that because the road was an

attracted overwhelming political, business, and labor support—its main advocacy group was cochaired by David Rockefeller, the CEO of Chase Manhattan Bank and brother of incumbent New York governor Nelson Rockefeller, and Harry van Arsdale, head of the city's council of unions. The project, however, also faced opposition—from a small but skilled group of neighborhood and environmentalist activists who argued that the project would attract more cars to the already congested city and that any interstate trade-in should be for transit rather than highway improvements.

For federal officials the combination of strong local support, a highway design that would displace fewer than a hundred people, and the provision of parks and other amenities made the project particularly appealing. Judith Connor, U.S. DOT assistant secretary for Environment, Safety, and Consumer Affairs in the Ford administration, for example, recalled that when DOT officials were reviewing the project's environmental impact statement,

> some of my staff had their doubts about the project's costs, but for years [the secretary's office] had been pressing the Federal Highway Administration to internalize the costs of making highways environmentally compatible. Here was the perfect example of how to do it in an urban area. They had adopted every principle we'd advocated—dedicated lanes for heavy traffic, bridle paths, bicycle paths, parks, etc. The federal government's policy was—we're willing to pick up costs to make highways environmentally compatible. On that basis I recommended to [DOT] Secretary [William] Coleman that he approve it [which he did]. What else could we do?[36]

Projects in Conflict

Despite Westway's apparently strong prospects, Sargent and Alan Altshuler, his secretary of transportation, doubted that the artery depression idea had much future in Boston. Its most obvious drawbacks were as follows. First, Sargent planned to use whatever trade-in money he could obtain for mass transit rather than alternative highway purposes. Second, federal highway officials were resistant to the idea of *any* federal funding for the artery proposal, even from the state's formula grant assistance. Whereas New York's elevated West Side Highway was old and had deteriorated so badly that it had been shut down for reasons of safety, they observed, the

interstate highway, it would lead to trucks on the Henry Hudson Parkway, where they were currently banned.

36. See Herzlinger (1979, p. 95).

Central Artery was only 15 years old and had many years left of useful life. Moreover, the champions of replacing it with a depressed facility had committed to eschewing any increase in capacity (from the existing three lanes in each direction). Thus the depression would be almost entirely for purposes of urban beautification. Third, the depression idea had little support in the business community. Its main supporters were the usual leaders of antihighway activism, whom the governor was satisfying in any event with decisions to kill previously planned interstate freeways and to invest very heavily in mass transit. Finally, it was hard to imagine how downtown traffic would flow during the many years between tearing down the existing artery and completing its replacement. (Downtown business leaders and the Boston Redevelopment Authority were particularly concerned about this issue, fearing gridlock during the years of construction and private disinvestment for years beforehand, due to anticipation of its effects.)

Sargent and Altshuler had no wish to be seen, however, as rejecting an idea that some of their most enthusiastic allies (in the wake of the governor's overall transportation decisions) found highly attractive. The governor was going to need all the support he could get to move his transit program forward, and it was still unclear where additional support would come from. (In the end most business and labor groups wrote off the rejected freeways as a lost cause and did come around to support the governor's transit initiatives.) Thus Sargent labeled the artery depression idea attractive on its face but not yet ripe for decision. Shortly thereafter, the state contracted with the Boston Redevelopment Authority to examine the feasibility of depression in greater detail and assess its compatibility with the city's other plans.

In contrast to their tepid interest in the artery depression, Altshuler and Sargent aggressively pursued the tunnel project because this segment was already on the interstate system and because they (along with the business community) viewed the airport access problem as urgent. This project, too, faced major obstacles, however. Notably, special-purpose roads were not eligible for interstate funding. Moreover, Edward King, the longtime, highly influential executive director of the Massachusetts Port Authority, which owns and operates Logan Airport, was adamantly opposed to the Sargent plan.[37] King did favor a new tunnel, but a general- rather than special-

37. The port authority is governed by a seven-member board appointed by the governor—but only one each year, for overlapping seven-year terms. The members had historically been drawn from business and labor leaders supportive of airport growth. In the early 1970s, in the context of controversies about Logan's expansion, Sargent began appointing people who had demonstrated commitment to transportation policies more sensitive to the environment and neighborhoods. (See chapter 5.)

purpose one that would emerge in the residential community of East Boston rather than within the airport itself. He maintained that Sargent's proposed tunnel would prove inadequate to handle future traffic and that its alignment would interfere with airport operations. A few antihighway activists also opposed the tunnel, most notably former state representative Michael Dukakis, a leading candidate for the Democratic gubernatorial nomination in 1974. Dukakis took the position that no additional expressway capacity should be built in or around the city of Boston, and that Sargent's proposed tunnel represented exactly such an expansion, whatever he chose to call it. Additionally, he argued, the state's priority should be constraining overall airport growth (about which its neighbors had long complained) before considering improvements in ground access to it.

The special-purpose tunnel plan did secure endorsements from the Port Authority Board of Directors and the Boston Chamber of Commerce in 1973. And the U.S. Congress, at the behest of U.S. House majority leader Thomas P. O'Neill, who represented the airport's immediate neighbors, authorized the inclusion of special-purpose freeways on the interstate system. In 1974, moreover, the Massachusetts state senate voted to authorize Sargent's tunnel proposal, though the state house of representatives (where King was particularly influential, and where some leaders were still angry with Sargent for killing other freeways) did not. Upon learning that King had played a major role in this defeat, the Port Authority board fired him.

At the end of 1974, Dukakis was elected governor (defeating Sargent) and announced that Salvucci would be his secretary of transportation. The new administration moved vigorously to implement most of Sargent's transportation plan—except for the tunnel—and it made the artery depression in particular one of its highest priorities. Whereas the BTPR had considered a $360-million plan, moreover, solely to depress 1.5 miles of elevated artery viaduct, Salvucci now advanced a much more ambitious proposal—including a new bridge over the Charles River, realigned highways in Charlestown (the Boston neighborhood on the north side of the Charles River), and additional tunneling near South Station. Planners estimated that the highway components of this plan would cost $800 million, with another $130 million needed for the rail link.[38]

In 1975 Salvucci sought federal interstate funding to develop this plan further. The Federal Highway Administration (FHWA) refused, citing two grounds. First, although the Central Artery was part of the interstate system, it was one of many segments funded by states prior to enactment of the

38. Boston Redevelopment Authority (1975).

interstate program, and such "designated segments" were generally not eligible for interstate funding. Second, the project would not provide significant transportation benefits. Salvucci, however, enlisted the aid of House majority leader O'Neill, who prevailed upon the FHWA and the House Public Works Committee to include the project in the 1975 interstate cost estimate (ICE). (The ICE was revised every other year, and only projects included on it were eligible for interstate money. Each revision was prepared by the FHWA with input from the states and, unless the House or Senate objected, it became official.)

The Central Artery estimate used, at the state's own suggestion, was one based on the original Sargent plan—now estimated to cost $360 million—rather than the new expanded project concept. The technical explanation for this lowball estimate, Salvucci later recalled, was that annual interstate funding allocations were based on the ICE and Massachusetts had no capacity to spend much interstate money at the time. The political explanation was that a larger estimate might attract unwelcome attention from other states and generate a controversy that would threaten approval.

Over the next several years Salvucci pushed ahead with detailed planning for the artery depression and with efforts to build support for it. In September 1978, however, former Port Authority executive director Ed King, running as a probusiness, socially conservative Democrat, defeated Dukakis in the Democratic gubernatorial primary and went on to win the general election. King made no secret in his election campaign of his desire to resurrect the old prohighway vision, including the general-purpose Third Harbor Tunnel through East Boston, and of his disdain for the Central Artery depression idea. His administration did move to revive the old tunnel plan but quickly encountered intense neighborhood opposition, bolstered by support from most of the state's other leading politicians, including O'Neill (now Speaker of the U.S. House of Representatives), the state's two senators, and Boston mayor Kevin White. King administration officials, moreover, neglected the technical side of transportation planning. Somehow they failed during their four years in office to produce even a first-draft EIS, a prerequisite for public hearings and serious federal consideration.

The Century Freeway Settlement

In 1978 the California Department of Transportation advanced a new set of ideas for resolving the Century Freeway dispute, with FHWA officials indicating their tentative support. It proposed to scale the freeway down from 10 to eight lanes, to depress it in part, to build a transitway in its median, to finance a job-training program for low-income corridor residents, and to guarantee an adequate supply of nearby affordable housing for displaced residents.

This proposal became the basis for settlement negotiations with the plaintiffs in the Century Freeway lawsuit. The litigants were disposed to bargain because they had little prospect of blocking the project entirely. The initial district court injunction had halted construction while the state prepared its EIS. Subsequent court decisions in unrelated cases, however, including a landmark decision by the U.S. Supreme Court, had made clear that a public agency, having prepared a valid EIS, had broad discretion in selecting its course of action.[39] Politically, moreover, the project still enjoyed broad support. When Governor Jerry Brown, in the mid-1970s, had suggested scaling it down to a four-lane boulevard with a transitway in the median, most localities in the corridor had taken the opportunity to register their support for a freeway—arguing that it would be far more effective as a spur to development and source of congestion relief.

The eventual settlement, concluded in 1979, provided for the Interstate Highway Program to fund 4,200 units of new or renovated affordable housing and ambitious programs of both job training and minority contracting. The project redesign and these ancillary elements helped fuel a threefold increase in the Century Freeway's cost, from about $500 million in 1977 to an estimated $1.6 billion in 1979. Despite this increase U.S. DOT secretary Neil Goldschmidt praised the settlement, noting, "we are building more than a freeway. We are building neighborhoods and better cities."[40]

Boston's Artery and Tunnel Projects Become One

In 1982 Dukakis reemerged, defeating King in the Democratic primary (in a reversal of what had happened four years earlier) and going on to win the general election easily. Once in office he brought back Salvucci as state transportation secretary. During his four years out of office, Salvucci had concluded that the best chance to revive the artery depression was to make it part of a vastly expanded project—enlarging the artery itself, combining it with a new general-purpose tunnel to the airport, and adding a new "seaport access" connector. Specifically, he now judged that the new artery should be

---

39. *Vermont Yankee Nuclear Power Corp. v. Natural Resources Defense Council, Inc.,* 439 U.S. 961 (1978); DiMento and others (1991); and Wenner (1982).

40. Timothy Ord, "Paving over 17 Mi of Urban Blight," *Business Week,* December 3, 1979, p. 32; see also Hestermann and others (1993); DiMento and others (1991, ch. 4); and Zamora (1989). On the impacts of the design and mitigation changes to the project's budget, see Taylor (1995, pp. 50–51).

at least four lanes in each direction and five in some sections, rather than three. This would entail abandonment of the Sargent and first Dukakis administration assurances that this project would not involve additional lane capacity. But Salvucci deemed such expansion essential as part of his campaign to persuade federal highway officials that the artery proposal was about more than urban beautification, and that indeed it was the only feasible way to ameliorate traffic congestion in downtown Boston. Some earlier advocates of depressing the artery were dismayed by this revision, particularly as it became clear that the roadway expansion would crowd out any new rail link between North and South Stations. Salvucci responded that the rail link was probably infeasible anyhow; it had gradually become apparent that the depressed artery would have to rise and fall as it passed over and under subway lines. While the grades were not a problem for vehicular traffic, they would be for trains. Additionally, the state now planned to cover the artery along its entire length, rather than just intermittently. The cost of ventilating for diesel trains, or (more plausibly) of electrifying the regional railroad system, would be prohibitive. And it had never been clear how the rail link would be funded in any event. In short, as Salvucci later put it, the rail link faced "any number of problems, each of which was fatal."[41]

He also proposed to build a general-purpose tunnel, running from an intown portal about a mile away from downtown to a site well inside the airport.[42] This plan simplified the tunnel design (by eliminating the need for curves), but it also created the need for a new connector—an extension of the Massachusetts Turnpike (I-90). Salvucci emphasized that the connector, while a costly addition, would have major development benefits. It would greatly improve motor vehicle access to industrial South Boston, an underused 900-acre area that city officials and private investors had long eyed as a promising direction for downtown expansion. It was separated from downtown, however, by a narrow waterway at which most streets deadended and from the airport by Boston Harbor. The new connector and airport tunnel would, in combination, make it one of the most accessible points in all of Greater Boston.

This was indeed a grand, vastly expansive vision, but one that just might be eligible for funding by the interstate program. The first obstacle that Salvucci had to overcome, however, was Governor Dukakis himself, who had just reiterated during the 1982 campaign his vociferous opposition to

41. Frederick P. Salvucci, interview by authors, Cambridge, Mass., March 17, 1992.
42. Salvucci claims that Bill Reynolds, who first proposed the artery depression, also was the first to suggest this alignment. Other planners, however, claim that the idea had been raised intermittently throughout the late 1970s and early 1980s.

Boston's Central Artery in the mid-1980s. Warning that the road was severely overloaded and would soon need to be rebuilt in any event, state transportation secretary Frederick Salvucci proposed replacing it with an underground highway, to be constructed underneath the existing road. Credit: Peter Vanderwarker.

a new harbor tunnel. Salvucci assured Dukakis that the tunnel he now had in mind would provide significant economic development benefits, that it would have no harmful impacts, and that support for it would greatly help to advance the artery depression. The major transit plans of the 1970s, he added, were by now in service or under construction, so the time was ripe for new initiatives. Moreover, both the artery and tunnel were still being carried in the federal interstate cost estimate, so a good prospect existed for 90 percent federal funding.

Dukakis, determined to build better relationships with business than during his first administration, knew that Boston's business leaders, while dubious about the artery depression, had long viewed a new airport tunnel as vital. So he authorized Salvucci to take soundings. In his discussions with the business leadership, Salvucci emphasized five themes. First, he said, if the business community hoped to obtain Dukakis's support for the tunnel, it would have to join him in support of the artery depression. Second, the federal deadline for filing environmental impact documents for unbuilt portions of the interstate system was September 30, 1983, so it was now or never. Third, only the combination of widening the artery and building the new general-purpose tunnel would significantly alleviate congestion in the urban core. Fourth, the project could be built without major traffic disruption, using a new technology known as "slurry wall" construction. This method would make possible construction of the new road below-grade while the existing elevated artery and most adjacent streets remained open to traffic. Finally, the existing artery was nearing the end of its useful life. Within a decade or two it would have to be at least redecked and possibly replaced, at far higher cost to the city and state (because this work would not be eligible for interstate program funding) and with much greater disruption than his plan would entail. John LaWare, then chairman of the Vault, the summit group of downtown business leaders, recalled that its members initially agreed to support the artery depression as the only way to get the tunnel. "But as we got further into it," he recalled, "the desirability of the whole program became obvious."[43]

The next major obstacle to be overcome was opposition in East Boston, the neighborhood immediately adjacent to Logan Airport. The most adamant tunnel foes had ties with Salvucci that went back to the late 1960s, and they had been Dukakis's strongest supporters in East Boston. Salvucci assured them that he would never sell out the neighborhood, but that a new

43. John LaWare, interview by authors, by telephone, April 17, 1992.

tunnel was inevitable in the long run and this was the ideal plan for it. Over a period of months, he gradually persuaded many, if not all, East Boston politicians and community leaders to adopt a stance of watchful neutrality.

Similar dynamics were at work in the North End, on the in-town side of Boston Harbor. Although the planned artery depression would not take any North End property, critics maintained that it would destroy the neighborhood's commerce and property values by making it all but inaccessible during the decade or more of construction. Salvucci explained the slurry wall construction method, promised to build replacement parking for spaces lost during artery construction, and pledged to involve the community in deciding how the new land to be created nearby, on top of the artery, would be developed. As in East Boston, the meetings and promises did not convince the most ardent critics, but they did persuade enough local opinion leaders to enable Dukakis to feel comfortable proceeding—at least to the next steps of environmental analysis, more detailed planning, and federal negotiations.

The region's environmentalists were largely silent. Of the leading environmental groups, only the Sierra Club testified at the major public hearing held during this period. Club officials, while lamenting the demise of the rail connector, generally praised the project for removing an eyesore from downtown Boston and lauded Salvucci for including disparate groups in the planning process.

With support mobilized and opposition muted, Dukakis officially endorsed the project in September 1983. State officials estimated that the expanded project would cost about $2 billion. Announcing his approval, Dukakis emphasized the differences between this and previous Boston-area highway plans: "We will not bulldoze neighborhoods," he stated. "We will not take one person's home. We will not make people so unsure about the future that they are afraid to fix the roof because they don't know if the state will show up tomorrow to take their home."[44]

Funding the Central Artery/Tunnel (CA/T) Project

The artery/tunnel project still faced daunting obstacles in Washington. Federal highway officials argued that the only improvements to the Central Artery authorized in the most recent (1981) ICE were for redecking, not replacement. State officials responded that ICE estimates for the artery had assumed depression ever since 1975, though at an artificially low figure based on the 1972 Sargent plan. They were able to document, moreover,

44. Laurence Collins, "Dukakis Offers $2.2B Tunnel Artery Plan," *Boston Globe*, September 28, 1983, p. 1.

that the FHWA had sought to strike this funding from each subsequent ICE, but that it had been added back in when the House and Senate Public Works Committees reviewed the FHWA's initial ICE proposals. The committees, of course, had been responding to senior Massachusetts Congress members, particularly O'Neill, who later recalled: "Let me tell you something about Washington. The squeaky wheel gets the grease. . . . Maybe it's not the way to run a government but that's the way the government runs."[45]

The Massachusetts story was not unique, moreover. In 1981 Reagan's Office of Management and Budget and the newly appointed FHWA administrator, Ray Barnhart, moved to scale back road plans across the nation that they deemed excessively costly. State and local project supporters, however, with the aid of their congressional delegations, were able to rebuff the great majority of these efforts, and even Barnhart's successes were partial at best. The Century Freeway was in the latter category. Its cost had risen to more than $2 billion. Barnhart announced that the FHWA would fund only about half the number of housing units specified in the 1979 legal settlement and that it intended to drop the project's transit and high-occupancy vehicle lane components, reduce the roadway from four to three lanes in each direction, and cut the number of interchanges by half. The road's principal advocates—a mix of state and local officials together with a coalition of construction firms—launched a bipartisan counteroffensive with the aid of Representative Glenn Anderson, a high-ranking member of the House Public Works Committee. The result was a compromise in which the FHWA achieved some of its proposed cutbacks—a 12 percent reduction in the number of housing units, a 30 percent reduction in the number of interchanges, and the lane reduction from four to three in each direction—but also took on a major new commitment, to fund the construction of 10 transit stations with adjacent park-and-ride lots.

More generally, the Reagan administration reversed course in 1983 and agreed to the first federal gas tax increase since 1959. A portion of this increase, moreover, was earmarked for transit, a program that Reagan had cut dramatically during his first two years in office. (Highway and transit advocates, who had been collaborating to secure larger appropriations than presidents desired since the early 1970s, had solidified their coalition during the first two Reagan years and were now able to capitalize on significant Democratic gains in the 1982 congressional election. The administration was responding to these realities.) As a result, federal spending on highways,

45. Thomas P. "Tip" O'Neill Jr., interview by authors, Washington, D.C., October 19, 1992.

which had fallen in constant dollars by nearly one-third in Reagan's first two years, surged back, reaching the highest level since the 1960s by fiscal year 1985. State and local highway spending also grew rapidly during this period, one of widespread concern about infrastructure deterioration.[46] (See tables 4-1 and 4-2.)

Even though they acknowledged that Governor Sargent's original plan for the artery depression had been included in federal interstate cost estimates since 1975, senior federal highway officials were adamant that this did not mean they had approved the project or that it was eligible for interstate funding. So once again the state turned to Congress, and again the vehicle was the ICE (which, in accord with a 1983 U.S. Supreme Court ruling on an unrelated matter, now had to be enacted in statutory form).[47] Speaker O'Neill first approached House Public Works Committee chairman James Howard, a longtime ally.[48] Howard's first inclination was to limit interstate financing of the Central Artery depression to planning and design. At O'Neill's strong urging, though, he quickly came around to the state's position that construction should be included as well.[49] His committee and the full House followed suit. But it also produced a bill loaded down with numerous other special projects (much smaller, to be sure, than the CA/T) favored by powerful House members. With the Senate resistant to so much earmarking and President Reagan threatening a veto, Congress early in 1984 enacted an ICE with controversial items omitted, agreeing to take up the latter in a few months. As the gridlock persisted, however, Congress and the administration eventually agreed to defer action on these items until 1986, when all federal highway and transit laws were due to be reauthorized.

Salvucci, now convinced that he needed Republican support, enlisted several downtown Boston property owners who were large donors to the Republican Party. He also retained the services of Roger Allan Moore, a

46. A series of influential reports in the 1980s decried the state of American infrastructure, most notably Choate and Walter (1981); Vaughan (1983); Vaughan and Pollard (1984); M. Kaplan (1984); and National Council on Public Works Improvement (1988).

47. *Immigration and Naturalization Service v. Chadha et al.*, 462 U.S. 919 (1983).

48. Howard had been elected from a generally Republican district in the 1964 Johnson landslide and faced several difficult reelection battles early in his career. O'Neill, who headed the Democratic congressional campaign committee in the mid-1960s, had aided Howard in those campaigns and the two formed a lifelong alliance.

49. Howard would later revive this issue as a means of persuading the state to yield on two lesser issues, billboard regulation and sludge disposal. In the first case, he appeared to be serving the interests of some major donors (who wanted state regulations weakened). In the latter, he insisted that the state drop a proposal to dump treated sludge off the New Jersey shore, near his congressional district. The state backed down in each case.

local attorney who had done work for Massport and who had long been active in national Republican politics, serving as parliamentarian at the 1980 Republican convention and as a senior adviser on delegate selection in Reagan's 1968, 1976, and 1980 presidential campaigns. Moore quickly discovered that FHWA administrator Barnhart was eager to resolve the CA/T dispute in advance of the congressional deliberations on surface transportation program reauthorization in 1986. With this in mind, he proposed—and Barnhart agreed to—a review by FHWA career officials with the following premise: that the artery depression should be approved for interstate construction financing if, but only if, its benefit/cost ratio proved at least equal to that of the harbor tunnel. The state claimed that, using standard FHWA criteria, the artery depression had a better ratio (1.63 versus 1.09 for the tunnel alone).[50]

In the spring of 1985, two of the FHWA's most senior planners came to Boston to examine the transportation models that underlay the state's benefit/cost analyses. They concluded that the artery alone and the tunnel alone each had a benefit/cost ratio of about 0.3—though because of synergistic effects the overall project would have a slightly better ratio, in the range of 0.4 to 0.5.[51] Though dismally low, these estimates suggested that the artery portion was no worse than the tunnel portion. And that was the threshold test.

In this context, Barnhart quietly agreed to support a legislative provision making most of the expanded CA/T project eligible for interstate funding and the rest eligible for funding with formula highway aid. The components eligible for interstate financing would be the tunnel, the new mile-long connector between it and the Massachusetts Turnpike, and both ends of the new Central Artery, including its massive interchanges with other elements of the regional highway system. The estimated cost of these elements was $1.85 billion. The component to be funded with formula aid was the depression of one mile of currently elevated viaduct through downtown Boston, at an

50. Massachusetts Department of Public Works (1985, pp. 38–39). These criteria were themselves debatable. The primary "benefit" of nearly all major highway projects is the expected time that motorists will save by comparison with a baseline alternative, but this presents two problems. First, since motorists and trip purposes vary widely, and since estimates are based on surveys rather than experiments with actual prices, there is no consensus on the dollar values that should be assigned to time in this context. Second, when people are enabled to travel at higher speeds, they tend to increase the number of miles they travel, keeping the amount of actual time they spend traveling more or less constant. The implication is that new roads should be valued for enhancing mobility (and facilitating low-density land use patterns) rather than saving time per se. See Altshuler (1979, ch. 9).

51. R. Barnhart, memo to John Bestgen, regional FHWA administrator, February 19, 1985.

estimated cost of $600 million. The state and the FHWA also forged a joint strategy to avoid floor debate on the CA/T project. Its essence was that the House—where O'Neill and Howard were firmly in control—would vote interstate funding for the entire project, the Senate bill would provide no funding for the artery portion, and the conference committee would adopt the state/FHWA agreement.

The peril associated with floor debate had recently been demonstrated with reference to the CA/T project's near twin, Westway. Several key New Jersey legislators, including Howard, had turned on Westway when environmental studies suggested that fish it displaced would move to the New Jersey side of the Hudson River, where their presence would complicate environmental permitting for planned commercial redevelopment. New Jersey and New York City officials were also engaged at this time in an angry dispute about New Jersey's use of federal Urban Development Action Grant (UDAG) funds to lure business from the city. Additionally, as a result of several rounds of litigation about a fill permit granted by the U.S. Corps of Engineers, national environmentalists had made the defeat of Westway a high priority. The result had been a House vote, in September 1985, to ban any additional federal aid for it. (On the same day a federal appeals court panel held for the plaintiffs in the latest permit litigation.) Several weeks later New York governor Mario Cuomo, with the approval of New York City mayor Edward Koch, gave up on Westway, agreeing to seek reallocation of its federal aid for a new surface boulevard and some transit investments.

The Barnhart-Salvucci agreement suggested a better outlook for the CA/T, except that Barnhart shied away from clearing it with his superiors, either in the Department of Transportation or the White House. When they learned of it, as they did relatively quickly, they let it be known that the administration was not on board. State officials took this as a signal to further intensify their bipartisan lobbying. Salvucci obtained assistance, for example, from the Chicago-based Pritzker family (owners of the Hyatt Hotel chain), which was seeking to develop a large mixed-use project adjacent to downtown Boston.[52] Harry Spence, who was project manager for the Pritzker group, recalls telling his superiors: "If you want Fred [Salvucci] to work on your agenda, then you have to work on his agenda."[53] The

52. The development failed due to bickering among the partners and the late 1980s collapse of the Boston real estate market. Subsequently, a new federal courthouse was built on part of the site, and as of this writing in early 2002 the Pritzker family had secured permits to build a new mixed-use development on it.

53. Harry Spence, interview by authors, by telephone, March 12, 1992.

Pritzkers' main contribution was to enlist the aid of former U.S. transportation secretary Drew Lewis, whose pre-Cabinet career had been in Chicago and who was active in the Republican Party's highest circles.

Senior DOT and White House officials remained unconvinced,[54] but Barnhart kept his word and the congressional deliberations proceeded just as he and the state had planned. The 1986 bill died for extraneous reasons. In the first months of 1987, however, a successor bill with the same CA/T provisions quickly moved through Congress. President Reagan vetoed the bill on March 27, citing its excessive total cost and "unjustifiable funding" for more than 150 special projects, nearly a tenfold increase from the last act reauthorizing surface transportation programs, in 1982.[55] The president specifically criticized the bill's CA/T provisions, moreover, charging that it was unfair to let Massachusetts add to the interstate highway system when federal law precluded any other state from doing so.[56]

The override battle took on great symbolic importance because Reagan—recently bruised by the Iran-Contra affair—was striving to reassert his primacy in domestic affairs while new House Speaker James Wright and new Senate majority leader Robert Byrd (the Democrats had just regained control of the Senate) were equally determined to advance a Democratic agenda. Both sides launched furious lobbying campaigns, with a particular focus on the 17 Republican senators who had voted for the bill. Most of these viewed the bill's provisions—particularly the relatively high funding levels for transit—as beneficial to their states, however, or were involved in side agreements. For example, there was great agitation at the time in many western states to increase the national speed limit of 55 miles an hour, and this did occur in 1987—with the margin of victory in the House being provided by a group of liberal Democrats. This group, led by Massachusetts representative Barney Frank, in effect traded its votes on the speed limit issue for the votes of two conservative Republican senators (Idaho's Steve Symms and Nevada's Chic Hecht) to override Reagan's surface transportation bill veto.

The House overrode the president's veto by a wide margin on March 31. The president prevailed in the Senate a day later, however, despite the defection of 13 Republicans (including Hecht and Symms), because one Democrat, Terry Sanford of North Carolina, sided with him. The Democrats now brought intense pressure on Sanford to switch. Leaders in the House

54. In late 1986, however, senior DOT officials did indicate that they were was willing to trade support for the CA/T project for help in their efforts to transfer control of National Airport from the federal government to a regional body.

55. See Evans (1994).

56. Reagan (1989, pp. 296–97).

even threatened to eliminate tobacco subsidies if he stood firm.[57] The pressure worked. Sanford switched, the veto was overridden, and the Barnhart-Salvucci agreement became law.

Regulatory Hurdles

Believing that they had resolved most key disputes, Dukakis and Salvucci hoped for clear sailing after 1987. The example of Westway, however, was never far from their minds. The attacks that finally killed Westway were not those that its advocates had viewed as most dangerous. State and federal regulators, for example, had concluded that there were no data to support opponents' primary criticism of the project—that it would lead to significant increases in air pollution and therefore violated federal air quality laws. Indeed, the regulators had rejected this claim, and federal district court judge Thomas Griesa had upheld their decision in 1981. Griesa had reserved judgment, though, on what appeared to be a minor challenge, having to do with the question of whether young striped bass wintered under rotting, unused piers that were scheduled to be removed by the project. The EIS concluded that few fish were present at all. Following a bench trial in 1982, however, Griesa found that this was at odds with the state's own studies and with comments filed by a number of federal agencies. He therefore ordered the state and the U.S. Army Corps of Engineers, which was responsible for issuing fill permits for the project, to conduct further studies.[58] Three years later, reviewing an amended EIS, Griesa concluded again that it failed to establish that the project would have no significant impact on the bass. Under the provisions of the Clean Water Act, this meant that the corps could not issue the permits the project needed to proceed.[59] Though the final blow for Westway was the negative House vote discussed above, this litigation was a major factor in its demise, contributing both to the vote itself and the more general exhaustion of Westway's supporters.

Massachusetts officials believed that the community process they had gone through in 1983 made such suits unlikely. They hoped to secure all

57. Barry (1989, p. 182); Brian Donnelly (Massachusetts member of Congress at the time), interview by authors, Quincy, Mass., September 25, 1992.

58. *Action for Rational Transit v. West Side Highway Project; Sierra Club v. United States Corps of Engineers,* 536 F. Supp. 1225 (D. N.Y. 1982).

59. Griesa's two decisions, moreover, contain remarkably detailed accounts of how project proponents and the corps, sometimes acting in response to political pressure brought by project proponents, repeatedly suppressed and downplayed data on the project's impacts on the striped bass. See *Sierra Club v. United States Army Corps of Engineers,* 541 F. Supp. 1367 (D. N.Y. 1982); and *Sierra Club v. United States Army Corps of Engineers,* 614 F. Supp. 1475 (D. N.Y. 1985).

required permits by the end of 1988, to start construction in 1990, and to complete it (including removal of the elevated artery) no later than 1998. Instead, they spent the remaining three years of the Dukakis administration (and 10 times the number of consultant hours originally budgeted) pursuing environmental permit requirements, and when they departed many loose ends remained. Eventually, state officials would estimate they had arrived at more than 1,500 separate mitigation agreements in more than 20 permitting processes, and that these accounted for at least one-third of the CA/T project's total cost. The great majority of these agreements fit the conventional definition of mitigation—that is, action to prevent or minimize harmful impacts. A minority, though, considerably expanded this definition, providing ancillary benefits—such as new parkland and commitments to rail transit expansion—that important stakeholders demanded as the price of their support or neutrality. There was, of course, some irony in the need for such concessions, given that the artery depression had itself been conceived as a beautification project and the new harbor tunnel had been relocated at enormous expense to avoid any neighborhood impacts.

Among the myriad CA/T mitigation controversies, we focus here on just three of the most prominent—involving regional air quality, the Charles River crossing, and a land taking in East Boston.

Since the late 1960s environmentalists had argued that even the most sensitively designed highways stimulate more driving and thus more pollution, whereas mass transit improvements tend to protect the environment. Neither regulators nor the courts ever based decisions on these sweeping claims, however, until the late 1980s, when environmentalists successfully challenged transportation plans in San Francisco and Phoenix on the ground that far more funding was available for their highway than their transit components.[60] Release of the CA/T project's draft EIS in early 1990 brought similar concerns to the fore in Boston. It projected that, by reducing congestion, the CA/T would actually improve air quality in Boston. The models underlying this projection included several transit projects, however, that were not yet formally authorized or funded and assumed that transit fares would rise no faster than the rate of inflation. The Conservation Law Foundation (CLF), a small organization specializing in the skilled use of litigation and publicity to achieve environmental goals, seized on these assumptions, demanding a guarantee that they would be realized.[61] The state's internal

60. See Garrett and Wachs (1996); Transportation Research Board and National Research Council (1995); Yuhnke (1991, esp. pp. 249–51).

61. The CLF, which had fewer than one thousand members, received the bulk of its funding from foundations. Its board, moreover, was very well connected—at the time including

analyses showed that the project would improve air quality quite aside from the transit assumptions. Salvucci was eager to avoid a public controversy about this issue, however, and thus chose not to go public with these analyses. Rather, he emphasized that the transit assumptions represented state policy and he was confident they would be realized.

The Charles River crossing controversy arose from two sets of considerations. First, it was necessary to connect the Central Artery with four other facilities—state Route 1 to the northeast, Interstate 93 to the northwest, Storrow Drive to the west (along the Charles River's southern bank),[62] and a pair of cross-harbor tunnels to the southeast. Second, the project had to make these connections in ways that protected parkland and recreational boating as well as residential and commercial land uses. An obvious question was whether these connections, like the artery itself and the new harbor tunnel, could be underground. It quickly became apparent, however, that tunnels would be phenomenally expensive and also technically risky—because several nearby structures, including a subway tunnel, a dam separating the Charles River from Boston Harbor, and a commuter railroad bridge, might be damaged. So the state focused on bridge options.

The standard design for the main interchange in a rural setting would have been a four-quadrant cloverleaf (two north of the river and two south). This was not feasible in the present case, however, because three of the potential quadrants were in active commercial or parkland use. So the engineers sought ways to compress the functions of all four quadrants into one—located in North Point, an industrial area on the north side of the Charles River. The resulting design (known as Scheme Z because it had been the twenty-sixth alternative developed) provided for a bridge 18 lanes wide, supported by 17 piers sunk into the riverbed, and an interchange spiraling 110 feet skyward. This portion of the project was to create more elevated roadway than the CA/T would eliminate in downtown Boston. It also provided for an extraordinarily convoluted movement between Storrow Drive and the Central Artery. Though both are on the same side of the river, vehicles moving from one to the other would have to cross it twice. Scheme Z had no natural advocates. Salvucci emphasized, however, that the corridor in question had long been devoted to heavy industry and transportation, and that every effort to identify a better alternative had failed.

---

former governor Sargent, former *Boston Globe* editor Tom Winship, and several senior attorneys specializing in environmental law.

62. Technically Storrow Drive turns into the Embankment Road before it meets the artery.

He faced opposition, however, even within state government itself. Julia O'Brien, director of planning for the Metropolitan District Commission (MDC), a state agency that had jurisdiction over the Charles River and its banks, concluded that Scheme Z would foreclose the MDC's long-standing (but never funded) plan to extend the existing riverbank park to the mouth of Boston Harbor. At her urging, MDC commissioner Ilyas Bhatti asserted that both the river and several MDC-owned parcels next to it qualified as protected parkland under Section 4(f) of federal transportation law. East Cambridge residents, meanwhile, charged that Scheme Z would thwart a long-standing plan for mixed-use redevelopment of the North Point area, and questioned why Cambridge should get elevated ramps while Boston was getting a depressed and covered roadway. Responding to these and other criticisms, the city of Cambridge filed negative comments on the draft EIS, implying that it would sue if necessary to block Scheme Z.

The third significant mitigation dispute involved a proposed land taking in East Boston. The new harbor tunnel would bring traffic from the south directly into Logan Airport. Traffic connections to the north, however, would be above ground, and would in part border residential East Boston. Seeking to avoid taking any buildings or parkland, Salvucci chose an alignment requiring a portion of Park 'N Fly, an existing off-airport commercial parking lot. Local activists then urged a more ambitious plan, replacing the entire lot with a new buffer park between the neighborhood and airport.

Richard Goldberg, who co-owned the lot with some out-of-town investors, opposed both of these plans and embarked on a three-part campaign to stop them. First, he launched an expensive lobbying effort in the state legislature, which voted to prohibit the state from acquiring the Park 'N Fly land. (Dukakis successfully vetoed this provision and Goldberg was later convicted of having bribed the Massachusetts House speaker, Charles Flaherty, in the course of pursuing it.)[63] Second, Goldberg threatened to litigate federal and state permit approvals, even where Park 'N Fly itself had no direct interest. Third, working through a consultant, he facilitated the organization of—and provided most of the funding for—a coalition of project critics who had not previously been allied. This group, known as the Committee for Regional Transportation (CRT), included Scheme Z opponents, advocates of the North/South rail link, bicycle activists, the owner of a downtown building adjacent to the existing artery, and some residents of

63. Flaherty was never convicted of taking the bribe, but after a major investigation by the U.S. attorney, he pleaded guilty to income tax evasion and resigned as speaker in 1995.

East Boston, the North End, and Cambridge. Goldberg's challenge was unusual in its variety of tactics but not its form. At exactly the same time, for example, Nicholas Contos, a property owner in South Boston, was mounting a similar if less ambitious campaign. In New York City a few years previously, Seymour Durst, a major West Side property owner and developer, had allegedly been the principal funder of Westway's environmental opponents as well as a formal plaintiff in some of their suits.

In mid-1990 these three issues (air quality, the Charles River crossing, and the Park 'N Fly land taking) began to converge—in part because of Goldberg's strategy but even more significantly because all parties realized that Salvucci was racing against time. Dukakis was not running for reelection, and each prior gubernatorial transition in the history of the CA/T had led to an abrupt shift in course. The best chance to prevent this from happening again, Salvucci judged, was to secure state EIS approval before the new administration took office. (State environmental law was in at least one key respect more stringent than federal; it required the mitigation of any harms identified in the review process. Federal law required only that such harms be thoroughly assessed.)

In addition to the permit hurdle, the project faced two referendum threats in November. The first, sponsored by the union that represented state highway engineers, proposed a tight cap on the state's use of outside consultants. Its main target was the Bechtel/Parsons Brinckerhoff consortium, which the state had hired to manage the CA/T project and which now had a budget almost equal to the rest of the state Department of Public Works. The second, sponsored by the state's leading antitax group and a coalition of high-tech firms, proposed repeal of a host of tax increases recently enacted to cover a state budget shortfall. The state was counting on one of these, an increase in the state gasoline tax of 10 cents a gallon, as a primary source of state funding for the CA/T.

During the late spring and summer of 1990, CA/T supporters sought to prepare the way for a smooth gubernatorial transition. Spearheading this effort was the Artery Business Committee (ABC), a group founded in 1988 by the owners of major properties along the artery corridor. ABC—whose members by now included the CEOs of more than 50 downtown firms with land use interests (ownership, development, professional services)—persuaded four of the five major candidates for governor, including both of those who prevailed in the September primary, to endorse the CA/T project. Obtaining the support of William Weld, the Republican nominee and eventual winner of the general election, represented a particularly significant triumph because early in his campaign he had suggested that the state should reconsider the artery depression.

A related coalition of construction, architectural, and engineering firms raised $1.4 million to oppose the ballot proposition restricting state use of consultants. Early polling and focus group research showed overwhelming public support for this measure. When the definition of a consultant was expanded to include human service providers, however, such as child care and home health care workers, most focus group members turned sharply against the proposition. With this information in hand, the coalition developed an ad campaign stressing the measure's potential human service impacts. Surprised, the measure's sponsors tried to amend it to apply solely to architectural and engineering contracts. But the deadline for changes had long passed. On Election Day the measure failed by a vote of 55 percent to 45 percent. Voters also rejected the tax rollback proposition. A broad coalition of public employee unions spearheaded the campaign against this measure. Salvucci contributed to this effort by ensuring that neither the CA/T project's final environmental impact statement nor a long-awaited CA/T project financing plan were released until after the election.

Salvucci also engaged in a whirlwind of negotiations to resolve the outstanding CA/T disputes. He persuaded MDC commissioner Bhatti, for example, to withdraw from his position that some land in the Scheme Z corridor was federally protected public open space in return for a commitment that the CA/T project would fund a host of open space improvements—estimated to cost about $75 million—along the banks of the Charles River. And he unveiled a new, more elegant design for the Charles River bridge. The price of this change, however, was a bridge 30 feet wider and the elimination of a key downtown on-ramp. This in turn outraged the leaders of ABC. Charlestown residents also opposed the new plan because it channeled additional traffic through their neighborhood.

Pressured from all sides, Salvucci concluded that his highest priority must be to eliminate the CLF as a potential opponent. He knew that its prime concerns were transit and transportation controls rather than any features of the CA/T project itself. As a longtime transit advocate, moreover, he was concerned that the incoming fiscally conservative governor would be tempted to curtail transit spending. So early in December he joined CLF executive director Douglas Foy in a formal Memorandum of Understanding (MOU). Salvucci, never elected and with just a few weeks remaining in office, committed the state to build 14 rapid transit and commuter rail extensions, 20,000 new parking spaces at commuter rail and rapid transit stations, and a regional system of high-occupancy vehicle (HOV) lanes. He also committed it to limit all future transit fare increases to the rate of inflation and to impose more stringent limits on the number of parking spaces in downtown Boston. For his part, Foy committed the CLF not to sue, and indeed to join the state in resisting legal challenges to the CA/T project—a pledge that drew bitter criticism from environmentalists still fighting Scheme Z. John DeVillars, the state's secretary of environmental affairs, quickly signaled his support for the MOU and his intent to incorporate its provisions into his EIS approval.

Several other key parties, however—including Governor-elect Weld, the Massachusetts Bay Transportation Authority (MBTA) Advisory Board (which represents the local jurisdictions with transit service in the Boston region), and the Massachusetts Taxpayers Foundation (a business-backed fiscal watchdog group)—were highly critical, noting that the MOU bound future administrations to invest $2 billion to $4 billion, not to mention the operating subsidies that these projects would require—and this in the midst of a severe state fiscal crisis. After intense Christmas-week negotiations, DeVillars amended his position slightly. He now indicated that the state would be authorized to replace specific projects listed in the MOU with others of comparable air quality benefit and that the state had to incorporate the projects and the replacement policy in its official plan for complying with the federal Clean Air Act. Given that transit expansion rarely yields significant air quality gains,[64] this provision could have been read as leaving future decisionmakers considerable discretion. Foy, however, warned that the CLF would sue to halt work on the CA/T if any future administration sought to modify the MOU in any significant way.

Finally, Salvucci agreed to convene a blue-ribbon citizen advisory committee to reexamine the bridge plans. On January 2, 1991, the next to last day of the Dukakis administration, DeVillars accepted the project's environmental impact report, conditional upon implementation of the recent CLF and Scheme Z agreements. He also required taking the entire Park 'N Fly site for a new East Boston park. Within days, the city of Cambridge, Park 'N Fly, and the CRT all announced that they would sue to stop the project from moving forward.

Surviving a Gubernatorial Transition

Governor Weld assumed office in the midst of a severe local recession and fiscal crisis. Several of his advisers, noting that the CA/T plan provided for

64. Altshuler (1979); and Meyer and Gómez-Ibáñez (1981).

the section now occupied by the elevated Central Artery to be funded out-side the framework of the interstate program, argued for dropping the whole artery depression component of the CA/T. (The plan envisioned reliance on a combination of federal formula highway aid and state match-ing funds for the segment in question. These funds were also in great demand for other projects across the state, however.) Others, including the new state secretary of transportation, Richard Taylor, maintained that this would be a mistake. Noting that the project enjoyed very broad support, particularly in the business community, they warned that any major recon-figuration would trigger a new permitting process, which could delay the entire project for years. In the short run, they added, the CA/T was an eco-nomic plus for the state's depressed economy because of the federal funding it brought into the state, while in the long term it would make the Boston area more attractive for investment by improving airport access, reducing central area traffic congestion, and improving the physical attractiveness of downtown Boston. After a brief pause for reflection, Weld decided to move full speed ahead.

The major challenge of 1991 was to secure additional earmarked fund-ing for the CA/T in the federal reauthorization of surface transportation programs scheduled for enactment that year (the first such reauthorization since the original project approval in 1987). This task would be greatly complicated if the project were beset by local controversy. So the new administration took up where the old had left off, striving to conciliate project critics. Most notably, it established a broad-based panel to review the Charles River crossing design. This panel, drawing on previously unpubli-cized options that had been developed by the state's own engineering consultants, eventually coalesced around several modifications to Scheme Z. These placed certain movements in land-based tunnels, thereby eliminating the double crossing of the river, reducing the scale of the North Point ramps, and allowing for reinsertion of the downtown on-ramp that Salvucci had found it necessary to delete the previous December.

The committee failed to reach a full consensus, however, splitting on the question of whether the Charles River bridge could be further downsized by placing a small portion of its traffic in a cross-river tunnel and on precisely how to make some key connections. Taylor allowed this dispute to simmer but his successor, James Kerasiotes, who moved up from the position of state highway commissioner at the end of 1992, quickly decided to proceed with an all-bridge scheme for the river crossing. The design he selected was con-siderably more elegant than Scheme Z, just a little bit smaller, and an estimated $1.3 billion more expensive. While some activists were critical and Cambridge brought an unsuccessful lawsuit, CA/T advocates applauded this decision and the controversy quickly faded. (It was assumed, of course, that the federal government would cover 90 percent of the added cost.)

At about this time as well the state concluded an agreement with Park 'N Fly, agreeing to replace its existing site with another, at least equally suitable for its business.[65] Park 'N Fly in return agreed to drop its environmental lawsuit and stop aiding the CRT, the broad group of project critics it had largely organized and funded. The CRT did not immediately dissolve, but it was never again a significant force.

Meanwhile, administration officials were sending mixed messages on the CLF agreement. Taylor pledged his personal support but—reflecting FHWA views—said he did not see how the federal highway agency could build future transit commitments into its project approval. (He did, however, pledge support for inclusion of the MOU provisions in the state's clean air plan and as permit conditions for the artery's ventilation buildings.) In keeping with this approach, FHWA administrator Thomas Larsen refused to make the MOU transit elements conditions of project acceptance. The CLF sued the state and the FHWA in response, claiming: "The public record on the project makes it perfectly clear that the project depends heavily on mass transit . . . to meet the requirements of the [Clean Air Act]."[66] In fact this greatly overstated the case. The state and the FHWA were vulnerable, however, because the models did not include any sensitivity analyses of what would occur if some or all of their transit assumptions failed to materialize.

Subsequent research and modeling, by both independent researchers and state agencies, indicated that the transit projects, park-and-ride lots, and fare-cap policies called for in the MOU would be extremely costly per unit of air pollution eliminated by comparison with such measures as improved vapor control systems on gasoline pumps, better motor vehicle inspection and maintenance programs, and reformulated fuels. State officials chose not to use these findings politically, however, because to do so would have

65. This swap was never completed, however, because of Goldberg's subsequent legal troubles. Massport eventually purchased the Park 'N Fly land in 2001. See Massachusetts Port Authority Pressroom, "Massport Completes ParkEx Transaction: Clears Way for Bremen Street Park and Reduced Traffic on East Boston Streets," January 10, 2001 press release (www.massport.com/about/press01/press_news_parex.html [February 2002]).

66. S. Burrington, letter attached to the CLF's notice of intent to sue sent to the U.S. Environmental Protection Agency, the Federal Highway Administration, Governor William Weld, the Massachusetts Executive Office of Transportation and Construction, and the Massachusetts Office of Environmental Affairs, May 29, 1991.

conflicted with their central aims of minimizing controversy and litigation. On the contrary, they moved to incorporate the MOU provisions into the state's clean air plan and ventilation building permits. With these efforts nearing finality, the CLF agreed in March 1992 to drop its suit. Foy reiterated as it did so, however, that the CLF would fight any future effort to substantially alter the MOU provisions, and no subsequent administration has seen fit to test him.

The lack of relationship between policy and research in this case was far from unique, of course, and had a direct parallel in the Century Freeway case. The legal settlement in that case, it will be recalled, included a large program of new housing development, justified on the ground that adequate replacement housing was unavailable for those displaced by the road. State-sponsored studies of those already displaced by the project, however, ran counter to this position. The judge overseeing this case in the early 1970s found these studies both adequate and accurate.[67] The plaintiffs persisted, though, and found allies in the administration of Governor Jerry Brown—which was unenthusiastic about the freeway but eager to build affordable housing. In this context, the state and the plaintiffs agreed that as a condition for implementation of the road project, the FHWA should finance an extensive program of affordable housing construction. Career federal highway officials resisted, but President Carter's secretary of transportation, Neil Goldschmidt, embraced the settlement as in keeping with the Carter administration's National Urban Policy. When Reagan administration officials subsequently explored the idea of abandoning this commitment, they found it enjoyed such strong local support that they decided to forbear.

The Cost of Consensus

As of 1991 the estimated cost of the CA/T had risen by two-thirds since 1987, from $3.1 billion to $5.2 billion. The interstate system was complete, except for several projects in the pipeline of which the CA/T was by far the largest—and the furthest from completion. Since 1956 states had been entitled to 90 percent of the cost of interstate projects, whatever this turned out to be. This pattern was unlikely to persist, however, with most of the money going to a single state, and the CA/T seemed vulnerable if its escalating cost became the specific focus of another congressional debate. After intensive state lobbying, however, the Bush administration opted to

67. See *Keith v. Volpe*, 352 F.Supp. 1324 (D.Calif. 1972), pp. 1346–47.

include the CA/T cost increase since 1987 in the reauthorization bill it submitted to Congress—judging that a battle with the state's powerful congressional delegation over this issue would cost more than it was worth (and might well end in a defeat for the administration). Its resistance was softened, moreover, by its desire to be helpful to the new Republican governor of Massachusetts.[68] Consequently, its submission included $2.5 billion in additional funding for the CA/T, bringing the total federal share to $4.2 billion.

State and federal officials disagreed, though, on how to address the possibility of still further cost escalation in future. The state pressed hard for an understanding that the historic Interstate Highway Program pattern of 90 percent federal participation in the cost to complete, however much it might escalate, would continue. But the administration, and eventually Congress as well, refused to go along. The Intermodal Surface Transportation and Efficiency Act (ISTEA) of 1991 specified explicitly that its interstate program allocations would be the last. This language received little attention in Massachusetts, however, and state officials professed not to view it as very significant. Their position was that the state's congressional delegation would simply have more work to do when the next reauthorization act came up in six years.[69]

The CA/T project also benefited from three other developments in 1991. First, the Bush administration decided late in the year, as an antirecession measure, to accept a considerably more expensive bill than it had originally recommended. Second, ISTEA included a provision guaranteeing that no state would experience a reduction in its total aid allotment of more than 10 percent in any year. Since ISTEA loaded interstate funding into its early years, this provision added $370 million to the state's formula aid during its later years. And the state received a final windfall as a result of Senate-House bargaining in conference over earmarked projects. In return for Senate acceptance of more than 500 such projects (mainly in the districts of powerful House members), the leader of the Senate delegation, Daniel Patrick Moynihan, obtained a provision reimbursing states for the cost of roads on

---

68. Thomas Larsen (federal highway administrator at the time), interview by authors, by telephone, December 20, 1993. The state's congressional delegation was less influential than it had been during the great CA/T debates of the mid-1980s, when it included the chair and ranking minority member of the House Appropriations Committee (Edward Boland and Silvio Conte) and, until his retirement in 1987, Speaker O'Neill. But it still included the chair of the House Rules Committee (Joseph Moakley) and one of the most influential members of the Senate (Edward Kennedy, chair of the Labor and Human Resources Committee).

69. Richard Taylor, interview by authors, Boston, December 22, 1993.

the interstate system that had been constructed without federal aid, generally before enactment of the Interstate Highway Program in 1956. (This provision had not been part of either the Senate or the House bill.) Moynihan's concern was the New York State Thruway, but since Massachusetts had also built its turnpike without federal aid, it stood to receive $200 million as a result of this provision during the six years of ISTEA, with the prospect of more to come in future transportation acts. Overall, the state stood to receive about $2.80 in federal highway aid (roughly half for the CA/T) for every highway tax dollar it sent to Washington during the six-year life of ISTEA, the highest ratio of any state in the continental 48.

The Expanding National Surface Transportation Coalition

ISTEA marked the end of the Interstate Highway Program, which had dominated federal transportation spending and planning for more than three decades, but it did not by any means signal a diminution in the federal role with respect to highway investment. Rather, it authorized significant real spending increases, from $17.5 billion in 1991 to $21 billion in 1997 (in constant 1997 dollars). It did continue a long-standing shift toward rehabilitation and reconstruction, however, as opposed to new construction. By 1995 about half of all spending on highways was for these purposes. And it greatly relaxed categorical restrictions on the use of highway aid, giving states far greater flexibility than ever before.

ISTEA was by no means just a highway bill, though. In addition to authorizing $124 billion for highway grants over its six-year life, it authorized $31 billion for urban mass transit. It required states, in developing their plans and spending priorities for urban areas with 200,000 people or more, to work closely with regional planning organizations. It set aside $2.4 billion for projects such as bicycle paths and historic and scenic preservation. And it specified that the highest priority of surface transportation spending was to facilitate the achievement of clean air objectives. As a result of these provisions, most environmental groups applauded ISTEA, an unprecedented development. The surface transportation coalition, broadened to include transit advocates during the 1970s and 1980s, now included virtually all of its former critics.

CA/T Costs Rise, Federal Aid Does Not

In November 1993, Massachusetts secretary of transportation James Kerasiotes announced that the CA/T cost estimate had risen another 40

Table 4-3. Cost Estimates of Central Artery/Tunnel Project, 1983–2002[a]

Year	Current dollars (billions)	Constant 2002 dollars (billions)	Overall federal share (percent)	Federal interstate program share (percent)
1983	2.3	3.7	85	85
1985	2.6	3.9	85	69
1987	3.2	4.5	85	69
1989	4.4	5.8	85	69
1991	5.2	6.4	85	69
1992	6.4	7.7	85	65
1993	7.7	9.0	85	54
1995	7.8	8.7	85	52
1996	10.4	11.4	85	40
1998	10.8	11.5	79	39
2000 (March)	12.2	12.6	70	34
2000 (April)	13.5	13.9	63	31
2000 (October)	14.1	14.5	61	30
2001	14.5	14.6	59	29
2002	14.6	14.6	58	29

Sources: Boston Redevelopment Authority (1975); Massachusetts Office of the Inspector General (2001); Green (1979); Massachusetts Highways Department (1994, 1996a, 1996b); Massachusetts Turnpike Authority (1999a, 2000, 2001); Federal Highway Administration, "Federal Task Force on the Boston Central Artery/Tunnel Project: Review of Project Oversight and Costs" (2000); and Office of Inspector General, Department of Transportation, "Top Ten Management Issues" (2001).

a. Through 1995 the cost estimates were in current dollars; more recently they have included estimates of future growth due to inflation. Costs of interest on state borrowing to finance the CA/T (both to finance the state share and in anticipation of future formula highway aid) are not included. The state inspector general estimated in 2000 that these costs might approach $4 billion.

percent since 1991, from $5.2 billion to $7.7 billion (see table 4-3). This was, of course, more than triple the $2.6-billion estimate on which the state had relied in its mid-1980s campaign for congressional approval. In a subsequent review, the state attributed about half this increase to design and mitigation changes and the other half to inflation. (The latter claim seemed high, as this had been a period of very low inflation; if one accepted it for the sake of argument, however, the real cost of the project had doubled.)

Though a shock locally, this revision was not out of the ordinary for a major highway project. The estimated cost of the Century Freeway, for example, rose from $502 million in 1977 to over $2 billion when it was completed in 1993—an increase of more than 100 percent even when inflation is taken into account.[70] In 2000 the official cost estimate for the new Woodrow Wilson Bridge near Washington, D.C., suddenly rose by two-

70. See Taylor (1995).

thirds, from $1.5 billion to about $2.5 billion—due, it was claimed, to unexpectedly high costs for dredging, for the reconstruction of water and sewer lines (many of them first identified during construction), and for environmental mitigation.[71]

In Massachusetts the new estimate triggered fears that construction of the CA/T would require deep cutbacks in other state roadwork or tax increases to avert them. State officials dismissed such concerns, observing that Congress generally protected states from any reduction in annual funding level from one surface transportation act to the next. So long, they maintained, as the state's projected highway allocation in the final year of ISTEA ($740 million) remained at least constant in subsequent years, there would be no need to consider such actions.

In 1994, however, Republicans gained control of both houses of Congress and the state's delegation—all Democrats except for two freshmen elected that year, both of whom lost their seats two years later—was reduced to impotence. The Republican heartland, moreover, included a group of Sunbelt states that had long contributed more in highway taxes than they received in highway aid. These "donor" states in the highway program were almost all "recipient" states in the overall federal system, but many of them—fast-growing Sunbelt states—had ambitious highway plans and were resolved to alter the highway program in their favor.

As a result, debates about the successor to ISTEA revolved around the issue of funding formulas. The result, enacted in mid-1998, was the Transportation Equity Act for the 21st Century, more commonly known as TEA-21. TEA-21 retained the basic programmatic structure of ISTEA and accentuated the trend toward earmarking funds for "special" projects—1,850 in number, with an estimated total cost of $9 billion. As usual, Congress authorized considerably more spending than the administration had requested—guaranteeing $162 billion for highways and $36 billion for mass transit over six years, nearly 40 percent more than ISTEA, and authorizing even larger expenditures for highways if gas tax revenues came in higher than projected. This increase in aggregate spending enabled Congress to solve its most urgent political problem: how to satisfy the claims of traditional donor states (now ascendant in Congress) while avoiding absolute cutbacks in aid to the traditional recipient states.[72] In the end, only one

71. See Alan Sipress, "The Incredible Ballooning Price Tags," *Washington Post,* October 5, 2000, p. B1.

72. For example, 12 states—Alabama, Delaware, Georgia, Idaho, Kentucky, Michigan, Montana, Nevada, South Carolina, Tennessee, Texas, and Virginia—saw their federal highway aid increase by more than 60 percent.

state experienced an absolute reduction—Massachusetts. It had done so remarkably well in ISTEA that there was little sentiment in Congress for protecting it from a return to more typical aid levels. Most notably, Congress refused to earmark another penny for the CA/T. Overall, the state's highway aid allotment was to decline from an average of $830 million a year under ISTEA to $525 million a year under TEA-21—a cut of 35 percent in nominal dollars, but roughly 50 percent in real terms. The immediate effects in Massachusetts included public dismay and escalating controversy about the CA/T's management, but not any serious consideration of halting or slowing the pace of construction, now well under way. State officials, downtown business and labor interests, and the press were unanimous that work should proceed full speed, arguing that the large investments already made would not yield benefits until the CA/T opened to traffic, that costs would continue to escalate during any period of delay, and that it was urgent to complete the unsightly, disruptive work of construction itself (within and adjacent to downtown) as quickly as possible.

The state's Republican governors since 1990 had taken an absolute position against any and all tax increases, so state officials were compelled to devise other options. The plan on which they settled called for the state to use two-thirds of its formula highway aid under TEA-21 for the CA/T ($2.1 billion of $3.2 billion) and to borrow another $1.5 billion against subsequent federal highway aid. Federal law permitted such borrowing, though at the state's own risk since aid allocations after the expiration of TEA-21 in 2003 remained purely speculative.[73] The state also exacted contributions totaling $1.55 billion from the Massachusetts Turnpike Authority and the Massachusetts Port Authority, which they planned to raise by issuing revenue bonds, to be serviced from increased tolls and fees. Meanwhile, the state was spending about $60 million a year of general revenue to service debt on CA/T-related bonds, and its debt service costs for Boston-area transit had tripled over the course of a decade (from $90 million in 1989 to $268 million in 1999), in large part because of projects specified in the CLF agreement.[74]

While attracting substantial media coverage, these developments did not engender much controversy until early 2000, when Kerasiotes, now chairman of the Turnpike Authority but still in charge of the CA/T, announced that the project's estimated cost had risen by $1.4 billion to more than $12 billion. It soon became apparent, moreover, that top CA/T managers had

73. Massachusetts Turnpike Authority (1999, p. 13).
74. Massachusetts Taxpayers Foundation (1999, pp. 23–24).

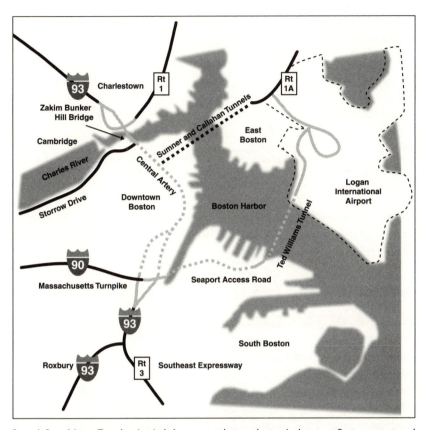

Boston's Central Artery/Tunnel project includes a new, underground artery in downtown Boston, a new tunnel under Boston Harbor, a new bridge over the Charles River, and a new connector between the artery and the tunnel. Credit: Robert B. Levers.

withheld this information from state and federal officials and from investors in state bonds. This triggered an FHWA investigation, which concluded in April that the actual projected increase was nearly $3 billion, to $13.5 billion. At this point Kerasiotes was forced to resign. In subsequent months, as the project's new managers probed further, its estimated cost rose to $14.1 billion. At this writing, in 2002, the CA/T's estimated cost is $14.6 billion (see table 4-3).

With these recent increases, the projected cost of the CA/T, after adjusting for inflation, has more than tripled since 1987 when Congress approved its financing. The estimated share to be financed by the Interstate Highway Program, moreover, out of competition with other state highway priorities, has declined from 69 percent to 29 percent. These figures exclude, moreover,

Table 4-4. Metropolitan-Area Population, Land Area, Highway Miles, and Travel, 1980 and 2000

Area characteristic	1980	2000	Change (percent)
Population (millions)	178	217	18
Land mass (millions of square miles)	565	706	20
Lane miles of urban highways and principal arterials (millions)	220	302	27
Vehicle miles of travel in urban areas (millions)	855	1,665	49

Sources: Authors' calculations from Bureau of the Census, *Statistical Abstract of the United States: 2001* (2002, table A, p. 894); Federal Highway Administration, "Highway Statistics Summary to 1995" (1997, tables HM-220, HM-260, VM 202, and "Highway Statistics 2000" (2001, tables HM-20, HM-60, VM-2).

the billions spent on transit projects specified in the CLF agreement and projected interest costs—which may total as much as $4 billion—on project-related debt.[75]

Conclusion: Paradigm or Anomaly?

At one level, the Central Artery/Tunnel project was, and continues to be, an anomaly. It is, by far, more expensive than any other highway project ever undertaken in the United States, and it was inspired by a federal aid program that no longer exists. Yet the forces that produced the CA/T have by no means entirely abated, as evidenced by the continuing growth in highway spending at all levels of American government and the continuing expansion of urban highway mileage. Indeed, from 1980 to 2000 urban highway and principal arterial mileage increased more rapidly than urban population and land area—though at little more than half the rate of motor vehicle travel (see table 4-4).

At the national level, there was considerable debate as the Interstate Highway Program wound down about whether the overall federal role in highway investment ought sharply to decline. The interstate program had been enacted, after all, to underwrite the development of a specific freeway network, which was now essentially complete and unlikely to be significantly expanded. Yet exactly the opposite occurred. Aside from a dip in the early Reagan years, real federal highway spending has consistently grown, and since 1990 even more rapidly than state and local expenditures. ISTEA, moreover, defined a new 163,000-mile National Highway System (inclusive of but far more expansive than the interstate system), including 3,800 projected new miles.

75. Massachusetts Office of the Inspector General (2001, pp. 2–3).

There have, on the other hand, been very significant changes in recent decades. Federal highway programs, in particular, are now authorized in the context of much broader surface transportation legislation, the key constituencies for which include mass transit, environmental, and other traditional critics of disruptive highway investment. The result has been a need for continual adjustment to minimize conflict among these constituencies and provide substantial funding for their respective priorities. The purposes for which highway grants may be used have become increasingly flexible, moreover, and local governments, participating in metropolitan planning organizations, have gained increasing influence on how they are used. This program structure encourages a wide distribution of available resources rather than their concentration on a few major projects. (States can also pursue "special" congressional project earmarks, but the projects so favored tend to be numerous rather than individually massive.)

Most planned new highways as of 2002 are on the outskirts of fast-growing urban areas such as Atlanta, Charlotte, Denver, and Houston. Some in-town facilities are also planned, however, typically with features reminiscent of the CA/T. Ohio, for example, recently rebuilt an existing waterfront expressway in Cincinnati as a depressed and partially decked facility.[76] Wisconsin is replacing a mile-long elevated freeway spur in Milwaukee with a surface boulevard and mixed-use development. Several urban areas are also making highway and rail freight improvements to improve traffic flow in the vicinity of busy seaports. Los Angeles and Long Beach, most notably, have recently—at a cost of more than $2 billion—eliminated all grade crossings in a 22-mile rail corridor connecting their seaports with rail and truck marshalling yards.[77] The state of Washington and the port authorities of Seattle and Tacoma have plans for a similar project, expected

76. The $314 million Cincinnati project, which was completed in August 2000, was designed to support an ambitious waterfront redevelopment program, costing in excess of $1 billion, that included two new stadiums and a new museum. See Aileen Cho, "Where There's a Will, There's a New Fort Washington Way in 34 Months: 'Impossible' Fast Track Job Spurs Cincinnati Urban Revival," *Engineering News-Record,* April 3, 2000, pp. 36–39; and www.riverfrontplanning.org.

77. The project was carried out by an authority, the governing board of which included representatives of both cities, their port districts (which have jurisdiction over different portions of the same harbor), and the county's transit authority. The largest sources of funding were local bonds and a federal loan secured by anticipated revenue from the railroads using the corridor, and grants from the ports and the regional transit authority (primarily with funds from state and federal transit aid programs). Lesser sources included an up-front payment from the railroads as well as small federal and state highway grants for some of the grade-crossing and road-widening work that accompanied the project. See Alameda Corridor Transportation Authority (1999, pp. 24–26).

to cost about $400 million. And New Jersey is moving forward with a plan (costing three quarters of a billion dollars) for a truck-only route between its port facilities and nearby rail yards and highways.[78]

Ambitious ideas for replacing elevated in-town expressways with new facilities in tunnel, on the CA/T model, are also currently under study (along with other options) in several areas—most notably in Seattle, where the state and city announced in July 2002 that they favored a plan to replace the aging two-mile Alaskan Way viaduct and its approach roads with a four-mile-long depressed and covered roadway, estimated to cost $10.1–11.6 billion.[79] The New York State DOT is studying a similar proposal for the Gowanus Expressway in Brooklyn, and regional planning agencies in both San Francisco and Los Angeles have recently raised the possibility of building new freeways in tunnels.[80] Each of these proposals, of course, faces daunting obstacles. None is likely to receive truly serious consideration unless it attracts a core of intensely committed supporters, including key elements of its downtown business leadership. Even if built largely underground, each is likely to encounter serious permitting obstacles and expensive demands for mitigation. And funding will be an even greater problem than it was for the CA/T, given the absence of a federal program like the interstate, which appeared to promise near-complete federal financing out of competition with other state road priorities. As highway congestion continues to worsen, however, the pressure for such projects seems likely to increase as well, setting the stage for new campaigns to enhance their feasibility—by developing new funding streams, relaxing regulatory constraints, or both. Such efforts, it need scarcely be added, are certain to be intensely controversial.

78. These access projects are elements of much broader port modernization programs driven in large measure by fierce competition for the growing, but increasingly centralized, container freight business. See Luberoff and Walder (2000).

79. The depression plan is one of three being studied by the state DOT. See Washington State Department of Transportation, "SR 99 Alaskan Way Viaduct and Seawall Project" (www.wsdot.wa.gov/projects/viaduct/plans.htm [September 2002]).

80. The New York State Department of Transportation, while agreeing that the existing road must be rebuilt or replaced, initially rejected tunneling as impossible to finance. After local advocates brought suit, however, it agreed in January 2001 to include one or more tunneling alternatives in its draft environmental impact analysis, due to be completed in 2003. See New York Department of Transportation (NYSDOT), "The Gowanus Project" (www.dot.state.ny.us/reg/r11/gowanus/index.html [March 2002]); and Elizabeth Hays, "Gowanus Rehab a Puzzlement; There's No Easy Solution to Replacing Old Expressway," *New York Daily News*, January 7, 2001. On San Francisco, see Ralph Lewis, "San Francisco Could Go Down Same Road as Boston," *Boston Globe*, April 22, 2000, p. B3. On Los Angeles, see Jeffrey Rabin, "Unlocking Gridlock: MTA Is Crafting 25-Year Blueprint for Freeway, Mass Transit Projects to Lessen Growth-Related Congestion," *Los Angeles Times*, November 20, 2000, p. B1.

CHAPTER FIVE

Building New Airports and Expanding Older Ones

Denver International, the first passenger airport built in more than two decades to serve a major U.S. metropolitan area, opened in February 1995. Leaders of the national aviation industry, together with local business and political leaders, celebrated Denver's success in overcoming the obstacles that had stymied all other recent efforts to build major new passenger airports. But they doubted that many others would follow. Though proposals were under discussion in several other urban areas, none was close to final approval. And Denver's advantages would be hard to replicate. Few of the regions with serious air traffic congestion had vast, flat, largely uninhabited sites fewer than 30 miles from downtown. Critics emphasized, moreover, that the projections of demand used to justify Denver's new airport now seemed excessive, and that its development had been marked by substantial cost overruns and delays.

Denver business and political leaders had been engaged in a campaign for additional airport capacity since the 1960s. The prospect of expanding Stapleton, though, Denver's existing airport, had generated intense opposition from local environmentalists and potentially affected neighborhoods. The region's dominant airlines had been at best ambivalent, moreover, about both the desirability of additional capacity, which would facilitate the entry of new competitors, and the airport's cost, which would doubtless show up largely in the form of higher landing and terminal fees. The result, for more than two decades, had been political gridlock. This scenario was paralleled in urban areas across the country from the 1960s through the late 1980s. In the 1990s, however, the gridlock began to dissolve amid growing concern about airport congestion, and numerous regions embarked on massive programs of airport expansion and reconstruction, some even more expensive than Denver's new airport. So the Denver case, while unique in its details, was also representative of a much broader trend.

Origins of the National Airport System (1918–45)

In 1918 the U.S. Postal Service began offering rudimentary airmail service with army fliers and publicly owned aircraft, having failed to attract private contractors. Seven years later, with airmail volume growing rapidly, Congress mandated postal service reliance on private contract carriers to encourage the development of commercial aviation and to eliminate direct competition between the federal government and the railroads. A year later, in 1926, it authorized federal development of a national system of air navigation aids, while explicitly prohibiting federal aid for airport development. (The model was federal maritime policy.)

When common carrier air service first came into being during the late 1920s, even major city airports generally consisted of little more than a short runway, graded but unpaved, and one or two simple buildings. Local business campaigns to stimulate airport improvements and attract federal airmail routes were already common, however. Postal service contracts were essential because air carriers could rarely survive without them. Thus, for example, Atlanta leaders mobilized successfully to ensure that their city, not Birmingham, would be the terminus for southeastern airmail service (beyond which the "air" mail traveled by land).[1] If local business leaders united to lobby Congress and the postal service, however, they routinely competed fiercely when it came to airport siting. Roughly a dozen groups of real estate interests, for example, advanced proposals for a municipal airport to serve Los Angeles. The group that prevailed favored a site in Inglewood, northwest of downtown Los Angeles, adjacent to land that its members planned to develop for factories with air transportation needs.[2]

These early siting choices often endured because as larger airports were needed in later years the path of least resistance was usually to expand the airfields developed in the 1920s rather than build from scratch on a new site. As urban areas sprawled over the generations, moreover, the relative prox-

1. Braden and Hagan (1989, p. 37).
2. Friedman (1978, pp. 19–20).

imity of these original sites to downtown commerce came to be appreciated as an asset that could never be replicated. Many of the original sites were so small and difficult to expand that they were eventually superseded, but even today 12 of the nation's 31 "large hub" airports are on expanded versions of sites chosen in the 1920s.[3] (See tables 5-1 and 5-2.)

Air travel grew rapidly from a small base during the Great Depression, with the number of enplaned passengers rising eight times from 1930 to 1940. Federal aid for airport improvements was still ostensibly prohibited but in practice, under the guise of work relief, the federal government provided most of the money expended for airport improvements during this decade. About 4 percent of the grants distributed by the Works Progress Administration (WPA)—$440 million out of $11 billion—was used for airport projects, a sum that represented about three quarters of all capital spending on civilian airports during the decade. Other New Deal programs provided significant funding for air traffic control improvements.[4]

With enactment of the Civil Aeronautics Act (CAA) in 1938, the federal government also assumed broad responsibility for the economic welfare of the airline industry. The strategy embodied in the CAA (in line with common New Deal practice in other industries) was to nurture existing carriers by restricting price competition and the entry of new competitors. In this case the new agency established by the act was also charged with setting airmail rates at levels calibrated to ensure the carriers' financial viability. This body—the Civil Aeronautics Authority, later renamed the Civil Aeronautics Board (CAB)—quickly became the focus of intense lobbying by, among others, localities seeking regional dominance. For decades, for example, Dallas and Fort Worth interests battled before the CAB over which city's airport would gain route allocations befitting its (desired) status as the region's dominant facility.[5]

During World War II the federal government spent about $3.25 billion developing military airfields (about half of which it turned over to states and localities after the war) and another $400 million improving civilian airports for wartime military use. To illustrate, the site of an airplane factory (with airfield) complex built near Chicago by the military in 1942 and 1943 and

3. The Federal Aviation Administration (FAA) defines large hub airports as those airports that serve at least 1 percent of enplaned passengers; for at least the past several decades, about two-thirds of all enplanements have been at such hubs. Airlines use the term "hub" differently, to describe airports with significant amounts of connecting traffic. In this chapter, unless otherwise indicated, we employ the FAA definition.

4. Figures from Couch and Shughart (1998, p. 113); and Martin (1965, p. 91). Also see Komons (1978, pp. 241–42); and Karsner (1993, ch. 2, pp. 12–32).

5. Fairbanks (1992, pp. 176–78).

Table 5-1. Acreage of U.S. Large Hub Airports[a]

Airport	Year opened	Acres at opening	Acres in 1972	Acres in 2001
Salt Lake City	1920	400	4,270	6,823
Boston (Logan)	1923	189	2,400	2,400
Minneapolis/St. Paul	1923	100	2,930	3,100
St. Louis (Lambert)	1923	170	1,850	1,980
Atlanta (Hartsfield)	1925	287	3,750	4,200
Philadelphia	1925	125	2,500	2,300
Honolulu	1927	885	3,900	4,672
San Francisco	1927	150	5,207	5,000
Los Angeles	1928	640	3,006	3,500
Newark	1928	68	2,300	2,300
San Diego	1928	n.a.	480	480
Tampa	1928	160	3,300	3,300
Detroit	1929	774	4,800	4,800
Ft. Lauderdale	1929	1,400	1,400	1,400
Miami	1929	116	2,699	3,000
Charlotte	1935	n.a.	n.a.	n.a.
Phoenix	1935	285	n.a.	2,232
New York (LaGuardia)	1939	550	580	650
Washington (Reagan National)	1941	860	860	860
Cincinnati	1947	n.a.	n.a.	n.a.
Seattle/Tacoma	1947	906	1,800	2,500
Las Vegas (McCarran)	1948	n.a.	1,470	2,820
New York (JFK)	1948	4,900	4,900	4,930
Baltimore	1950	3,200	3,200	3,200
Pittsburgh	1952	1,600	3,100	10,000
Chicago (O'Hare)	1955	7,000	7,000	7,700
Washington (Dulles)	1962	10,000	10,000	10,000
Houston (George Bush)	1969	8,000	7,200	8,000
Orlando	1970	n.a.	n.a.	14,672
Dallas/Fort Worth	1973	17,500	n.a.	17,637
Denver	1995	34,000	n.a.	34,000

Sources: Stroud (1956, p. 6-111); Gentry, Howell, and Taneja (1977); and Federal Aviation Administration and ARP Consulting, "Aviation Capacity Enhancement Plan, 2001: Building Capacity Today for the Skies of Tomorrow" (2002).

n.a. Not available.

a. A large hub airport handles at least 1 percent of national enplanements. This table lists all U.S. airports so classified by the FAA as of 2001.

Table 5-2. Large Hub Airports, Ranked by Enplanements, 2000[a]

Airport	Enplanements (millions) 2000	Rank 2000	Rank 1971
Atlanta (Hartsfield)	39.3	1	4
Chicago (O'Hare)	33.8	2	1
Los Angeles	32.2	3	2
Dallas/Fort Worth	28.3	4	8
San Francisco	19.6	5	5
Denver	18.4	6	13
Phoenix	18.1	7	29
Las Vegas (McCarran)	17.4	8	25
Detroit	17.3	9	11
Newark	17.2	10	12
Minneapolis/St. Paul	17.0	11	19
Miami	16.5	12	7
Houston (George Bush)	16.4	13	21
New York (JFK)	16.2	14	3
St. Louis (Lambert)	15.3	15	15
Orlando	14.8	16	59
Seattle/Tacoma	13.9	17	18
Boston (Logan)	13.6	18	10
New York (LaGuardia)	12.7	19	6
Philadelphia	12.3	20	14
Charlotte	11.5	21	44
Cincinnati	11.2	22	31
Honolulu	11.2	23	17
Pittsburgh	9.9	24	16
Baltimore	9.7	25	28
Washington (Dulles)	9.6	26	36
Salt Lake City	9.5	27	34
Tampa	8.0	28	27
San Diego	7.9	29	26
Ft. Lauderdale	7.8	30	40
Washington (Reagan National)	7.5	31	9

Sources: Federal Aviation Administration and ARP Consulting, "Aviation Capacity Enhancement Plan, 2001: Building Capacity Today for the Skies of Tomorrow" (2002, appendix B); and Uhl (1972, appendix A).

a. From 1971 to 2000 nine airports grew into the large hub category, serving at least 1 percent of nationwide enplaned passengers. These were Phoenix, Orlando, Charlotte, Cincinnati, Baltimore, Washington (Dulles), Salt Lake City, Tampa, and San Diego. Three other airports—Cleveland, New Orleans, and Kansas City—dropped out of the large hub category.

then leased to Douglas Aircraft became the core of today's O'Hare International Airport.[6] Similarly, an air force training field in northern Kentucky became Cincinnati's main airport; and the military financed a doubling of the size of Atlanta's airport along with numerous other improvements.[7] Two other wartime developments were even more significant in laying the basis for postwar air travel growth. First, military research and development generated a host of new technologies, including jet engines and radar.[8] Second, direct federal responsibility for air traffic control became firmly established, including federal ownership and operation of both airport control towers and regional centers to manage the flow of traffic between airports.[9]

Thus, as World War II ended, the basic structure of the nation's civil air system was in place. Aircraft production, ownership, and operation were private. The federal government managed the air traffic control system, regulated airline routes and fares, provided airmail contracts that included an element of subsidy, and financed research and development (though with military rather than commercial objectives). Localities owned and operated nearly all common carrier airports but had little tradition of carrying out major capital projects without federal assistance. The states, with rare exceptions, were not involved.

The Early Postwar Years (1945–60)

Even before the war's end, local business and political leaders in many cities developed aggressive plans for airport improvements and sought to ensure that federal aid would be available to assist in their realization. In the latter effort they were allied with the nation's airlines, aircraft manufacturers, and construction industry associations, and Congress did enact an airport aid program in 1946. The fruits of this victory proved extremely modest, however. Appropriations over the seven-year life of this act averaged only $18 million a year, and only about one quarter of this amount was available for use at major airports.[10]

6. Doherty (1970, ch. 1).
7. See the Cincinnati/Northern Kentucky International Airport website at www.cvgairport.com/history.html; and Braden and Hagan (1989, p. 109, 114).
8. See Heppenheimer (1995, pp. 75–109, 137–57, 173–74); Rochester (1976, pp. 57–78); and J. R. M. Wilson (1979, pp. 217–43, 286–87).
9. See Heppenheimer (1995, pp. 123–24); and J. R. M. Wilson (1979, pp. 113–16).
10. See J. R. M. Wilson (1979, pp. 171–84); Martin (1965, pp. 94–108); and Ripley (1969, pp. 24–26).

The site of what became Chicago's O'Hare International Airport in the late 1940s. The runways and buildings had been part of a federal airplane factory that was turned over to the city after World War II. Credit: Courtesy of Landrum & Brown.

At the local level, disputes were common about whether to expand existing, close-in airfields that had been sited in the 1920s or to build new, much larger facilities on the urban fringe. Local business groups, led by downtown interests, almost invariably preferred the former course, but expansion was typically difficult because these older airports were now surrounded by residential and commercial development. Consequently, many cities began to examine larger, more distant sites. In Chicago, for example, controversy raged in the mid-1940s about whether to expand, replace, or supplement Midway Field—a 600-acre facility 10 miles southwest of downtown that was, at the time, the nation's busiest airport. Four potential sites for a new airport received serious consideration along with the option of expanding Midway. The Douglas Aircraft site, owned by the army, was the easiest to acquire and seemed adequate to meet projected needs for many years to come, but it was 17 miles from the central business district. Business community concerns were finally assuaged by city and state assurances that an expressway connecting this site with downtown would be constructed simultaneously with improvements to ready the airport for scheduled service. Chicago officials lobbied successfully to have the army turn 1,080 acres (70 percent of the total Douglas site) over to the city in 1946. Over the next several years the city acquired 5,300 adjacent acres from civilian owners at a total cost of about $7.6 million, but it still lacked funding to build the promised new expressway or bring the airport itself up to commercial use standards. So the airlines remained at Midway. For years the new airport—renamed in 1949 to honor the late Edward "Butch" O'Hare Jr., a World War II Congressional Medal of Honor recipient whose politically influential father had been one of Al Capone's business associates—languished, with little traffic, few capital improvements, and poor connections to downtown.[11]

New York City had built LaGuardia Airport, mainly with WPA funding, in the late 1930s.[12] At 550 acres, it was five to 10 times larger than most of the municipal airports developed in the 1920s, but it quickly became severely congested. During World War II the city developed plans for a second airfield, on 4,900 acres of filled marshland, to be known as Idlewild (later John F. Kennedy) Airport. The estimated cost of this project was in excess of $100 million, however, and it was unclear where this money would come from. Robert Moses, the city's longtime construction coordinator, concluded that the solution was to raise airline rental payments at LaGuardia, which were extremely low, and to use both these and future payments at Idlewild to finance revenue bonds. The airlines balked at paying more, however, and there things stood for a time.

Austin Tobin, executive director of the Port Authority of New York and New Jersey, now launched a quiet campaign to gain control of the region's airports, including the projected Idlewild. Tobin persuaded key business leaders that only an agency with control of all the region's major airports could prevent destructive competition of the sort that had characterized prewar airport battles between New York City and Newark, and that the Port Authority was a bastion of professional and managerial competence by comparison with the patronage-ridden governments of New York City and Newark. Further, he won the support of airline officials with his contention that the Port Authority's strong financial position would enable it to construct the new Idlewild Airport and also expand LaGuardia without raising fees or rents. Over intense opposition from Moses, in 1947 New York agreed to lease its airports to the Port Authority for 50 years. (Newark signed a similar deal a few months later.)

---

11. See Doherty (1970, chs. 2–4); and Czaplicki (1998).
12. The following account is based principally on Doig (2001, ch. 12); and Kaufman (1952, pp. 145–97).

It was long-standing Port Authority policy, however, that each project should be self-supporting, and the authority soon concluded that it would have to impose sharply increased landing fees and terminal lease payments at Idlewild to satisfy this criterion. The airlines were outraged, but after New York governor Thomas E. Dewey directly intervened, they reached agreement with the authority in 1949 on a revised schedule of payments. Robert Tuttle, a senior official at the time with American Airlines, later observed: "Settlement of the bitter Port Authority/Airlines dispute literally revolutionized airport development throughout the United States and many countries overseas. . . . It made possible and encouraged every major airport to become self-supporting . . . [and] it meant that financing [for] large new airports or [major improvements at] old ones was now readily available."[13]

Other cities concentrated on expanding and modernizing their existing airports. Los Angeles, for example, added over 2,000 acres to its original 640-acre airport site between 1946 and 1954, and in 1956 (after two defeats) secured voter approval for a program of major improvements, including a new runway and extensions of two others.[14] Still others wavered for a time between expansion and new airport options. In Dallas, notably, the question was whether to improve Love Field or join with Fort Worth to construct a new regional airport roughly midway between the two cities. The federal Civil Aeronautics Board strongly favored the latter option, and Fort Worth at times indicated that it might proceed even if Dallas refused to participate. At the urging of its chamber of commerce, Dallas in 1951 hired James Buckley, a former senior official of the New York Port Authority, to advise on the airport options. Buckley concluded that the city would do best to improve Love Field and urged a vigorous lobbying effort in Washington, D.C., to ensure that Love remained the Dallas–Fort Worth region's dominant airport. The city's business and political leaders took this advice to heart, and in 1953 the city council asked voters to approve a $10-million bond issue for Love Field improvements—including a new runway, extension of an existing runway, a new terminal building, and a new general aviation airport to relieve congestion at Love Field. The business community spent more than $50,000 in support of this measure, and Robert Thornton, a leading local banker, expressed its message well: "We must go forward or we will be like some of the towns that the railroads passed up."[15] The ballot proposition passed by a wide margin.

13. Doig (2001, pp. 311–12).
14. For a detailed account of the history of Los Angeles International Airport until the mid-1970s, see Friedman (1978).
15. Fairbanks (1992, p. 175). See also Fairbanks (1998); and Scott and Davis (1974).

Table 5-3. Enplaned Passengers and Scheduled Departures, 1926–2000

Year	Enplaned passengers (millions)	Change (percent)	Flights (millions)	Change (percent)	Passengers per flight	Change (percent)
1926	6	n.a.	n.a.	n.a.	n.a.	n.a.
1930	418	6,867	n.a.	n.a.	n.a.	n.a.
1935	790	89	n.a.	n.a.	n.a.	n.a.
1940	2,966	275	n.a.	n.a.	n.a.	n.a.
1945	7,052	138	n.a.	n.a.	n.a.	n.a.
1950	19,220	173	2,457	n.a.	n.a.	n.a.
1955	41,709	117	3,276	n.a.	12.7	n.a.
1960	62,258	49	3,853	18	16.2	27
1965	102,920	65	4,198	9	24.5	52
1970	169,922	65	5,120	22	33.2	35
1975	205,062	21	4,705	-8	43.6	31
1980	296,903	45	5,353	14	55.5	27
1985	380,024	28	5,835	9	65.1	17
1990	465,557	23	6,924	19	67.2	3
1995	547,384	18	8,062	16	67.9	1
2000	665,513	22	8,992	12	74.0	9

Sources: Civil Aeronautics Board, "Handbook of Airline Statistics, 1973" (1973, tables 46, 48); Office of Airline Data, "Historical Air Traffic Data: 1954–1980," Bureau of Transportation Statistics, November 2001 (www.bts.gov/oai/iindicators/airtraffic/annual/1954-1980.html [October 2002]); and Office of Airline Data, "Historical Air Traffic Data: 1981–2001," Bureau of Transportation Statistics, November 2001 (www.bts.gov/oai/indicators/airtraffice/annual/1981-2001.html [October 2002]).

n.a. Not available; data not collected.

Commercial air passenger trips rose by nearly 800 percent between 1945 and 1960 (see table 5-3), surpassing the number of intercity railroad passenger trips after 1955. In consequence, pressures intensified at nearly all major airports for runway, terminal, and access-road improvements on the one hand, and fee increases to help finance them on the other. In 1956, for example, Mayor Richard Daley persuaded the airlines serving Chicago to accept a package of fee increases to finance major improvements at O'Hare, to commit that they would move all their operations to O'Hare once the improvements were carried out, and—in a provision that became a staple of major airport financing nationally over the next several decades—to guarantee the airport improvement bonds.[16] (The new facilities opened in 1963.)

In 1956 as well, the nation's airlines announced that they planned to launch commercial jetliner service within about two years and to expand it rapidly thereafter. The new aircraft would require longer, stronger runways

16. See Doherty (1970, ch. 6, esp. pp. 193–97).

Table 5-4. Total Airport Spending and State/Local Share, 1956–99

Billions of 2002 dollars, except as noted

Year[a]	Total	State/local share (percent)	Capital	State/local share (percent)
1956	0.9	90	0.6	86
1960	1.7	83	1.2	77
1965	1.9	83	1.2	73
1970	3.7	91	2.6	88
1975	4.0	80	2.3	66
1980	4.8	76	2.7	58
1985	5.6	80	2.8	58
1990	8.2	81	4.4	64
1995	9.4	78	4.3	52
1999	13.3	88	6.5	77

Sources: Authors' calculations from Office of Management and Budget, "Budget of the United States Government, Fiscal Year 2003: Historical Tables" (2002, tables 9-6, 12-3); Congressional Budget Office, "Trends in Public Infrastructure Spending" (1999, tables 1, 2, 3, 4); Bureau of the Census, *Government Finances: 1998–1999* (2001, table 1), *Statistical Abstract of the United States: 2001* (2002, tables 426, 427), *Statistical Abstract of the United States: 2000* (2001, tables 495, 496), *Statistical Abstract of the United States: 1991* (1992, tables 451, 452), *Statistical Abstract of the United States: 1982* (1983, table 468), *Statistical Abstract of the United States: 1967* (1967, tables 578, 581); and authors' estimates for 1999 capital spending figures.

n.a. Not available.

a. Figures are for the fiscal year ending in the year shown.

and would carry significantly more passengers than existing planes, thereby increasing the strain on terminal and baggage systems. In response, real capital spending on airport improvements doubled between 1956 and 1960 (see table 5-4), and efforts to find new airport sites were intensified in numerous regions. In Houston, for example, after the business elite concluded that the city's existing airport would not suffice for the jet age, a few of its members moved privately to assemble a site north of the city that planners had identified as optimal. Their idea was to accomplish this quickly and then sell the site at cost to the city. City officials balked at first, suspicious that the investors—who insisted that their motivation was purely to serve the city—were seeking to profit from this transaction. Amid intense business lobbying, however, in 1959 the city did purchase the site and 5,000 adjacent acres as well, for what became Houston Intercontinental Airport (later renamed George Bush Intercontinental Airport/Houston).[17]

The prospect of the jet age also intensified demands for change at the federal level. The Eisenhower administration was supportive of proposals—pressed particularly by the airlines and aircraft manufacturers—to improve

17. For more on the Houston airport, see Pratt and Castaneda (1999, pp. 167–70).

the air traffic control system, but it viewed airport development as a local responsibility. As a result, federal airport aid averaged just $14 million a year during the mid-1950s (fiscal years 1953 through 1955). Dissatisfied, major airport operators and a group of big-city mayors launched a campaign for dramatic increases, which over the next several years brought about a near-quintupling of the program scale. This funding still accounted for a very small proportion of national airport investment, however, and it was not focused on improving nationally significant airports. Though both the Eisenhower and Kennedy administrations favored such targeting, Congress insisted on retaining historic formulas guaranteeing that most of the money would go to smaller airports—and the greatest possible number of congressional districts.[18]

Growth Becomes Controversial (1960–75)

The new jets were a great commercial success, and air travel almost tripled over the course of the 1960s (see table 5-3). The jets were much noisier than propeller aircraft, however, and had more shallow trajectories during landings and takeoffs. As a result of these factors in combination—more flights, noisier aircraft, flatter trajectories—the land area affected by aviation noise increased about sevenfold, exposing (by various estimates) 6 million to 15 million people to significant noise levels.[19] Airport neighbors won an important victory in 1962 when the Supreme Court ruled that the owners of airports were liable for noise-related damages to nearby areas, including reductions in property values.[20] Within a decade more than 70 airports faced noise-related lawsuits. In Los Angeles, for example, plaintiffs were claiming damages in excess of $2.8 billion, and the airport's general manager testified that noise, not congestion, was the airport's greatest problem.[21]

This was, moreover, a period of rising citizen activism, so it became far more difficult to expand existing airports even as commercial pressures intensified to do so. The Federal Aviation Administration (FAA), which oversaw airports and airways, and the Civil Aeronautics Board, which regulated airline operations, urged—even forced—state and local officials to

18. See Ripley (1969, pp. 20–71, esp. 24–26, 63–71); and Rochester (1976, pp. 89–90, 232–33).

19. The lower figure is from Federal Aviation Administration, "Aviation Noise Abatement Policy" (1976, p. 1). The higher figure is from U.S. Aviation Advisory Commission (1973, p. 36). For a good discussion of the issue, see Harrison (1983, pp. 43–143).

20. *Griggs* v. *Allegheny County,* 369 U.S. 84 (1962).

21. Testimony as cited by Rhoads (1974, p. 23).

Construction work at Chicago's O'Hare International Airport in 1961,two years before it replaced Midway as Chicago's primary airport. Credit: Courtesy of Landrum & Brown.

consider instead building new airports on outlying sites—as the federal government itself had done in the late 1950s, developing Dulles International Airport on 10,000 rural acres 30 miles from downtown Washington, D.C.[22] In 1962, for example, FAA administrator Nejeeb Halaby announced that the FAA would make no more grants to either Dallas or Fort Worth until they agreed to join in building a large new regional airport. Shortly thereafter the CAB launched an investigation of airport options for the region; two years later, following extensive and often acrimonious hearings, it ruled that the two cities should be served by a single facility—and that unless they agreed on a site within 180 days, the CAB would choose one for them.

22. See Rochester (1976, pp. 114–16, 165–66).

Dallas business leaders—concerned in any event that Houston and Kansas City, two regions they viewed as direct competitors, were currently building new airports—now relaxed their opposition. This cleared the way for an agreement between the two cities, cemented by state legislation authorizing a regional airport authority. Establishment of the authority required voter approval, however, and Dallas County voters rejected it in 1967. The cities got around this obstacle by directly establishing a bicity airport board, reporting to their city councils. The board in turn quickly selected a site of 18,000 acres for the new airport, mainly in rural jurisdictions about halfway between downtown Dallas and downtown Fort Worth. Development of this site required the displacement of about 730 people, but little opposition materialized, apparently because the cities provided generous compensation and because most other property owners in the vicinity believed the airport would greatly increase the value of their land.[23]

Most other efforts to site new airports failed, however, in the face of local resistance. In 1960, for example, the Port Authority of New York and New Jersey announced that it planned to build a fourth jetport for the New York region on 10,000 acres centered in the Great Swamp, a largely undeveloped wetland in Morris County, New Jersey, about 25 miles west of New York City. Regional business and labor leaders were strongly supportive. Affluent neighbors of the proposed site, however, allied with local conservation groups to oppose the project. They were quickly joined by the area's members of Congress and state legislators. A small group of wealthy residents, moreover, purchased portions of the swamp, which they promptly donated to the Department of Interior as a wildlife refuge. Though Port Authority officials continued to seek a fourth airport site through the 1960s, they were never able to make significant progress.[24]

In 1968, similarly, the Port Authority of Dade County, Florida, proposed a new airport for the Miami area on 25,000 acres just north of the Everglades National Park. The Greater Miami Chamber of Commerce and other local business groups quickly endorsed this project as critical to south Florida's future economic vitality. National as well as local environmental groups mobilized in opposition, however, arguing that the proposed facility, together with the development that it would inevitably stimulate nearby, would impose grievous harm on the Everglades. They found important

23. See Fairbanks (1992, pp. 179–82; 1998, pp. 236–37); Feldman and Milch (1982, pp. 55, 231); and Scott and Davis (1974, chs. 6, 7).
24. See Cavanaugh (1978); and Feldman and Milch (1982, pp. 164, 183–87, 194–99, 202, 265–68).

allies in the U.S. Department of the Interior, which was responsible for the Everglades, and among elected officials. Senator Henry Jackson (D-Wash.), most notably, held hearings to air charges that the project had been planned without any environmental analysis or consultation with national parks officials. President Nixon personally intervened, finally, in late 1969, directing senior officials of the Interior and Transportation Departments to reject the Port Authority's plan, while pledging federal aid for a second Miami jetport when a suitable site was determined. County officials subsequently proposed a 7,500-acre site northwest of Miami—but again failed to overcome environmental opposition.[25]

Efforts to develop new airports likewise failed in Los Angeles, Chicago, Minneapolis/St. Paul, and St. Louis during the late 1960s and early 1970s. In other areas, such as Boston, where aviation and local business leaders strongly favored construction of a new airport, elected officials, observing the instant mobilization against every site raised for consideration, shied away from even advancing a formal proposal.

Efforts to expand existing airports were generally more successful, but this too began to change in the late 1960s. Starting in 1967, for example, the city of Denver sought to expand Stapleton Airport into the Rocky Mountain Arsenal, a military facility of 18,000 acres. Potentially affected residents, however, supported by officials in adjacent jurisdictions—most notably Adams County, a largely rural area on the other side of the arsenal from Stapleton—mobilized vigorously in opposition. Their main concern was noise, but Adams County interests noted as well that virtually all the economic benefits of Stapleton expansion would accrue to Denver—since the arsenal would continue to block easy ground access between the airport and Adams County. In 1971, the city won a partial victory when the army agreed to relinquish 622 acres (roughly 10 percent of what the city had sought) for airport expansion. This enabled the city to build an additional north-south runway, but so close to an existing runway that only one could be used in bad weather (when, because of instrument landing rules, additional capacity was most needed).[26]

Meanwhile, the Port Authority of New York and New Jersey was seeking to build two new runways at Kennedy Airport, in part on land to be created with fill in Jamaica Bay. Buffeted by intense community and environmental criticism and with prodding from the U.S. secretaries of

25. See Gilmour and McCauley (1976).
26. See J. Miller (1983, pp. 107–11, 116–20); and City and County of Denver (1989, pp. 1.5–1.6).

Chicago's O'Hare International Airport in 1970. Its basic runway configuration has remained unchanged since that time because opposition by neighbors has derailed all proposals for new runways. Credit: Courtesy of Landrum & Brown.

transportation and the interior, the authority asked the National Academies of Science and Engineering to convene an expert study panel. This panel, chaired by MIT engineering professor James Fay, concluded in 1971 that the authority's plan would "cause major irreversible ecological damage to the Bay."[27] Noting further that 700,000 people were already exposed to significant noise from Kennedy, and that this number would increase under the authority's plan, it stated that "there can be no further excuse for continuing the present disastrous policy."[28] As an alternative to physical expansion, the panel urged a focus on economic, management, and technological measures to enhance capacity within the airport's existing physical

27. Jamaica Bay Environmental Study Group (1971, p. 1).
28. Jamaica Bay Environmental Study Group (1971, p. 21).

configuration—such as congestion pricing, pressure on the airlines to con-solidate schedules (thereby increasing the proportion of occupied seats on each flight), and air traffic control improvements. On the day after this report became public, the Port Authority abandoned its Kennedy expansion plan.[29]

The shifting sands of airport expansion politics were nowhere more evi-dent than in Boston. Its Logan Airport had been a city facility until 1948, when it was turned over to the state because the city lacked funds to make needed improvements. Direct state operation proved no solution, though. Finally, in 1956, at the urging of local business leaders, the state created the Massachusetts Port Authority, an independent agency empowered to fund improvements with revenue bonds—secured not only by airport earnings but also by surplus revenues from a toll bridge that the state legislature included in its portfolio. Though Logan was mostly surrounded by water, it also abutted a densely settled working-class neighborhood, East Boston, and several other such neighborhoods lay beneath its flight paths. As Mass-port moved to expand Logan, consequently, its plans generated loud protests. Business and labor interests were highly supportive, though, and the authority prevailed invariably through the 1960s.[30]

The balance shifted, however, in the early 1970s, when Massport sought to implement a host of additional expansion projects, including a new runway pointed directly at East Boston. Again the neighborhood mobilized in oppo-sition, while regional business and labor leaders were solidly behind Massport. Now Logan's neighbors were able to draw on the resources of two regionwide movements, however, for environmental protection and against new express-way construction. In 1970 Governor Francis W. Sargent, who had succeeded Volpe when the latter became U.S. secretary of transportation, appointed a committee of experts to examine the region's airport controversies, and in July 1971 he accepted its unanimous recommendation against the new runway. [31] (Like its Kennedy Airport counterpart, the committee urged alternative strate-gies not requiring airport expansion, including in this case efforts to secure federal funding for high-speed rail service to New York City.)[32] Sargent did not control Massport, whose board members served long, staggered terms, but his views—which were echoed by several of the state's other leading elected offi-cials, including Representative Thomas P. "Tip" O'Neill Jr. (then the House majority leader), whose district included East Boston—were certain to carry

29. Robert Lindsey, "Port Authority Drops Bay Plan," *New York Times*, February 18, 1971, p. 70.

30. Nelkin (1974, pp. 47–50, 63–87).

31. One of the present authors, Altshuler, served as a member of this committee.

32. See Governor's Task Force on Intercity Transportation (1971, pp. iv–xx).

great weight in Washington. And this mattered a great deal, even though Massport did not need federal money—because it did need a fill permit from the U.S. Army Corps of Engineers. Facing a likely rebuff from the Corps of Engineers, Massport withdrew its permit application.[33]

It continued to pursue numerous other expansion proposals, however, including runway extensions, a new short runway for commuter and general aviation aircraft, a new taxiway, new terminals and parking facilities, and new freight handling facilities. Sargent was receptive to the terminal and freight handling projects, but generally sided with the community and environmental critics of new runway and parking facilities. Further, in making his annual appointments to the Massport board, he chose candidates likely to support his new approach. In 1973, most notably, he appointed James Fay, who had chaired the National Academies' committee on Kennedy Airport expansion, to head the Massport board. Business, labor, and legislative leaders criticized the governor for injecting "politics" into the supposedly apolitical authority, but he stood firm. (Previous governors had routinely appointed business community nominees to six of the seven Massport board positions. By law, the seventh seat was reserved for a labor representative, and governors had normally appointed someone with strong construction or transportation industry ties.) Sargent finally gained a clear board majority in 1974. Longtime executive director Edward King, however, now openly defied the board on major issues, as a result of which it fired him immediately after the 1974 election—which, ironically, Sargent lost. But the new governor, Michael Dukakis, had been even more critical of Massport over the years than Sargent. Shortly after his inauguration the new board majority cancelled all of Massport's pending controversial projects.[34]

Many localities in this period also pressed their airport operators to limit flights and ban particularly noisy planes. Though the courts imposed significant constraints on the authority of local jurisdictions to dictate such regulations,[35] by the mid-1980s about 400 of the nation's airports had done so, leading to the FAA's chief counsel to complain that local concerns had overwhelmed national in the management of the nation's air transportation system.[36]

33. See Nelkin (1974, pp. 87–93).

34. One of these, the proposed commuter runway, gained new life as the Massport board majority shifted once again in the 1990s and remains mired in controversy.

35. The courts found that operators could impose restrictions only if they responded to a demonstrable problem, did not discriminate among classes of users, and did not constitute an undue burden on interstate or foreign commerce. See *City of Burbank* v. *Lockheed Air Terminal*, 411 U.S. 624 (1973); Harper (1988, pp. 117–66); and Bennett (1982, pp. 449–93).

36. See Ellett (1987); and Blackman and Freeman (1987).

Airport critics also urged increasingly that the federal government mandate quieter engines on new aircraft. FAA officials resisted this campaign through most of the 1960s, arguing that such requirements might compromise safety, but Congress acted nonetheless in 1968, directing the FAA to establish aircraft noise standards consistent with both safety and economic feasibility. The first such standards were promulgated in 1969. Technology to retrofit existing aircraft soon became available as well, but the FAA, responding to claims of financial incapacity by the airlines, allowed them to delay full implementation until the mid-1980s. When finally implemented, these measures more than halved the number of people exposed to what the FAA considered unacceptably high levels of noise. They did not, however, lead to any significant reduction in noise complaints or decrease opposition to airport expansion plans.[37]

In the mid- to late 1960s, finally, growing air congestion—highlighted by two catastrophic midair collisions—led representatives of the airlines, airport operators, and aircraft manufacturers, together with federal aviation officials and key congressional committee members, to revisit some longstanding controversies about how to fund airport and air traffic control improvements. Though Congress had imposed taxes on airline tickets since 1983 and on airline fuel since 1941, the revenue from these levies covered less than one-half of the federal government's expenditures for civilian air traffic control and airport improvements.[38] Federal budget officials maintained, consequently, that a precondition for any significant growth in spending should be aviation user tax increases.

The airlines bitterly opposed such increases for several years. At the very end of the 1960s, however, they relaxed their opposition in return for a commitment to earmark aviation user tax revenues exclusively for aviation system improvements.[39] Finally, in 1970, the Nixon administration, Congress, and key interest groups agreed on legislation authorizing $2.65 billion over five years for aviation, including $1.4 billion for airport improvement grants. The nation's 27 large hub airports, though, which served 64 percent of all trips, were—in a continuation of the historic pattern—to receive only 25 percent of this grant total, with the rest going to several thousand smaller

37. Federal Aviation Administration, "Performance Goal: Aircraft Noise Exposure" (www.api.faa.gov/STRATEGIC/docs/SUP-Sup-30-EnvGoal(1).html [October 2002]); and Shapiro (1992, pp. 1–61).

38. See Rhoads (1974, p. 34).

39. To this point aviation tax revenues had been deposited in the government's general fund account. Henceforth they would be deposited in a trust fund, like that for highways (since 1956).

airports spread across the congressional firmament.[40] Even as federal grants increased during the 1970s, moreover, states and localities cut back their own capital spending for airport improvements by roughly half—due in part to project controversies and in part to more general pressures for fiscal stringency. As a result of these trends in combination, capital spending for airport improvements, in real terms, declined in the first half of the decade before returning in 1980 to virtually the same level it had been a decade earlier (see table 5-4).

Coping with Congestion (1975–95)

Both passenger enplanements and real capital spending on airport improvements roughly doubled from 1975 to 1990 (see tables 5-3 and 5-4).[41] But efforts to construct new airports and even new runways at existing airports generally stalled. It was two decades after the completion of Dallas/Fort Worth International Airport in 1974 before another new jetport for scheduled passenger service opened in a major market. There was, as well, a dramatic slowdown in the construction of new runways and the expansion of old ones. The air transport system continued to function without significant congestion increases in these years, however, due to three factors: airline deregulation, the introduction of wide-body jets, and air traffic control improvements.

Deregulation

For 40 years beginning in 1938, airlines needed the permission of a federal regulatory board to serve any route or change any fare, and the central thrust of policy was to ensure industry prosperity by limiting competition. Federal regulators became far more open to competition during the mid-1970s, how-

40. The FAA, it will be recalled, defines large hub airports as those serving at least 1 percent of the national total of enplaned passengers. More generally, see Weiner (1975, pp. 200–11); and Rhoads (1974, pp. 17–61).

41. Some of the spending, it should be noted, was for noise mitigation. Federal legislation enacted in 1979 authorized the use of federal airport aid to develop and carry out noise mitigation plans—including purchases of existing structures for demolition or relocation and soundproofing. By the late 1990s more than 200 airports had allocated about $4.8 billion for these purposes, including $2.8 billion in federal aid (12 percent of all federal airport assistance during the 1980s and 1990s). Through at least the 1980s, however, these efforts were not accompanied by any reduction in noise complaints, and they contributed less to reducing noise, in any event, than the phasing out of older jets. See General Accounting Office, "Aviation and the Environment: Transition to Quieter Aircraft Occurred as Planned but Concerns about Noise Persist" (2001); Falzone (1999, pp. 796–800); Creswell (1990); Schoen (1986, pp. 310–27); and Shapiro (1992, pp. 1–61).

ever, and statutory deregulation followed in 1978. Now airlines were free to enter any markets and to charge whatever fares they wished.[42] Of the many consequences, three profoundly affected the nation's major airports.

—First, airlines (including new entrants to the industry) rushed into the most heavily traveled markets, in many cases offering new options such as superlow, no-frill fares. Constrained by gate availability at dominant airports in the largest urban areas, moreover, some began to offer service from secondary airports such as Midway in Chicago and Love Field in Dallas.

—Second, the major carriers adopted hub-and-spoke route structures, in part to build up their load factors (the proportion of seats filled on each flight), but increasingly as well to create market niches radiating out from "fortress hubs." In the latter, by providing far more frequent service and a much wider array of connections than any competitor, and often as well by controlling most available terminal capacity, they could greatly reduce their vulnerability to price competition. Four airports, each dominated by one or two carriers, eventually emerged as the nation's most significant hubs—Atlanta's Hartsfield, Chicago's O'Hare, Denver's Stapleton, and Dallas/Fort Worth—while several others, such as St. Louis, Minneapolis/St. Paul, Pittsburgh, and Charlotte, developed as important "secondary" hubs.[43]

—Third, the airlines developed and gradually refined the practice of "yield-management" pricing, offering a bewildering array of prices on each flight, and often adjusting them by the minute, to ensure by takeoff that all or nearly all available seats were filled. The result was in part to enhance airport passenger capacity directly (by increasing the number of occupied seats on each flight), but it was also to accelerate market growth by making very low fares available to the most price-sensitive consumers.

Deregulation also proved to be a boon for regional carriers, offering short- and medium-range service (250 to 750 miles) on smaller planes. Initially these carriers—most of which eventually became subsidiaries of major airlines—used propeller or turboprop aircraft with 30 or fewer seats. By the 1990s, however, they were rapidly shifting to jet aircraft with 50 to 100 seats, able to compete with the major carriers in serving moderate density

42. On the politics of deregulation, see Derthick and Quirk (1985, esp. pp. 147–74); Baily, Graham, and Kaplan (1985, ch. 2); Brown (1987); Behrman (1980); and Altshuler and Teal (1979).

43. See Pickrell (1984, pp. 168–73). The standard definition of a hub is that more than half its passengers are merely connecting. Thus some airports with very large numbers of connecting passengers—such as Los Angeles, Phoenix, San Francisco, and Miami—are not usually counted as hubs. See "Analysis of Local and Connecting Traffic and Top 50 U.S. Airports," *Aviation Daily*, April 3, 2001, p. 10.

routes. The combination of deregulation, new aircraft, and close affiliation with the major carriers (which could economize by ceding routes to these lower-cost subsidiaries) enabled the regional carriers to more than triple their share of the national air travel market, from 4 to 13 percent, between 1978 and 2000.[44]

Wide-Body Jets

Improvements in jet engine technology made it possible to build wide-body aircraft with many more seats than their predecessors, far less expensive per seat mile to operate, and able to land on runways of no greater length. These new jets required different terminal configurations from their predecessors, however, even as continued rapid passenger growth and rising amenity expectations were also giving urgency to terminal expansion efforts. Terminal improvements did not have direct noise impacts and rarely involved new land takings, so they typically generated little opposition. As a result, the share of airport investment accounted for by terminal improvements rose dramatically. Before 1965 airport capital expenditures generally were divided about 75 percent for runways and taxiways versus 25 percent for terminals and related facilities. By the early 1970s, however, with runway projects stalled and terminal demand growing, these ratios were entirely reversed, with three quarters of investment going toward new and improved terminals; and this ratio persisted thereafter.[45]

Air Traffic Control (ATC)

During the late 1960s and through the 1970s the FAA established regional facilities to provide unified air traffic control in each of the nation's major urban areas, completed an upgrade of its computer system, and invested heavily in runway instrumentation at major airports. In part these organizational and electronic improvements were able to substitute for the paucity of investment in new airports and runways—but not entirely. The agency reported in 1981 that eight of the nation's major airports were already handling traffic in excess of their effective capacity and that 16

---

44. Data on market share from Stanford Transportation Group, "Regional Aviation: A Vital Past, a Challenging Future" (paper prepared for the 26th Annual Federal Aviation Administration Forecast Conference, Washington, March 16–17, 2001 (http://api.hq.faa.gov/conference/conference2001/proc2001/bernstein.pdf [October 2002]); Federal Aviation Administration, "Twenty Years of Deregulation, 1978–1998" (1999, pp. 2, 5); General Accounting Office, "Regional Jet Service Yet to Reach Many Small Communities" (2001, p. 9); and Davies and Quastler (1995, pp. 115–78).

45. De Neufville (1976, p. 97).

more would probably be over capacity by 1990.[46] The ATC system itself lost capacity in 1981, moreover, when the Reagan administration fired striking air traffic controllers; for years afterward the system was not fully staffed. The administration's proposed solution was a massive upgrade of the FAA's computer system, which it estimated would enable it to handle future demand without adding significant numbers of controllers.

Congress approved this upgrade in 1982, quintupling the level of spending for air traffic control improvements, from $250 million to $1.2 billion a year. The most ambitious elements of the FAA's improvement program were plagued from the start, however, by management and procurement problems, and they are still in development at this writing two decades later.[47] But the agency did identify and implement numerous incremental ATC improvements—working with the airlines, for example, to sequence traffic more effectively and to improve ground taxiway procedures. At Dallas/Fort Worth, illustratively, such process adjustments made possible a 40 percent increase in hourly arrival rates.[48] It also became clear over time that the methods used to gauge effective airport capacity from the 1960s into the 1980s had yielded estimates that were far too low. In 1972, for example, FAA and Massport officials estimated that Boston's Logan Airport would ultimately be able to accommodate 313,000 flights a year. Two decades later, in 1992, the airport accommodated 486,000 operations, and the FAA now estimated that its capacity was roughly 500,000 operations a year.[49]

Within this broad frame—of rapid traffic growth, deregulation, changing aircraft configurations, and incremental air traffic control improvements—local strategies and circumstances of course varied widely. To convey some sense of this diversity, we now turn to developments in four major air travel markets: Atlanta, Chicago, Boston, and Denver.

---

46. Office of Technology Assessment, "Airport System Development" (1984, p. 10). Those deemed over capacity already were the dominant airports in Chicago, Denver, Detroit, Los Angeles, Philadelphia, San Francisco, St. Louis, and Washington, D.C.

47. See Transportation Research Board and National Research Council (1991b, pp. 221–25); Office of Technology Assessment, "Airport System Development" (1984, pp. 60–79); Congressional Budget Office, "Improving the Air Traffic Control System" (1983); and Federal Aviation Administration, "National Airspace System Plan" (1983). On delays in putting the system in place, see Office of Inspector General, Department of Transportation, "Top Ten Management Issues" (2001, pp. 34–44); and General Accounting Office, "Annual Report on New Starts Proposed Allocation of Funds for Fiscal Year 2002" (2001, pp. 25–30).

48. See Federal Aviation Administration, "Aviation Capacity Enhancement Plan 1998" (1999, pp. 32, 64).

49. See Dawson, Dean, and Meyer (1995, pp. 13–16).

Atlanta and Chicago Debate New Airports, Expand Their Old Ones

Through the 1980s and early 1990s airport operators nationwide cited Atlanta, which opened a massive new terminal complex in 1980 and a new runway four years later, as perhaps the prime model for regions wishing to compete successfully in the modern economy. Atlanta was in fact one of the nation's fastest growing regions, and its airport expansion was extraordinary for the time. Even its business and political leaders, however, had been unable to develop the second regional airport that many of them deemed essential.

Atlanta's location made it a natural transfer point for travelers between the Southeast and other parts of the country, and it had long sought to maximize this role. Its airport (named for former mayor William Hartsfield) was the first anywhere to gain a traffic windfall from hub-and-spoke service, moreover, which both Delta and Eastern Airlines pioneered from Atlanta in the 1950s.[50] Though the city, which owned and operated the airport, had opened a new terminal in 1961 and another runway in 1964, its top officials and local business leaders soon concluded that more terminal and runway capacity would be required.[51] They viewed airport expansion as part of a broad strategy, relying significantly on public investment, to position Atlanta as the convention and corporate office center of the Southeast. At the time they were also promoting construction of a new rail transit system, a new convention center, and new professional sports facilities.[52]

In the mid-1960s consultants hired by the city and the regional planning agency developed plans to enlarge the existing airport by acquiring about 1,200 acres of adjacent land (which held 900 homes), constructing a new terminal complex, and adding two new runways. In 1967 the airlines agreed to fee increases adequate to fund the third runway and begin preparing the new terminal site, while reserving judgment on the fees proposed to fund the fourth runway and the terminal building. Two years later, concerned that cost estimates for the new terminal were coming in much higher than anticipated, the airlines opposed its construction. They suggested, instead, that the city

---

50. There is some dispute as to whether Delta or Eastern was the first to develop a hub-and-spoke system in Atlanta. See Braden and Hagan (1989, pp. 125–26).

51. Most of the actual planning was done under the auspices of the Atlanta Regional Metropolitan Planning Commission, a public entity, which was very close to the city's business community, particularly the Greater Atlanta Chamber of Commerce. (As discussed in chapter 6, the commission, with the strong support of the city's business leaders, also played a major role in developing the initial plans for Atlanta's rail-transit system.)

52. Many of these projects are discussed elsewhere in this book. For an overview, see Stone (1989, pp. 32–46, 55–64); and Allen (1996, pp. 152–55, 161–72).

modestly improve the existing terminal and build the planned third runway but focus over the longer term on developing a second regional airport.

After some debate, city officials concurred and hired a consultant to identify potential sites. The consultant came up with four—three to the north and west of the city, where most growth was occurring, and one in a low-income rural area to the south. An advisory committee appointed to review these options eventually settled on the last, arguing that it would be cheaper, easier to build on, and less politically controversial than any of the northern sites—the mention of which had already stimulated intense local opposition. The airlines protested, however, that this site was too distant and in the opposite direction from growth in the air travel market.

Faced with this impasse, local officials kept an eye out for additional sites. An opportunity arose in 1972; the city purchased 10,000 acres about 50 miles north of downtown from the Lockheed Corporation. Meanwhile, a consortium led by developer Tom Cousins was assembling a site of 30,000 acres 15 miles closer in, with the idea of selling some to the city for an airport and developing the rest. Cousins and his allies mounted a skillful campaign, and by late 1973 both Delta Airlines, the dominant carrier at Hartsfield, and the city's chamber of commerce had joined them in championing this site. But it too soon faced serious obstacles. Although it was very large and lightly developed, its few residents quickly mobilized in opposition. There was also dissent within the Atlanta business community, most visibly from architect-developer John Portman, who argued that any airport so far from the city would accelerate sprawl and further weaken downtown.

A further complication was that relationships between the city government of Atlanta and its business leadership were in flux. Traditionally, mayors had been drawn from the business community or at least elected with its strong support, and they had worked together harmoniously. The city now had a black majority electorate, however, which in 1973 had elected its first black mayor, Maynard Jackson. With few ties to the business community, Jackson arrived in office committed to shifting the balance between neighborhood and downtown and between black and white interests in the city. While prepared to support the business community's development agenda, he was determined to ensure that benefits accrued to the city's minority residents to the greatest degree possible. Observing that the main direction of white residential and business migration was northward while that of the city's black population was to the south, Jackson began touting the southern site that the advisory committee had previously recommended. It was a battle he could not win, however. The airlines and

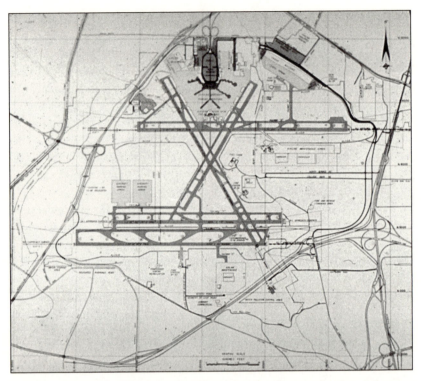

Atlanta's Hartsfield International Airport in the late 1960s. Judging that the city could not easily expand runway or terminal capacity on the Hartsfield site, local officials and business leaders sought to acquire a much larger site for a new airport. Credit: Courtesy of the City of Atlanta/Department of Aviation.

the city's business leadership were dead set against any southern site, and local opposition to the specific site was growing as well. Within a few months of his inauguration, therefore, Jackson accepted the viewpoint of the business community and airlines. The city purchased two-thirds of the Cousins site (20,000 acres) in 1974.[53]

Concerned, however, that construction of a new airport would be long delayed, the airlines now supported the city's earlier plan for a large new terminal at Hartsfield in addition to the new development. Regional business leaders were enthusiastic, and Mayor Jackson was as well, not least because Hartsfield was located on the city's south side. But Jackson insisted that one-fourth of all contracts be set aside for minority-owned firms. The airlines and the city's business community adamantly opposed this proviso, and at their instigation the governor and key state legislative leaders resurrected some long-standing proposals for a state takeover of the airport. The stand-

53. See Reed (1987, pp. 208–09).

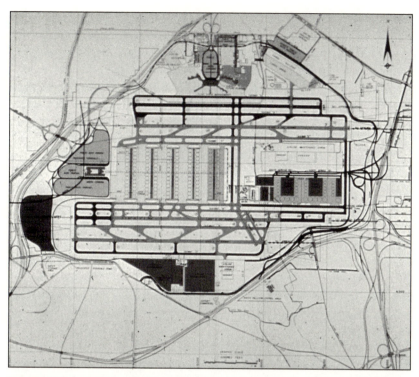

During the 1970s, local officials concluded that siting a new airport would be even more difficult than expanding Hartsfield. The expansion plan's most prominent features were a new midfield terminal and a new runway built on the site of the old terminal. Credit: Courtesy of the City of Atlanta/Department of Aviation.

off was finally resolved in 1976. Jackson agreed to scale back his affirmative action demand from a minimum of 25 percent participation by locally owned minority firms to a more loosely defined "goal" of 20 to 25 percent. In addition, he agreed to appoint the business community's designee to oversee the airport project and to fire an African-American city official who had aroused business enmity with her aggressiveness on behalf of affirmative action. Local business leaders in turn agreed to oppose any effort to remove the airport from city control and to support Jackson's 1977 bid for reelection (which proved successful by a large margin).[54]

By this time Atlanta, the nation's nineteenth largest metropolitan area, was home to its second busiest airport, after Chicago's O'Hare. Accordingly, the final plan for Hartsfield modernization, completed in 1977, called for construction of the largest terminal complex in the world—to consist of a

54. See Reed (1987, p. 211); Braden and Hagan (1989, pp. 181–82); and Stone (1989, pp. 87–88).

main building for landside access, ticketing, baggage handling, and retail commerce, five concourses with 138 gates, and an automated people mover to whisk travelers among these component parts. This was the world's first terminal complex designed explicitly for hub-and-spoke operations, reflecting the fact that about 70 percent of enplaned travelers at Hartsfield were merely changing planes. Actual construction proceeded with little controversy, and the new terminal opened in September 1980—at a total project cost of about $750 million.[55]

The fourth runway, which was built in part on the site of the old terminal, was stalled for several years by local controversy and litigation but finally opened in 1984. In order to secure its environmental approvals, the city committed to an extensive noise mitigation program with three key components: the acquisition of about 2,500 homes (including the entire village of Mountain View), the soundproofing of another 10,000, and easement purchases to preclude new development. Taken together, these efforts ultimately cost more than $355 million.[56] The city, meanwhile, retained ownership of both the Cousins and Lockheed parcels, but as of this writing there are no active plans to develop either site as a second regional airport.

In contrast to Atlanta, Chicago's magnetism as an aviation hub reflects both its scale and mid-country location. From the early 1930s to 1998 (when it was superseded by Atlanta), its major airport—first Midway, then O'Hare—was the world's busiest. Within several years of its opening in 1963, however, and despite adding a sixth runway in 1968, O'Hare was severely congested. Early in 1969 the FAA stepped in, capping the total number of operations during peak hours and establishing a system to allocate the available slots. At the same time it imposed similar arrangements at Kennedy, LaGuardia, Newark, and Washington National Airports. Committees of airline representatives allocated the commercial slots—roughly 80 percent of the total—while the remainder were kept available for private aircraft on a first-come, first-served basis (with 48 hours' notice).[57] Though announced as temporary, and in fact terminated at Newark less than a year later, this system remained in operation at all of the other affected airports until July 2002—when pursuant to a statutory directive (enacted in 2000), it was eliminated at O'Hare.[58]

55. Of this $750 million total, about two-thirds was for the terminal complex itself. The other one-third was for access roads and a new control tower.

56. B. Hollaway (Office of Noise Mitigation, Atlanta Hartsfield International Airport), telephone interview by authors, November 15, 2001. Also see Cidell and Adams (2001, pp. 41–45).

57. See *Federal Register*, February 26, 1969, pp. 2602–03.

58. See Mietus (2001, pp. 231–33).

In the mid-1970s Chicago's airport planning consultant, Landrum and Brown, concluded that to accommodate projected growth over the next 20 years O'Hare would require two additional runways. The construction of these runways, it estimated, would require the acquisition of 500 homes in nearby communities, while their usage would expose tens of thousands of others to increased noise. The consultants also recommended a host of other projects, including modernization and expansion of the airport's terminals, new parking facilities, and ground access improvements. These proposals all required state approval, however, and the airport's neighboring communities were primed for battle. As a result, in 1981 Chicago mayor Jane Byrne announced that she would pursue only a "constrained" version of this plan, with no new runways but a price tag of $1.3 billion nonetheless—the most expensive project in the city's history.[59] Key elements included two runway extensions (of about 500 and 1,500 feet), one new terminal and the expansion of three others, a people mover system for circulation within the airport, and an array of highway, parking, and transit investments.[60]

O'Hare's neighbors immediately revived a long-stalled lawsuit over existing noise impacts, which resulted in a 1982 consent decree. The city committed in this decree to prepare a comprehensive plan for airport development, subject to approval by the FAA, to formalize participation by its surrounding communities in the planning effort and to proceed with major airport improvements (even if funded without federal aid) only after compliance with all procedures specified in the National Environmental Policy Act. Despite considerable controversy and additional litigation, the O'Hare expansion plan moved forward thereafter, but even as it did evidence accumulated that it would not prove adequate.

In 1987, consequently, the state of Illinois convened a committee of officials from the FAA, three states (the others were Indiana and Wisconsin), the city of Chicago, the Chicago regional planning agency, and the airlines to consider the possibility of a third regional airport.[61] A majority of this panel concluded that a new facility was needed and that its consultants should begin examining potential sites. The city, its business leadership, and the airlines strongly dissented, however. As the debate heated up, for example,

59. See "O'Hare Airport Expansion Takes Off: Chicago's $1.4 Billion Public Works Program Is Largest Ever," *Engineering News-Record*, May 10, 1984, p. 26; and Pat Wingert, "Suburbs Lose Appeal in Suit to Block O'Hare Expansion," *Chicago Tribune*, March 14, 1986, p. 1.

60. See. *Suburban O'Hare Commission* v. *Dole*, 787 F.2d 186 (7th Cir. 1986).

61. Specifically, the committee included representatives of the state departments of transportation in Illinois, Indiana, Wisconsin, and Chicago, the Chicago Area Transportation Study Council of Mayors, the FAA, and the Air Transport Association.

George Tidmarsh of the Chicago Association of Commerce and Industry warned that the panel was making a "monumental mistake" because the demand forecasts used to justify a third airport were unrealistic and the funding plan assumed an unusually large amount of federal assistance.[62] In a similar vein, Russell Mack, vice president of United Airlines, warned, "We can't afford duplicate facilities. We'll either stay at O'Hare or move to the third airport."[63]

With gubernatorial support the panel proceeded nonetheless, announcing in 1989 that it was focusing on four possibilities, all outside of Chicago, 35 to 55 miles from downtown; cost estimates for the new airport ranged from $2 to $6 billion.[64] When Richard M. Daley became mayor of Chicago in April 1989, he altered the debate in three ways. First, he reopened the issue of adding runways at O'Hare. Second, he proposed that the third airport study consider a new alternative: construction by the city itself (enabling it to retain control of all three regional airports) on a 9,400-acre site in southeast Chicago. This site, in an area known as Lake Calumet, included a mix of derelict industrial property, low-income residential neighborhoods, and wetlands. City officials estimated that a new airport there would cost $4.9 billion and require the displacement of about 8,500 homes (more than 20,000 people). Third, Daley threw his support behind a proposal recently advanced by U.S. transportation secretary Samuel Skinner, an Illinois native for whom national airport capacity expansion was a top priority. Skinner, who had assumed office in 1989, favored authorizing local airport operators to impose head taxes on passengers as a source of revenue for airport capital improvements.

It was the head tax idea that played out first. Skinner favored it as a source of significant new funding for the nation's most congested airports that did not involve direct federal imposition of a tax increase. (The highest visibility campaign promise that his president, George H. W. Bush, had made in 1988 was "no new taxes.") For Daley the attraction was that a $3 tax on each inbound and outbound passenger would, in Chicago, generate about $100 million a year. His support for Skinner's proposal, moreover, increased the chances that the secretary would support his positions in the

62. See George Tidmarsh, "Should We Push Ahead with the 3rd Airport?" *Chicago Sun-Times*, October 29, 1988, p. 14.

63. Elizabeth Whitney, "Plans Get off the Ground for a New Chicago Airport," *St. Petersburg Times*, July 30, 1989, p. A1.

64. See Fran Spielman, "Panel Says Go on 3rd Airport," *Chicago Sun-Times*, August 13, 1988; Jennifer Wolff, "Third Airport Flying High Down South," *Crain's Chicago Business*, February 13, 1989, p. T1; "Airport Fight Seen as Rural v Urban," *Pantagraph*, December 2, 1991, p. A4.

Chicago airport wars. But there was a major hurdle to be overcome. Congress had banned head taxes in 1973 at the explicit behest of the airlines, which viewed them as a way for localities to siphon revenue from aviation to support other governmental functions.[65] Most of the airlines were still resistant, even if the revenues were now to be earmarked for airport investment, arguing that such taxes would drive up the effective cost of air travel and encourage unneeded projects. Some were more open than formerly, however, provided the tax levels were firmly capped and the revenues directed to airport capital improvements. And the major airport operators were highly enthusiastic.

Daley quickly persuaded Chicago's congressional delegation, led by Daniel Rostenkowski, chair of the House Ways and Means Committee, to support Skinner's proposal. After extensive bargaining—and some pointed reminders, apparently, that Secretary Skinner had power of approval over lucrative overseas route assignments and airline mergers—the fees were incorporated into a package that included substantially higher federal airport spending, a requirement for airlines to phase out their noisiest planes by 2000, and tighter restrictions on the authority of airport operators to pursue noise reduction by regulating airplane operations.[66] In order to obtain the support of members of Congress whose districts did not include major airports, the new act skewed federal aid allocation even further toward small ones. And for each dollar of head tax—now relabeled passenger facility charge (PFC)—revenue that a major airport collected, it would have to forfeit 50 cents of its formula federal aid entitlement.[67] Within several years, nonetheless, virtually every one of the 71 airports classified by the FAA as a large or medium hub imposed the maximum permissible PFC ($3 for each arriving and departing passenger) and by 2000 PFC revenues nationwide exceeded $2 billion a year.[68]

In the immediate aftermath of this legislative struggle, Skinner assisted Daley in ensuring that the committee examining potential sites for a third Chicago airport consider the Lake Calumet site. The committee concluded in the site's favor, even after finding that an airport there would cost at least $10.8 billion, more than twice Daley's original estimate. The airlines

65. Congress passed the ban after the U.S. Supreme Court ruled that under current laws such taxes were legal. See *Evansville-Vanderbergh Airport Authority District v. Delta Airlines Inc.*, 405 U.S. 707 (1972); and Kent (1980, pp. 257–58).

66. See Mike Mills, "House OKs Passenger Fees to Boost Airport Funding," *Congressional Quarterly Weekly Report*, August 4, 1990, pp. 2510–11.

67. See Falzone (1999); Jenkins (1994); and Basil Talbott, "How the Airport Tax Took Off," *Chicago Sun-Times*, January 27, 1991, p. 17.

68. Federal Aviation Administration (FAA), "Key Passenger Facility Charge Statistics" (www.faa.gov/arp/pfc/reports/stats/htm [March 2002]).

adopted a stance of neutrality, concerned about the price tag but attracted by the site's relatively close-in location. They insisted, however, that the long-term possibility of a third airport should not stand in the way of O'Hare improvements. O'Hare's neighbors, not surprisingly, argued the reverse.

In 1992, Daley, Illinois governor James Edgar, and Indiana governor Evan Bayh reached agreement that all three Chicago-area airports—O'Hare, Midway, and the projected third airport at Lake Calumet—would be governed by a new nine-member authority. Initially the mayor would appoint five members, the governors two each. Once the airport plan received all needed approvals, however, the board structure would shift to one of equality, with the mayor and the two governors each appointing three members. This agreement, of course, did not end the controversy, particularly as it required approval by the Illinois and Indiana state legislatures. Most Lake Calumet–area residents and their representatives opposed it, as did the long-time critics of O'Hare expansion, who observed that it ignored their concerns entirely. Additionally, some Chicago-area business groups and airline representatives judged that the new commission structure would confer too much power on suburban interests, which were likely to seek restrictions on O'Hare operations and growth.[69] In the end, despite intensive lobbying by Edgar and Daley, the agreement failed in the Illinois state senate—mainly because the leader of the Republican minority, James Philip, represented several communities close to O'Hare. In the face of his opposition, not a single Republican supported the bill. And despite Daley's best efforts, a few Democrats opposed it as well.

A few days later, Daley announced that he would no longer pursue the Lake Calumet plan. At the time many viewed this as a ploy to bring additional pressure on Governor Edgar and state senate Republicans. The measure never reemerged, however, in part because Republicans gained control of the state senate in 1992 and Senator Philip became the majority leader. After this election Governor Edgar announced that he now supported one of the greenfield sites previously considered, in Peotone, about 35 miles south of downtown Chicago. His successor, George Ryan (1999–2003), pursued the Peotone idea with even greater enthusiasm. City officials feared, however, that a new airport in Peotone would adversely affect O'Hare and become a magnet for far-suburban development. The air-

69. See Michael Gillis, "Area Merchants Say Airport Authority Rules Favor Edgar," *Chicago Sun-Times*, June 23, 1992, p. 4; and Michael Gillis, "3rd Airport Bill Faces Tougher Go in Senate," *Chicago Sun-Times*, June 28, 1992, p. 4.

lines were opposed on fiscal grounds and would not commit to using Peotone. And residents of the Peotone area were sharply divided, with many dreading the transformation that a new jetport would bring to their semi-rural area.[70]

Daley and the airlines resisted the Peotone plan in Washington, D.C., as well as locally, aided from the beginning of 1993 by Daley's brother, William, who was one of President Clinton's most valued political operatives (and, in Clinton's second term, secretary of commerce). The Clinton administration in 1997 removed Peotone from the list of projects eligible for federal airport planning funds. Meanwhile, though Daley continued to support new runways at O'Hare, he did not advance formal proposals to build them, knowing that they would face gubernatorial vetoes. Through the 1990s, in short, Mayor Byrne's guidelines of 1981 held—permitting terminal, taxiway, and parking improvements within the existing airport boundary and some ground access improvements extending beyond it, but neither new runways nor a new airport.

Boston Considers Congestion Pricing

In the early 1970s both the National Academy's panel on Kennedy Airport expansion and Massachusetts governor Sargent's committee on intercity transportation had urged consideration of pricing strategies to limit peak period demand for available runway capacity.[71] If pricing reflected the value of runway time, virtually all economists believed, the scheduled airlines and their passengers would greatly benefit from reduced congestion—at the expense, to be sure, of some general aviation users, but these would mainly be diverted to other time slots or secondary airports. It also seemed reasonable to anticipate that, in a congestion pricing regime, commuter airlines would channel some of their growing demand into larger aircraft rather than ever more frequent flights. With the scheduled airlines also continuing to increase average aircraft size, existing runway capacity might suffice for decades to come.

The only test of this idea, and a very crude one at that, had briefly occurred in 1968, when the Port Authority of New York and New Jersey,

---

70. See Andrew Buchanen, "Opponents Rally against Proposed Third Airport," *Associated Press Newswire*, May 12, 2001; and Tamara Kerrill, "Rural Runway Rumor Persists, Many Ready to Fight to Save a Way of Life," *Chicago Sun-Times*, August 29, 1994, p. 6.

71. Jamaica Bay Environmental Study Group (1971, vol. 1, pp. 12–13, vol. 2, pp. 22–25); and Governor's Task Force on Intercity Transportation (1971, pp. 48–50).

which operated LaGuardia, Kennedy, and Newark Airports, sought to divert small planes by increasing the minimum landing fee during peak periods (8–10 a.m. and 3–8 p.m.). After the fee was imposed, general aviation operations had declined by one-third overall and much more sharply during the time periods in which the new fee was in effect. This brief experiment had ended, though, when the FAA imposed slot controls early in 1969.

Though general aviation interests had failed in a lawsuit to overturn the Port Authority's 1968 fee structure, the 1973 act banning head taxes had added a new complication. It specified merely that landing fees had to be reasonable and nondiscriminatory, but the FAA and the courts interpreted this to mean that (1) airports could only seek fee revenue sufficient to recover their historic capital and current operating costs; and (2) the allocation among users had to be based on a nondiscriminatory principle such as aircraft weight.[72] The resulting fees were invariably too low to have much effect on airline or private pilot choices. The law could in principle have been amended, of course, but general aviation interests were fiercely opposed to congestion pricing and there was no significant constituency for it. The scheduled airlines were at best ambivalent—in part because they too benefited from fee structures far below what investor-owned airports would have levied, but also because they were reluctant to engage in battles with general aviation interests—in particular, many members of Congress and corporate executives who were important allies on many other issues.[73]

Nonetheless, in 1988, the Massachusetts Port Authority, which had long been unable to expand Logan Airport physically or to build new runways, adopted a new fee structure intended to reduce general aviation traffic. Massport, like every other major airport operator, had traditionally based its fees entirely on aircraft weight. The new fee structure—designed to yield the same amount of revenue overall—included both a fixed fee (about $100 for each landing or takeoff) and a weight-based charge. The typical landing fee for a very small plane would rise from $25 to slightly more than $100, while that for a jumbo jet would decline from over $800 to about $450.[74]

Commuter airline and general aviation interests quickly persuaded U.S. transportation secretary James Burnley to order an official inquiry—and brought suit as well. In June 1988, however, a federal district court judge authorized Massport to proceed. As its officials had predicted, the new fees

72. For a discussion of these legal issues, see Creager (1983, pp. 322–26); and Hardaway (1991, pp. 67–72).

73. See Hahn and Kroszner (1989).

74. *New England Legal Foundation* v. *Massachusetts Port Authority*, 883 F.2d 157, 159 (1st Cir. 1989).

had a dramatic impact on operations and delays. During the first three months they were in effect (July–September 1988), general aviation traffic declined by 34 percent and the number of small commuter aircraft operations declined by 6.5 percent (though the commuter airline passenger count actually rose). The overall percentage of Logan flights delayed fell from 31 percent a year earlier to 14 percent.[75] In November, however, a DOT administrative law judge concluded that Massport's fees failed the "fair allocation" test, and this decision was subsequently upheld both by the secretary's office and a federal appeals court.[76]

This could have been just an interim setback. Secretary of Transportation Samuel Skinner let it be known informally that he would be open to a revised pricing scheme, designed in accord with standard utility pricing practices—which routinely include peak pricing. Massport, encouraged, contracted with a leading consultant to develop such a proposal. Just as the study was completed, however, the state administration changed. Governor Michael Dukakis, who had been highly supportive of Massport's pricing initiative, was succeeded by Governor William Weld, a Republican, at the beginning of 1991. Though firmly committed to market solutions in principle, Weld made it clear that he did not believe pricing was appropriate in this case. His Republican successors, to this writing in 2002, have maintained this view as well.[77] Critics note that while Massachusetts is a heavily Democratic state, those of its citizens who vote on Cape Cod and many others who vacation there tend to be disproportionately Republican, frequent patrons of commuter airlines, and general aviation fliers.[78]

Denver Builds a New Airport

Denver's regional planning agency and its consultant, Peat Marwick Mitchell and Company, arrived at two central conclusions in the late 1970s.

75. Jerry Ackerman, "Logan Landing Fees Biased, Judge Says," *Boston Globe*, November 11, 1988, p. 29.

76. *New England Legal Foundation* v. *Massachusetts Port Authority*; and Transportation Research Board and National Research Council (1991b, pp. 225–31).

77. A recent ruling by the state secretary of environmental affairs, however, approving a proposed new Logan runway, calls on the airport to impose some form of congestion pricing as well. See Massachusetts State Secretary, Environmental Affairs (2001, pp. 3, 6–8). The governor supported the runway but did not comment on the secretary's pricing recommendation.

78. See Charles M. Sennott, "Small Planes a Big Factor in Airport Congestion, but the Battle over New Runway vs Peak Pricing Mires Progress," *Boston Globe*, April 14, 1996, p. 24; and Michael Rezendes, "Planes, Pains, and Automobiles: Logan's Booming but the Idea of a Second Airport for Boston Just Won't Fly," *Boston Globe*, June 19, 1994, p. 74.

First, even if a way could be found to expand Stapleton Airport further into the Rocky Mountain Arsenal, it would remain too small to accommodate projected air traffic growth over the next two decades. Second, even with the rapid growth anticipated, the Denver market would be unable to support more than a single large common carrier airport, so construction of a new one would mean phasing out scheduled service at Stapleton.[79]

The city of Denver, which owned and operated Stapleton, was determined to retain its role as owner-operator of the regional airport, and judged as well that a close-in airport tended to benefit its economy. Yet a new airport would clearly have to be sited well outside the city, threatening both these assets. Moreover, the three airlines currently serving Denver were united in their preference for improving Stapleton—with its close-in location, low fee structure, and severely limited gate capacity for additional competitors. Local business groups concurred. So for city officials the choice seemed clear: keep Stapleton viable. Thus in 1982 Mayor William McNichols announced a $1.4-billion Stapleton expansion plan, including two new runways and a new midfield terminal with 100 gates.

The airlines and local business leaders, both city and regional, were enthusiastic. As they had in the late 1960s, however, Stapleton's neighbors, more distant residents who anticipated adverse noise impacts from the new runways, regional environmental groups, and numerous officials in adjacent Adams County quickly made clear their adamant opposition. They were encouraged when Mayor McNichols, for unrelated reasons, failed in his 1983 bid for reelection.

The new mayor was Federico Peña, a little-known former state representative whose main base of support was a multiethnic neighborhood-based coalition. Peña, though, had been lobbied heavily by business groups during the campaign, and had pledged just before the final election that he would support Stapleton expansion. One month after his inauguration, accordingly, he voted with most other members of the regional planning agency board (over the objections of Adams County) to endorse the Stapleton expansion plan. He also met a few days later, though, with the commissioners of Adams County and the mayor of Commerce City, its largest municipality. They strongly urged Peña to take a fresh look at the issue, particularly their proposal for a new airport in Adams County, and he agreed.[80]

---

79. See Denver Regional Council of Government (1983, pp. 1–2); and Dempsey, Goetz, and Szyliowicz (1997, pp. 45–49, 54–60).

80. See Wallis (1992a, pp. 72–74); and Judith Brimberg, "Adams Softens Stand on Airport Site," *Denver Post*, June 26, 1983, p. B1.

The staff group to whom he entrusted this task quickly concluded that because of the Rocky Mountain Arsenal's severe toxic contamination, the idea of further Stapleton expansion onto it was highly problematic. At the very least opponents would be able to delay such expansion for many years, and they might well succeed in blocking it altogether. George Doughty, the only member of Peña's group with direct aviation experience—he had run Cleveland's airport—added that he agreed with the conclusions of the regional planning agency's consultants of a few years earlier: even if Stapleton were expanded, a new airport would ultimately be needed.

Determined to maintain city ownership and operation of the region's airport, Peña now authorized his aides to explore whether this might still be possible if a new airport were developed in Adams County. Adams County officials were receptive to this idea, but they had two primary concerns: to minimize environmental impacts, both from the new airport and from Stapleton, and to ensure that the county would reap substantial economic benefits. The result, in December 1985, was an agreement with the following main provisions:

—Denver would annex and purchase from its private owners a site of 11,000 acres in Adams County, just east of the arsenal. Most of this site was currently in use as ranch and dry wheat farmland, though a portion was on uncontaminated land within the arsenal. The annexation would, under state law, require a referendum in Adams County.

—The city would construct, own, and operate a new airport on this site, with eight to 10 runways.

—Upon completion of the new airport—no later than the year 2000— Denver would permanently close Stapleton.

—Adams County would not challenge two proposed new runways at Stapleton (one for commuter and general aviation only) that Denver claimed were needed to avert severe congestion in the years pending completion of the new airport.

—All commercial development, except that integrally related to airport operations, would be kept off the airport site, ensuring that Adams County would collect the local tax revenue it generated.

—Adams County would prohibit new residential development in areas likely to be affected by noise from the new airport.

—The city and Adams County would equally split all nonaviation tax revenues generated within the airport site.

Denver officials estimated that the new airport would cost $1.5 billion— about half to be financed with airport landing fees and rental income, one-

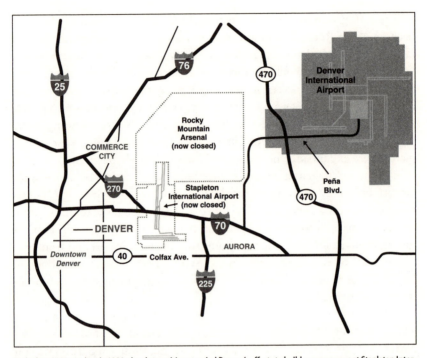

In the late 1970s and early 1980s, local opposition stymied Denver's efforts to build new runways at Stapleton International Airport. Denver's mayor, Federico Peña, took the lead in developing a new airport on a largely uninhabited 53-square-mile site, 24 miles northeast of downtown Denver. Credit: Robert B. Levers.

third with federal aid, and the remainder with proceeds from the sale of Stapleton's site for redevelopment. As an interim measure, the airlines agreed to pay a surcharge on Stapleton landing fees both to finance the plan's Stapleton improvements and to advance land acquisition for the new airport.

In 1986 the Greater Denver Chamber of Commerce took the lead in organizing the Greater Denver Corporation to advocate both the airport and other pending capital projects (of which the largest were a new convention center, baseball stadium, and water supply dam). Over the next several years this group attracted more than 500 corporate sponsors and spent more than $2.5 million to advance its agenda. Major donors included U.S. West Communications ($400,000), the Public Service Company of Colorado ($300,000), Silverado Savings and Loan ($95,000), and at least four major developers with substantial holdings near the proposed airport site (each of whom gave more than $50,000). In addition, one of the area's metropolitan daily newspapers contributed $60,000 while the other gave $12,000, and each strongly backed the several projects on its editorial pages.

In 1987, finally, major landowners near the proposed airport site made significant last-minute contributions that helped Peña win a come-from-behind victory in the city's mayoral election.[81]

All was not smooth sailing, however. Critics in both Adams County and some Denver neighborhoods argued that the new airport as planned would not on balance ameliorate noise impacts, and indeed might even worsen them. Environmentalists discovered that one of the proposed interim runways to be built at Stapleton would damage a bald eagle habitat, thereby running afoul of the Endangered Species Act. The U.S. Air Force expressed concern that flights from the new airport might interfere with defense radar systems at one of its nearby bases. And some major real estate investors in Adams County argued forcefully that the new airport should be located at a greater distance from Denver, where more land would be available for collateral development.

Meanwhile, air traffic was stagnating. The region's energy-oriented economy, hard-hit by declining oil and gas prices, lost 30,000 jobs from 1986 through 1988. One of its three main air carriers, moreover, People Express, shut down in 1986, and enplanements at Stapleton, which had grown steadily for decades, declined in 1987. As the regional recession deepened, advocates of the new airport shifted their rationale as well. Rather than emphasizing the need to accommodate projected traffic growth, they now claimed that it would provide badly needed construction jobs and, by making Denver more attractive to service enterprises, help free it from its historic dependence on the cyclical natural resource economy. Citing these arguments, Peña announced in September 1986 that he would make every effort to accelerate the project timetable.

The region's two remaining carriers, however, United and Continental, demurred. With the addition of just a general aviation runway, they now judged, Stapleton would be adequate for at least two decades. (This was the less controversial of the two new runways specified in the city's 1985 agreement with Adams County, in part because it was scheduled to be built within the airport's existing boundaries. The other, a full-service runway, was to be constructed in part on arsenal land.) Moreover, they contended, the fees required to finance the projected new airport would drive fares to unacceptably high levels. Both airlines also announced that they would no

81. See Wilmsen (1991, pp. 140–41); Dempsey, Goetz, and Szyliowicz (1997, pp. 94–95); and Robert Kowalski, "Silverado-MDC Deals Entangle Prime Airport Land," *Denver Post,* January 1, 1989, p. 1.

longer pay the Stapleton surcharge to which they had agreed two years earlier for preparatory work on the new airport.[82]

City officials responded that the airlines' real motive, now that they had
a profitable duopoly in Denver, was to preclude expansion that might facilitate the entry of new competitors. While reiterating his intent to speed
construction of the new airport, moreover, Peña cancelled the proposed
Stapleton improvement program, including the general aviation runway
that the airlines considered essential. He also vowed that if United and Continental did not sign terminal leases for the new airport, he would recruit
other airlines to do so.

In the early months of 1988 the city and Adams County arrived at a
somewhat different, and considerably more detailed, set of agreements than
those announced in 1985.[83]

—The new airport would be located several miles further from Denver
than projected in 1985, on a site nearly three times as large. At 34,000
acres, this site would be twice that of the nation's largest existing airport,
Dallas/Fort Worth, and indeed larger than the island of Manhattan.[84] The
new airport's central terminal would be 24 miles from the Denver central
business district. (Among American airports, only Dulles in the Washington,
D.C., area was more distant from its central business district, at 27 miles.
It was not strictly comparable, however, since Washington also had close-
in National Airport.)

—In addition to the airport site itself, Denver would annex nearly 4,000
acres for use as an access corridor, connecting with an interstate highway.

—All runway configurations and operating procedures would be
designed to minimize noise impacts. Adams County, moreover, would have
a veto over any changes the Federal Aviation Administration might require.
If agreement could not be reached, the airport would not be built.

—Once the airport opened, noise would be monitored at 101 sites. If the
agreed limits were exceeded, Denver would take steps to prevent future

82. The airlines, pending a court resolution of the dispute, paid the disputed fees into
escrow. In March 1989 a federal judge ruled that Denver could not use Stapleton landing fees
or airline surcharges to fund work on the new airport. Despite this ruling, Denver was able
to fund the airport plan in other ways, including bonds backed by anticipated fees the airlines
would pay at the new airport. See *City and County of Denver* v. *Continental Air Lines, Inc.
and United Air Lines, Inc.*, 712 F. Supp. 834 (D. Colo. 1989).

83. Space considerations prevent discussion of a midpath agreement unveiled in December 1986. Of note, however, is the fact it specified a third site, different from both that
announced in 1985 and that finally selected in 1988. For more detailed accounts of these negotiations, see Wallis (1992b).

84. Dempsey, Goetz, and Szyliowicz (1997, p. 232).

violations. If it failed to do so, it would be subject (after judicial review) to a $500,000 fine for each uncorrected violation.

—Denver would purchase the homes of all 559 people who lived in areas where noise from the new airport would exceed the FAA's threshold for acceptable noise impacts in residential communities.

—To avert future noise complaints while allowing for airport growth, Adams County would ban new residential development in an area of 25 square miles around the airport.

—Adams County would retain property tax jurisdiction over nonairport development on the land to be annexed by Denver.

Later in 1988 Denver's proposed annexation of the airport site and access corridor went before the voters of Adams County. Three groups mobilized in opposition—a small group of Denver and Adams County residents who wanted the airport moved even further away from the city; commercial property owners in the vicinity of Stapleton (particularly major hotels), who opposed any new airport; and some residents of Van Aire, an affluent subdivision with a small airstrip that would have to close if the new airport opened (to prevent airspace conflicts). These groups did not coordinate their efforts, however, and together spent less than $100,000.[85] In contrast, the new airport's advocates raised $1.5 million, mainly from the Greater Denver Corporation and individual corporations, and were able to deploy more than a thousand canvassers from development, real estate, construction, and professional firms likely to benefit if the airport were constructed. Substantial numbers of state and local officials also campaigned actively for a yes vote, most notably Colorado governor Roy Romer, who was very popular in Adams County. (In contrast, Peña, who as mayor of Denver was likely to be viewed with suspicion by Adams County voters, maintained a low profile.) With the state's economy just beginning to recover from the recent energy recession, the central theme of the campaign was jobs. All other issues faded into the background. Despite the proponents' overwhelming advantages in money and organization, the outcome was in doubt until Election Day—when the advocates prevailed by a margin of 56 to 44 percent.

No referendum was legally required in Denver, but airport foes demanded one and local officials, including Peña, eventually acquiesced. The city's electorate was asked, in May 1989, to vote yes or no on the following proposition: "In order to create more jobs, stimulate the local economy, and meet future air transport needs, should the city build a new airport using no city taxes?" The Adams County "yes" coalition reassembled, this time

85. See Moore (1989, pp. 14–17).

spending about $700,000. In opposition, the same group of Stapleton-area hotel owners who had been active in Adams County raised and spent about $150,000, mainly on negative television commercials. Additionally, a grass-roots group argued that the new airport would saddle the city with too much debt, but it raised only about $30,000 and made little apparent impression. On Election Day voters endorsed the new airport by a margin of 63 to 37 percent.

Thus by mid-1989 local support for the project appeared solid. Three important hurdles remained, however: environmental permitting, securing a large commitment of federal aid, and persuading the airlines to sign long-term lease agreements.

The main environmental issue was air pollution. Denver was in serious violation of national air quality standards for carbon monoxide, ozone, and particulates. The project's draft EIS projected that, because the new airport would be so much further from the city than Stapleton, its ground access traffic would generate more than five times as much pollution. Most of this pollution would be in outlying areas, however, that *were* in compliance with national standards.[86] Project critics—most notably the Environmental Defense Fund (EDF), the airlines (United and Continental), and the Stapleton-area hotel owners—highlighted the former point and urged rejection. Project supporters, of course, highlighted the latter, and it was their position that both federal and state regulators eventually upheld.[87]

The question now became whether any of the critics would sue. In the event, none did. EDF leaders recognized that the new airport would be preferable from an environmental standpoint to Stapleton, but they were tempted to sue for a binding commitment to build the region's planned new light rail transit system, including a link to the airport. (The EIS assumed that this would be built, but funding remained highly uncertain.) They were more concerned at the time, however, about another city project, a proposed new water supply dam on the Platte River, and they realized that the city had no capacity to guarantee funding for the transit system. So they decided to be satisfied with Peña's commitment to pursue realization of the transit plan as vigorously as possible.[88] The airlines were concerned that a suit to block the nation's only planned new regional jetport would undermine their efforts to

86. City and County of Denver (1989, p. 2.33).

87. The EPA did specify, however, that mitigation measures might subsequently be required if the region remained out of compliance with national air quality standards and airport-related traffic was one of the reasons. City of Denver, DIA (1989, p. 10.125).

88. R. Yuhnke (EDF senior attorney), interview by authors, by telephone, May 6, 1998.

bring about airport capacity increases elsewhere, and that it might also produce case law they would rue in other circumstances. They may also have
been reluctant to antagonize U.S. transportation secretary Skinner, whose
assistance they were eagerly courting on other matters, most notably ongoing efforts to secure new overseas routes. Skinner was known to view the
Denver project as both a vital addition to the national air traffic system and
a valuable demonstration that it was feasible to add new aviation capacity.
He warned the airlines that "the airport is going to happen" whatever they
might do.[89] The Stapleton-area hotel owners, finally, were mainly out-of-state
chains and decided not to invest any further in this apparently lost cause.[90]

The airport financial plan was premised on receipt of about $500 million
in federal aid, roughly 30 percent of the airport's now-estimated cost of $1.7
billion, plus about $200 million of direct FAA capital expenditures for air
traffic control purposes. This was roughly 10 times what Denver might
anticipate from its historic share of federal airport expenditures. Airport
supporters therefore launched an intensive lobbying effort. The city, for
example, hired Ron Brown, then chair of the Democratic National Committee, who eventually received several hundred thousand dollars for his
efforts.[91] Local and regional business groups, particularly the Colorado
Forum, an organization of the state's 50 largest companies, lobbied directly
in Washington and made substantial campaign contributions to the members of key congressional committees.[92]

The main argument for special funding was that, according to the FAA,
Denver's planned new airport capacity would reduce air traffic delays nationwide by about 5 percent—a remarkable contribution for any single project.
Politically, the advocates made common cause with a wide range of national
groups pressing for aviation system improvements. Where opportunities
arose, they engaged as well in classic logrolling. Denver Democratic Con-
gresswoman Patricia Schroeder, for example, who chaired the House Armed
Services Committee, let Florida Congressman William Lehman, the chair of
the Appropriations Subcommittee on Transportation, know that she would
approve some military construction projects he wanted in south Florida only

89. See "Denver Gets $60 Million to Proceed with Building New Airport," *Aviation
Daily*, September 28, 1989, p. 611.
90. J. Jensen (Stapleton Area Hotel Association), interview by authors, by telephone,
May 11, 1998.
91. See David Willman, "Probe of Airport Funds Put Peña under Scrutiny," *Los Angeles
Times*, March 12, 1995, p. A1.
92. See James A. Barnes, "Cleared for Takeoff," *National Journal*, September 18, 1993,
pp. 2237–41.

if he supported the Denver airport project. Similarly, Colorado senator Tim Wirth reportedly won the support of Senator Robert Byrd (D-W. Va.), the powerful chair of the Senate Appropriations Committee, in return for his vote in favor of a retraining program for unemployed coal miners.[93] In the end, the transportation appropriations act of 1989 specified that the federal government would grant about $500 million for the new Denver airport over the following eight fiscal years, and that the FAA would directly expend about $200 million to construct its air traffic control facilities.[94]

Federal aid was critical but half the revenue required to finance the new airport was slated to come from airline landing fees and rental payments, and the airlines continued to balk. Peña made clear, in response, that he was confident other airlines would jump at the chance to serve Denver if United and Continental decided not to lease space at the new airport. Indeed, to drive the point home he initiated construction activity at the end of 1989. At the same time, in recognition of the continuing stagnation in passenger traffic, the city scaled back from six to five runways and from 120 to 94 gates (14 fewer than Stapleton). Even so, the new airport would be able to accommodate three separate landings and takeoffs simultaneously, more than any other U.S. airport. And of course it would have vast reserves of land for future expansion.

Peña's judgment that the airlines would eventually participate received partial confirmation in March 1990, when Continental signed a lease for 30 gates. In return, it obtained the closest concourse to the airport's main terminal and a city commitment to add a 600-foot pedestrian bridge (over two taxiways) connecting the two. This would enable Continental's passengers to walk, if they wished, between the main terminal and the airline's gates; travelers using other concourses would have no choice but the airport subway. Additionally, the city agreed to lease Continental 75 acres for a maintenance hangar, a flight kitchen, and a freight facility at a highly favorable rate.[95]

93. See Burt Hubbard and Ann Carnahan, "Hard Sell Shoved DIA Down Denver's Throat," *Denver Rocky Mountain News*, February 7, 1995, p. 8A; and Beth Ferking, "Wirth's Intensive Lobbying for Airport Pays Off," *Denver Post*, September 12, 1989.

94. In the event Denver received about $50 million less than originally anticipated, because it made use of the passenger facility charge provision enacted a year later. This provision, it will be recalled, specified a partial loss of federal aid for each dollar of PFC revenue generated. Denver's PFC generated $30–40 million a year, offset by a loss of $8–10 million in federal aid.

95. William Ryan, "New Deals Draw Strong Demand: Prices Extend Secondary Gains," *Bond Buyer*, May 9, 1990, p. 1.

United continued to hold out, however. And in December 1990 Continental's parent company filed for bankruptcy. At this point bond-rating agencies downgraded Denver International Airport bonds to just above junk status, the lowest rating ever accorded debt for a major airport project.[96] Finally, however, in December 1991, after obtaining major concessions from the city, United agreed to lease 45 gates at the new airport, 15 more than it currently had at Stapleton. In return, the city agreed to spend $200 million for a United maintenance hangar and for a people mover along the length of United's concourse. It also agreed to cap landing fees at no more than $20 for each enplaned passenger, with future adjustments for inflation. (Even this, however, was more than three times the average fee at Stapleton, which was close to the average for major U.S. airports. But the airlines were expected to realize considerable savings as a result of reduced air traffic delays and shorter taxiing distances at Denver International.) The city and state also offered a $325-million package of inducements to United for a planned new aircraft maintenance facility, but United was negotiating with other jurisdictions as well and ultimately chose Indianapolis, where the subsidy offer was even better.

During the course of this negotiation United informed the city that its terminal would include an automatic baggage-handling system. City officials, concerned that this system would give United an undue competitive advantage, decided in response to install automated baggage handling for the entire airport—even though their own consultants warned that the technology for such a system was not yet reliable.[97] In the event, the system they built never worked. The failed efforts to debug it and the subsequent construction of a conventional system delayed the airport's opening by 16 months and raised its final cost by $461 million—$361 million in lost revenue (which the city had to borrow, in order to cover debt service payments), $63 million for the replacement manual baggage-handling system, and $37 million for change orders approved during the effort to get the automated system to work. Redesigning the terminal building to meet United's demands, including space to accommodate the automated baggage system, added another $150 million to that building's cost. These were the most conspicuous but only a few of the factors that drove the airport's cost to an eventual total of $4.8 billion, almost three times the $1.7-billion figure that

96. William Ryan, "Denver Airport Oversubscribed, Issue Increased to $500 Million," *Bond Buyer*, April 10, 1991, p. 1.
97. Glenn Rifkin, "What Really Happened at Denver's Airport," *Forbes*, August 29, 1994, p. 110; and Montealegre and others (1996).

city officials had projected in 1989 when both the Denver electorate and Congress registered their approval.[98]

By 1995 when Denver International Airport (DIA) opened, Continental had effectively withdrawn from Denver. United, completely dominant, was able to impose an extremely high fare structure. One consequence was a decline in boardings by comparison with the previous year at Stapleton. Indeed, passenger enplanements in 1995 were scarcely higher than a decade earlier, and the number of operations was lower. Even at this level of demand, however, the new airport turned a modest profit, and beginning in 1997 traffic turned upward. United reported, meanwhile, that Denver was one of its most profitable hubs.[99]

Investment Booms (1995–2001)

As might be expected, rates of air travel growth have declined as the airline industry has matured. But the growth trajectory remained very strong through the 1990s (3.7 percent a year, 43 percent over the decade as a whole), and the decade's growth was greater in absolute terms than any that had preceded it—200 million enplaned passengers, roughly equal to the total volume of airline patronage in 1975 (see table 5-3). By the mid-1980s, moreover, the airlines had largely exhausted the potential of yield management pricing to increase their load factors and of using larger aircraft to increase the average number of seats available on each flight; and they were increasingly attuned to the importance of service frequency as a competitive advantage. So the number of flights, which had risen just 14 percent from 1970 to 1985, rose nearly four times as rapidly (54 percent) from 1985 to 2000.

Runway capacity, gate shortages, ground access congestion, and crowding within terminals all became sources of growing concern. Airport operators and the major airlines, supported by local business interests, aircraft manufacturers, and most top state and local officials, pressed harder for airport capital improvements than they had in decades. The neighborhood and environmental opponents who had so commonly blocked airport capacity expansion since about 1970, they argued, must no longer be allowed to prevail. In a typical example, the Commercial Club of Chicago

98. See Dempsey, Goetz, and Szyliowicz (1997, pp. 424–31, 434–41, and 455–58); Gryszkowiec (1995); and General Accounting Office, "Denver International Airport: Information on Selected Financial Issues" (1995).

99. See Richard Williamson, "United, Flying Lower on Fare Structure," *Denver Rocky Mountain News*, December 9, 1997.

issued a report in April 2000 maintaining that failure to construct a long-discussed new runway at O'Hare would "jeopardize the economic future of our region in the 21st century."[100] Business groups in Cleveland, Atlanta, and Boston employed similar rhetoric in pressing for new runways at their main regional airports.

This campaign played out in the federal as well as state and local arenas. After several years of debate, in 2000 Congress reauthorized federal aviation programs at significantly higher levels of spending—nearly doubling the airport grant program from $1.9 billion in 2000 to an average of $3.3 billion a year over the next three fiscal years, and increasing the annual authorization for air traffic control improvements by 45 percent ($2 billion to $2.9 billion). While most of this aid, in accord with long-standing policy, was intended for smaller commercial airports and general aviation facilities—the nation's 71 largest airports handled 89 percent of all ticketed air passengers but received only two-fifths of federal airport grant dollars (see tables 5-5 and 5-6)[101]—the major airports did at least share proportionately in the program growth, and they secured a 50 percent increase in the maximum permissible passenger facility charge. (Such charges, first authorized by Congress in 1990, were by this time generating about $2 billion a year, almost all at large and medium hub airports, which by the mid-1990s were funding their capital improvement programs almost entirely with airport revenues and passenger facility charges [see table 5-6].)[102]

As the military closed large numbers of domestic bases, moreover—including 46 with airports—during the late 1980s and the 1990s, numerous aviation boosters hoped that some of these would prove viable sites for new commercial jetports. With rare exceptions, however (and none of these in the nation's largest travel markets), these hopes were dashed by local opposition.[103] In south Florida, for example, Miami–Dade County mayor Alex Penelas and local business leaders mounted a vigorous campaign for con-

100. See Ken Leiser, "Thunderstorms and Storms of Protest Affect Lambert Field's Operations and Its Plans for Expansion," *St. Louis Post-Dispatch*, January 16, 2000, p. B1; and "Chicago Business Leaders Release Booz-Allen & Hamilton Report Calling for New Runway at O'Hare," *PR Newswire*, April 19, 2000 press release.

101. See Kirk (2000, pp. 6–10); General Accounting Office, "Airport Financing: Funding Sources for Airport Development" (1998, pp. 8, 44–49); and Congressional Budget Office, "Financing Small Commercial-Service Airports: Federal Policies and Options" (1999, pp. 1–13).

102. For additional detail, see Federal Aviation Administration (FAA), "Key Passenger Facility Charge Statistics" (www.faa.gov/arp/pfc/reports/stats/htm [March 2002]).

103. See Federal Aviation Administration, "Report of Achievements under the Airport Improvement Program, 1997" (1998, table B-6).

Table 5-5. Distribution of Federal Airport Grants by Airport Size, 1996

Airport type[a]	Number of airports	Share of grants (percent)	Share of scheduled commercial enplanements (percent)
Large hub	29	24	67
Medium hub	42	17	22
Small hub	70	18	7
Nonhub	272	15	3
General aviation, relievers, and other commercial service	2,931	27	0

Source: General Accounting Office, "Airport Financing: Funding Sources for Airport Development" (1998, pp. 44–49).

a. A large hub airport handles at least 1 percent of national enplanements, a medium hub from .25 percent to 1.0 percent of enplanements, and a small hub from .05 percent to .25 percent of enplanements. A nonhub has more than 10,000 annual enplanements but less than .05 percent of the national total. General aviation, reliever, and other commercial service airports do not provide regularly scheduled commercial flights, though some house air taxi services.

Table 5-6. Sources of Funding for Major Airport Capital Projects, 1996

Percent

Revenue source	Large and medium hub airports $N = 71$	Small hub and nonhub airports $N = 3,233$
Airport revenue and passenger facility charges[a]	88	38
Federal grants	11	51
State grants	2	12
Share of all airport spending on capital projects	78	22

Source: General Accounting Office, "Airport Financing: Funding Sources for Airport Development" (1998, p. 8).

a. The airport revenue category includes both bonds secured by landing, rental, and other fee income and expenditures so financed on a pay-as-you-go basis.

version of the former Homestead air force base into a second regional airport. This proved to be a replay, however, of the failed effort three decades earlier to locate a new airport adjacent to the Everglades, attracting passionate opposition from national as well as local environmentalists. In January 2001, just before the Clinton administration left office, the air force determined that it would not release the base for use as a civilian airfield. Local advocates cried foul and the new Bush administration agreed to a fresh review, but in December 2001 its air force secretary, James Roache, decided to let his predecessor's decision stand. Similarly, in Orange County, California, growth advocates proposed replacement of the extremely crowded John Wayne Airport with a new facility on the former El Toro marine base. Local opposition in the vicinity of El Toro was intense, however, and in March 2002 Orange

County voters backed a measure that called for turning most of the base into parkland.[104] The most significant exception to this pattern occurred in Austin, Texas, which replaced its existing airport in 1999 with a new facility built on the former Bergstrom air force base—but Austin ranks forty-eighth among U.S. air passenger markets.[105]

The pressure for new airside capacity in significant markets did find an outlet in the 1990s, however, as airport operators succeeded—for the first time since the 1960s—in advancing substantial numbers of new runway projects. The nation's 31 large hub airports, which accounted for the great majority of air traffic congestion, added just three new runways in the 1980s but 11 in the 1990s, and 12 more are scheduled for completion between 2000 and 2006 (see table 5-7).[106] Many of the new runways, additionally, were elements of much broader investment programs. The plan for O'Hare, for example, included four new full-length runways (partially offset by decommissioning two full-length and one general aviation runway), extending another two, building a new terminal and western entrance to the airport, constructing additional access roads, and improving mass transit to downtown. Estimates of the ultimate cost of this plan (from the city and state, respectively) ranged from $6 to $12 billion. Similarly, Atlanta's new runway was part of an overall expansion plan to cost in excess of $5 billion.[107] Other major airports, still unable to advance new runways,

104. See William Fulton, "The Airbase to Airport War," *Governing*, December 1999, pp. 38–42.

105. Other military airfields converted for commercial passenger service were in Guam; Alexandria, Louisiana; Myrtle Beach, South Carolina; Gwinn, Michigan; and Portsmouth, New Hampshire—which in 2000 ranked 70th, 94th, 205th, 275th, and 291st in passenger enplanements nationally. One converted for air cargo usage, in Columbus, Ohio, ranked 57th nationally among air cargo facilities. Eighteen others, mainly in rural areas, were in use as general aviation airports. See L. Sandelli, letter to D. Luberoff re Status of Transition of Military Airfields to Civil Airports for Years 1988, 1991, 1993, 1995; Federal Aviation Administration, "Report of Achievements under the Airport Improvement Program, 1997" (1998, table B-6); and Federal Aviation Administration and ARP Consulting, "Aviation Capacity Enhancement Plan, 2001: Building Capacity Today for the Skies of Tomorrow" (2002, appendix B).

106. As of early 2002, moreover, another eight were in advanced stages of planning or environmental review. Federal Aviation Administration and ARP Consulting, "Aviation Capacity Enhancement Plan, 2001: Building Capacity Today for the Skies of Tomorrow" (2002, fig. 3-3, table D-1, pp. 37–38, 112–13); and Mead (2002a, pp. 13–14).

107. Overall, air travel delays radiated out primarily from eight major airports: LaGuardia, Newark, and Kennedy in the New York region, Chicago's O'Hare, Atlanta's Hartsfield, Boston's Logan, San Francisco, and Philadelphia. Only one of these, Philadelphia, managed to build a new runway in the 1990s, and that was a short runway for small aircraft use. As of 2002 work had started on a new runway at Hartsfield and new runways were planned for O'Hare and Logan, but both of the latter were still mired in controversy.

Table 5-7. Runways Built or under Construction at Large Hub Airports after 1975

Airport	Year opened or year scheduled to open
Atlanta (Hartsfield)	1984, 2005
Charlotte	1979, 2004
Cincinnati	1991, 2005
Dallas/Fort Worth	1996
Denver	1995[a], 2003
Detroit	1976, 1993, 2001
Houston	2003
Las Vegas (McCarran)	1987
Las Vegas	1991
Miami	2003
Minneapolis/St. Paul	2004
Orlando	1989, 2003
Philadelphia	1999 (GA)[b]
Phoenix	2000
Salt Lake City	1995
Seattle/Tacoma	2006
St. Louis (Lambert)	2006

Sources: Federal Aviation Administration and ARP Consulting, "Aviation Capacity Enhancement Plan, 2001: Building Capacity Today for the Skies of Tomorrow" (2002, pp. 36–38, appendix D); and Mead (2002a, pp. 12–13).

a. The new Denver airport, which opened in 1995, had five full-length runways, one more than the airport it replaced.

b. GA indicates that this is a short runway for use only by general aviation, not commercial airlines.

nonetheless embarked on massive terminal and ground access improvement programs. As of 2001 more than half the large hub airports were either engaged in or in advanced planning for improvement programs—with projected price tags of $1 billion or more.[108]

Some of the new runways entailed significant residential displacement and exposed new areas to serious noise impacts. St. Louis's plan, for example, required the taking of more than 2,000 homes; Atlanta's, 650; and Chicago's, 600. Airport operators sought to defuse the resultant opposition in four ways. First, they noted that although air traffic had grown steadily during the 1990s, the phaseout of older aircraft and better land use planning

---

The projected Logan runway, moreover, was not full service. It was to be half-length, for small aircraft, and available for use only in the over-water direction, to avoid any noise impacts over land.

108. Authors' calculations from James S. Gilliland and others, "U.S. Airports in the 21st Century: Secure at What Cost?" Fitch ICBA, April 10, 2002, p. 2 (www.fitchratings.com [February 2002]).

around airports had reduced the number of people exposed to what the FAA considered high levels of airplane noise from about 2.7 million people in 1990 to 448,000 in 2000.[109] This argument was rarely persuasive, though, for the simple reason that many people living near airports disagreed with the FAA's definition of acceptable noise levels. Indeed, major airports reported that there had been no reduction whatever in the number of noise complaints they received.[110]

Second, airport operators emphasized their commitment to noise and other types of environmental mitigation. Minneapolis/St. Paul, for example, set aside $200 million to soundproof as many as 14,000 homes.[111] San Francisco, which proposed filling two square miles of the bay to relocate its runways (and thereby allow both runways to be used during bad weather conditions), promised to create 45 square miles of new wetlands along the bay's shoreline.[112]

Third, adopting one of the strategies that Denver had employed, some airport operators found ways to share the economic benefits of airport development with affected local jurisdictions, particularly in connection with off-airport real estate development. Throughout the 1990s, for example, Cleveland sought to build a new runway and extend an existing runway at its airport. This project required expansion into the adjacent city of Brook Park (population 22,646), however, and takings within it of several hundred houses and an active trade show hall. After intense controversy and a lawsuit, which Brook Park won,[113] the two jurisdictions finally arrived at an agreement in 2001: the airport expansion will proceed, but Cleveland will cede to Brook Park 50 acres of nearby undeveloped land, along with an existing NASA research center, and Brook Park will receive 50 percent of all property tax revenue collected from a planned airport industrial park within the boundaries of Cleveland. The voters of Brook Park approved this agreement by 55-45 percent in August 2001 after a campaign financed on the pro

109. See General Accounting Office, "Aviation and the Environment: Transition to Quieter Aircraft Occurred as Planned but Concerns about Noise Persist" (2001); Falzone (1999, pp. 796–800); Creswell (1990), and Schoen (1986, pp. 310–27).

110. Federal Aviation Administration, "Performance Goal: Aircraft Noise Exposure" (www.api.faa.gov/STRATEGIC/docs/SUP-Sup-30-EnvGoal(1).html [October 2002]); and General Accounting Office, "Aviation and the Environment: Transition to Quieter Aircraft Occurred as Planned but Concerns about Noise Persist" (2001, p. 13).

111. See Department of Transportation, "Minneapolis–St. Paul International Airport, Dual Track Planning Process, New Runway 17/35 and Airport Layout Approval" (1998, pp. 9–11).

112. See Michael McCabe, "Salt of S.F. Bay, Plan to Restore Marsh as Trade for Airport Fill," *San Francisco Chronicle*, January 4, 1999, p. A13.

113. See *City of Cleveland* v. *City of Brook Park,* 893 F. Supp. 742 (D. Ohio 1995).

side largely by the region's leading business group.[114] Atlanta made similar concessions to obtain a fifth runway for Hartsfield, a project that also required land acquisition beyond the city's boundary. It agreed to pay the city of College Park about $82 million over 10 years to offset the decline in its property tax base and to cover the cost of moving its convention center, to pay Clayton County about $28 million over the same period, to place a new airport terminal where it was most likely to generate off-airport development in these communities, and to assist Clayton County in its efforts to attract high-tech jobs.[115]

Fourth, the champions of new runway construction argued that a failure to relieve local airport congestion would severely impair regional competitiveness in the local economy. This argument rarely persuaded environmental or neighborhood critics of airport expansion, but it proved more effective in the courts and state political forums than at any time since the 1960s. Upholding the plan for a new Seattle runway, for example, a county superior court judge concluded that it was "the region's only feasible solution for its air transportation needs."[116] Similarly, a state appellate court judge in Missouri found that the regional economic benefits of a proposed new runway at St. Louis's Lambert Airport "clearly outweigh[ed]" the localized costs it would impose on neighbors.[117] Even where runway advocates lost in court, moreover, they were frequently able to prevail legislatively. In 1993, for example, after Texas courts ruled that localities adjacent to the Dallas/Fort Worth airport were empowered to prevent airport expansion into their territory, the state legislature conferred annexation authority on the airport's board. In a similar vein, explaining his decision to acquiesce in the expansion of Atlanta's Hartsfield Airport, the chair of Clay-

114. See Rena Koontz and Sarah Treffinger, "Airport Deal Approved, Land Swap with Cleveland Wins Easily in Brook Park," *Plain Dealer*, August 8, 2001, p. A1; and Thomas Sheeran, "Voters Approve Land Swap for Airport Expansion," *Associated Press State and Local Wire*, August 7, 2001.

115. See City of Atlanta and City of College Park, "Memorandum of Understanding," December 5, 1999; City of Atlanta and Clayton County, "Intergovernmental Agreement," March 16, 2000; Gary Hendricks, "Clayton OK a Major Runway Step: Hurdles Remain; Atlanta, College Park, and the FAA Have Yet to Sign Off on the Airport Project," *Atlanta Journal-Constitution*, November 11, 1999, p. 5; Gary Hendricks, "Runway Deal Near Takeoff," *Atlanta Journal-Constitution*, December 5, 1999, p. D1; and Gary Hendricks, "Hartsfield Runway: Project Gears Up Despite Hurdles High and Long: First Step in Massive Expansion," *Atlanta Journal-Constitution*, April 18, 2001, p. A1.

116. See Scott Sunde, "Challenges to 3rd Runway Thrown Out," *Seattle Post-Intelligencer*, July 10, 1998, p. C1. The runway's foes have continued to attack the project in court, thus far without success.

117. See *City of Bridgeton* v. *City of St. Louis*, 18 S.W.3d 107, 114 (2000). For a good overview of recent cases, see Tuegel (1998, esp. pp. 310–16).

ton County's commission said he feared the alternative would have been state authorization for Atlanta to annex the land in question, without any serious quid pro quo for the county.[118]

The momentum for new runway construction appeared to pick up further steam at the beginning of 2001 with the arrival of the new Bush administration, which was strongly inclined toward "streamlining" environmental procedures that stood in the path of economic development. It seemed probable that even if efforts to amend key statutes proved fruitless, the Bush team's orientation would profoundly affect their administration— just as conservative appointments over the previous two decades had affected their judicial interpretation. On September 11, 2001, however, a far more urgent set of aviation concerns emerged. So we conclude this examination of developments over the past half century at what may be a historic turning point. We examine developments since September 11 and cautiously venture to peer ahead in chapter 9.

118. See Hendricks, "Runway Deal Near Takeoff."

CHAPTER SIX

The Political Rebirth of Rail Transit

In November 1980, on the same day that Ronald Reagan was elected president on a platform that emphasized tax cuts, Los Angeles–area voters approved a sales tax increase to fund a long-discussed rail transit system for their sprawling region. With this decision, Los Angeles joined a host of cities—including San Francisco, Washington, D.C., Baltimore, Miami, Atlanta, Baltimore, Buffalo, Pittsburgh, St. Louis, Dallas, Denver, San Diego, San Jose, Sacramento, and Portland—that built or were planning to build new subway and light rail lines in the 1970s and 1980s. This was a remarkable burst of activity in at least two respects. First, very little investment in rail transit had occurred during the great mega-project era or indeed at any time since the 1920s. Second, the boom in such investment that got under way in the 1970s took off just as it was becoming all but impossible to build most other transportation mega-projects, such as new expressways and airports.

At the national level, central-city mayors, business leaders, and major transit providers, both public and private, had coalesced in the early 1960s to lobby for a program of federal transit aid. This coalition, expanded to include environmental and neighborhood-based interests, achieved its greatest victories in the early 1970s—mainly by threatening to oppose continued federal highway aid unless prohighway forces joined them in securing large-scale funding for transit as well. Though highway interests resisted at first, they eventually acquiesced as part of a strategy to counter the dual effects of growing antihighway sentiment in major cities and presidential efforts, for general budgetary reasons, to curtail highway spending. As participants in this enlarged coalition, transit advocates succeeded in obtaining dramatic increases in federal transit assistance during the 1970s, defending the transit program in the 1980s against sharp cutbacks proposed by the Reagan administration, and resuming momentum in the 1990s.

Protransit coalitions were equally successful at the subnational level, inducing many state governments to provide large-scale transit aid for the first time and persuading the voters of many regions to approve earmarked taxes for the construction of new rail systems. Such victories did not, to be sure, come easily, and numerous campaigns failed. Suburban interests often judged that they would bear disproportionate costs for modest benefits, or that transit would stimulate unwanted development and migrations from the central city, while inner-city leaders often concluded that the systems proposed were designed almost entirely to serve affluent white suburbanites. After setbacks, however, transit backers routinely adapted and returned to the fray—altering their route structures to win over key opponents, packaging rail transit plans with promises to improve local bus services, obtaining more state and federal aid to mitigate local resistance based on tax concerns, and mounting increasingly sophisticated political campaigns. And eventually they often succeeded.

The transit investment boom, accompanied by significant increases in transit operating subsidies, stemmed the headlong decline of transit ridership as measured in absolute terms, though the transit share of urban passenger travel, already meager, continued to diminish. Since the mid-1970s transit has consistently received about one-half of all public money spent on surface transportation in urban areas though it currently serves less than 2 percent of all urban passenger movements (and no freight). In a few locales, escalating costs and social critiques have, over time, forced a reexamination of rail projects even after their construction has begun. In many others, though, the demand for rail remains strong, with dozens of urban regions looking to build new rail systems or expand existing ones.

Transit's Rise and Fall (1900–70)

From the middle of the nineteenth century to the beginning of the twentieth, transit systems helped define the shape of American cities, facilitating the development of dense central business districts and of suburbs clustered along radial rail lines. Indeed, in many locales streetcar systems—privately owned regulated utilities—were loss leaders developed mainly in connection with land development schemes. For example, Henry Huntington, who built and operated a 1,164-mile streetcar system in Los Angeles, lost money on the streetcars and adjacent water lines but made millions developing land that the lines had made newly accessible.[1]

By the 1920s, however, most electric railways were in financial trouble as car ownership increased and land development opportunities along the older lines were exhausted. Streetcar firms were commonly vilified as monopolies, moreover, leading government regulators routinely to deny fare increases even in periods, such as World War I, of significant inflation.[2]

In response to growing downtown traffic problems and incipient suburbanization during the 1920s, downtown property interests in many locales pushed for new, publicly funded rapid transit investments. In 1925, for example, the Los Angeles Chamber of Commerce, the city's Downtown Businessmen's Association, and its Central Business District Association jointly proposed a comprehensive regional system of grade-separated rail rapid transit. Unlike a companion plan that called for improved roadways in Los Angeles, however, this proposal went nowhere, largely because of opposition from property owners in the commercial districts that had begun to grow up outside central Los Angeles.[3]

Transit ridership fell from about 17 billion people a year in 1925 to 12 billion during the Great Depression (1935), before rising to about 13 billion in 1940 and then surging—in a context of gas rationing—to an all-time peak of more than 23 billion riders in 1945. A decade later, in 1955, ridership was back at the 1933 level despite substantial population growth and great national prosperity (see table 6-1). The industry was mainly private at this time, and even the few public systems were expected to get by with minimal subsidization. So the consequences of this decline were fiscally devastating. Operators cut back services, raised fares, and deferred maintenance. Capital investment was virtually nil.[4]

---

1. See Fogelson (1967, pp. 104–07); Jackson (1985, pp. 120–24); Barrett (1983, pp. 114–15, 172–73); and Warner (1978, p. 60).

2. See Bottles (1987). For an excellent early view of transit politics, see Dreiser (1914).

3. See Bottles (1987, pp. 122–57); and Fogelson (1967, pp. 176–78).

4. A few cities, such as Detroit, Seattle, and San Francisco, had been operating public streetcar lines since the early part of the century, and New York had taken over its privately run subway system in 1940. Boston's transit system, in publicly supervised receivership since shortly after World War I, became public in 1947, the same year Chicago took over its transit system. For background on Chicago, see Banfield (1961, pp. 91–125); and Barrett (1983); on Boston, see Gómez-Ibáñez (1994); and on New York, see Hood (1993); and Doig (1966).

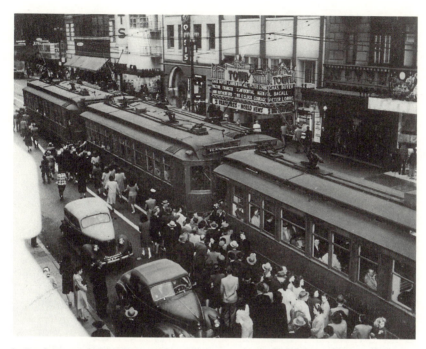

Los Angeles streetcars in 1945. Due to gasoline rationing, transit ridership surged during World War II. By the mid-1950s, however, it had fallen by more than half. Credit: Los Angeles County MTA, Dorothy Peyton Gray Transportation Library.

Nonetheless, central area business interests in a number of cities—most notably Los Angeles, Atlanta, and San Francisco—mounted campaigns in this period for the development of new downtown-oriented rail systems. These did not generally prove feasible in the absence of large-scale aid from higher-level governments, but there was a singular exception. In San Francisco the Bay Area Council, a regional planning group funded mainly by the largest downtown-based corporations, took the lead in developing plans for rapid transit during the late 1950s and early 1960s. In 1957 it persuaded the state legislature to create a five-county Bay Area Rapid Transit (BART) District, with a mandate to build, operate, and finance rapid transit. Four years later BART released its detailed plan, upon which two of its suburban counties, Marin to the north and San Mateo to the south, chose to withdraw. Voters in BART's three other counties were asked at the polls, in November 1962, to approve both the plan and property tax increases to finance its capital cost. (They were assured that farebox revenue would be sufficient to cover operating costs.) Downtown business groups and the region's major construction firms led the campaign for a "yes" vote, joined by the region's

Table 6-1. Transit Ridership, by Mode, 1925–99[a]
Millions of passengers

Year	Bus	Heavy rail	Light rail	Commuter rail	Other[b]	Total[c]
1925	1,484	2,264	12,924	n.a.	n.a.	16,672
1930	2,497	2,559	10,530	n.a.	n.a.	15,586
1935	2,721	2,236	7,286	n.a.	n.a.	12,243
1940	4,773	2,382	5,943	n.a.	n.a.	13,098
1945	11,130	2,698	9,426	n.a.	n.a.	23,254
1950	11,078	2,264	3,904	n.a.	n.a.	17,246
1955	8,452	1,870	1,207	n.a.	n.a.	11,529
1960	7,082	1,850	463	n.a.	n.a.	9,395
1965	6,119	1,858	276	n.a.	n.a.	8,253
1970	5,216	1,881	235	n.a.	n.a.	7,332
1975[d]	5,162	1,673	124	260	n.a.	7,219
1980[e]	5,706	2,108	122	280	67	8,283
1985	5,580	2,290	131	275	99	8,375
1990	4,877	2,346	300	328	115	7,966
1995	4,698	2,034	249	344	179	7,504
1999	5,111	2,521	289	374	227	8,523

Sources: American Public Transport Association (1978, table 8; 1987, table 9; 2001, table 26); Urban Mass Transit Association, "National Urban Mass Transportation Statistics, Second Annual Report, Section 15 Reporting System" (1982, pp. I-59–I-63; 1988, p. 71); and Federal Transit Administration, "National Transit Summaries and Trends for the 1990 Section 15 Report Year" (1992, pp. iv, 29–34), "National Transit Summaries and Trends for the 1995 National Transit Database Report Year" (1996, pp. 14–17), "Annual Report on New Starts Proposed Allocation of Funds for Fiscal Year 2002" (2001, table 28).

n.a. Not available.

a. Data for 1940–75 are for "total passenger rides as reported to the American Public Transit Association (APTA) and its predecessors"; data for 1980–2000 are for "unlinked passenger trips" by mode as reported to the Urban Mass Transit Administration (UMTA) and its successor, the Federal Transit Administration (FTA).

b. "Other" includes demand-responsive transit, cable cars, ferryboats, monorails, and van pools.

c. Totals first include commuter rail riders in 1975 and riders on other modes in 1980.

d. Most of the increase in heavy rail transit ridership from 1975 to 1980 (which represented 44 percent of the entire increase in transit ridership over this period) was due to changes in the method of counting such riders. The reported growth in bus ridership in the same period (which represented almost half the increase in ridership in this period) appears to be due in part to the change in reporting methods described above.

e. Because of special problems with the 1980 UMTA data, 1980 ridership figures are estimated using both UMTA and APTA data. In all years after 1980, the government figures are about 10 percent lower than those reported by APTA. According to APTA officials, the reason is that small transit operators (almost all providers of solely bus and demand responsive services) are not required to file reports with FTA on ridership, funding, or costs.

four newspapers, most leading civic groups, the incumbent governor, Edmund G. (Pat) Brown, and his challenger that year, Richard Nixon. Organized opposition was negligible, but the plan required a 60 percent favorable vote to pass. On Election Day this margin was exceeded by just 1 percent, but BART was now in position to build the first new urban subway system in the United States since the 1920s.[5]

5. For more on BART, see Hall (1982); Zwerling (1974); Whitt (1982); and Wirt (1974).

Federal Aid Commences

Federal policymakers ignored mass transit through the 1950s, with two conspicuous exceptions. In 1956 they exempted transit operators from the new federal excise taxes adopted to finance the Interstate Highway Program. And in 1958 they acted to facilitate the elimination of commuter rail services by intercity railroads. The latter action became the spark that first ignited national transit mobilization.

Faced with burgeoning truck competition and burdened with a regulatory structure inherited from the days when many railroads were effective monopolies, nearly all of the nation's railroads were struggling during the 1950s. Those in greatest difficulty, however, were the operators of substantial commuter rail services (nearly all in the New York City, Philadelphia, Chicago, Boston, and San Francisco areas). Fare increases and service reductions invariably provoked local protests, supported by state legislators from the affected area, so state regulators routinely disapproved railroad petitions or delayed action on them as long as possible. Defending this approach, they typically maintained that the railroads were still quite capable of offsetting passenger service losses with their freight profits. By 1957 passenger subsidies were absorbing an estimated 44 percent of the net freight revenues of those railroads with commuter rail operations, and much more in some cases.[6] For their part, the railroads maintained that this drain severely impaired their capacity to invest in freight operations and that it was driving those with the largest passenger rail commitments into bankruptcy. Their complaints did not cut much ice at the state level, but Congress was far more receptive. The federal Transportation Act of 1958, legislation focused centrally on the health of the railroad industry, authorized the Interstate Commerce Commission to overrule state regulators whose actions were impairing the economic viability of interstate carriers.

In the months after enactment of this legislation, carriers moved to discontinue most of the nation's commuter rail operations. If services were to be preserved, it appeared, the only solution was public subsidization. Political and business leaders in the affected central cities, with support from their commuter operators and railroad employee unions, quickly mobilized to pursue such assistance, and they typically obtained very limited state aid in the form of operating assistance, reduced taxes, and low-cost financing for new cars.[7] They made no headway in Washington, however, until a new

6. See Smerk (1991, p. 59, n. 8)

7. See Danielson and Doig (1982, pp. 215–26; Doig (1966, pp. 192–231); and Smerk (1991, pp. 60–61).

Democratic administration took office in 1961. In that year, with administration backing, Congress authorized $75 million for modernization loans and grants to commuter rail lines, the first ever direct federal aid for urban mass transit.[8]

The transit industry as a whole was in trouble, however, and it was clear that enactment of a more substantial program of assistance would require a wider coalition. With a sympathetic administration in the White House, this expansion gradually occurred—promising major cities without rail transit the possibility of constructing new systems, and smaller cities the possibility of modernizing their bus systems. In 1962 President Kennedy proposed a three-year, $500-million program of federal grants for transit capital investments. In fairly typical testimony on behalf of this legislation, Atlanta mayor Ivan Allen maintained that Atlanta would eventually need 120 expressway lanes radiating from downtown and a 28-lane belt highway if it failed to put a rapid transit system in place. "If you . . . multiply this situation throughout every metropolitan area in the nation," he warned, "you can readily see that the requirements of a federal highway program [without a companion transit program] would be of such staggering proportions as to bankrupt every level of government in the nation."[9]

The transit bill stalled for more than two years nonetheless, confronting opposition from fiscal conservatives, legislators from areas with little or no transit, and even transit labor unions. The latter feared that new rail systems and other modernization investments would result in layoffs. The breakthrough to enactment occurred in 1964, when advocates reached an agreement with transit labor (and, on its behalf, the AFL-CIO) on unprecedented labor protection language. This language, which became section 13(c) of the Mass Transit Act, made it prohibitively expensive for transit operators to use federal aid for purposes that led to adverse impacts on transit employees.[10] As strictly interpreted by the Department of Labor, this provision has frequently been cited since as an important barrier to productivity improvement in the transit industry. To this day, however, it remains politically untouchable. In 1964 it enabled a coalition of northern

8. The funding was administered by the Housing and Home Finance Agency, which became part of the new Department of Housing and Urban Development in 1966. In 1968 transit programs moved to the new Department of Transportation, where they were housed in the new Urban Mass Transit Administration (UMTA). For more on the coalition and the law, see Danielson (1965); Altshuler (1963); Adler (1993); and Smerk (1991).

9. Ivan Allen, testimony to the Senate (1962).

10. See Woodman, Starke, and Schwartz (1995); Smerk (1991, pp. 64–65); and Richmond (2001a).

Democrats and moderate suburban Republicans narrowly to enact a $375-million, three-year program of capital grants for mass transit, including rapid transit and bus as well as commuter rail.

The federal legislation reenergized longtime supporters of rapid transit in a number of cities and sparked new efforts in many others; but proposals for new systems generally required direct voter approval, and this frequently proved difficult to obtain. During the late 1950s, for example, the Atlanta region's Metropolitan Planning Commission, at the urging of downtown business leaders, had developed an elaborate rapid transit proposal. In 1962, as a first step toward realization of this plan, the legislature placed on the ballot a state constitutional amendment authorizing the creation of urban area transit authorities. This proposition failed in the face of suburban and small-region opposition, combined with conservative resistance to the very idea of publicly owned mass transit.[11] Two years later, however, after enactment of the federal Mass Transit Act, the state electorate approved a transit agency for the five-county Atlanta region alone; and in 1965 voters in four of these counties approved membership in the Metropolitan Atlanta Regional Transit Agency (MARTA). (Voters in suburban Cobb County opted out.) In 1968, MARTA—chaired by Richard Rich, whose flagship downtown department store was three blocks from the proposed central station—proposed a property tax increase to fund phase 1 of the rail system, expected to cost about $900 million.[12] Many suburbanites remained unenthusiastic, however, and African American leaders charged that the proposal ignored the needs of inner-city residents, who would remain dependent on privately operated bus service. The ballot question failed by a margin of 55 to 45 percent.[13]

Transit proposals in other locales encountered similar fates. In 1965, for example, the Los Angeles Chamber of Commerce established the Citizens' Advisory Council on Public Transportation, which included representatives of some of the city's largest businesses. Two years later the council published a report calling for a new rapid transit system, which it claimed would increase property values, enhance mobility, and reduce traffic congestion. In

11. See Hebert (1972, pp. 111–13).

12. For background on Atlanta, see Hebert (1972); and Hamer (1976).

13. The defeat was across the board—the measure lost in both the city itself and the surrounding counties. Clarence Stone, the preeminent analyst of Atlanta's politics, called this episode a major watershed in the city's political history because it marked the emergence of the minority community as a political force whose support the business elite could no longer take for granted. See Stone (1989, pp. 74, 78, 98–102); Almy, Hildreth, and Golembiewski (1981, pp. 1–10); Keating (2001, pp. 118–22) and Coogan and others (1970).

1968 the new Southern California Regional Transit District proposed a half-cent increase in the sales tax to fund a downtown-oriented 89-mile rail system, even larger and more expensive than BART. Supporters raised almost half a million dollars to finance the inescapable referendum campaign, roughly 60 percent from downtown businesses. The opponents raised only about $25,000 but prevailed. The measure received a favorable vote of only 44.7 percent, far short of the 60 percent required for passage.[14]

In areas with existing rail systems, on the other hand, states were more disposed to contribute financially and to dispense with referendum requirements. As a result, these states reaped by far the greatest benefits from the new federal program. New York State, for example, provided operating subsidies for its ailing commuter railroads from the mid-1950s, acquired and began modernizing the bankrupt Long Island Railroad in 1964, and created the new Metropolitan Transportation Authority (MTA) in 1968. The MTA, with large amounts of state as well as local funding, was to exercise comprehensive responsibility for the New York region's mass transit system, including suburban services within New York State.[15] Similarly, in 1964 Massachusetts expanded the number of cities and towns in its Boston-area transit district from 14 to 79, thereby expanding the local property tax base over which transit subsidy costs could be spread, and it committed to provide state aid as well: up to 90 percent of the nonfederal cost of new transit extensions and a portion of the commuter rail subsidy.[16] The regions with existing rail systems, overall, garnered well over two-thirds of available federal transit aid in the late 1960s and early 1970s.[17]

The Funding Breakthrough (1970–80)

Transit spending by all levels of government rose sharply from 1960 to 1970, increasing from $3.7 to $6.1 billion in constant 2002 dollars (see tables 6-2 and 6-3). Capital spending, moreover, almost tripled, rising from $0.5 to $1.4 billion, with the federal share rising from zero to 33 percent (see table 6-4). Yet the transit funding crisis continued to worsen, and private operators in particular (who still provided most bus services) aggressively curtailed their services.

14. See Whitt (1982, pp. 84–92).
15. See Danielson and Doig (1982, pp. 231–33); Moses (1970, pp. 256–58); and Caro (1974, pp. 1138–39).
16. See Gómez-Ibáñez (1994); and Gómez-Ibáñez and others (1994).
17. See Hilton (1974, pp. 55–71).

Table 6-2. Transit Spending and Funding Sources, 1950–99[a]

Billions of 2002 dollars

Year	Total spending	Fares	Federal	State and local
1950	3.6	3.0	0.0	0.6
1955	3.3	3.0	0.0	0.3
1960	3.7	2.9	0.0	0.8
1965	4.8	3.6	0.1	1.2
1970	6.1	4.3	0.4	1.4
1975	11.0	3.9	3.0	4.1
1980	14.7	4.6	6.0	4.1
1985	20.7	6.3	4.9	9.4
1990	23.9	6.6	4.7	12.5
1995	28.9	7.3	4.9	16.6
1999	30.0	8.1	4.4	17.5

Sources: Authors' calculations from Office of Management and Budget, "Budget of the United States Government, Fiscal Year 2003: Historical Tables" (2002, tables 9-6, 12-3); Congressional Budget Office, "Trends in Public Infrastructure Spending" (1999, tables 1, 2, 3, 4); and Bureau of the Census, *Government Finances: 1998–1999* (2001, table 1), *Statistical Abstract of the United States: 2000* (2001, tables 495, 496), *Statistical Abstract of the United States: 1998* (1999, table 506), *Statistical Abstract of the United States: 1991* (1992, table 456), *Statistical Abstract of the United States: 1986* (1986, table 452), *Statistical Abstract of the United States: 1982* (1983, tables 468, 469), *Statistical Abstract of the United States: 1967* (1967, tables 578, 581), *Statistical Abstract of the United States: 1957* (1957, table 491).

a. Figures are for the fiscal year ending in the year shown. Constant-dollar spending is based on the Bureau of Economic Affairs' GDP price deflator. Where data reported by the Bureau of the Census and the Office of Management and Budget (OMB) differ from those reported by the American Public Transit Association, all tables in this chapter use the former.

Table 6-3. Sources of Transit Revenues, 1950–99

Percent

Year[a]	Fares	Federal	State and local
1950	82	0	18
1955	91	0	9
1960	77	0	23
1965	74	1	24
1970	70	6	23
1975	35	28	37
1980	31	41	28
1985	31	24	46
1990	28	20	52
1995	25	17	58
1999	27	15	58

Source: Authors' calculations from table 6-2.

a. Figures are for the fiscal year ending in the year shown.

Table 6-4. Transit Capital Expenditures, 1950–99[a]

Billions of 2002 dollars, except as noted

Year	Total	Federal	Federal share (percent)
1950	0.7	0.0	0
1955	0.6	0.0	0
1960	0.5	0.0	0
1965	1.1	0.1	5
1970	1.4	0.5	33
1975	3.8	2.4	62
1980	3.7	3.9	106
1985	5.7	4.1	71
1990	6.9	4.0	58
1995	8.4	4.0	48
1999	9.2	4.3	46

Sources: See table 6-2.

a. Figures are for the fiscal year ending in the year shown. Constant-dollar spending is based on the Bureau of Economic Affairs' GDP price deflator. The data indicate that federal capital grants exceeded total capital spending in 1980. The apparent explanations are two: delays between the receipt of federal money by local recipients and its use, and differences between federal, state, and local fiscal years.

In 1969 the U.S. Conference of Mayors and the National League of Cities made increased federal transit aid one of their highest priorities. Supported in most cases by their downtown business associations, they were also quickly joined at the national level by industry groups representing rail manufacturers, rail rapid transit operators, and private bus companies.[18] They also attracted broader support from organized labor, most notably by persuading the Laborers International Union (LIU), which represented construction workers, to push for the transit program on the grounds that it would create many construction jobs. This was particularly important because the LIU was larger and more influential than the transit and railway workers' unions, which had become part of the transit coalition in the mid-1960s. The environmental movement was a rapidly growing force at this time, moreover, and emphasized transit as the preferred alternative to urban highway construction. Together these allies threatened to oppose upcoming efforts to reauthorize the federal highway program unless highway advocates supported significantly increased funding for transit. (This was a particularly significant threat because the Nixon administration and budget

18. These were the Institute for Rapid Transit, which represented both the manufacturers and operators of rapid-rail transit systems; the Railway Progress Institute, which represented manufacturers of railway equipment; and the American Transit Association, which primarily represented private bus operators.

hawks in Congress were seeking to cut back highway spending as part of their efforts to constrain overall federal spending.)

The administration proved surprisingly receptive, viewing transit as a component of urban policy with an unusually broad support base, including business groups and affluent suburbanites as well as traditional Democratic constituencies. Fred C. Burke, chief lobbyist in this period for the transit coalition, observed to a reporter in 1970: "There [is] no question that the realization by politicians of who is going to benefit from the program—the middle and upper middle class—is an enormous tactical aid for us in working with Congress, especially among Republicans and Southerners."[19] Alan Altshuler, who participated in these activities as Massachusetts secretary of transportation, observed more generally:

> Transit proved to be a policy for all perspectives on the urban problem. Though its direct constituency was relatively small, its ideological appeal proved to be extremely broad. Whether one's concern was the economic vitality of central cities, protecting the environment, stopping highways, energy conservation, assisting the elderly and handicapped and poor, or simply getting other people off the road so as to be able to drive faster, transit was a policy that could be embraced. This is not to say that transit was an effective way of serving all these objectives, simply that it was widely believed to be so. Additionally, because the absolute magnitude of transit spending was so meager at the beginning of this period, it was possible to obtain credit for rapid program growth with quite modest increases in the absolute level of expenditures.[20]

The transit coalition won its first important victory in 1970, with legislation authorizing $3.1 billion in new transit capital grants over five years—roughly five times the annual level of funding in the late 1960s. By 1972 several governors and their secretaries of transportation were mounting a campaign for flexibility in the disposition of federal aid long earmarked for urban interstate highway segments that had become fiercely controversial. Massachusetts governor Francis Sargent, having stopped nearly all of the remaining interstate projects planned for the Boston area, took the lead. As a result of his decisions, and to the dismay of powerful business and labor interests, the state stood to lose nearly $700 million in federal aid (equivalent

19. William Lilly III, "Urban Report: Urban Interests Win Transit Bill with 'Letter Perfect' Lobbying," *National Journal*, September 1970, p. 2021–29.

20. Altshuler (1979, p. 36).

to $2.4 billion in 2002). New York and Maryland, which also had controversial projects awaiting decision, joined with Massachusetts in seeking authorization to use their projected interstate allocations for alternative transit or highway projects. Leaders of the highway coalition at first considered this a preposterous idea, but the state officials persisted, arguing that it was unfair to penalize states that—because of changing political circumstances and new federal environmental laws—were unable to build controversial highways. Sargent, in particular, concentrated on lobbying his state's powerful congressional delegation. In response, House majority leader Thomas "Tip" O'Neill, through whose district two of the controversial Massachusetts highways passed, and Senator Edward Kennedy asked the key committee chairmen—Representative James Wright (D-Tex.) and Senator Jennings Randolph (D-W.Va.)—to include the transfer provisions in pending legislation to reauthorize the federal highway program. Wright and Randolph proved receptive. Altshuler, who conceived this provision and, on Sargent's behalf, managed the effort to secure its enactment, wrote several years later:

> Their [Wright and Randolph's] central concern was that urban expressway controversies had become a significant threat to the consensual and veto-proof dominance of the highway coalition in Congress. . . . This is by no means to minimize the victory achieved by urban anti-highway and transit interests. . . . But it should be emphasized that these were minority actors who achieved influence by maximizing their nuisance potential. Their triumph occurred when a few far-sighted leaders of the highway coalition, which remained politically dominant, discerned that a mutually beneficial solution was possible and persuaded the rest of the coalition to accept it.[21]

In 1974, finally, after the oil shock of 1973, which dramatically worsened transit operating deficits, the transit coalition was able to achieve its last major objective, federal operating subsidies. In order to maximize congressional support, this aid was to be distributed by formula, even to localities with little transit use: urban areas with fewer than 100,000 residents were to receive 12 percent of the aid though they accounted for only 4 percent of national transit ridership.[22] Overall, transit spending grew faster than virtually any other federal budget category during the 1970s—rising in constant (2002) dollars from about $400 million in 1970 to about $6 bil-

---

21. Altshuler (1979, p. 38).
22. Meyer and Gómez-Ibáñez (1981, p. 46).

lion in 1980. State and local transit spending, exclusive of fares, rose as well in this period, but much more gradually, from $1.4 billion to $4.1 billion (see tables 6-2 and 6-3).

The federal statutes enacted in this period guaranteed that virtually all metropolitan areas would receive some transit assistance, but the lion's share of the money went to the largest urban areas. From 1965 to 1983, for example, more than half of federal transit capital aid and 40 percent of transit operating assistance went to five metropolitan areas—New York, Chicago, Philadelphia, Boston, and Washington, D.C. These regions accounted, it bears note, for nearly two-thirds of national transit trips; the New York region alone, including northern New Jersey, accounted for nearly 40 percent.[23]

Rail Comes to Atlanta

The prospect of far more generous capital grants than had been available in the 1960s energized rapid transit advocates across the country. In Atlanta, for example, advocates were able to project a two-thirds federal share for the region's long-proposed new system, and this proved decisive in the successful 1971 referendum campaign to secure its approval.[24] This was not the entire story, however. In contrast to 1968, the 1971 vote was the culmination of a long, carefully crafted campaign in which MARTA's backers and officials reached out to elected officials and community groups they had previously ignored. This effort began not long after the 1968 referendum, when Richard Rich resigned from the MARTA board and was replaced (as a member, though not as chair) by Jesse Hill, a prominent black businessmen who had also been a leading opponent of MARTA's 1968 plan. Hill pressed MARTA to hire more minorities, both in staff positions and as contractors. He insisted as well that MARTA must be more than a rapid rail system for suburbanites who worked downtown. In particular, he supported the city's black leadership in resisting a consultant proposal that the system's main north-south line (which served primarily white areas) be built as a rail line while the east-west line, which served largely minority communities, be built as a lower-cost busway. As a result, MARTA opted for rail in both

23. Authors' calculations from Federal Transit Administration, "Statistical Summaries, 2001: FTA Grant Assistance Programs" (2002, p. 108); and Urban Mass Transit Administration, "National Urban Mass Transportation Statistics, Second Annual Report, Section 15 Reporting System" (1982, sec. 1, pp. 15, 159–62, sec. 2, pp. 176–77).

24. The section on Atlanta is drawn mainly from Almy, Hildreth, and Golembiewski (1981); Hebert (1972); and Stone (1989).

corridors.[25] Additionally, it agreed to purchase the city's existing private bus system and spend $45 million upgrading it.

Atlanta mayor Sam Massell, a white liberal elected in 1969 with strong support from the black community, favored reliance on the property tax to finance the local share of MARTA's cost, as had been proposed in 1968. This was unacceptable to most suburban officials, however, who preferred a regional sales tax. Massell eventually concurred, despite his concern that a sales tax would unfairly burden Atlanta's poor; but he extracted a collateral agreement to reduce the local bus fare from 40 cents to 15 cents.

As the referendum approached, MARTA and the city's business leadership formed a campaign organization called the Committee for Sensible Rapid Transit. The committee's business-financed campaign, which cost about $300,000, emphasized the federal role in financing the proposed new rail system and paid special attention to winning over the city's minority community. In contrast, opponents—suburbanites who feared that the new rail system would facilitate minority dispersal and minority leaders still convinced that it would bypass their constituents—spent only a few thousand dollars. The measure passed, but very narrowly, attracting just enough votes in the two highly urbanized counties to offset overwhelmingly negative votes in the two that were mainly exurban and rural.

Los Angeles Tries Again

Tom Bradley became mayor of Los Angeles in 1973 after a campaign in which he made rail transit a top priority, stressing its promises of congestion relief, downtown revitalization, and federally financed job creation. At his urging the Southern California Regional Transportation District commissioned a new study, which recommended a 250-mile rail system, projecting that its creation would boost the transit share of trips to and from downtown from the current 38 percent to 65 percent. This plan, together with a proposal for local sales tax financing of the local share, was put to the vot-

---

25. MARTA also agreed to build a spur from the east-west line to serve the Proctor Creek area, particularly Perry Homes, a large public housing project, once the basic system was complete. In later years MARTA balked at fulfilling this commitment on the ground that its studies showed patronage would be low. Local activists persisted, and a portion of the spur was finally constructed in 1992. It was never completed, however, and the Perry Homes project itself, which had become one of the city's least desirable, was demolished in 2001. At this writing, in 2002, the Atlanta Housing Authority is seeking to develop a mixed-use community on the site. See Stone (1989, p. 168); Joe Dolman, "Proctor Creek Bill Comes Due," *Atlanta Journal-Constitution*, August 20, 1986, p. A14; and David Pendered, "Broad Renewal Planned for Perry Homes," *Atlanta Journal-Constitution*, April 1, 2002, p. F1.

ers in 1974. The campaign for a "yes" vote was, as usual, led and mainly funded by downtown business interests.[26] A group of mayors and chambers of commerce from Pasadena, Glendale, Beverly Hills, and various smaller communities, however, organized a modest opposition campaign, charging that the proposal was "regressive, inflationary [and] for the benefit of major corporations along Wilshire Boulevard and downtown Los Angeles."[27] The proposition failed, as did a slightly different proposal initiated by County Supervisor Baxter Ward two years later.

Los Angeles rail advocates now shifted away from the idea of securing authorization for an entire regional system toward pursuit of a "starter" line. They could not agree, however, on which line this should be. Mayor Bradley and the Los Angeles Chamber of Commerce supported a route heading west from downtown under Wilshire Boulevard, the nation's densest corridor west of Chicago, then extending north to Hollywood and the San Fernando Valley. Numerous suburban officials preferred a north-south line, however, running from the San Fernando Valley through downtown to Long Beach, mainly on existing at-grade rights-of-way; and they counted among their number U.S. Representative Glenn Anderson, a Long Beach Democrat who was a senior member of the House Public Works Committee. There were, as well, proposals for a downtown people mover, for improved bus service, for the construction of HOV lanes, and for transportation demand management programs designed to encourage carpooling.

At the behest of Los Angeles rail advocates, in 1976 the state legislature created the Los Angeles County Transportation Commission (LACTC), a body charged solely with developing a rail transit plan for the region. Commission member Kenneth Hahn, who was also a county supervisor representing low-income neighborhoods on the south side of Los Angeles, now took the lead in crafting a package that would include something for all of the region's active transit constituencies. He proposed that the commission seek a half-cent sales tax increase for transit (which would raise about $225 million a year), with the understandings that (1) the top two rail priorities would be lines from downtown out the Wilshire corridor (the Red Line) and to Long Beach (the Blue Line); (2) a portion of the new revenue would be used to lower bus fares immediately (with only a three-year guarantee, however); and (3) one quarter of the new revenue would be distributed to localities for transportation improvements of their own choice. With modest amendments this package was put to the voters in November

26. Whitt (1982, pp. 97–99).
27. Whitt (1982, p. 98).

1980, along with a conceptual map showing the corridors in which the new rail lines would be located. It received endorsements from the Los Angeles Taxpayers Association (an organization of nearly 250 of the county's major business and civic leaders), the city's two daily newspapers, the AFL-CIO, and the League of Women Voters, but the city's business leadership—discouraged in the wake of its previous defeats—chose not to campaign aggressively this time, spending only $21,000 overall. The measure passed nonetheless with 54 percent of the vote, attracting its strongest support from inner-city residents (attracted by the immediate bus fare reduction) and those along the proposed rail corridors.[28]

The Impact of Interstate Transfers

The 1973 interstate transfer provision, allowing states to reallocate funds long earmarked for interstate highway projects to alternative highway or transit projects, also changed the political and planning dynamics in several locales, ultimately providing more than $6.8 billion in funding for more than 50 transit projects, most notably in the Washington, D.C. ($2.1 billion), Boston ($1.5 billion), Chicago ($882 million), New York City ($848 million), Baltimore ($485 million), and Philadelphia ($354 million) urban areas.[29] The Boston region, for example, used it to fund an extension of its Red Line subway and a relocation of its elevated Orange Line as a depressed facility paralleled and in places covered by a linear park. Interstate transfers also provided about one quarter of the funding for Washington, D.C.'s long-discussed subway system.

In Portland, Oregon, the availability of the transfer option heightened a long-standing dispute about the proposed Mt. Hood Freeway, which was to provide access to the city from its eastern suburbs—and take 1 percent of Portland's housing stock. Mayor Neil Goldschmidt, elected in 1972 on a platform calling for neighborhood preservation and downtown renewal, seized on the enactment of interstate transfer to urge a reconsideration of options in this corridor. Ultimately he brokered a deal in which the state agreed to trade in the Mt. Hood funding for 140 alternative road and transit improvements. On the transit side, the central agreement was to build either a busway or rail line in an abandoned freight railroad corridor running from downtown Portland (parallel to the Banfield Freeway) east to Multnomah County.

28. For more on the 1970s transit debates in Los Angeles, see Richmond (2003, ch. 6); Wachs (1996, pp. 136–39); and Fulton (1997, pp. 136–39).
29. Federal Transit Administration, "Statistical Summaries, 1999" (2000, table 60, fig. 60A).

The Light Rail Renaissance

In many cities too thinly populated for rail rapid transit to seem feasible, the growth in federal funding after 1970 spurred interest in "light rail" transit (LRT)—essentially the modern form of streetcar service. The main technological difference between "light" and "heavy" rail systems was that the former drew power from overhead wires while the latter used an electrified third rail at ground level. Consequently, light rail vehicles could run on existing streets whereas heavy rail vehicles needed exclusive grade-separated corridors. Where light rail did run on existing rights-of-way, its per-mile capital costs might be as little as one-tenth those of heavy rail systems. LRT systems with at-grade intersections, on the other hand, tended to run at lower average speeds than heavy rail systems, and thus were likely to have considerably higher labor costs for each mile of service.

LRT plans invariably assumed that the federal government (or in the case of San Diego, the state) would provide most of the required capital funding and that farebox revenues would cover all (or nearly all) operating costs. While the politics varied from place to place, the support coalitions generally included downtown business interests, environmental and anti-highway (neighborhood-based) groups, and local transit operators. Advocates maintained that LRT vehicles provided greater capacity than buses at comparable labor costs, that trains would attract more riders than buses because they were inherently more appealing, that they were less polluting, and that train stations (unlike bus stops) were likely to spur nearby redevelopment. To construction interests specifically, they argued as well that light rail projects generated far more work than bus service improvements.[30] Critics, on the other hand, insisted that buses using dedicated rights-of-way could provide all the benefits of light rail at far less cost and might attract even greater ridership if they fanned out at either end of the busway to serve more dispersed origins and destinations.

This debate was played out in Portland after the region's leaders agreed to build transit in the Banfield Freeway corridor. A task force established by Governor Tom McCall concluded that light rail in this corridor would generate 59,700 daily riders while a busway would produce 71,100. On this basis, the local council of governments and state Department of Transportation endorsed the busway option. Environmental and neighborhood activists were adamant in favor of rail, however, and were joined by two important allies. Tri-Met, the regional transit operator (formed in the late 1960s from the vestiges of several private bus firms), maintained that trains

30. See Richmond (2001b).

would have lower operating costs than buses and that it was bad public relations to place an uncongested busway adjacent to a congested highway. Additionally, commissioners in Multnomah County—believing that rail was more likely to spur desired development than a dedicated busway—threatened to sue unless the state considered rail in the corridor. This combination turned the tide. The task force, Mayor Goldschmidt, and Governor McCall all opted for rail in the end, and it was built with interstate transfer funding.[31]

Buffalo also turned to light rail after federal transit officials rejected its proposal for a heavy rail line as too expensive. As studies indicated very limited patronage potential, the rationale for this line gradually evolved from congestion relief to its alleged value as a spur to revitalization of the city's ailing central business district, and this argument carried the day.[32] Sacramento, San Diego, St. Louis, San Jose, Pittsburgh, and Houston all began preparing downtown-oriented plans for light rail in this period as well, while Miami and Detroit developed plans for downtown people movers.[33]

Disappointing Results

Even as these projects moved forward, however, evidence was accumulating that rail investment had very limited potential to affect automobile usage. Only about one-third of those using San Francisco's new BART system, for example, had previously driven, and they were replaced on parallel highways within months by motorists who had previously been deterred by congestion.[34] Nationally, reported transit ridership did rise from 7.3 billion annual trips in 1970 to about 8.3 billion riders in 1980, with all the increase coming at the end of the decade. At least 40 percent of the reported increase, however, was due to two changes in the way the data were reported, and most of the remainder occurred on buses (see table 6-1).[35] Transit usage

31. Edner and Arrington (1985, chs. 3, 4). For a more detailed account of Tri-Met's formation and its link to long-standing efforts by the business community and public officials to improve both highway and transit access to downtown Portland, see Bianco (1994).

32. See Paaswell and Berechman (1982).

33. In an early 1980s survey of 12 U.S. and Canadian cities with rail projects that were either recently built, under construction, or planned, Robert Cervero found that officials in eight—San Diego, Buffalo, Pittsburgh, Portland, Toronto, Sacramento, San Jose, and Orange County—reported that their projects were part of larger downtown redevelopment efforts. See Cervero (1984, p. 140).

34. Webber (1979, p. 102).

35. While some of the increase may have been caused by new spending and high gasoline prices in the late 1970s, a large share was also due to changes in the way riders were counted. Commuter rail was first included in the transit data in 1975; this change accounted for about 29 percent of the ridership increase between 1970 and 1980. Until the late 1970s, moreover, rapid transit patrons who transferred from one train to another were counted as making one

actually declined, moreover, by the measure of passenger *miles* traveled, and the transit share of overall urban travel continued to fall (see table 6-5). Total operating costs (in constant dollars) rose more than 16 times as rapidly as farebox receipts during the 1970s, moreover: 131 percent versus 8 percent (see table 6-6). About half this cost increase could be attributed to inflation; the remainder was due mainly to a surge in labor costs.[36] The meager growth in farebox revenue reflected two factors: intense political resistance to fare increases, even to keep up with inflation, and transit operators' own belief that such increases were self-defeating—because they tended to be largely offset by patronage losses.[37]

Construction costs also proved higher than anticipated. BART, for example, cost more than twice as much as projected at the time of its 1962 referendum. The first phases of the Washington, D.C., and Atlanta systems exceeded their estimates by even wider margins. Again inflation was in part to blame, but in constant dollars the Washington subway cost 83 percent more than estimated while Atlanta's cost 58 percent more than estimated.[38]

Finally, the focus on rail typically produced far greater per-trip subsidies for suburban commuters than less affluent inner-city transit patrons.[39] The gap was particularly noteworthy because transit operating subsidies were rarely financed by progressive taxes. Melvin Webber calculated that BART's funding system, which relied on sales and property taxes, ensured that the lowest-income households paid a higher share of their income to support the

---

trip, but thereafter they were counted as making a separate trip on each vehicle; this seems to have accounted for another 24 percent of the increase. A substantial growth in reported bus ridership between 1975 and 1980 accounted for the remaining increase. It is unclear whether some of this was also due to changes in reporting methods (most notably, by reporting transfer bus trips as multiple trips), but the overall increase from 1975 to 1980 seems anomalous. Urban areas were sprawling, auto trip distances were increasing, and the transit category was expanded to include commuter rail, which involves much longer trips than other forms of transit—yet if these figures are to be believed, transit trips on average became 15 percent shorter. The abrupt, dramatic ridership increase (14 percent) reported for this period only briefly reversed a long-term decline. Over the next 15 years transit ridership resumed its downward trend—until another reversal occurred in the late 1990s. See tables 6-1 and 6-6. Also see American Public Transit Association (1978, p. 26; 1987, table 9).

36. See Urban Mass Transit Administration, "The Status of the Nation's Local Mass Transportation: Performance and Conditions" (1987, pp. 83–97); Lave (1981); and Meyer and Gómez-Ibáñez (1981, p. 49).

37. Fare increases did generally yield some new revenue, but numerous studies found long-term elasticities in excess of 0.5, meaning that a 10 percent fare increase would typically generate a falloff in patronage of 5 percent or more over time. See P. B. Goodwin (1992, pp. 160–61).

38. See Pickrell (1990, table 6-1, p. 62).

39. See Pucher (1981); and Altshuler (1979, pp. 277–302).

Table 6-5. Urban Surface Transportation, Passenger Miles[a]

Billions of miles, except as noted

Year	Transit	Auto	Transit share (percent)
1945	130	245	34.7
1950	90	406	18.2
1955	60	518	10.4
1960	48	606	7.3
1965	43	807	5.1
1970	41	1,179	3.4
1975	38	1,333	2.8
1980	37[b]	1,431	2.5
1985	38	1,658	2.2
1990	38	1,975	1.9
1995	38	2,199	1.7
2000	45	2,337	1.9

Sources: Transit data for 1945–75: Altshuler (1979, p. 22; see also pp. 478–79 for more on methodology). Transit data for 1980–2000: Urban Mass Transit Administration, "National Urban Mass Transportation Statistics, Second Annual Report, Section 15 Reporting System" (1982, pp. I:59–63), "National Urban Mass Transportation Statistics: 1985 Reporting Year" (1988, p. 71); Federal Transit Administration, "National Transit Summaries and Trends for the 1990 Section 15 Report Year" (1992, pp. iv, 29–34), "National Transit Summaries and Trends for the 1995 National Transit Database Report Year" (1996, pp. 14–17), "Annual Report on New Starts Proposed Allocation of Funds for Fiscal Year 2002" (2001, table 28); and American Public Transit Association (1987, table 10). See also American Public Transit Association (2001, table 30). Highway data: authors' calculations from Federal Highway Administration, "Highway Statistics Summary to 1995" (1997), "Highway Statistics, 2000" (2001, table VM-1, VM-2), "Report No. 1, Automobile Occupancy, 1969: Nationwide Personal Transportation Study" (1972, table 1), "Report 6, Vehicle Occupancy, 1977: Nationwide Personal Transportation Survey" (1981, p. 1), "Personal Travel in the United States, 1983–1984: Nationwide Personal Transportation Survey" (1986, table 8-7), "National Personal Transportation Survey Databook, 1990," vol. 2 (1993, table 7-7), "National Personal Transportation Survey, 1995: Summary of Travel Trends" (1999, table 15).

a. The Federal Highway Administration reports vehicle miles of travel and average vehicle occupancy. Average occupancy, as reported by successive Nationwide Personal Transportation Surveys, declined from 2.2 in 1969 to 1.55 in 1995. Based on trend lines between surveys, the estimated ratios of passenger to vehicle mileage used in this table are 2.15 in 1970; 1.92 in 1975; 1.76 in 1980; 1.66 in 1985; 1.62 in 1990; 1.55 in 1995; and 1.48 in 2000.

b. The American Public Transit Association reports slightly higher figures for transit from 1980–2000. Even if accepted, however, these would increase the transit share of urban passenger mileage by just 0.1–0.2 percent.

system than the region's highest-income households. "Clearly," he concluded, "the poor are paying and the rich are riding."[40]

Transit Aid under Attack

By the late 1970s the combination of rising costs and disappointing results was generating some reappraisal, even in liberal circles, of federal transit aid. President Jimmy Carter, for example, wrote in 1977 (in a leaked memo): "Many rapid transit systems are grossly overdesigned. We should insist on off-street parking, one-way streets, special bus lanes, and surface rail-bus as

40. Webber (1979, p. 115). Also see Merewitz (1973); and Hall (1982).

Table 6-6. Transit Operating Expenditures and Funding, 1950–99[a]

Billions of 2002 dollars, except as noted

Year	Total	Fare box receipts	Fare box share (percent)	Federal share (percent)	State and local government share (percent)
1950	2.9	2.95	101	0	0
1955	2.7	3.03	112	0	0
1960	3.3	2.88	89	0	11
1965	3.7	3.59	97	0	3
1970	4.7	4.30	91	-1	11
1975	7.2	3.88	54	9	37
1980	11.0	4.62	42	19	39
1985	15.0	6.34	42	6	52
1990	17.0	6.64	39	4	57
1995	20.4	7.34	36	4	60
1999	20.8	8.10	39	1	60

Sources: See table 6-2.

a. Figures are for the fiscal year ending in the year shown. Constant-dollar spending is based on the Bureau of Economic Affairs' GDP price deflator.

preferable alternatives to subways. In some urban areas, no construction at all would be required."[41] The program's political base remained firm, however, until 1981 when President Reagan assumed office. The Reagan administration declared transit aid one of its prime targets for domestic spending reduction. David Stockman, Reagan's first director of the Office of Management and Budget, later wrote:

> Mass transit operating subsidies were a special abomination, costing [federal] taxpayers over $1 billion per year. Every study showed that the only effect of these gifts from the federal larder was to raise the already monopoly-level wages of local transit workers—or to reduce arbitrarily the transit fares paid by rich and poor alike. Similarly, the multi-billion dollar transit capital grants were encouraging the construction of new subway systems all over the country, when there was no hope that these economic white elephants could ever pay for even their operating costs, let alone the billions it cost to build them. But with 80 to 90 percent "free" financing from Washington, city fathers and chambers of commerce types were tripping over each other to get in line at Uncle Sam's money kitchen. . . . [So] if there was any single clear-cut case of what the Reagan Revolution required, it was dumping this vast local transportation pork barrel.[42]

41. Smerk (1991, pp. 148–49).
42. Stockman (1987, p. 149)

San Francisco's Bay Area Rapid Transit system, which opened in 1972, was designed to bring suburban workers into the downtown core. Subsequent analyses showed that the system had at most negligible effects on automobile usage and patterns of regional development. Credit: Courtesy of Bechtel Corp.

Reagan called upon Congress in 1981 to eliminate transit operating subsidies, sharply reduce transit capital grants, and place a moratorium on new rail starts. The national transit coalition mobilized quickly to resist, aided by the fact that Democrats controlled the House of Representatives; and they were successful in blunting the new administration's attack. In the end, Congress cut back transit aid by 20 percent in fiscal 1982, Reagan's first full year in office, mainly on the capital side. It neither reduced operating assistance significantly nor placed any special constraints on new rail starts. Indeed, it instructed the Urban Mass Transit Administration (UMTA) to begin funding planned new rail projects in Portland, Miami, Baltimore, and Buffalo, downtown people movers in Detroit and Miami, and planning studies in six more cities.[43] These instructions reflected a combination of local lobbying on behalf of the projects in question and the position of powerful members of Congress—such as Republican Mark Hatfield of Ore-

43. "Congress Reaches Agreement on Major Construction Cuts," *Engineering News-Record*, June 11, 1981, p. 17.

gon, who chaired the Senate Appropriations Committee,[44] and Democratic Representative William Lehman of Miami, who chaired the House Appropriations Committee's subcommittee on transportation.

In 1982, President Reagan returned to the fray with a proposal for states and localities to assume full responsibility for transit (and most highway) projects, and to receive in return some federal gas tax revenue—less, however, than the total of grants to be phased out. William Niskanen, who served on Reagan's Council of Economic Advisors at the time, later wrote:

> [The proposal] received no support from the state and local officials because they preferred federal money, especially in the form of block grants, to raising additional funds from their own voters. The proposal also received no support in Congress, which preferred the illusion of doing good with federal money to confronting colleagues and potential opponents in state capitals. For these reasons, the proposal died as quickly as it was formulated and it was never renewed.[45]

Even as President Reagan was seeking to curtail surface transportation spending (though not to the same degree) in 1982, Secretary of Transportation Drew Lewis was lobbying for a five-cent a gallon increase in the federal gasoline tax to finance increased expenditures. Lewis and Representative James Howard, chair of the House Public Works Committee, agreed that one cent of the increase, which would raise about $1 billion a year, would be allocated for transit. With this commitment, Lewis was able to assemble a very broad coalition, extending from highway contractors to the American Public Transit Association, the U.S. Conference of Mayors, and the Congressional Black Caucus.[46]

Within the administration Lewis argued that increased capital spending for highway and transit purposes would create needed jobs in the ongoing recession. Reagan's economic advisers viewed this as a baseless argument for a permanent tax and spending increase, however, and the president himself remained adamantly opposed to all new taxes—at least until the Democrats gained 26 House seats in the November midterm election. Then he abruptly

44. See Howard Kurtz, "Budget Knife Only Nicks Road and Harbor Projects," *Washington Post,* January 26, 1982, p. A1.

45. Niskanen (1988, p. 59).

46. See David Broder, "Invisible Budget," *Washington Post,* May 30, 1982, p. C7; Rochelle Stanfield, "Mass Transit Lobby Wins a Big One, but Its Battles Are Not Over Yet," *National Journal,* January 29, 1983, p. 224; and Jo Mannies and Phil Sutin, "$1 Million Reported Approved for Streetcar Plan," *St. Louis Post-Dispatch,* January 5, 1983, p. 1.

changed his mind.[47] In December the lame-duck Congress enacted the tax increase as part of a general four-year reauthorization of federal highway and transit programs. The new legislation authorized more than $4 billion a year in transit spending, nearly the level that had prevailed at the end of the Carter administration.

Although two-thirds of the new transit spending was to be allocated by formula (and available for either capital or operating purposes), the law also authorized roughly $1 billion a year for discretionary capital grants. With the Democrats back in control of both houses of Congress and with local demands far exceeding authorized expenditures,[48] a fierce struggle now developed between Congress and the administration for control of this money. The Urban Mass Transit Administration sought to rank projects on the basis of formulas that it considered economically rational, assigning greatest weight to per-passenger costs and the willingness of regions to bear substantial costs themselves—that is, more than the minimum shares required by law. On this basis, Ralph Stanley, who became UMTA administrator in mid-1983, proposed that Congress shift money from proposed new rail starts in Los Angeles, San Diego, St. Louis, Miami, and Jacksonville to several rail renovation projects and bus system expansions in other locales.[49]

Not surprisingly, advocates of the low-ranked projects—including many within the president's own party—sharply disagreed. Senator John Danforth (R-Mo.), for example, charged that UMTA's St. Louis analysis was based on an "unworkable and unrealistic" bus plan. In focusing on ridership alone, he added, UMTA had totally ignored the multiplier effects that the rail project would have on the local economy.[50] In this he echoed the St. Louis project's EIS, which argued that light rail would have "more potential for economic development" than buses and would improve the city's image, thereby making it easier to "compete for conventions and tourists."[51]

47. See Niskanen (1988, p. 51).

48. In the mid-1980s *Business Week* magazine calculated that the total cost of the proposed new rail systems for which campaigns were in progress was more than $11 billion, with each group hoping that the federal government would pay 75 percent of its project costs. In addition, champions of the existing systems in Washington, D.C., San Francisco, Boston, Atlanta, Chicago, Miami, New York, Philadelphia, Cleveland, and Baltimore were lobbying for projects with an estimated total cost of $12 billion. See "Mass Transit: The Expensive Dream," *Business Week*, August 28, 1984, pp. 62–69.

49. For a detailed description of UMTA's efforts, see Kennedy (1984).

50. "Danforth Supports Light Rail Transit System," *United Press International*, July 31, 1984.

51. Department of Transportation and others, "St. Louis Central/Airport Corridor: St. Louis City and County, Missouri, and East St. Louis and St. Clair County, Illinois: Alternatives, Analysis, and Draft Environmental Impact Statement for Major Transit Capital Investments" (1984, pp. 38–39).

Rail advocates in other regions made essentially the same case, and Congress proved receptive to it. Throughout the mid-1980s Congress appropriated larger sums for transit than the Reagan administration sought and earmarked large sums for specific rail projects—such as those in Miami and St. Louis—that UMTA opposed as costing far more than their benefits could justify.

Stanley did succeed in imposing two policies designed to limit federal exposure. First, he required that transit agencies build projects in usable segments. (Previously, they had often built disconnected parts so as to maximize the pressure for additional funding.) In Los Angeles, for example, officials agreed to divide their proposed $3.3 billion, 18.4-mile "starter" subway—the Red Line—into several parts, with federal funding initially directed to a 4.4-mile segment that they insisted would be valuable even if nothing further were built. Second, he required as a condition of federal aid that localities sign "full-funding" agreements pledging that they, not the federal government, would be responsible for cost overruns.

The Reagan administration and Congress had one more major battle over transit aid when highway and transit programs were again up for reauthorization in 1987. President Reagan vetoed the measure sent to him by Congress on the grounds that it authorized too much money and was packed with earmarks for wasteful pork barrel projects. On the transit side, the administration had recommended capital grant spending of about $1.2 billion a year over the projected four-year life of the act. Congress, instead, had authorized more than $4 billion a year. In his veto message, the president singled out two projects as particularly egregious and illustrative of his general argument: Boston's Central Artery/Tunnel and the Los Angeles subway. As discussed in chapter 4, Congress overrode the veto, with the decisive vote coming in the Senate, where 13 Republicans joined every Democrat in voting against the president. At least seven of these Republicans were from states that stood to receive significant amounts of transit aid from the bill.[52]

Competing for Capital Grants

With virtually all capital funding now earmarked by Congress, local transit advocates had to mount legislative as well as executive branch lobbying campaigns if they hoped to compete. The Los Angeles regional transit district, for example, paid a variety of lobbyists more than $1 million between 1983 and 1986 in its effort to secure federal aid for its proposed

52. The seven were Pete Wilson of California, John Danforth and Kit Bond of Missouri, Arlen Specter and John Heinz of Pennsylvania, Alfonse D'Amato of New York, and Lowell Weicker of Connecticut.

$3.3-billion Red Line, which was to run from downtown to North Holly-wood.[53] Downtown property owners joined with engineering and construction firms that stood to benefit from subway contracts to form the Los Angeles Transportation Coalition. This group brought important members of Congress to Los Angeles, where they received generous speaking fees, campaign contributions, or both.[54]

It was imperative for local rail advocates to maintain the appearance of consensus, because senior elected officials tended to defer action when confronted with local controversies. One consequence in Los Angeles was relocation of the second segment of the proposed starter subway line, which became a far less optimal route from the standpoint of attracting passengers.[55] As originally conceived, this segment was to run for about five miles under Wilshire Boulevard, the most densely developed corridor west of the Mississippi River, before turning north toward the San Fernando Valley. In the mid-1980s, however, homeowners in a mid-Wilshire neighborhood (Hancock Park) objected that the line would stimulate too much development in their vicinity and might expose them to more crime by facilitating travel from low-income areas. Residents and businesses along Fairfax Avenue, where the plan called for particularly massive cut-and-cover construction, protested the interim disruption that this would entail. Lew Wasserman, chair of the MCA Corporation and a renowned local power broker, objected that the proposed route bypassed MCA's rapidly growing Universal City entertainment and retail complex.

Then in 1985 a major explosion occurred at a (nonsubway) construction site in the mid-Wilshire district, killing 22 people. Subsequent investigation revealed an underground pocket of methane gas, a legacy of the years before World War II when much of the area had been working oil fields. Though technical experts concluded that future problems could easily be avoided, opponents of the Wilshire alignment seized on the methane issue to argue that implementation of the current plan would be unacceptably dangerous. Representative Henry Waxman, a powerful Democrat who represented the area, took up their cause and secured a provision in the 1986 transporta-

53. These lobbyists included Stuart Spencer, who had been a senior Reagan campaign strategist, and Mickey Kantor, a prominent Democrat who went on to head the Commerce Department in the Clinton administration from 1996 to 1997. See Rich Connell and Tracy Wood, "RTD Funds Vast Lobbying Effort with Bus Revenues," *Los Angeles Times*, February 15, 1987, part 1, p. 1.

54. See Rich Connell, "House Debate on Metro Rail Funds Stalls," *Los Angeles Times*, November 15, 1985, part 1, p. 1; and Lionel Van Deerlin, "L.A. Misses the Big Red Cars," *San Diego Union-Tribune*, May 17, 1984, p. B11.

55. This account is primarily drawn from Taylor and Kim (1999).

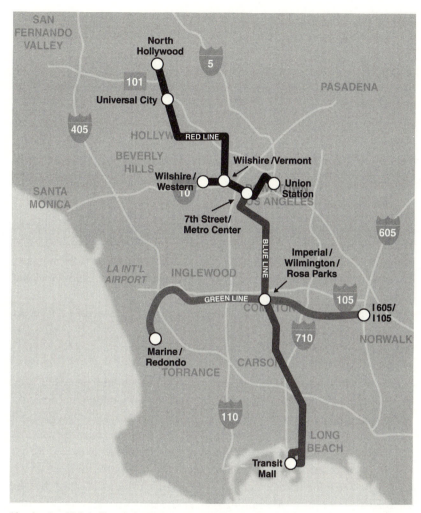

After decades of failed efforts, in the 1980s Los Angeles County began to construct a rail transit system. Major components include the Red Line subway and the above-ground Blue and Green light-rail lines. Credit: Robert B. Levers.

tion appropriations bill banning construction of the line until local officials could prove that an earthquake would not trigger an underground methane explosion. When Congress did eventually approve funding for the line, it did so with a proviso (inserted by Waxman) that it could not pass through the mid-Wilshire area. Instead, it would now turn north before it reached the neighborhoods in which substantial opposition had emerged, and it would serve the Universal City area. Because the new alignment was through less dense areas, it had considerably lower patronage potential than the original routing, but it faced no significant opposition—and that was what counted politically.

In a similar vein, localities frequently minimized controversy by siting new transit lines in existing rail or freeway corridors, chosen for their availability rather than their optimality from a patronage standpoint. This strategy was used, for example, in Portland and Sacramento and for portions of Los Angeles's new Blue Line (from downtown to Long Beach). Though federal transit officials expressed concern in each case, they ultimately let the lines proceed as planned.

States and Localities in the Lead

Though Congress prevailed in most specific transit battles during the 1980s, the Reagan administration succeeded in reversing the overall trend toward increased federal funding for transit. Such aid, adjusted for inflation, declined by 23 percent from 1980 to 1990. States and to a lesser extent localities moved into the breach, raising their combined transit expenditures by more than 200 percent in real terms over the decade. Whereas federal transit spending had been nearly 50 percent larger than spending by states and localities in 1980, it was less than half as great in 1990 (see tables 6-2 and 6-3).

The extraordinary growth of state and local spending reflected a rising sense of urgency, but the battles to achieve it were commonly hard-fought nonetheless. In the Philadelphia region, for example, Southeastern Pennsylvania Transportation Authority (SEPTA) general manager Louis Gambaccini developed a 10-year, $4.5-billion capital program requiring a funding source that SEPTA could pledge as backing for revenue bonds. First he sought a regional sales tax. When suburban legislators blocked that, he pursued state gasoline tax funding. Under the state's constitution, gas tax revenue could be expended only for highway purposes, but Gambaccini was not deterred. He mobilized a campaign to amend the constitution, organizing the Southeastern Pennsylvania Area Coalition for Transportation (ACT), composed of business, labor union, civic, religious, and consumer groups. ACT's cochairs were a white insurance executive and a black minister. Polls indicated, however, that this proposal would fail if put to state voters in a referendum. SEPTA and its allies therefore shifted tactics again, toward straight legislative logrolling. Philadelphia-area representatives agreed to support tax increases to balance the state's budget and finance increased highway spending in return for an assured revenue flow of $120 million a year to SEPTA. (The most significant source, in the end, was an increase in the state tax on public utility property.) Greater Philadelphia First (GPF), an association of the city's top business leaders, and its member companies spent $500,000 on a public relations campaign in support of this package, while ACT mobilized a telephone campaign to individual legislators. The most controversial component of the package, a tax bill, passed narrowly in the end, with Philadelphia-area legislators—who voted more than 3-1 in favor—providing the margin of victory.[56]

SEPTA's strategy and success were paralleled in numerous other regions, though the details varied. New York's Metropolitan Transportation Authority (MTA), for example, secured dedicated funding from a state mortgage recording tax, a tax on petroleum products sold in the state (other than home-heating oil), and a "temporary" surcharge on certain franchise taxes. Chicago's Regional Transportation Authority (RTA) obtained dedicated funding from a regional sales tax, which now provides about half of its operating funds and about one-third of its capital funds.[57]

New Data, Old Controversies

Rail transit ridership (including commuter rail) rose from 2.5 billion riders a year in 1980 to 3.4 billion in 2000. Declines in bus ridership offset more than 60 percent of this gain, however, with the result that overall transit patronage increased by little more than 5 percent (see table 6-1). The decrease in bus ridership in part reflected population decline in older cities, but it was also attributable to transit management decisions. Transit agencies routinely eliminated parallel bus routes as they opened new rail lines, while rerouting many others (to the detriment of some passengers) to feed rail stations.[58]

Most of the post-1980 gains in rail transit ridership, furthermore, occurred in two metropolitan areas: New York and Washington, D.C. In the former, bus patronage surged as well, and it declined only slightly in the latter. In contrast, more modest increases in rail transit ridership in San Francisco, Atlanta, and Baltimore were more than offset by declines in bus patronage, and rail usage actually fell in Chicago and Philadelphia.

In a study of eight new rail lines—four of them heavy rail, four light rail—Don Pickrell found that costs were generally higher than estimated, and patronage lower. More significantly, the total cost for each new passenger

56. See McLaughlin (1999, pp. 511–47).
57. Authors' calculations from Federal Transit Administration, "Annual Report on New Starts Proposed Allocation of Funds for Fiscal Year 2002" (2001).
58. See Richmond (2001b, pp. 159–60).

attracted to transit was extremely high—ranging from $9.49 in Portland to $34.64 in Pittsburgh. For example, Portland's new light rail line, which opened in 1986, cost 54 percent more (in constant dollars) to build than its planners had estimated, had annual operating costs 45 percent greater than forecast, and carried fewer than half the riders projected. Sacramento was a partial exception in that its capital cost came in only 13 percent above estimate (in constant dollars) and its annual operating costs were actually 10 percent below, but its ridership was 71 percent lower than projected. Consequently, its total cost per passenger was more than four times as great as originally forecast.[59]

Light rail advocates typically pointed, on the other hand, to a success story: the light rail line between downtown San Diego and the Mexican border (at Tijuana). This line, which opened in 1981, had significantly lower operating costs and greater patronage than the bus lines it replaced. Consequently, it was recovering more than 70 percent of its operating cost from the farebox, nearly twice the average of the San Diego region as a whole.[60] Critics maintained that even this was less of a success than it appeared, however. José Gómez-Ibáñez calculated that ridership growth on this route was merely in line with that of other bus lines in the rapidly growing southern portions of San Diego. Though the trolley service had lower operating costs than the bus service it replaced, moreover, it had much higher capital costs, entirely financed by taxpayers.[61]

Rail systems in Portland, St. Louis, Sacramento, and San Jose also reported lower costs or higher farebox recovery ratios than their bus systems. As in San Diego, however, these comparisons failed to pit rail performance against equivalent bus lines or to take account of policy decisions to reroute bus lines to feed rail transit. In St. Louis, for example, light rail covered 39 percent of its costs from fares in the 1996 fiscal year, while buses covered only 21 percent, but transit fares overall covered a lower proportion of system costs than in 1993, before light rail service began.[62]

---

59. Pickrell could not identify common sources of the forecasting errors he reported, noting that the most obvious candidates, such as project delays and reductions in downtown employment, generally explained "very little of the typically wide margins separating forecast and actual levels of cost and ridership." See Pickrell (1990, tables S-1, 3-4). For a summary version, see Pickrell (1992).

60. See Cervero (1984, p. 146); and Gómez-Ibáñez (1985, pp. 340–42).

61. Gómez-Ibáñez (1985, p. 349).

62. Richmond (2001b, p. 168).

Transit's (Political) Momentum Resumes (1989–Present)

Despite such critiques, the public seemed to embrace advocates' arguments for transit investment. In the late 1980s, for example, California voters approved two statewide bond referendums for transit, and Los Angeles voters approved an increase in the local sales tax for transit in 1990. Meanwhile, Los Angeles regional air quality planners developed an ambitious plan to combine massive rail transit investment in the region with employer regulation to decrease the share of workers driving alone to work. In keeping with these plans, the L.A. County Transportation Commission in 1992 approved a $183-billion, 30-year plan calling for 400 miles of new rapid transit and commuter rail service as well as major bus improvements.[63]

In Portland, Oregon, transit advocates claimed that contrary to Pickrell's analysis, the new east side light rail line was a tremendous success because it carried substantially more people than had been predicted in revised (more cautious) ridership forecasts made just before it opened. They argued as well that the line had both strengthened downtown Portland and helped spur the revitalization of a nearby warehouse district.[64] Local elected officials, transit agency managers, and environmental and community activists began to push for a long-discussed second line on the west side.[65]

Rail critics' arguments prevailed, at least for a while, in Dallas, where the Dallas Area Rapid Transit (DART) agency proposed a $2.6-billion, 91-mile rail system to be funded with a mix of federal aid and local receipts from a proposed sales tax increase. The agency published highly optimistic ridership forecasts, but a citizens' group discovered and forced the release of much more sober internal analyses, which concluded that the rail system would attract barely more patronage than the existing bus system. DART fought back, but its proposal for the sales tax increase met defeat at the polls. DART was not finished, however; it developed a scaled-down light rail proposal, with the local match funded on a pay-as-you-go basis with revenue from existing taxes. This option did not require a referendum.[66]

Houston was perhaps the most notable example of a region decisively rejecting rail. Throughout the mid-1980s local controversy raged about a

63. For more on these transportation plans and their potential to affect air quality in the Los Angeles area, see Wachs (1996, pp. 138–43); Scott (1993); Bae (1993); and Fulton (1997, pp. 142–50).

64. Arrington (1995, pp. 44–45).

65. Adler and Edner (1990, pp. 100–102).

66. Kain (1990, p. 184).

Portland, Oregon, has emphasized light rail as an instrument to constrain sprawl and revitalize its downtown.
Credit: Courtesy of Tri-County Metropolitan Transportation District of Oregon.

transit plan developed by the city's chamber of commerce. In 1983 local voters rejected a $2.4-billion version of this plan calling for an 18.5-mile heavy rail system, even though no new taxes were required to finance its construction (a sales tax increase for transit having been approved in 1978). Houston transit advocates then took a cue from the strategies used previously in Los Angeles and Atlanta. Led by Alan Kiepper, executive director of the local transit agency; developer Gerald D. Hines; and Robert Lanier, a prominent Houston businessman who had chaired the state Highway and Public Transportation Commission, they proposed a package with elements to satisfy diverse constituencies: $1 billion for a 20-mile light rail system but also $560 million for street improvements, $340 million for exclusive bus lanes, and $310 million for new buses and maintenance facilities. Reaching out effectively to black leaders, they ultimately obtained an important endorsement from the Metropolitan Organization, a coalition of inner-city churches and civic organizations. They also mounted an elaborate public relations campaign, funded by the largest downtown property owners and local construction companies. With these adjustments, the plan easily passed in early 1987.[67]

67. For a detailed account of the referendum, see Laird (1990).

Matters became more complicated later in the year, however, after Mayor Katherine Whitmire, a rail supporter, appointed Lanier to the local transit board. Concluding that bus improvements would make more sense for Houston than the proposed rail system, Lanier called on the transit agency's planners to develop a detailed all-bus alternative—and then persuaded the transit board to adopt it. Whitmire retaliated by dropping Lanier from the board when his term expired. Lanier then challenged Whitmire for the mayoralty in 1991, prevailed, and moved to implement the all-bus plan.[68] But that proved not the end of the story either. Rail plan backers continued to press their case and eventually, after Lanier himself left office, achieved a partial victory. In 2001 Houston's transit agency initiated construction of a $325-million, 7.5-mile light rail line.

Increased Federal Support

At the national level, the continuing strength of transit support was evident in the 1990 Clean Air Act Amendments (CAAA) and the 1991 Intermodal Surface Transportation Efficiency Act (ISTEA). Environmentalists and transit advocates secured provisions in the former measure preventing states from undertaking federally funded transportation projects inconsistent with their obligation to meet national air quality standards. Many environmentalists read this provision as requiring urban areas with air quality problems to reduce motor vehicle travel, a feat they believed could only be accomplished by developing alternatives such as rail transit.[69]

After enactment of the CAAA, environmentalists, transit officials, and other transit advocates formed two new umbrella organizations—the Surface Transportation Policy Project and Transit Now—to pursue favorable provisions in the upcoming highway-transit reauthorization bill. Their goals were to increase federal funding for transit (the Bush administration wished to increase highway spending but hold transit expenditures virtually level), secure broader authorization for states to use highway aid allocations for transit, and increase the local role in urban transportation decisionmaking. The Bush administration and highway interests resisted these proposals, but key congressional Democrats supported them—notably Senator Daniel Patrick Moynihan of New York, who chaired the Senate subcommittee

68. Academic analysts John Kain and Jonathan Richmond later concluded, in separate analyses, that Houston's all-bus system had proven notably more cost effective than rail transit systems built in other cities at about the same time. See Kain and Lui (1995); and Richmond (2001b).

69. See Yuhnke (1991, p. 247); and Garrett and Wachs (1996, pp. 20–22).

with responsibility for surface transport legislation, Representative Robert Roe of New Jersey, chair of the House Public Works Committee, and Representative Norman Mineta of California, a former mayor of San Jose who chaired the Public Works subcommittee on surface transportation.

Moynihan, who was broadly supportive of all the transit coalition's objectives, became the principal architect of the new act. Roe and Mineta (along with ranking Republicans on the House Public Works Committee) had more expansive funding objectives, though, and were eager to earmark new money for specific "demonstration" projects—many of them promised to members who had backed Roe's successful 1990 campaign to oust the committee's former chairman, Glenn Anderson. The final compromise satisfied all their aims. Moynihan crafted the main new policy elements and secured major project earmarks for his own state. House members secured a very large increase in spending together with hundreds of demonstration projects. Bush administration officials initially resisted the package that emerged but ultimately accepted most of it—primarily because a recession was under way by late 1991, when the measure finally passed, and the president was unwilling to take responsibility for an interruption of highway and transit programs.

ISTEA increased the annual authorization for transit spending by roughly one quarter, from $4 to $5 billion a year, and earmarked most of the capital grant component for projects desired by leaders of the key committees and of Congress as a whole.[70] It also granted states considerably greater flexibility to use highway aid for transit purposes and conferred substantial authority on metropolitan planning organizations in urban areas with 200,000 people or more. Finally, the law required states to use a portion of their highway aid for "transportation enhancements" such as scenic byways, bicycle trails, and historic preservation.

The transit provisions of both the CAAA and ISTEA were mainly driven by clean air concerns. After their enactment, however, more careful model-

70. Roe, for example, secured $635 million for a variety of rail projects in northern New Jersey. Mineta—along with Senator Alan Cranston, chair of the Senate Banking, Housing, and Urban Affairs Committee, which oversees transit legislation, and Glenn Anderson, whom Roe had ousted as committee chairman—secured $580 million for an extension of BART to the San Francisco International Airport and $695 million for an extension of the Red Line subway in Los Angeles. Representative Dan Rostenkowski, chair of the Ways and Means Committee, which had to reauthorize gas taxes that funded the bill, secured $260 million for a central area circulator project in Chicago. Moynihan, together with Alfonse D'Amato, the ranking Republican on the Senate Banking, Housing, and Urban Affairs Committee, obtained $464 million for a project connecting commuter and subway lines in Queens. See Stewart (1995, pp. 376–77).

ing indicated that rail transit investments were a particularly expensive way to achieve air quality goals—costing over $200,000 for each ton of hydrocarbon removed from the air, more than 10 times the cost of other measures such as improved vehicle emission testing and better timing systems for traffic lights.[71] Because these costs were so high and rail transit improvements generally had lead times of a decade or more (while the Clean Air Act focused on improvements within a shorter time period), most regions did not make transit a significant part of their clear air attainment efforts.[72]

Continuing Controversy in Los Angeles

The Los Angeles Metropolitan Transportation Agency (MTA) came into being in 1993 via a merger of the county transportation commission and regional transit district.[73] Affirming its commitment to the county commission's $183-billion, 30-year transit plan, it recruited Franklin White, a former New York State commissioner of transportation, to serve as executive director. White soon concluded that projected MTA revenues were insufficient to finance both this plan and existing services. He pressed to scale back the capital plan, but the board refused to go along—in part, apparently, because it was reluctant to anger constituents who had been promised rail lines and in part because construction, engineering, and consulting firms that stood to benefit from the rail construction program had rewarded board members with more than $500,000 in campaign contributions. (More lobbyists, it bears mention, had registered with the MTA than with the California state legislature.)[74]

The board decided, over the objections of White and most transit advocacy groups, to address the budget shortfall by raising bus fares. One result was a lawsuit alleging racial and ethnic discrimination brought by advocates for Los Angeles's minority communities.[75] The Los Angeles bus system was the nation's second largest, and in the mid-1990s it still accounted for more

71. Howitt and Altshuler (1999, p. 245).
72. Howitt and Moore (1999, pp. 80–83).
73. The MTA is governed by a 13-member board that includes the mayor of Los Angeles, the five Los Angeles County supervisors, three members appointed by the mayor, and four members selected by officials of the county's other 87 localities.
74. See David Willman and Eric Lichtblau, "MTA Contractors Dispense Thousands in Political Gifts," *Los Angeles Times*, December 27, 1994, p. A1; and Bill Boyarsky, "The MTA: New Mecca for Lobbyists," *Los Angeles Times*, September 1, 1993, p. B2.
75. The plaintiffs included the Bus Riders Union, the local chapter of the National Association for the Advancement of Colored People (NAACP), and the Environmental Defense Fund (EDF), an environmental group that had generally supported major rail transit investments.

than 90 percent of the MTA's total ridership. Of those who rode Los Angeles buses, 83 percent were minorities and more than half had household incomes below $15,000 a year. They received an average subsidy of $1.17 a trip. In contrast, 72 percent of the riders on the MTA's commuter rail line were white and their average income was about $60,000 a year. They received an average subsidy of $21.62 per trip. Overall, the MTA spent about 70 percent of its budget on rail transit, mainly to service debt for lines still in development and thus not yet carrying passengers.[76] The plaintiffs argued further that bus overcrowding was rampant because the MTA had devoted nearly all its capital resources to rail. Federal district court judge Terry Hatter issued a temporary injunction against the planned MTA bus fare increases in 1994, though he did authorize modest fare increases in 1995.

Meanwhile, rail construction costs were escalating rapidly, and problems emerged with the quality of construction in several Red Line tunnels. With the agency now a lightning rod for public and media criticism, the board responded at the end of 1995 by firing White. In a parting shot, he publicly observed that the board was a group of elected officials concerned with little more than obtaining benefits for their next election campaigns. "That's why," he continued,

> the last long-range plan was $183 billion. That's why the plan had a rail line in virtually every district of every member. . . . From the moment I arrived . . . one of the persistent rumors that I received was, "Things aren't straight over at the MTA." . . . People did not, and many do not, believe that the way we make decisions is fair. They believe insiders have a track. They believe this is a money train and, to a large degree, it is. . . . If you get between the people who want the money and the people who have the money . . . you've got problems.[77]

In November 1996, the MTA entered into a consent decree with the bus fare plaintiffs freezing fares for at least two years, cutting the prices of monthly bus passes, and adding enough buses to nearly eliminate peak-period standing on all lines. The last of these provisions ultimately required the purchase of more than 2,500 buses at a cost of about $1.5 billion.[78]

76. Jeffrey Rabin, "MTA Borrowing Puts the Agency $7 Billion in Debt," *Los Angeles Times*, June 21, 1998, p. A1.

77. See *Labor/Community Strategy Center et al. v. Los Angeles County Metropolitan Transportation Authority*, Plantiff's Revised Statement of Contentions of Fact and Law, p. 154 (http://legacy.environmentaldefense.org/programs/Transportation/Equity/g_download.html [October 2002]).

78. For a good overview, see *Labor/Community Strategy Ctr. v. L.A. County Metropolitan Transportation Authority*, 263 F.3d 1041 (9th Cir. 2001).

By this time the estimated cost of the 18.4-mile Red Line had risen to $6 billion, nearly twice the amount projected a decade earlier in nominal dollars and more than 25 percent higher in real terms. In addition, the state had recently diverted some local sales tax revenue from transit to help finance the county's hospitals.[79] After intense and bitter debate, the MTA board early in 1998 suspended construction on two planned Red Line extensions, both to areas with predominantly minority populations. It allowed work to proceed, however, on a partially built extension to Hollywood and North Hollywood.

Board member and county supervisor Zev Yaroslavsky, a one-time subway supporter whose district included both Hollywood and North Hollywood, now organized a referendum initiative to ban the use of sales tax money for any new subway construction. (It did not, however, limit spending on segments currently in construction or future extensions above ground.) This campaign generated some curious political alliances. Supporters of the initiative included the Bus Riders Union, which favored generous spending for transit though with much less emphasis on rail; Howard Jarvis's Taxpayers Union, a conservative group dedicated to cutting taxes; state senator Tom Hayden, a progressive Democrat; and county supervisor Mike Antonovich, a stalwart Republican. Opponents included the Sierra Club, construction trade unions, and elected officials and activists from Los Angeles's east side, a largely Hispanic area that been anticipating service by one of the suspended rail lines. Opponents emphasized that Yaroslavsky was seeking to cut off new rail construction only after the planned lines through his own district were too far along to be stopped. On Election Day, however, his initiative attracted 68 percent support, winning by large margins throughout the city, including the east side.[80]

The issues raised in the Los Angeles lawsuit and referendum were by no means unique to that region. Nationwide, new rail systems and line extensions were absorbing the lion's share of public transit investment and policymaker attention, though as of 2000 buses and a half-dozen rapid transit systems dating from before World War II carried nearly nine of every 10 transit riders (including nearly all of those most dependent on transit).[81]

79. See General Accounting Office, "Los Angeles Red Line: Financing Decisions Could Affect This and Other Los Angeles County Rail Capital Projects (1996)" and "Surface Infrastructure: Costs, Financing, and Schedules for Large-Dollar Transportation Projects" (1998).

80. See Jeffrey Rabin and Richard Simon, "Backing for Anti-Subway Measure Equally Strong in All Areas of the City," Los Angeles Times, November 5, 1988.

81. As of 2000, 58 percent of transit trips occurred on buses and 31 percent on older rail systems that were essentially in place before World War II—serving New York City, Chicago, Philadelphia, Boston, San Francisco (MUNI), and Cleveland.

Table 6-7. Transit Ridership and Expenses, by Mode, 1999[a]

	Bus	Heavy rail	Commuter rail	Light rail	Other[b]
Key indicators					
Unlinked trips (millions)	5,111	2,521	396	289	206
Operating expenditures (millions of dollars)	11,056	3,885	2,703	564	1,550
Fare revenue (millions of dollars)	3,941	2,162	1,218	152	235
Farebox recovery ratio (percent)	36	56	45	27	15
Operating subsidy (millions of dollars)	7,115	1,723	1,485	412	1,315
Capital expenditures (fully subsidized, millions of dollars)	2,955	2,810	1,683	1,038	278
Total subsidy (millions of dollars)	10,070	4,533	3,168	1,450	1,593
Share of key indicators (percent)					
Unlinked trips	60	30	5	3	2
Operating expenses	56	20	14	3	8
Operating subsidy	59	14	12	3	11
Capital subsidy	34	32	19	12	3
Total subsidy	48	22	15	7	8
Subsidy per passenger trip (dollars)					
Operating	1.39	0.68	3.75	1.43	6.38
Capital	0.58	1.11	4.25	3.59	1.35
Total	1.97	1.80	8.00	5.02	7.73

Sources: Authors' calculations from Federal Transit Administration, "1999 National Transit Database" (2000, tables 1, 6, 28); American Public Transit Association (2000, tables 14, 18, 25); and Bureau of the Census, "Government Finances: 1998–1999" (2001, table 1).

a. Figures are for the fiscal year that ended in 1999. The Bureau of the Census reports overall spending, fare revenue, and subsidy figures but does not break them down by mode. The Federal Transit Administration reports all these figures except fares by mode, and the American Public Transit Association reports all these figures by mode. The overall spending levels in each of these sources, however, differs. In keeping with other spending data in this book, this table uses the overall Census Bureau spending and revenue figures, relies on the FTA for data on ridership and modal shares of operating and capital spending, and on APTA for modal shares of fare revenues.

b. "Other" includes demand-responsive transit, cable cars, ferryboats, monorails, and van pools.

Light rail and commuter rail systems, most notably, were carrying just 7 percent of all transit users but absorbing 31 percent of capital expenditures. Their patrons, meanwhile, were benefiting from by far the largest per-trip subsidies of any transit users. Subsidies in practice averaged $1.80 a trip for heavy (mainly old) rail systems, $1.97 for buses, $5.02 for light rail, and $8.00 for commuter rail (see table 6-7).

Defenders of these disparities noted that bus users, because they make relatively short trips, benefited from greater subsidies per *passenger mile* than any other transit patrons except those using light rail. Bus service advocates viewed this, however, as a transparent rationale for the greater subsidization of affluent suburban commuters (and the process of urban sprawl) than of more needy transit users. Aside from Los Angeles, such controversies had generated lawsuits in Philadelphia at the end of the 1980s and in New York in 1995. The plaintiffs did not prevail in either case, but the controversies continued.[82]

New Strategies

Los Angeles voters were by no means alone in derailing long-planned transit initiatives during the late 1990s. Transit funding measures were also defeated in Seattle in 1995, Portland (Oregon) in both 1996 and 1998, St. Louis in 1996, Denver in 1997, and Miami in 1999.

Transit advocates rarely gave up, however. More frequently, they scaled back and reconfigured their plans to attract greater support in the suburbs. After voters in the Denver area rejected a massive downtown-oriented rail program in 1997, for example, transit planners scaled back to a single line, which could be funded without a tax increase (though it did require extension of a tax otherwise scheduled to expire in 2005), and they embedded the transit proposal in a package authorizing suburban highway improvements as well. After Seattle voters rejected a $6.7-billion rail plan in 1995, transit advocates returned with a $3.9-billion version a year later, with 80 percent of the funding to come from increased sales and motor vehicle excise tax revenues and the rest from federal transit grants. In contrast to the previous proposal's reliance on rail to connect all the region's urban centers, the new plan substantially expanded bus service and included funding for suburban HOV ramps and lanes. Bob Watt, president and CEO of the Greater Seattle Chamber of Commerce, explained that while he preferred a more expensive plan with greater spending on rail, "it was perfectly obvious that something wasn't sitting well with our voters and we needed to change. You can have the best transit plan in the world and if people won't vote for it, it doesn't count."[83]

Other locales responded to referendum defeats by devising funding plans that did not require voter approval. As of this writing in late 2002, for example, Portland is proceeding with a $125-million, 5.5-mile light rail line from downtown to the regional airport, financed mainly with a mix of available transit and redevelopment agency funds and revenue from an airline ticket surcharge. In addition, a consortium of private developers has committed to invest $28 million in return for a 99-year lease on 120 acres

82. See *Committee for a Better North Philadelphia v. Southeastern Pennsylvania Transportation Authority*, 935 F.2d 1280 (3d Cir.1991); and *New York Urban League, Inc. v. Metropolitan Transportation Authority*, 71 F.3d 1031 (2d Cir. 1995).

83. Gordon Oliver, "New Transportation Challenge Is Getting the Public on Board," *Portland Oregonian*, November 15, 1998, p. B1.

of airport-owned land adjacent to both the rail line and a major highway interchange. Similarly, though Portland-area voters have twice rejected tax increases for a light rail line to the city's southern suburbs, the region's transit agency (with support from many political leaders) has continued to study rail transit options, including funding plans that might allow the project to proceed without a referendum.[84]

Staying the Course at the Federal Level

The Republican takeover of Congress in 1994 appeared to threaten the gains that transit had made in ISTEA, especially since the leadership of the new majority was both intensely committed to scaling back traditional Democratic programs and centered in Sunbelt areas where transit usage was very low. During early discussions about the reauthorization of federal highway and transit programs, which were due to expire in 1997, some highway advocates and their allies in the Republican leadership attempted to revisit earlier decisions on the scale of transit support, particularly as it involved gas tax usage. In response, environmental, community, and protransit groups quickly mobilized. The transit coalition prevailed in the end, primarily for three reasons. First, Republican leaders, having been bruised in a series of environmental battles during 1995 and 1996, were reluctant to take on another. Second, highway interests were eager to increase spending levels far beyond the levels desired by President Clinton and the congressional leadership, and thus were disposed to maintain their solidarity with protransit groups. Third, the Republican majority itself included key members with a strong interest in transit. Of these the most notable was New York senator Alfonse D'Amato, who chaired the Senate Committee, on Banking, Housing, and Urban Affairs, which has jurisdiction over federal transit programs. D'Amato, up for reelection in 1998, was determined to expand the transit program, which benefited New York more than any other state. The bill ultimately enacted, the Transportation Equity Act for the 21st Century (TEA-21), guaranteed that transit would receive at least $36 billion over six years, a significant increase from ISTEA. It also approved more than 200 rail projects for funding, though this was just a stage in the competitive process since the expenditure levels authorized were far less than required to fund them all.

---

84. See Dennis McCarthy, "Happy Valley–Area Leaders Mostly Argue for Light Rail," *Oregonian*, February 25, 2002, p. B2; and George Passadore, "As Region Grows, Transit Options Must Expand," *Oregonian*, November 30, 1999, p. D13.

Conclusion

Four decades after a handful of urban mayors and railroad executives began mobilizing to secure funding for commuter rail lines, urban mass transportation is almost entirely owned and operated by governmental entities, it has been substantially modernized and expanded at public expense, and it is well established as a financial commitment at all levels of government. These public commitments have stemmed the absolute decline in transit usage and have doubtless facilitated the revitalization of some historic downtowns. The share of urban travel served by transit has continued to decline, however, to under 2 percent (see table 6-5), as has transit usage per capita. Given the continuing decentralization of urban America and the unlikelihood of further rapid growth in transit spending, it is difficult to imagine circumstances in which these trends might be reversed.[85]

So why has transit enjoyed such political success in recent decades? It appeals to interests across the political spectrum: downtown and construction-related businesses, construction and transit labor unions, environmentalists, good-government organizations, advocates for the poor, and a wide variety of others who perceive transit as a way of reconciling development, equity, and amenity goals. There are major tensions within this coalition, of course, often leading transit advocates to stress rail improvements for suburban commuters to the neglect of bus improvements for inner-city residents, but leading as well at times to packages responding to the key demands of both constituencies.

This remains very much a minority coalition, but one with great nuisance potential from the standpoint of far more powerful highway interests. In practice, the highway and transit coalitions established a strong, enduring alliance in the 1970s, dedicated to the maximization of surface transportation spending and respect for each other's priorities. This broad coalition has routinely prevailed at the federal level even when confronted with severe budget-cutting pressures from the executive branch, and highway-transit coalitions have become common at the state and local levels as well. Transit interests have managed to obtain an extraordinarily large share of surface

85. Anthony Downs has calculated that even if policymakers could find the resources to halve transit fares, double service, and reduce running times by half, transit ridership would not even double. Downs (1992, pp. 42–43). Alan Altshuler carried out a similar analysis, arriving at similar conclusions, in the late 1970s. Altshuler (1979, pp. 430–41). Doubling transit ridership, moreover, would offset only about one year's growth in urban motor vehicle usage. See Federal Highway Administration, "Highway Statistics, 2000" (2001, table VM-1); and American Public Transit Association (APTA) (2001, tables 18, 30).

transportation resources, moreover—since the mid-1980s, about one quarter of public spending nationally on surface transportation (all levels of government combined) and almost half of such spending in urban areas.[86] There is no reason to anticipate that this pattern will change in the foreseeable future. Stated another way, the political if not the behavioral resurgence of mass transit appears highly robust.[87]

86. Federal Highway Administration, "Highway Statistics, 2000" (2001, tables HF-10, SF-12); and supplemental calculations by the authors.

87. The Federal Highway Administration and Federal Transit Administration have reportedly examined the 20–25-year surface transportation plans of the nation's nineteen largest metropolitan areas. Ten plan to allocate more than one-half of their projected budgets for transit capital and operating costs; seven others plan to allocate between one-third and one-half. Kenneth Orski, "The Myth of Underfunded Mass Transit," *Innovations Briefs*, July–August 2002.

CHAPTER SEVEN

Common
Patterns

The three preceding chapters are both mode-specific and densely detailed; this chapter, in contrast, draws out some common themes.[1] To recapitulate: the 1950s and 1960s witnessed an unprecedented boom in urban mega-project investment, much of it highly disruptive of the existing urban fabric. This period, here labeled the great mega-project era, came to an abrupt end during the late 1960s and early 1970s, as new social movements erupted and local residents rose up to defend their neighborhoods. Numerous new policies and procedures were adopted to safeguard environmental, neighborhood, and preservationist values.

While subject to increasing challenge in subsequent decades, particularly the 1990s, the constraints erected circa 1970 mainly held through the remainder of the century. Cities adapted in part by altering their mix of developmental tactics—relying far more on such inducements as tax abatements, low-interest loans, and direct subsidies to lure private investment and less on direct capital investment. They moved away, in particular, from the mega-project types most emblematic of the great mega-project era: new expressways, airports and airport runways, and clearance-based urban renewal. Direct capital investment did not wither away, however. On the contrary, it expanded in such categories as rail transit, airport terminal improvements, professional sports facilities, and convention centers. If few

1. Citations in this chapter are limited to points that have not been documented previously.

new highways were constructed in the highly urbanized portions of metro-politan areas, moreover, those that were involved extraordinary resource commitments. During the 1990s, finally, federal aid (and, in the airport case, federally authorized but locally imposed head tax revenues) for all three transportation modes examined in this book ratcheted sharply upward.

What were the principal sources of impetus and support for mega-projects after 1970? How did their champions adapt to the constraints put in place during the backlash against great mega-project era disruption? How did the projects themselves change to satisfy these constraints? There are no definitive answers to these questions, but certain patterns do emerge from the political histories examined in chapters 4–6 (and, for purposes of comparison with nontransportation projects, chapter 2).

—Urban mega-projects ceased to be routine after 1970. Their imple-mentation hinged far more on the case-by-case initiative and skill of their advocates than had those of the great mega-project era.

—Mega-project support coalitions were, with rare exceptions, spear-headed by business enterprises with very direct interests at stake. The exceptions—at least among the projects examined in this book—involved leadership by environmental groups on behalf of mass transit projects.

—Mega-project ideas frequently originated in the public sector and were then "sold" to prospective constituencies. Even when private groups provided the initial impetus, energetic and deft public sector leadership was generally required as well—to widen the base of public support, mollify critics, secure resources at higher levels of government, and generally manage conflict through the many years of planning, authorization, and implementation. We (and others) refer to such leadership as "public entrepreneurship."

—However broad their support coalitions, mega-project proposals rarely proceeded to implementation if they imposed more than trivial costs on neighborhoods or the natural environment. We label this the "do no harm" paradigm.

—Even the most sensitively planned mega-projects generated some neg-ative impacts, however, and it became widely accepted that these should be "mitigated" as far as possible. The line between offsetting harms and con-ferring net benefits was often blurred, though, and project advocates were strongly motivated to dampen controversy. So the norm of mitigation fre-quently became an important source of leverage for groups with other concerns than merely repairing or counterbalancing project damages.

—Though often funded in large part by the federal government, urban mega-projects almost invariably originated and drew their main constituency support locally, with little if any regard for national purposes. We refer to this pattern as "bottom-up federalism."

—The central imperative of mega-project finance was to avoid increases in broad-based local taxes—particularly if levied on host city residents alone, and most specifically property and income taxes. Alternatives of growing importance during this period included local taxes crafted to fall mainly on visitors, state aid, regional sales taxes, and in at least a few cases lottery revenues.

—Mega-project costs rose dramatically in the years 1970–2000 and generally exceeded official estimates at the time of project authorization by a considerable margin. It is striking that this long-standing pattern, which appears to prevail worldwide, continues unabated despite major improvements in the technical capacity for cost estimation—suggesting that its causes lie primarily in the realm of politics rather than those of engineering or accounting.

Urban Mega-Projects Became Nonroutine

In the evolution of any project, choices must be made at every turn. When the project is of a common, noncontroversial type, though, and standard decision rules are firmly in place, most choices can be treated as merely technical. All but a very few can be delegated to bureaucratic professionals (for example, highway engineers), and politicians can take credit for overall "progress" while denying responsibility for specific decisions that offend some constituents. These conditions are never fully satisfied, of course, but during the great mega-project era they were approximated far more frequently than before or since. Highway engineers, most notably, were able to plan and construct new urban expressways in relative cookie-cutter fashion, confident in their assignment to implement portions of a national plan (as represented by a national Interstate and Defense Highway map), in their possession of 90 percent federal funding, and in a set of precise decision criteria developed by members of their own profession under Federal Highway Administration auspices. Even strategies for dealing with local officials, business leaders, neighborhood groups, and individuals threatened with displacement were cut and dried. Local business and political leaders were so eager for these projects, moreover, that they could be relied upon to close ranks against critics.

Other officials charged with mega-project responsibilities were somewhat less insulated from politics, but still much more so than their post-1970 successors. Urban renewal officials, for example, could not claim that they were bound by a national plan; nor could they count on an automatic flow of federal funds. They had to apply for discretionary federal funding, to identify funding sources (even if in-kind) for a one-third local match, and frequently to deal with internal business community conflicts (about precisely where, for example, to site projects). Still, cities everywhere were planning similar projects, federal funding was generally adequate to satisfy local demand, local business groups were usually eager for renewal, it seemed safe to ignore the slum residents and small business proprietors threatened with displacement, and environmental protection had not yet become an issue.

In contrast, the advocates of mega-projects after 1970 generally had to forge consensus from an initial base of intense controversy. They could rarely count on an easily accessible flow of federal funding;, indeed, by the mid-1980s such aid was rarely available at all for urban revitalization projects outside the domain of transportation (for example, stadiums and convention centers).[2] Even where federal aid was a realistic possibility, project champions generally had to mount an intense campaign—in both Congress and the executive branch—to obtain it. They also had to satisfy a myriad of environmental, housing, historic preservation, and citizen participation rules, while demonstrating (because federal decisionmakers usually insisted on it) that project opponents were very few and politically insignificant. Far more creative and politically adept leadership was required to advance a project in this new context than during the great mega-project era.

Core Constituencies

The mega-project support coalitions discussed in this book were almost invariably led by business. The exceptions were several West Coast transit projects that won approval with merely tepid business support. We did not come across any cases, though, in which projects went forward in the face of business community opposition.[3] The enterprises most commonly in the vanguard were major land developers and commercial property owners,

2. Localities were able to secure Urban Development Action Grants (UDAG) for some projects of this type during the late 1970s and the 1980s. The UDAG program, however, which was created as a limited follow-on to urban renewal by the Carter administration, dwindled in the Reagan years, finally being terminated in 1988.

3. This is consistent with Clarence Stone's comment on Atlanta politics—that while organized business was far from all-powerful, it was the indispensable constituency without which substantial initiatives could very rarely succeed. Stone (1989, p. 196).

especially those with strong downtown interests, often joined by utilities and banks. In some cases their interests were quite general—for example, airport expansion to enhance the accessibility of the region as a whole. Nearly all projects conferred disproportionate benefits on specific enterprises and locations, however, and the support coalitions for these tended to be led by companies that stood to be prime beneficiaries. These were not always, of course, drawn from the groups just mentioned. Sports team owners were typically the key players in campaigns for new stadiums and arenas, for example, while hotel, restaurant, and other hospitality enterprises—often individually small but joined together in strong trade associations—were prominent in convention center campaigns. What all such businesses had in common, though, was a local market focus. Nearly all, furthermore, depended heavily on state and local public actions to permit and in some cases subsidize their projects, to provide access and other needed infrastructure improvements, to certify their compliance with health and safety standards, to determine their tax assessments, and to maintain or improve their environs. Other active coalition members typically included the core constituency's suppliers, professional firms, and financiers along with construction industry associations and labor unions. General business associations were invariably supportive as well, as were the local media (excluding small "alternative" publications).

The pool of business leadership for development initiatives appears to have contracted since the great mega-project era. Most of the large banks, department stores, utilities, and even newspapers that once anchored local business coalitions have since been absorbed into national conglomerates; and branch managers are less likely to engage in local politics than the owners and top executives of locally headquartered enterprises.[4] This trend is observable in the land development and commercial property investment industries as well, although less so. Additionally, the proportion of regional business located downtown has greatly diminished over the past half century. Enterprises diffused across the suburbs participate in regional and wider business associations, but they seem to be less engaged in local development politics than those clustered downtown.

We did, as mentioned above, come across a few successful mega-project coalitions that were not business-led, all in the field of transit. The

4. See Heying (1997, pp. 657–68). More anecdotal accounts include DiGaetano and Klemanski (1999, pp. 142–48); Rob Gurwitt, "The Rule of the Absentocracy: The Eclipse of Hometown Leadership and How Some Places Are Coping with It," *Governing*, September 1991, pp. 52–58; and Nicholas Lemann, "No Man's Town: The Good Times Are Killing Off America's Local Elites," *New Yorker*, June 5, 2000, pp. 42–48.

Sacramento and Portland (Oregon) light rail transit systems, notably, both originated in the public sector as a response to pressure from environmental and community groups. Local business groups, while supportive, were not conspicuous in the campaigns for local approval. In Los Angeles downtown business leaders had long promoted rail transit without success. Discouraged, however, and dubious about some plan details, they played little role in the 1980 referendum campaign that finally generated serious local funding for rail transit. In all of these cases, however, once local approval was secured, business leaders played key roles in lobbying for federal aid.

Public Entrepreneurship

For all that well-mobilized constituencies were indispensable to the success of mega-project proposals, so in most cases were aggressive, deft government officials. Indeed, it was frequently they who originated project ideas and first sparked the formation of support coalitions. Even when others initiated, they commonly took the lead in crafting strategies, tactics, and plans; in lobbying for federal and state aid; in securing other types of needed legislation; in obtaining regulatory permissions; and in dealing with project critics.

Though business groups initiated some mega-projects, they seemed more frequently to "invest" in proposals originated by others. They were by no means easy marks, of course. Rather, like venture capitalists in the private sector, they considered a great many ideas brought to them by entrepreneurs—most commonly senior public officials, who in turn drew on the ideas of subordinates, consultants, and a wide variety of private interests—but they invested in few. What they sought, apparently, were proposals that looked very good for their businesses, were to be carried out mainly or entirely at public expense, and had a reasonable chance of securing the myriad approvals required.

The knowledge that such support was possible doubtless encouraged public entrepreneurs to develop proposals. The knowledge that it was indispensable provided a powerful incentive to shape them with an eye toward serving business priorities. In contrast to the great mega-project era, however, public entrepreneurs after 1970 were also under great pressure to conciliate prospective project victims. Citizens had become skeptical of claims that decisions were merely technical. They insisted on having their voices heard, they were primed to mobilize if ignored, and they were empowered to litigate effectively by numerous laws and regulations adopted in the late 1960s and early 1970s. Even the media, while highly supportive of most projects on their editorial pages, were no longer content to report agency and business press releases; where controversy existed, they were generally inclined to give it prominent play. So public entrepreneurs, operating in a fishbowl, had to become adept at satisfying the demands of multiple constituencies simultaneously.

To illustrate, the idea to demolish Boston's elevated Central Artery and rebuild it below ground was conceived in 1971 by a civil engineer in the city's employ (then advising the mayor on transportation policy) and a highway contractor with whom he became acquainted in a citizen participation process. Their common desire was a highway project that community, environmental, business, and labor interests might all support. Their idea was quickly taken up by community and environmental groups but not the others. For more than a decade, therefore, it languished—even though the engineer (Fred Salvucci) spent four of those years as state secretary of transportation and had the support of his governor (Michael Dukakis) to make it a top priority.

Gradually, Salvucci realized that nothing could be done without business support. When he returned to office (with Dukakis) in 1983, he proposed combining the artery depression with another mega-project idea: a new expressway tunnel to Logan Airport. The tunnel idea did enjoy business support, but it faced serious opposition from an important community group and (on its behalf) from Dukakis and leading members of the state congressional delegation, including Speaker of the House Thomas P. "Tip" O'Neill Jr. and Senator Edward Kennedy. In combining these ideas, however, Salvucci brought the governor and leading downtown property interests together. He also reconfigured the tunnel project to alleviate the community's concerns. Within months the business-led artery/tunnel coalition came together, and the politicians came aboard.

O'Neill and Kennedy played key roles in securing congressional authorization and funding for the project. The business coalition, led by owners of property adjacent to the artery alignment, played a critical role as well, particularly in lobbying the Reagan administration and brokering solutions to local controversies. Salvucci conceived and orchestrated strategy at every step of the way. Once federal funding was assured, he turned to marathon negotiations with community and environmental groups—determined to head off litigation or even serious controversy. Still later, as Dukakis and Salvucci prepared to leave office, the business coalition persuaded William Weld, the conservative Republican who became governor in 1991, to adopt the project as one of his own top priorities—and so it has remained for his successors through this writing in 2002.

In reflecting on this continuity of commitment, one must be struck by the "robustness" of the project formulation that Salvucci crafted and nurtured in the 1980s—that is to say, its capacity to survive major shifts in policy, economic and fiscal conditions, and political leadership. The longer a project's lead time, the more certain it is to pass through such changes, and thus the more critically its chances hinge on the robustness of its framing ideas. Few proposals are born robust. More commonly, variants contend for years, often a decade or two, before a robust version emerges, if it ever does; and even then, of course, it requires continual tweaking along the way. In this particular case, the Massachusetts Turnpike Authority proposed a new harbor tunnel and it was incorporated into official state plans during the late 1960s, the artery depression idea emerged in the early 1970s, tunnel and artery advocates faced off from the mid-1970s through the early 1980s, Salvucci combined variants of both ideas with some new elements in the early 1980s, details of the new plan were negotiated over the following decade, construction got seriously under way in the mid-1990s, and the project is scheduled (as of late 2002) for completion in 2005.

The quest for additional airport capacity in Denver followed a similar— if somewhat briefer—path. For nearly a decade local officials and business leaders pressed hard for the expansion of Denver's existing airport, Stapleton. Airport neighbors stymied these efforts, however, with legal and political maneuvers. Finally, in the mid-1980s, Mayor Federico Peña and Steve Kramer (a commissioner in nearby Adams County, many of whose residents feared adverse impacts if Stapleton were expanded) brokered a solution. Denver would annex a site in the county for construction of an entirely new airport, a site so large and undeveloped as essentially to obviate the issue of noise impacts. Adams County would reap nearly all the tax benefits from business and residential development in the airport vicinity. Stapleton Airport would be shut down and its site redeveloped with a mix of commerce, housing, and public open space. Everything else followed from these core ideas, though the site eventually selected was different from that originally planned, and it took several years to work out numerous other details. Though by no means acting alone, Peña was the principal leader of this effort throughout, steering the project through a major downturn in the regional economy, separate referendums in the county and then the city (though he adopted a very low profile during the former campaign), a series of environmental challenges, and a successful campaign to attract large-scale federal participation (ultimately about $650 million).

In other cases public entrepreneurs played key roles in forging more robust plans without having had significant roles as project originators. A long-standing effort in Los Angeles to build rail transit, for example, was not resolved until County Supervisor Kenneth Hahn crafted a funding plan and a package of projects that, taken together, were able to attract majority support in a regional referendum. Similarly, Portland mayor Neil Goldschmidt took the lead in ending that region's highway controversies during the 1970s, developing a more balanced and environmentally sensitive highway-transit package in consultation with a mix of business, environmental, and community groups.

Not every project discussed in this book had a conspicuously effective public sector champion. But most did, particularly the largest projects, those with intergovernmental funding, and those with the widest community side effects (especially airports and highways). Assembling the authorizations and resources needed to implement such projects, and mediating the numerous conflicts they generate, is typically beyond the capacity of business coalitions acting alone, or even in concert with merely competent officials. Creative, highly adept public leadership is typically a key component of the successful mix.[5]

"Do No Harm" Planning

Through the 1950s and much of the 1960s, mega-project planners could focus almost exclusively on ensuring business support. Since these were programs to which leading business groups were thoroughly committed, moreover, such support was rarely in question. The prevailing ideology was that projects should be undertaken if, in the judgment of civic elites, they benefited the public on balance. This was not to deny that virtually every project inconvenienced some people: the occupants of homes acquired by eminent domain, for example, and those living under new flight paths. In a popular phrase of the time, however, "you can't make an omelet without breaking eggs."[6] Residents of areas threatened with harmful impacts, environmentalists, and other potential critics were not yet in possession of the

5. Mark Schneider and Paul Teske emphasize that antigrowth as well as growth coalitions are frequently assembled and led by entrepreneurial leaders. Schneider and Teske (1995, pp. 137–43). We concur, but have not focused on the internal dynamics of opposition groups in this research.

6. This proverb (author unknown, dating at least to the mid-nineteenth century) is today most commonly associated with Robert Moses, who liked it so much that for two years in the 1960s he had it posted on highway signs near the site of the New York World's Fair. See Knowles (1999, p. 615); and Caro (1974, pp. 849, 1227).

ideologies that in later years would attract widespread support to their causes. Nor were they mobilized except in occasional ad hoc responses to immediate threats. Nor did they have significant access to the courts.

After 1970 the planning of mega-projects occurred in a very different climate. Groups fearful of harmful side effects were well armed with persuasive ideologies and new legal protections, already mobilized or primed to do so, and highly formidable in court if all else failed. In this context, the dominant paradigm of public investment planning shifted dramatically, to one best characterized by the phrase "do no harm." The essence of this paradigm was that even projects of the sort that had traditionally been most disruptive, such as new expressways and airports, should be sited, designed, and mitigated so as to leave no victims in their wake. If that was not feasible, the projects should be scrapped.

Groups differed, of course, on the precise degree to which this injunction should prevail and in what circumstances it might be relaxed. In practice, it was most likely to be relaxed when localities were competing for the favor of footloose private corporations—Detroit clearing massive sites for new automobile assembly plants during the 1980s, for example, or Chicago siting a new baseball stadium for the White Sox a few years later. During the 1990s it was relaxed as well in some cases where airport operators, with broad business support, insisted that a critical need existed for new runway capacity that could only be achieved by extending outward from their existing sites. These were exceptions, however, to a pattern that very generally prevailed—particularly in the 1970s and 1980s but only marginally less so thereafter.

As early as the mid-1960s, highway planners began striving in a few cases to mollify critics by embedding their projects in broader, amenity-enhancing design plans. New York City mayor John Lindsay, for example, backed an effort to combine development of the controversial Cross Brooklyn Expressway with adjacent land use improvements. California and Chicago officials made similar efforts in connection with the Century Freeway and Crosstown Expressway, respectively. The New York and Chicago projects were never built, however, and the Century Freeway remained highly controversial through the 1970s.

Facing such obstacles, some planners went further, proposing that new urban freeways be placed below grade and intermittently covered with parks or other amenity improvements. In the mid-1960s, for example, Mayor Lindsay supported a plan of this type for the proposed Lower Manhattan Expressway, and several years later Massachusetts planners did so for sections (mainly within public parks) of Boston's Inner Belt. In all but one or two cases, however—notably the Delaware Expressway along Philadelphia's waterfront—these efforts also failed.

Beginning in the 1970s, therefore, some highway planners went further, proposing construction not merely below grade but in tunnels. After early plans for New York's Westway proved highly controversial, for example, its planners designed it with a full cover of new development and parkland. Similarly, while early plans for Boston's depressed Central Artery called for intermittent decking, the plan that gathered broad approval in the 1980s specified tunneling—with a guarantee, moreover, that 75 percent of the new surface land created would be devoted to public open space uses. This approach was central as well to the settlement of long-standing highway disputes in suburbs of Seattle and Detroit during the 1980s.[7]

The most important component of "do no harm" planning, though, tended to be siting—the placement of projects at some distance from groups with the potential to block them. Beginning in the 1960s, for example, it became extremely difficult to expand existing airports, which generally were located close to residential communities. Consequently, the promoters of airport capacity expansion shifted focus, seeking the construction of new airports on very large sites (to minimize neighbor exposure to noise) just beyond the zone of urban settlement.[8] All the new airports built in major U.S. urban areas during the 1960s and early 1970s (Houston, Dallas/Fort Worth, and Dulles Airport outside Washington, D.C.) were sited in accord with this model. Even this strategy failed to suffice in most cases, however, and 20 years intervened between the opening of Dallas/Fort Worth International Airport in 1974 and the next major passenger airport in the United States, Denver International (DIA). The DIA site is nearly twice that of Dallas/Fort Worth, the largest such airport built previously, and roughly 50 times the size of New York's LaGuardia Airport.[9]

Airports are unique, of course, in their locational flexibility. Other forms of urban infrastructure require placement much closer to their users in order to attract sufficient patronage. Specific alignments and building sites can still be selected, however, to minimize community impacts. The planners of New

7. For Seattle, see Talbot (1983, ch. 1); and Donald Merwin, "Problems Solved: Massive I-90 Project Springs to Life," *Highway and Heavy Construction*, October 1995, p. 32. For Detroit, see William Schmidt, "Pleasant Ridge Journal: The Freeway It Took a Generation to Build," *New York Times*, December 15, 1989, p. A20.

8. See Feldman and Milch (1980, pp. 215–38; 1982, esp. p. 235). In the latter (p. 51), Feldman and Milch maintain as well that the proposed new airports reflected a desire to build signature facilities.

9. See table 5-1.

York's Westway and Boston's Central Artery/Tunnel, for example, managed to avoid nearly all existing homes, parks, and major business structures. New rail lines are intrinsically less disruptive than highways, but even they are likely to generate impassioned opposition if placed in brand-new corridors at ground level or above. Consequently, numerous rail lines built in recent decades follow historic rail rights-of-way even at considerable sacrifice of potential patronage, and many others have been placed underground at great expense.

It is much easier to site new buildings—even stadiums, convention centers, and shopping malls—away from sensitive neighbors than airports, highways, or rapid transit systems because they require neither mammoth sites nor continuous corridors. Thus they can be placed in older industrial, warehouse, or skid row–adult entertainment districts, which occupy a great deal of land in and around the typical urban core but which are sufficiently distant from residential enclaves and high-end commerce to allay most potential opposition.[10]

Mitigation and Beyond

Even where post-1970 mega-projects were planned from the outset to minimize harm, demands for mitigation were invariably numerous and impassioned, and it was generally accepted that such impacts should be fully offset. Because the boundary between mitigating harm and providing net benefits was often indistinct, however, this norm provided leverage as well for skilled activists whose demands were at times tangential to mitigation. Project advocates, eager to achieve consensus and avoid litigation, were frequently open to such demands, particularly if they anticipated that all or most of the cost would be borne by higher-level governments. The latter were often receptive as well, because key officials at once hoped to have approvable projects and to avoid becoming embroiled in local disputes. Local consensus was also a useful criterion for agencies and legislative committees determining how to allocate limited resources.

Mitigation first became a statutory requirement in 1968 with respect to housing displacement alone. The Federal Aid Highway Act of that year (section 501) mandated adequate relocation housing for those displaced by projects, even if this required new construction at highway program expense. The purpose, it specified, was "to insure that a few individuals do not suffer disproportionate injuries as a result of programs designed for the

10. See, for example, Frieden and Sagalyn (1989, pp. 299–300).

benefit of the public as a whole."[11] No federal environmen
in the early 1970s specifically called for mitigation, but tl
ronmental Policy Act (NEPA) of 1970 required decisionm
thorough analyses of the environmental consequences of p
comparing a reasonable number of alternatives in each cas_. ɪvɪany states
enacted "little NEPAs" over the next several years, often more ambitious
than the original in requiring the mitigation, not merely the analysis, of
adverse impacts.[13] Numerous other federal statutes enacted, or in some
cases freshly interpreted, in the 1970s established "bright line" substantive
standards that had to be satisfied in order for projects to go forward, and
typically authorized both citizen and class action suits to bring about vigorous enforcement. These statutes, of course, had to be satisfied in
combination, not merely one by one.

With lawsuits a high probability, mitigation emerged as a strategy to
avoid total gridlock. It was almost never possible to carry out public investment projects without causing some collateral harm, so the courts gradually
came to insist on adequate offsets.[14] In a landmark 1975 case, for example,
a federal appellate court ruled that while a proposed highway in Mississippi
violated the Endangered Species Act of 1973, it could proceed if a mitigation program included land acquisition for a wildlife refuge.[15]

There was always room for controversy, though, and thus litigation
uncertainty, about whether mitigation was adequate—leading many to conclude that the critical imperative, even at extremely high cost, was to settle
disputes before they went to court. The case that drove this point home
more than any other was that of New York's proposed Westway. Research
carried out in the preparation of Westway's environmental impact statement
(EIS) revealed that fill work in the Hudson River would substantially harm

11. This provision was superseded in 1970 by section 201 of the Uniform Relocation
Assistance and Real Property Acquisition Act of 1970 (which applied to virtually all federal
programs). See Kahn (1982, pp. 164–65).

12. The courts have generally treated NEPA requirements as purely procedural since the
1980s, and the predominant view of close observers is that their direct effect—spurring officials to think harder about alternatives and consequences—has been modest. There is no
question, however, that NEPA requires public agencies to gather, analyze, and disseminate vast
amounts of data about each project—which in turn provides ammunition for project critics.
See Rosenbaum (1995, pp. 212–15); and McSpadden (1995, pp. 245–48).

13. Among the states with such provisions were California, New York, Michigan, and
Massachusetts. See Fogleman (1990, ch. 7).

14. For a good overview, see Schoenbaum and Stewart (2000, pp. 249–95).

15. See *National Wildlife Federation v. Coleman*, 400 F. Supp. 705 (D. Miss. 1975); and
National Wildlife Federation v. Coleman, 529 F.2d 359 (5th Cir. 1976).

its population of striped bass. This work—making it possible to place the road in part over a portion of the existing riverbed—seemed essential politically to insulate human neighbors from project impacts. To acknowledge it fully, however, would almost surely have led to rejection of a needed permit by the U.S. Army Corps of Engineers. Westway's planners, therefore, ignored the striped bass finding in the project's initial EIS. Project critics cared little about the fish, but this omission gave them leverage in federal court, where they succeeded in having both the EIS approval and the corps permit overturned. In a revised EIS, Westway planners acknowledged the striped bass issue but downplayed its significance. Project foes again sued, and the court rejected the new EIS as well. Consequently, the project was stalled as of 1985 with a critical federal deadline looming—after which the state would no longer be eligible to trade in Westway funding for substitute highway and mass transit projects. The obvious solution was to pursue a congressional extension of the deadline. The Westway environmental studies made clear, however, that if the striped bass habitats on the New York side of the Hudson River were removed, the only remaining habitat for the fish would be existing piers on the New Jersey side. In this scenario it would be almost impossible for New Jersey to obtain permits for redevelopment of its shoreline. So Congressman Frank Guarino, who represented Jersey City, opposed a deadline extension for Westway, enlisting other key members of the New Jersey delegation in support of this position—one of whom chaired the House Public Works Committee. In September 1985, consequently, the House of Representatives rejected any deadline extension. At this point the backers of Westway gave up, and New York officials hastily applied for a Westway trade-in.[16]

Because Westway was the nation's most prominent pending highway project at the time of its demise, its history loomed large in the minds of mega-project advocates elsewhere. Denver mayor Peña's decision to seek construction of a new regional airport, for example, was driven largely by concerns about the volatile mix of environmental litigation and community opposition he would face if he sought to pursue Stapleton expansion. And Central Artery/Tunnel project leaders negotiated more than 1,500 separate mitigation agreements, ranging from soundproofing to the construction of new parks and transit lines, in their successful effort to avoid litigation. These accounted for half or more of the entire project cost.[17]

16. For references and additional detail, see chapter 4.

17. The official project estimate was one-third, but this notably omitted billions of dollars for collateral transit improvements (see below) and more than $1 billion for a major bridge redesign, mainly (though not entirely) to improve its aesthetic impact.

Environmental and community groups have, not surprisingly, applauded the expansion of "mitigation" as a component of public investment planning. Planner Daniel Carlson writes, for example, that such efforts "offer successful and inspirational models for grassroots organizations and agency professionals who are interested in thinking and acting holistically when faced with proposed transportation projects."[18] This is a fair characterization, as far as it goes. What it leaves out is that the mitigation process has become a political arena in which numerous actors maneuver for benefits, many of which go well beyond ameliorating harmful impacts.

In the artery/tunnel case, for example, the Conservation Law Foundation (CLF)—a nonprofit, mainly grant-funded group whose favored instruments are lawsuits and publicity—contended that the project would worsen air quality and demanded billions of dollars in rail transit investment to prevent this from occurring. There was little reason to believe that its charge was valid or its proposed remedy effective. The CLF was able to extract the commitment it sought, however, because project advocates were determined to avoid the threat of litigation.[19] Similarly, advocates for improving the Charles River watershed obtained project commitments of about $100 million to develop additional parkland along its shores. The Century Freeway in Los Angeles was litigated, but the result was a settlement in which the state agreed to fund extensive add-ons—transit in the highway median, an ambitious program of project-related affirmative action, and large amounts of subsidized housing.

Private business interests have also found it convenient, on occasion, to seek leverage in the environmental permitting process. The owners of an open-air parking lot near Boston's Logan Airport, for example, filed suit challenging the artery/tunnel project's environmental approvals and financed a coalition of community and environmental organizations opposing the project. Their motive was simply to keep their land from being taken. The proof of the pudding was that, when the state agreed to a land swap (providing them with a new site even closer to the airport), they abandoned both their suit and putative allies. In a similar vein Seymour Durst, a major New

18. Carlson, Wormser, and Ulberg (1995, p. 4).

19. In its final form this agreement left room for the substitution of listed projects with others of comparable air quality value—an easy criterion to satisfy, critics believed, since most of the listed projects were likely to yield negligible air quality benefits. The CLF kept on the pressure for these projects in subsequent years, however, and no administration has seen fit to risk its wrath by proposing substitutions. The list, to be sure, consisted of projects that the state itself had identified during the 1980s, but its negotiation as a firm set of commitments occurred behind closed doors without public input, and was driven from the state's standpoint entirely by the aim of averting artery/tunnel litigation.

York property owner and developer, was concerned that Westway might reduce the value of his holdings by creating new prime development sites on the west side of Manhattan, so he apparently financed the key lawsuit against the project.[20]

It is not our purpose to criticize this expansion of mitigation conflict and policy. Mitigation agreements, including those that provide benefits only loosely related to project harms, clearly facilitate the achievement of consensus, and the purposes served are in most cases laudable. At the same time, they drive up project costs and provide ammunition to critics of public spending, who view mitigation as increasingly a euphemism for "green pork."[21] Finally, of course, they add a major new element of complexity to mega-project planning.

Bottom-up Federalism

A naive observer of American politics might assume that the federal government distributes grants to achieve national goals (and that states do so to achieve state goals). In fact, however, the grantor-grantee relationship is usually much more complicated than that. Recipient jurisdictions are typically active participants in the coalitions that bring new programs into being, refine them over time, and provide them with critical support each budget season. Where they are able to exercise discretion within the framework of such programs, moreover, they typically assign far greater priority to satisfying the preferences of local constituents than federal overseers.

The federal aid programs examined in this book were all distinguished more by their openness to local initiative than by their sharp definition of national purpose. Although the thrust of urban renewal was toward central-city revitalization, for example, it was part of an omnibus housing policy that on balance encouraged suburbanization. Nor was there any semblance of a national plan for urban renewal. Few localities had general plans either, so the federal government required only "workable programs"—in effect, project lists and justifications. There were federal guidelines, to be sure, but these were quite flexible to begin with, became increasingly so, and were

20. Explaining his father's use of a similar strategy in efforts during the mid-1980s to stop Times Square redevelopment plans, Durst's son Douglas recalled that since "the things we were unhappy about weren't things you could sue about," his father sought more promising legal grounds to challenge major projects, even if the legal issues raised in the suit did not comport directly with his business concerns. See David W. Dunlap, "Developers' Hazard: Legal Hardball," *New York Times*, December 8, 1996, sec. 9, p. 1. On Durst's financial support for Westway's foes, see Pescatello (1985, p. 202).

21. The origin of the phrase *green pork* appears to be McCool (1992, pp. 85–102).

weakly enforced. The requirement for projects to be "residential," for example, could be satisfied by clearing away slums to make way for commercial redevelopment. When even this proved too constraining for some renewal agencies, the proportion of projects that had to satisfy it was progressively relaxed. And federal authorities relied almost entirely on local officials to determine whether sites targeted for renewal were (as required) currently blighted.

The normal drift toward a blurring of federal purpose was, to be sure, reversed for a time in the renewal program. After the riots of the mid-1960s federal officials adopted a more directive stance: assigning priority to projects that promised to improve neighborhoods for existing residents, restricting slum clearance, and imposing strong requirements for citizen participation. This new program design was of little interest to local business leaders, however, and provided weak benefits by and large to local elected officials. So it proved just a step down the path toward program termination.

The Interstate Highway Program embodied a clear objective at birth—to provide the nation with a specifically mapped network of limited-access expressways connecting all of its states and metropolitan areas (including extensions into their downtown cores). The project corridors had been negotiated with the states and through them with major localities, but the overall concept was clear, and both specific alignments and designs were to be selected on the basis of strict engineering criteria. Over the years, however, as the adverse effects of urban highway construction became apparent and aggrieved groups multiplied, Congress responded by layering on numerous additional requirements (citizen participation, environmental protection, historic preservation, adequate relocation housing, and the like) that had nothing to do with traffic service. In 1973, finally, it authorized states to "trade in" controversial interstate segments for alternative highway or transit projects that they preferred. In brief, the federal commitment to finance each interstate route had become a tradable entitlement.[22]

Except for its scale, federal airport assistance, even today, more closely resembles the pre-1956 national highway program than the Interstate Highway Program. Federal highway grants in this period, it will be recalled, were almost entirely for rural roads even though most traffic occurred on urban streets and highways. In a similar though less extreme vein, federal airport assistance has always gone far more to small-city airports than could

22. No criticism is intended. Indeed, one of the present authors (Altshuler), then a Massachusetts state official, actively lobbied for this provision. In the longer term, let us note, federal highway law was trending in a block grant direction, a trend that became particularly apparent in the reauthorization act of 1991, known as ISTEA (see chapter 4).

be justified by the numbers of travelers they serve or the user taxes they generate, and this pattern was accentuated in the 1990s. Congress authorized airports in 1990 to levy a "passenger facility charge" (PFC) on each arriving and departing passenger, with the revenue to be used for airport improvements. This decision considerably expanded the fiscal capacity of major airport operators to undertake capital projects. It provided as well, however, that airports using PFC revenue (raised locally) had to sacrifice a portion of the federal airport grants to which they would otherwise have been entitled—thereby releasing additional federal aid for smaller airports. PFC revenues can be expended only on projects approved by the Federal Aviation Administration, but the federal role is basically to ensure that they are directed solely to airport improvement purposes. Aside from that, there is scarcely any pretense of national airport planning.

Local initiative and discretion have likewise been ascendant in the federal transit program. Originally a program of discretionary grants for capital investment purposes, the transit program acquired a large formula component in 1974, available to localities for either operating or capital purposes. Since the early 1980s, moreover, all capital grants have been directly earmarked by Congress, rather than left to the discretion of the Federal Transit Administration. This federal decision process, not surprisingly, is one dominated by local initiative and pork barrel bargaining. Benefit-cost analyses are at best of minor importance, at worst irrelevant.

If grantee jurisdictions have a great deal of influence collectively on program structure, they have even more when it comes to projects, and they are generally able to exercise it individually. This is, of course, as one might expect; projects must be tailored to specific sites even when national guidelines are tightly prescriptive. It goes much further than this, however: every project examined in this book was initiated by subnational officials and interest groups. It was they who took the lead at every stage in the decision process. And while sensitive to federal program rules, they were alert as well to the possibility of securing waivers, statutory amendments, or add-on funds with the aid of their congressional delegations. Stated another way, when federal aims are diffuse and weakly defended, principal-agent theory (as applied to the intergovernmental system) needs to be read bottom-up rather than top-down.

Locally Painless Project Financing

The hallmark of successful mega-project finance is that projects should appear costless, or nearly so, to the great majority of local voters. The easiest way to achieve this result, of course, is to rely on funding from higher-level governments. Where such aid is unavailable or insufficient, the challenge is to identify other sources of revenue to which local voters are generally insensitive—which means, above all, avoidance of local property and income taxes and spreading the burden well beyond the host city. This challenge became increasingly salient after 1970 with rising antitax sentiment, the end of federal renewal aid, the collapse of new expressway construction in highly urbanized areas, and the surge in capital spending for such facilities as stadiums, arenas, convention centers, and festival malls—for which federal aid was only rarely available. In the growing domain of mass transit, additionally, federal matching ratios declined after 1980. Nor was the revenue challenge purely local. State and federal officials as well felt increasing pressure to avoid raising broad-based taxes. So efforts to identify sources of revenue outside the attention zone of most voters proceeded at all levels during this period.

The most attractive source politically was private investment. It was rarely available, though, even in part, except for projects to accommodate profit-making activities (urban renewal, festival malls, professional sports facilities). In some cases, furthermore, it was illusory in that other government commitments to the investors—in the conditions of their long-term leases, for example—rose in tandem with the more visible commitments of private capital. So most of the new revenue for urban mega-projects had to be public. Host localities, insofar as they were responsible for funding, turned increasingly to special excise taxes on hotel rooms, restaurant and bar tabs, and auto rentals—all paid mainly by nonresidents (including, in the restaurant case, local suburbanites). Airport passenger facility charges were in the same category—and enabled Congress, which authorized this financing method in preference to increasing federal aid, to avoid any blame for raising taxes. Where states assumed partial responsibility, as they increasingly did, they also commonly sought to avoid voter blame—by tapping nontax sources such as toll and lottery revenues or authorizing marginal increases in regional sales taxes, often subject to voter approval.

Obtaining funding from higher levels of government generally required a two-stage process: (1) participation by urban interests nationally (or statewide) in a coalition to secure funding for a general class of investments (for instance, highway improvements); and (2) lobbying by specific jurisdictions to obtain large allocations from these programs.

Except for transit, the national coalitions discussed in this book were led by producer interests with little interest in cities per se. The housing coalition that produced urban renewal, for example, was dominated by homebuilders, suppliers of building materials, bankers, and realtors; and the overall set of programs it spawned is generally agreed to have encouraged suburbanization. The national highway coalition was led principally by the automobile industry in the run-up to enactment of the Interstate Highway Program and in later years by construction interests. The aviation coalition was led by airline and aircraft manufacturing interests, and even general aviation and small-city interests tended to outweigh those of major urban airports. As participants in these coalitions, however, urban interests were able to realize key objectives: the urban renewal and subsequent programs of aid for central-city revitalization, new expressways penetrating to the hearts of cities rather than terminating in outer circumferential highways, and at least modest amounts of federal aid for capital projects at major airports.

Transit, on the other hand, was specifically urban, and its coalition was organized initially by big-city mayors (soon joined by transit labor unions and equipment producers). This narrow coalition struggled, however, until, in the 1970s, it joined in strategic alliance with the national highway coalition—which for its part had become receptive because of widespread antihighway protests and presidential efforts to limit highway spending. The resulting "surface transportation" coalition was generally able to produce veto-proof majorities in Congress, and—quite remarkably, in view of transit's minuscule share of travel—it enabled transit to secure a funding level one quarter that of the federal highway program.[23]

The advocates of specific mega-projects worked, of course, within program frameworks that had generally been established years earlier, and could generally tweak these frameworks only marginally. Their mission, rather, was to draw, in the service of local objectives, upon the resource flows that these programs made available. What was surprising was that this mission commonly required lobbying and logrolling similar to that required to bring the programs into being in the first place. As part of their four-year effort to secure Interstate Highway Program funding for Boston's artery/tunnel project, for example, state officials, local business leaders, and the Massachusetts congressional delegation joined in a broad coalition to secure enactment of a federal surface transportation act that, in its final form, earmarked funding for more than 150 highway projects across the nation and

---

23. The transit share of *urban* highway and transit passenger mileage is 1.9 percent (see table 6-5). Its share nationally, however, including rural as well as urban travel, is just 1.1 percent, and of course its share of freight movement is essentially zero. Authors' calculations from Federal Highway Administration, "Highway Statistics, 2000" (2001, table VM-1); and Federal Transit Administration, "National Transit Summaries and Trends for the 2000 National Transit Database Report Year" (2001, table 28).

authorized significantly more money for transit than the Reagan administration desired. The state's congressional delegation supported increased speed limits on rural highways and subsidies for tobacco farmers in return for some critical votes to override Reagan's veto of this omnibus bill. The resulting legislation did not alter the basic rules of the Interstate Highway Program. It enabled Massachusetts to add the most expensive project in the program's history, though, and one with a very weak ratio of benefits to costs, at a time when interstate highway construction was complete or nearly so in every other state.

Similar logrolling marked enactment of the 1990 legislation authorizing airports to impose head taxes (now relabeled passenger facility charges). The core constituency for this measure was a coalition of major airport operators organized and led by Chicago officials, whose concerns were to finance major improvements at O'Hare and possibly develop a new airport as well. The federal secretary of transportation, who was from Illinois and for whom national airport capacity expansion was a major priority, was enthusiastic. The White House was receptive so long as the new charges were not labeled taxes or levied directly by the federal government—the president having famously promised "no new taxes" in his 1988 campaign. But the airlines were strongly opposed initially. What brought them around in the end was the addition of a provision they had long sought—placing tighter control on the authority of local operators to control airport noise—plus an implicit threat that the secretary of transportation might penalize holdouts when they sought lucrative overseas routes (which are assigned by the federal government). In the final push for votes in Congress, completely extraneous deals were cut as well, including a key legislator's pledge to keep cigarette tax increases off the table in planning to reduce the federal deficit.[24]

During the mid-1980s, finally, big-city mayors, transit operators, and business leaders from a group of jurisdictions with existing or planned rail transit systems—including New York, Chicago, Boston, Philadelphia, Houston, Los Angeles, Portland, and St. Louis—mounted a campaign for increased federal aid in the face of Reagan administration efforts to cut or even eliminate such funding. With the aid of their congressional delegations, they not only succeeded in this objective but also derailed an administration proposal to allocate aid on the basis of cost-benefit analyses. Congress strengthened its control of the project approval process, moreover. The key to designation as a project eligible for federal aid was advocacy by a senior member of at least one of the congressional committees with jurisdiction over

24. For details, see chapter 5.

transit legislation and appropriations or in the leadership of Congress as a whole.[25]

Where federal aid was unavailable or insufficient, mega-project advocates looked first to their state governments, but here too they generally had to forge wider alliances. In the 1980s, for example, as Philadelphia pursued state aid for a new convention center, Pittsburgh saw an opportunity to obtain state aid for major expansion of its airport. Joining forces, both succeeded.[26]

State officials were rarely willing to assume direct responsibility for tax increases to finance local mega-projects. So their methods of assisting were most commonly to assign project responsibilities to authorities with access to special revenues other than state taxes or to authorize—without themselves imposing—new local taxes. Massachusetts, for example, assigned responsibility for building the artery/tunnel project to its turnpike authority, pressed it to issue bonds secured by projected toll increases, obtained contributions from its port authority as well, and borrowed years ahead against the state's anticipated federal highway aid. Maryland created a stadium authority empowered to run sports lotteries. Illinois empowered the city of Chicago to issue nearly $1 billion worth of bonds for expansion of its convention center and to impose an array of new excise taxes to service them.[27] Numerous states, finally, authorized localities to increase sales (and other) taxes to fund new rail transit systems, such as those in Los Angeles, Atlanta, and Dallas.

When host localities had to finance projects themselves, their preferred mode was long-term borrowing, to be serviced with the proceeds of excise taxes and fees falling mainly on nonresidents—including visitors from their own suburbs as well as more distant places. The Chicago convention center bonds, for example, were backed by a 2.5 percent increase in the city's hotel tax, a new tax on restaurant meals in downtown Chicago, and a new tax on trips by taxi, limousine, or bus to and from Chicago airports.[28] Major airport improvements were typically financed by a combination of landing fee revenues, terminal and retail concession lease payments, and (beginning in the

---

25. See Kennedy (1984).

26. See Lubove (1996, p. 49); and McLaughlin (1999, pp. 479–82, 496–98, 507).

27. Even to secure this legislation, which cost the state nothing, Chicago legislators had to support a companion bill subsidizing scrubbers for coal-fired power plants to facilitate their use of high-sulfur coal produced in downstate Illinois. See Patrick Gauen, "Illinois Senate OKs Bill for Coal Scrubbers," *St. Louis (Missouri) Post-Dispatch*, July 19, 1991, p. A10; and Karl Oxnevad, "McCormick Convention Center Wins Approval for $935 Million of Issuance for Expansion," *Bond Buyer*, July 22, 1991, p. 22.

28. Oxnevad, "McCormick Convention Center."

1990s) passenger facility charges. The first two of these were corporate costs of doing business, ultimately passed on to consumers but never broken out in price quotes. Passenger facility charges were slightly more visible, but even they were collected by the airlines and paid largely by out-of-towners (overwhelmingly so in the case of connector hubs like Atlanta, Chicago, and Denver). Thus, although it would rely on all of these revenue sources and require higher local charges than any other airport in the country, Denver International Airport was marketed successfully to local voters in 1989 as a project that would use "no city taxes."[29] With this assurance, the electorate approved the project by a margin of 2-1.

Other ways to avoid the appearance of burdening local taxpayers were to convey publicly owned land at below-market prices, to channel public infrastructure resources into projects of value to favored developments, to subsidize development with tax abatements and tax-increment financing arrangements rather than appropriated funds, to provide loans or access to credit at below-market rates, and to encourage increased private capital commitments in return for (much less visible) long-term lease concessions.

The first of these was, of course, a practice of very long standing. The federal government relied mainly on public land grants to bring about construction of the nation's railroads in the nineteenth century,[30] and through the 1950s and 1960s land-cost write-downs and targeted infrastructure investments were the principal instruments of the urban renewal program. During the final quarter of the twentieth century, though urban renewal was no more, these methods remained in common use and were supplemented by a raft of others. Bernard Frieden and Lynne Sagalyn estimate, for example, that the median public share in financing 39 downtown shopping mall projects that they studied during the 1970s and 1980s was 32 percent. Cities rarely made outright cash grants; instead they offered tax abatements and tax-increment district financing, below-market leases of city-owned land or buildings, loans to be repaid at below-market rates or on deferred schedules, federal aid (until it dried up in the 1980s), collateral infrastructure investments, and commitments to improve surrounding districts. They also became investor-partners in certain facilities, sharing the burdens of financing and risk with their chosen private developers.[31]

Similar arrangements have been used more recently to finance sports stadiums and arenas. At first glance, it appears that the private contribution to

29. Quotation from the ballot proposition put to the Denver electorate in 1989.
30. See Goodrich (1965); and Gates and Swenson (1968).
31. See Frieden and Sagalyn (1989, chs. 5–8)

those projects has grown—rising in aggregate from just 11 percent of capital costs for stadiums and arenas built in the 1970s to 34 percent in the 1980s and 43 percent in the 1990s. A closer look reveals a much more complicated story, however. The proponents of San Francisco's new baseball stadium, which opened in 2000, argued successfully in their final referendum campaign—having previously encountered defeat on several occasions, before they learned to segregate the public and private roles so deftly—that the project would not involve any local tax contribution. Off-budget, however, its development was facilitated by public assembly of the land on which it sits, a long-term lease of this land to the team at below-market value, full exemption of the land and the stadium from property taxes, and publicly funded transit improvements. More generally, Long estimates that while the reported public share of new stadiums and arenas built after 1990 was nine percentage points *lower* than for those built earlier (but still in use as of 2001), the actual share was 11 percentage points *higher*.[32]

Transit was an exception, in that local contributions for new systems were most commonly financed by regional sales taxes. Federal aid ratios trended downward after 1980—from 80 percent to one-half or even less—as local demand far exceeded appropriations. Local reliance on user revenues was not an option, though, since not one of the nation's large transit agencies came close to covering even its operating costs from fares.[33] Nor was there a corporate constituency for visitor taxation, since the hospitality industry was generally indifferent to transit. So transit promoters were regularly driven to seek voter approval for regional sales tax increases. While local voters rejected most of these ballot propositions—about 75 percent from 1988 to 2000[34]—transit advocates frequently modified their plans, came back if necessary on multiple occasions, and eventually prevailed.

Voters in the Atlanta region approved MARTA, for example, on a second try in 1971, after its plan was expanded to include new lines serving minority areas, public acquisition of privately owned bus companies, bus fare reductions, and strong commitments to affirmative action in both

---

32. J. G. Long (2002, table 4-1). The figures are reported in chapter 2.

33. Of the nation's 27 largest transit agencies, 25 raised less than half their operating costs at the farebox in 2000. The two exceptions were San Francisco's BART system, which recovered 62 percent, and New York's Metropolitan Transit Authority, which recovered 57 percent. Authors' calculations from Federal Transit Administration, "Statistical Summaries, 1999" (2000).

34. Wendell Cox Consultancy, "U.S. Urban Rail Referendum Results to November 2000," *Public Purpose Urban Transport Fact Book* (www.publicpurpose.com/ut-railv.htm [February 2002]).

employment and contracting. Los Angeles–area voters authorized a sales tax for rapid transit in 1980, but only after the package was broadened to include lower bus fares, a network of light rail lines reaching far into the suburbs, and funding for local road projects in suburbs outside the rail corridors. Seattle-area voters approved a sales tax increase for rail transit in 1996, but only after the plan was scaled back from one they had defeated, reconfigured to include a variety of bus and high-occupancy lane projects, and adjusted to ensure that taxes raised in the suburbs would be spent there. In each of these cases the advocates maintained that local residents could expect a bargain because federal aid would cover a large share of project costs. The federal share estimates often turned out to be overly optimistic, however. In Seattle, for example, the ballot proposition indicated that federal transit grants would finance about 35 to 40 percent of a proposed $1.7 billion, 23-mile light rail system. By 2000 local planners were estimating that it would cost $2.6 billion just to build the project's first phase—a 7.2-mile segment in downtown Seattle. In January 2001 the Federal Transit Administration (still headed by Clinton appointees) agreed to a federal share of $500 million for this segment (including $100 million previously authorized by Congress). The Bush administration refused to recommend congressional authorization of the remaining $400 million, however, and there the matter stood as of late 2002.[35]

Cost Escalation and Underestimation

"Do no harm" design and mitigation strategies, along with rising amenity expectations for such project types as sports facilities and convention centers, generated sharp increases in real project costs in the concluding decades of the twentieth century, calling into serious question the sustainability of mega-project investment (see also chapter 9). Additionally, final project costs routinely exceeded estimates by a considerable margin.

Dramatic escalation of costs appears to have begun in the 1980s—perhaps because it took that long for major projects planned in the new circumstances of the 1970s to reach construction and perhaps as well because many jurisdictions were mired in fiscal difficulties from the mid-1970s through the early 1980s. In any event, the magnitude of the escalation is breathtaking. The average constant-dollar cost for each mile of new urban expressway, for example, appears to have increased only slightly from the

35. See Federal Transit Administration, "Annual Report on New Starts Proposed Allocation of Funds for Fiscal Year 2002" (2001); Rosegrant (2001).

1950s through the 1970s.[36] By contrast, according to a careful study by Brian Taylor, the average cost for each centerline mile increased by more than 600 percent in the 1980s and early 1990s, from about $7 million a mile to about $54 million a mile (in constant 2002 dollars).[37] This is because relatively few new segments were constructed in this period, but some of those that were—such as the Century Freeway in Los Angeles which, in constant 2002 dollars, cost about $176 million a centerline mile, and the decked portion of Interstate 90 outside Seattle, which cost about $272 million a centerline mile—were phenomenally more expensive than prior urban highways. The costs of these projects, moreover, are dwarfed by the Central Artery/Tunnel project, which is estimated to cost $1.9 billion a centerline mile, while a proposal to replace Seattle's Alaskan Way viaduct with a tunnel is estimated to cost almost $3 billion a centerline mile.[38]

There is not a great deal of experience with airports, but Denver International (completed in 1994) cost more than twice as much in real terms as its immediate predecessor among major new U.S. passenger airports, Dallas/Fort Worth (completed in 1974).[39] As for transit, San Francisco's Bay Area Rapid Transit (BART) system, built in the 1960s and 1970s, cost about $81 million a mile; Atlanta's MARTA system, built in the 1970s and 1980s, cost $152 million a mile; Washington, D.C.'s system, built in about the same period, cost $197 million a mile; and the Los Angeles Red Line subway, built in the 1980s and 1990s, cost more than $300 million a mile (all figures in 2001 dollars).[40] Light rail lines, which can operate on city streets, cost far less but their costs have escalated substantially as well. A recent survey of 19 such lines constructed between 1983 and 2000 found a 37 percent increase in real terms from the 1980s to the 1990s ($23.6 mil-

36. Authors' calculations from Owen (1966, table 6, p. 44); Meyer, Kain, and Wohl (1965, table 62, p. 205); Meyer and Gómez-Ibáñez (1981, table 11-8, p. 205); and Gómez-Ibáñez and O'Keeffe (1985, table 3-3, p. 35).

37. Taylor (1995, p. 51); personal communication with Brian Taylor, September 10, 2001; and authors' calculations.

38. Authors' calculations.

39. Authors' calculations from General Accounting Office, "Denver International Airport: Information on Selected Financial Issues" (1995, table 1, p. 5); and Feldman and Milch (1982, p. 70).

40. Authors' calculations from Merewitz (1973, pp. 78–86); Pickrell (1990, table 3-1, p. 33, table S-1); General Accounting Office, "Surface Infrastructure: Costs, Financing, and Schedules for Large-Dollar Transportation Projects" (1998, pp. 23–30); Jeffrey Rabin, "Subway's Arrival in Valley Ends a Long Costly Journey; Transit: Final Leg of $4.7 Billion System Opens Saturday but Impact on Cahuenga Pass Traffic Remains to Be Seen," Los Angeles Times, June 18, 2000, Sunday edition, p. A1; and Richmond (2001b, pp. 163–66).

lion a mile to $37.4 million).[41] The average cost of new stadiums and arenas rose from $51 million in the 1950s to $226 million in the 1990s (2001 dollars). And while no similar comparison is available for convention centers, those built toward the end of the century were orders of magnitude larger and more lavish than those built several decades earlier. Chicago's McCormick Place, for example, increased in scale from 320,000 square feet of exhibition space at the time of its opening in 1960 to 2.2 million in the late 1990s, while Atlanta replaced a 70,000 square foot center opened in 1967 with one of 950,000 square feet in the 1990s (and had 700,000 more on the drawing board).

The issue of faulty cost estimation is perhaps even more significant, in that it calls into question the bases for political decisions to undertake megaprojects. The estimated price tag for Boston's artery/tunnel project nearly tripled in real terms from 1987, when Congress approved funding for it, to 2002. The constant-dollar cost of Denver International Airport more than doubled from the late 1980s, when it received voter approval and federal funding commitments, to its completion half a dozen years later. And the projected real cost of Seattle's planned new light rail line increased by more than 50 percent in the five years (1996–2001) after its approval—even before the commencement of construction.

Such increases are neither new nor specifically American. Bent Flyvbjerg, Nils Bruzelius, and Werner Rothengatter recently examined the cost histories of 258 large road and rail projects (both urban and intercity) in 20 countries on five continents, built between 1927 and 1998. Their principal findings: costs were underestimated in 90 percent of these cases—routinely more than 40 percent and often by much more—and the tendency toward underestimation did not diminish over this 70-year period. These authors also conducted a secondary source review of large nontransportation projects, finding an even more pronounced pattern of cost overruns.[42]

Edward Merrow carried out a similar examination in the 1980s of 52 major projects (both in the United States and abroad) completed over the previous two decades, ranging in cost from $500 million to $10 billion (in 1984 dollars). The projects included a mix of public and private facilities (though only two, an airport and a seaport, were in the field of transportation).[43] Average cost growth in real terms, from the beginning of detailed engineering (which generally followed project authorization) to project com-

41. Authors' calculations based on Pilgrim (2000, p. 2).
42. Flyvbjerg, Bruzelius, and Rothengatter (2003, pp. 11–22).
43. The great majority of these projects were manufacturing, mining, mineral processing, and nuclear power plant facilities. See Merrow (1988, ch. 2).

pletion, was 88 percent, and public projects experienced greater proportional increases than private. On the basis of a regression analysis, Merrow concluded that about 80 percent of the cost escalation he identified had been attributable to three factors: unforeseen mitigation costs (often required by regulatory changes subsequent to project authorization), decisions to use new technologies, and perverse incentives built into public financing systems.[44]

Noting the consistency of observed errors over time, Flyvbjerg and others conclude that these are most likely, in general, to have been tactics in the pursuit of project approvals rather than innocent mistakes. As they baldly put it, "the cost estimates used in public debates, media coverage, and decision making for transport infrastructure development are systematically and significantly deceptive."[45] In a similar vein, Martin Wachs, one of the nation's most thoughtful and balanced observers of urban transportation policymaking, wrote some years ago:

> I have interviewed public officials, consultants, and planners who have been involved [in transit project cost and ridership forecasting] and I am absolutely convinced that the cost overruns and patronage overestimates were not the result of technical errors, honest mistakes, or inadequate methods. In case after case, planners, engineers, and economists have told me that they have had to "revise" their forecasts many times because they failed to satisfy their superiors. The forecasts had to be "cooked" in order to produce numbers that were dramatic enough to gain federal support for projects whether or not they could be fully justified on technical grounds.[46]

There are at least a few, it bears mention, who argue that cost underestimation is functional. Leonard Merewitz, for example, opined in a 1972 article (after showing that cost overruns were endemic): "I believe that keeping costs low is more important than estimating costs correctly. Therefore,

44. Specifically, he estimated that cost growth equaled 1.04 + .78 x number of project elements subject to stringent regulations (for example, environment, public health, labor), + .56 if a publicly owned project, + .59 if new materials, construction methods, or both are used, + .42 if first-of-a-kind technology is used. See Merrow (1988, ch. 4, esp. pp. 38–39). Recall also, from chapter 6, the separate findings by Don Pickrell and Jonathan Richmond that rail transit project costs have consistently been underestimated while ridership has regularly been overestimated.

45. Flyvbjerg, Bruzelius, and Rothengatter (2003, p. 20).

46. Wachs (1990, p. 144; 1989, pp. 476–79). C. Ernest Fitzgerald, who gained fame as a whistle-blower in the Department of Defense, once observed that "there are only two phases of a weapons program: 'too early to tell' and 'too late to stop.'" Cited in Tim Weiner, "The Nation Warbucks: How to Build Weapons When Money Is No Object," *New York Times*, April 16, 2000, sec. 4, p. 3.

if a low cost estimate acts as a restraint on costs, then it is better than a more realistic one."[47] Similarly, James Kerasiotes, who headed the artery/tunnel project through most of the 1990s, frequently admitted that he favored the use of aggressively low cost estimates as a way to keep pressure on project managers. (He never admitted that they were "unrealistic," but in the end he was fired for having concealed cost increases he could not bring under control.) We are aware of no studies testing this proposition. Recall that Merrow found lower cost overruns in the private sector, however, suggesting that it has less standing in the corporate than the governmental world. In our own view, consistent underestimation is an example of the "tragedy of the commons." It corrodes public confidence in government overall, and especially in proposals with long time frames, even as it helps advance specific projects.

47. Merewitz (1973, p. 280); and Wachs (1990, p. 152).

CHAPTER EIGHT

Urban Theory Redux

This chapter returns to the theories reviewed in chapter 3, specifying those we have found most helpful to an understanding of mega-project politics over the past half century. The discussion is organized around four themes: the main sources of change; patterns of initiative, support, and resistance; the bidirectional flow of influence in the federal system; and the shifting balance between elite initiative and pluralistic constraints.[1]

The Long View: Mega-Project Politics in Flux

Postwar theorists of urban politics have, with rare exceptions, focused on patterns at the time of their own research, and they have predominantly conveyed an impression of great stability. The focus of this book, however, is on change over the course of five eventful decades—in particular, the very limited capacity of local governments to implement major capital projects before the great mega-project era (roughly 1950–70), the relative brevity of this era, and the "do no harm" requirement that obtained through the remaining decades of the twentieth century.

---

1. To minimize duplication of material in chapter 2 and to economize on space, notes are generally limited in this chapter to new material and specific quotations.

The Pre-1950 Era

Few of the theorists under review say much about urban policy during the first half of the twentieth century. Those who do, though, invariably portray it as minimalist—that is, characterized by parsimony, great deference to property owners, and a nearly exclusive focus on basic service provision. (Though we concur in this general portrayal, chapter 2 reports quite a different pattern in the specific arena of local infrastructure investment—one of rapid growth through the first half of the twentieth century, interrupted only by the Great Depression and World War II.) They differ in whether to interpret this as evidence of pluralism or elite dominance, but not on the rarity of ambitious government efforts to stimulate economic or social change.

Dahl, for example, observes that a radical democratization of New Haven politics occurred in the first half of the twentieth century, made possible by the voting power of working-class ethnics. The result, he maintains, was a shift from the predominant nineteenth-century pattern of rule by a cohesive elite to one in which widely diverse interests, with little overlap in leadership, had to be accommodated. These interests "managed to avoid severe conflict by tacit agreements on spheres of influence." The city's economic notables, though, were able to veto both tax and expenditure increases "for anything more than minimal traditional city services."[2] Business regulation does not seem to have been on the policy agenda at all.

In a similar vein, Norman and Susan Fainstein observe that "directive" urban regimes, able to pursue large-scale redevelopment, emerged only when federal aid for renewal and highway construction became available in the 1950s. Previously, they write, the fragmentation of local authority structures and the multiplicity of local interests precluded bold local efforts to counter economic decline.

The Great Mega-Project Era

Several things changed in the years after World War II. First, rapid suburbanization and motorization deprived most older cities of the fruits of the postwar economic boom. Second, the New Deal and World War II had left an afterglow of belief that bold government action was often necessary and efficacious. In this context, federal aid did not seem out of the question. If it could be secured, the problem of taxpayer resistance to financing major ventures might dissolve. Third, there were numerous ideas in the air for such ventures, notably around the themes of slum clearance, redevelopment,

2. Dahl (1961, pp. 82, 190). More generally, see chs. 4, 16.

expressway construction, and airport development. Fourth, among the lega-cies of World War II was a tax system that generated vast amounts of money. As the nation disarmed in the years between VJ Day and the Korean War, this left considerable room for new initiatives. (By 1956, when the Interstate Highway Program was enacted, it was necessary to come up with new rev-enue to finance it, but highway users as a group were well able to finance their own benefits.) Finally, there was great concern that without new gov-ernment spending programs, the nation would slip again into depression.

In this context, national coalitions with significant urban elements came together in support of programs for large-scale investment in housing, urban renewal, freeways, and airports. These coalitions were not primarily urban. Then as now, central-city residents accounted for only about three in ten Americans, and not all central cities were in crisis. The coalitions them-selves, however, were diverse and open. Their leaders, aspiring to near-consensual support in Congress, were more than willing to accommo-date central-city recruits.

The housing coalition, for example, was led by bankers, materials sup-pliers, homebuilders, and construction labor unions, but it also included advocates of public housing and urban renewal. The omnibus housing acts that it lobbied into being were primarily about housing finance. Urban renewal was an add-on, justified officially by its housing elements (not just new construction but also clearance, then viewed as a benefit in its own right).[3] The highway coalition was led from Detroit, but it included oil companies, truckers, automobile dealers, highway contractors, autowork-ers, state and local public officials, organizations of farmers, and highway-related businesses in every congressional district. Some advocates of the interstate program, including President Eisenhower himself, would have preferred limiting the federal role to aid for intercity highways, ending at the outskirts of each metropolitan area. Federal studies indicated, how-ever, that travel on urban streets and highways would generate roughly half of national user tax revenue.[4] So local interests were able to become inte-gral (if still junior) partners in both these coalitions.

In their turn, the new aid programs often transformed local politics. The most powerful check on proposals for activist intervention had always been taxpayer resistance. From the local standpoint, however, federal aid was vir-tually "free." State governments, for example, took responsibility for the nonfederal share of highway expenditures, and the required local contri-

3. See Von Hoffman (2000, pp. 300–10).
4. See Taylor (2000, pp. 199–203).

bution to renewal projects could usually be finessed by counting in-kind contributions or infrastructure expenditures that the city would have incurred even in the absence of renewal.[5] So local officials could now distribute (or share in distributing) new benefits of enormous value to powerful claimants without provoking taxpayer displeasure. This was a political earthquake.

No theory under review provides a fully adequate explanation of this story, but several are quite helpful in considering aspects of it. Public choice theorists, for example, persuasively explain the congressional preference, at least in allocating divisible benefits (like federal aid dollars), for packages that command near-universal support. Bare-majority (minimum-winning) coalitions offer each member a larger payoff, but universalism maximizes the chance of inclusion for each member of Congress.[6] It also maximizes the strength of the legislative branch as a whole, since veto threats are hollow if the congressional majority comfortably exceeds two-thirds.

Norman and Susan Fainstein convincingly analyze the effects of federal aid on local politics from the 1950s through the 1970s. Except when federal aid is available, they write, and directed to agencies that are well insulated from normal politics, "municipal governments are incapable of a highly directing role in shaping cities, regardless of the potential profitability that can result."[7] These conditions were first realized in the 1950s with enactment of the urban renewal and interstate highway programs. Building on them, local regimes mobilized public power to reestablish the functional importance of the central business district (CBD), to attract white middle-class residents back to the city, to remove low-income and minority households from areas thought to have high redevelopment potential (primarily the CBD but also the environs of such institutions as universities and medical complexes), to maintain and reinforce segregation (deemed vital to a healthy economy), and generally to reinforce commercial property values.

The Era of Transition

Though these programs were highly disruptive to lower-income neighborhoods, it took 10 to 15 years for effective opposition to materialize.

---

5. Federal aid was much less important in the development of metropolitan area airports, but they too were generally financed by other means than local taxation—user fees paid mainly by nonresidents of the host locality, for example, and direct federal financing for the air traffic control system components. The factor that was new in the 1950s and 1960s was spectacular growth in air travel volume, which provided both the demand and user tax revenue base for major airport investments.

6. See Ferejohn (1974, p. 247); Shepsle and Weingast (1981, pp. 96–111); and Fiorina (1981, pp. 197–221).

7. Fainstein and Fainstein (1983, p. 248).

Lower- and working-class interests have always been hard to mobilize in American politics—in part due to ethnic and racial tensions within their ranks, and in part due to features of the larger political system that discourage class-based political organization.[8] Additionally, the redevelopment programs themselves kept lower-income people continually on the move, disrupting their social networks and thus their capacity to mobilize.[9] But opposition to each of the great mega-project era programs did erupt in force during the mid- to late 1960s. Urban renewal was effectively brought down by the riots of the mid-1960s. The Interstate Highway Program encountered widespread resistance to its urban segments by the late 1960s, which intensified after 1970. The airport case is even more striking: only one major passenger airport has been constructed since the early 1970s, and there was a near-moratorium on new runway construction until the 1990s.

A satisfactory explanation of these program reversals must, we judge, be organized around two themes: the general and to date unique surge in citizen activism that occurred during the 1960s, and social learning. The Fainsteins highlight the former, concluding that the protests of this period brought a widespread shift from directive to concessionary regimes—which increased redistributive expenditures, adopted affirmative action programs, developed programs of citizen participation, and shifted the emphasis of urban renewal from CBD redevelopment to neighborhood rehabilitation. This was, they judge, merely a tactical shift, but the highest priority of business now was insulation from popular attacks. We concur but think nearly equal weight must be assigned to the activism of middle-class and affluent urban residents that underlay the movements for environmental protection and historic preservation. Group learning over time was also of critical importance. At the beginning, virtually no one imagined the disruption that the great mega-project programs would entail. Liberals, for example, were part of the original coalition for redevelopment, focusing on its potential as a source of new housing for urban residents while failing to anticipate its actual devastation of low-income housing supply and neighborhoods. The Fainsteins note this but do not elaborate.[10] What seems clear, however, is that as the bulldozers rolled, lessons were gradually drawn and narratives shaped that could serve as effective springboards for mobilizing protest.

There is an alternative view, with which we do not agree, that while the protests served as triggers, the primary reasons for the end of the great

8. Fainstein and Fainstein (1983, esp. p. 273); and Katznelson (1981, chs. 2, 3).
9. Fainstein and Fainstein (1983, p. 254).
10. Fainstein and Fainstein (1983, p. 248).

mega-project era were economic. Even the Fainsteins, having first argued that clearance-based urban renewal was brought down by lower-class protests, add that these protests were able to succeed only because the importance of the program to local capital had sharply declined. The renewal program "had already achieved its objective of making the CBD suitable for development."[11] Paul Peterson makes essentially the same argument with respect to urban freeway construction. Though many observers attributed the post-1970 slowdown in such construction to grassroots protest activity, he writes, they were mistaking a superficial symptom for the root cause—namely, that new highways no longer had much value as instruments of economic development. Local governments, understanding this, became far more open to environmental and other interests opposed to highway development.[12]

Both arguments are plausible but not ultimately persuasive. As for renewal, some downtowns had indeed been brought back from the grave by 1965, and investors were generally more receptive to the idea of downtown investment than in 1950. By the early and mid-1960s, moreover, numerous critics were questioning the economic cost-effectiveness of renewal. There was no evidence before the urban riots, however, that cities were backing off from the program, or that their local business communities had lost faith in it. Nor did the end of clearance-based renewal signal a long-term government retreat from the promotion and subsidization of downtown private investment. Indeed, the years since have witnessed an intensification of local competition for such investment. So the argument that CBDs were fully established as attractive investment sites by 1975 is not convincing. Peterson, incidentally, in his 1995 book on federalism, attributes the decline of urban renewal to the racial turmoil it provoked.[13]

As for the freeway program, it is true that new roads in a well-developed network tend to add less value than did their predecessors, and by 1970 most U.S. metropolitan areas had numerous expressways in place. Whether this explains the abrupt retreat from urban freeway construction in the early 1970s, though, is another matter. The highway program was not under significant attack on economic grounds, nor is there any evidence that business support for it was flagging. Permit us also to share a bit of firsthand evidence. One of the present authors, Altshuler, served as Massachusetts secretary of transportation during this period, as Governor Francis W. Sargent

11. Fainstein and Fainstein (1983, p. 259).
12. P. E. Peterson (1981, p. 135).
13. P. E. Peterson (1995, p. 5).

(a liberal Republican) rejected nearly all of the remaining freeway increments planned for Greater Boston. In this capacity, Altshuler attended all significant meetings between the governor and business leaders in which transportation issues were discussed, and he well recalls the business leaders' fury. He cannot recall a single instance, moreover, in which the idea came up that highways were becoming less valuable as instruments of economic development. Sargent, certainly, knew nothing of this idea and fully anticipated that his decisions would cost him dearly with the business community (although he hoped, of course, to offset this loss with gains among environmental, good-government, minority, and other groups that had coalesced in opposition to the rejected highways).[14]

More generally, it should be borne in mind that even as new expressway construction declined, rail transit investment expanded—despite a clear predominance of negative economic opinion.[15] Jumping forward to the present, few political or business leaders seem to care what economists think about the value of public investments in convention centers and sports stadiums. Unlike these facilities, moreover, the freeways were entirely funded by higher levels of government.[16]

The Era of "Do No Harm"

In October 1973 war broke out in the Middle East. The Organization of Petroleum Exporting Countries (OPEC) severely curtailed production, provoking a worldwide recession and ushering in nearly a decade of stagflation. In U.S. domestic politics, the result was a dramatic shift of focus from issues of amenity, ecology, and social justice to those of economic revival and competitiveness. Locally, the Fainsteins write, concessionary regimes were succeeded by conserving regimes, which adopted a tough stance toward lower-class demands and assigned top priority to fiscal retrenchment. These regimes did not, though, attempt to revive the development policies of the 1950s and 1960s. Rather, fearful of provoking new protests, they shifted from a primary reliance on public investment schemes in striving to lure investors toward an emphasis on financial and regulatory incentives. This strategy, the Fainsteins argue, was a great political success: "As the state

---

14. For a more complete account, see Altshuler (1989, pp. 156–58).

15. See Meyer, Kain, and Wohl (1965, esp. pp. 99–106, 341–43, chs. 9–11); Moses and Williamson (1963); and Hilton (1974).

16. These observations can be fitted comfortably into the Fainsteins' theory as supportive evidence for their view that local governments are mainly instruments of specific business interests. They are much harder, though, to reconcile with Peterson's view that they are guided by a rational understanding of the community's long-term economic interests.

ceased to be the direct agent of redevelopment, it became a less important target for class conflict over use of the city. The conflict was now played out in a disaggregated manner between landlords and tenants, working-class residents and gentrifiers, small shopkeepers and big developers. Even where popular forces were strongest, local regimes could claim correctly that they had only limited control over private market actors."[17]

This analysis is persuasive with respect to urban redevelopment, the Fainsteins' central concern. It does not apply, however, to such programs as highway and airport development, where private investment was rarely an option. Nor do the Fainsteins explain why development subsidies and regulatory concessions generally attract so little attention; the main reasons, we judge, are as follows. First, these are policy instruments whose exercise business has always dominated (except for zoning in established residential neighborhoods). Second, they are quite abstract, and therefore hard for most residents to grasp. Third, as hard public choice theorists would note, the average resident bears only a trivial portion of the cost of such actions in any particular case. Finally, since private developers are unable to exercise eminent domain, they tend to shy away from sites with large numbers of established property owners—and particularly settled neighborhoods whose residents are committed emotionally as well as economically to their current locations.

Historical-institutional theory most satisfactorily accounts for the continued avoidance of state-sponsored disruption since 1973. Statutes and judicial doctrines adopted in the period of transition provided that in cases of conflict, environmental values should generally prevail over developmental objectives, and empowered very small minorities to throw sand in the gears of public development initiatives. The courts have, to be sure, gradually pulled back from expansive interpretations of these provisions,[18] but what most requires explanation is their continuing significance—and in a few cases even their strengthening—long after the passing of the unique circumstances in which they originated.[19]

17. Fainstein and Fainstein (1983, p. 268).

18. See McSpadden (2000, pp. 145–64); and also Greve (1996).

19. A complete list of major federal environmental statutes through 1998 appears in Vig and Kraft (2000, pp. 389–95). Important statutes enacted after 1973 include the Superfund Act of 1980 (and 1986 amendments), the Nuclear Waste Policy Act of 1982, the Resource Conservation Amendments of 1984, the Safe Drinking Water Act of 1986 (and 1996 amendments), the Pollution Prevention Act of 1990, the Clean Air Act Amendments of 1990, the Omnibus Water Act of 1992, and the Food Quality Protection Act of 1996.

A primary reason, certainly, is that large segments of the public have remained strongly supportive of environmental values and are ready to mobilize in defense of their neighborhoods. But another is that highlighted by historical-institutionalist theorists: given the checks and balances of American government, policies once adopted tend to persist long after the forces that gave rise to them have waned.[20] Such persistence is most feasible, of course, when the provisions constrain government action, since minority veto is a pervasive, well-accepted feature of American politics. Most positive actions, on the other hand, require the assembly of diverse coalitions and the neutralization of all those who might otherwise exercise their own minority vetoes. Such cooperation is difficult to obtain even for causes at the height of fashion—and virtually impossible for those that have fallen out of favor or become intensely controversial.

In sum, business-government coalitions have adapted to new political and legal, far more than economic, factors since the period of transition. With some old strategies blocked, they have identified new ones—equally developmental but tailored to avoid conflict with neighborhood, minority, and environmental interests. Over the years, mega-project investment has revived, but mainly as a result of its champions learning how to minimize such conflict.

Patterns of Initiative, Support, and Resistance

We are concerned in this section with three phenomena. First, public officials were the most frequent initiators of the mega-projects examined in this book (excluding sports facilities), and commonly took the lead as well in mobilizing support, developing strategies, and assembling resources for them. Second, the private support coalitions for these projects were almost invariably business-led. Third, while "use value" interests, as Logan and Molotch label them, were often able to impose constraints, they were very rarely active as project initiators or support coalition members.

Public Entrepreneurship

It is to public choice theory that we owe the term *public entrepreneurship* and the idea that its functions are analogous to those of entrepreneurship in business. There is no work in this tradition, however, on public entrepreneurship in urban settings; for that we must turn to other theorists, employing different terminology.

20. See Vogel (1993, pp. 267–68).

Dahl emphasized Mayor Lee's initiative, along with that of several top aides, in jump-starting New Haven redevelopment during the 1950s. Local business leaders had for some years favored redevelopment, he writes, but they had failed to provide realistic solutions to the question of how public money should be raised, the local press remained hostile to redevelopment, and those displaced seemed likely to fight. So local officials held back, and nothing happened. Lee was an enthusiast for redevelopment, though, and quickly moved to organize support for it after his election in 1954. This proved to be more difficult than one might have expected if redevelopment were truly a business initiative. It took him a year just to stimulate the formation of a business-led Citizens Action Committee. In the end, however, he assembled a very broad coalition, with business at its core but extending as well to include working-class and ethnic (including African American) groups, labor unions, educators, and even good-government groups like the League of Women Voters. With this support in place the program took off, but most initiative remained in the public sector. Reviewing 57 specific actions through 1958, Dahl reports that more than half were initiated by the mayor or his development administrator, Edward Logue. Other public officials initiated half the remaining actions, bringing the total public share to about three quarters.[21]

Dahl concludes that Lee's organization and leadership of the "executive-centered coalition" made possible, for the first time, the effective pursuit of "rapid, comprehensive change in the physical pattern of the city"—a "minor revolution" that was quintessentially political.[22] Dahl made no claim that executive-centered coalitions were common. He did suggest, however, that great projects are likely to move forward only when political executives take the lead—not just in developing plans but in mobilizing and then nurturing the private support coalitions on which their efforts ultimately depend.

The Critical Support Role of Business

Elite theorists counter, of course, that even where public officials can be observed performing entrepreneurial functions, they are merely responding to incentives structured by or at the behest of business interests. Indeed, sociologist G. William Domhoff developed this argument with a focus on Dahl's own case, New Haven in the 1950s.[23] Logan and Molotch argue more gen-

21. Dahl (1961, pp. 124–29).
22. Dahl (1961, p. 202).
23. See Domhoff (1978).

erally that in order for local officials to thrive politically and create a record of accomplishment, they must generally associate themselves with growth machine objectives. For the truly ambitious, furthermore, support is not enough; it is essential as well to demonstrate leadership in the identification and pursuit of attractive development opportunities. The other side of the coin is that officials who seriously antagonize growth interests routinely find themselves pilloried in the media, short of allies and funds, and driven from office.[24]

Stone adds a detailed portrayal of business co-optation tactics in his examination of the Atlanta growth coalition. In order to ensure wide support for its leadership, the coalition distributes a diverse array of incentives (ranging from contracts to club memberships to philanthropic contributions), not merely within the business community but also to local professionals, small businesses, churches, colleges and universities, cultural institutions, and social service nonprofits. In the modern "reformed" city, he observes, government officials have little patronage to distribute. The business community, however, deploys a great deal.[25] Thus when it unites around major projects, other local organizations (unless they are direct project victims) tend to fall in line.

The public leaders who sparked such projects as the Central Artery/Tunnel and Denver International Airport did not, as nearly as can be determined, perceive themselves as tools of business, but they clearly recognized that business support was indispensable and were highly skilled in calibrating their proposals to attract it. It is useful to think of them as entrepreneurs in need of venture capital. The local business leaders to whom they looked for support were inundated with proposals and could invest in just a few. But their investment criteria were known (at least to skilled participants in local politics), and the potential rewards of their favor were such as to constitute, for skilled mega-project entrepreneurs, an overwhelming incentive.

The Defensive Role of Use Value Interests

For obvious reasons "use value" interests—organized around the desire to preserve (and where possible enhance) urban amenities and in-place social networks—are the primary sources of opposition to mega-project proposals. The question that follows is whether they can often be mobilized for support purposes as well. We came across a couple of light rail cases in

24. See Logan and Molotch (1987, pp. 66–69, 230–36).
25. Stone (1989, pp. 186–91, 213–15).

which they were, but no more. Among the theorists under review, Logan and Molotch most persuasively explain why. For exchange value participants in local politics, who derive their livelihoods from property ownership or development, the pursuit of favorable government actions—whether investment, tax, or regulatory—is a routine aspect of business. So they tend to be politically active and well mobilized on a continuous basis. Use values can be powerful motivators of political action as well, but in general far more sporadically. Without a financial incentive to participate in local land use politics, most potential members of use value coalitions pay little attention except when threatened. So their mobilization capacity is almost entirely for purposes of defense. Stated another way, while preservationist concerns constitute the primary check on rampant development, they rarely constitute an alternative basis for positive or enduring political leadership.[26]

Bottom-up Federalism

Among the theories here under review, only two—hard and soft public choice theory—consider policy initiative in the federal system systematically. Theorists in the other traditions call attention at times to instances of local lobbying in the federal arena, and of local actions responsive to federal incentives, but their observations tend to be ad hoc rather than systematic.[27]

Hard public choice theory, it will be recalled, emphasizes the pursuit of district benefits as a driving motive for congressional action, and the tendency for projects to originate at the local level. It argues as well that when federal agencies press local applicants to demonstrate consensus, they are not merely seeking to protect themselves from criticism. They are, more fundamentally, responding to their congressional overseers, who are loath to become embroiled in local controversies. These observations are precisely on target.

Paul Peterson and colleagues, in elaborating what we have labeled "soft" public choice theory, argue that federal programs vary greatly in

26. Logan and Molotch (1987, pp. 134–41, 215–28). For a city-specific analysis of the difficulty of assembling use value interests into a stable governing coalition, see DeLeon (1992).

27. Logan and Molotch (1987, pp. 55–56) cite examples of localities obtaining federal grants to bolster their positions vis-à-vis competitive jurisdictions. Domhoff (1978, pp. 73–75) argues that the decisive factor in the takeoff of urban renewal in New Haven after 1954 was federal amendments of that year to the urban renewal law rather than Mayor Lee's accession to the mayoralty. Fainstein and Fainstein (1983, p. 248) state briefly that local directive regimes were made possible by federal renewal legislation.

permissiveness, depending on the extent to which federal and grantee government aims coincide. Because states and localities are primarily oriented toward development, developmental programs have always been administered permissively. The constituencies for redistributive programs, on the other hand, have traditionally pressed for more directive administration, characterized by extensive regulation and formal evaluations.[28] So far we concur, but we believe the argument should be qualified in two respects. First, development programs have been far more subject to regulation since the 1970s than previously—not, it is true, to prevent drift from their central purposes, but to ensure their synchronization with other social and environmental values (whose constituencies are oriented no less toward directive federal administration than those for redistributive programs). Second, Peterson and colleagues maintain that as redistributive programs mature, grantor-grantee tensions tend to dissolve because recipient governments, spared the need to finance these new missions, gradually become committed to them.[29] The record is more ambiguous, however, particularly in programs such as public housing and school busing to promote racial integration. In these cases, obviously, the conflicts with local preferences were never overcome, and it was the federal will that eventually dissolved. Federal reductions in oversight, moreover, seem at times to reflect political shifts away from a commitment to redistribution as opposed to improvements in grantee compliance. Welfare reform as enacted in 1996, during a period of conservative Republican ascendancy, is perhaps the most salient recent example. It transformed the program into a virtual block grant, but the central motives were to cap federal spending and reduce the welfare rolls rather than to acknowledge a growing state commitment to long-standing program objectives.[30]

Elite Initiative and Pluralistic Constraints: The Shifting Balance

The great mega-project era, it seems clear, was an anomaly—a period in which many of the normal constraints on local action in the development policy arena, and on business dominance, were suspended. The far more

28. Peterson, Rabe, and Wong (1986, pp. 12–20, chs. 4–6).
29. Peterson, Rabe, and Wong (1986, chs. 6, 7).
30. Peterson addressed the possible enactment of this legislation, which was pending as he completed *The Price of Federalism*. In view of its conflict with his theory, he ventured to doubt that if enacted it would long endure. P. E. Peterson (1995, p. 182). So far it has, though, and President Bush has recently (2002) proposed even more stringent requirements on states to move their dependent populations from welfare to work in the years ahead.

common pattern, both before and since this interlude, is more nuanced, with business constituting the main constituency for development initiatives but subject to a fairly tight web of pluralistic constraints. Stated another way, while business has a near-monopoly in organizing support for development proposals, the potential to derail proposals is far more diffused. Neighborhood, environmental, ethnic, preservationist, and other interests with little or no capacity to mobilize support coalitions can, if aroused, generally block or modify initiatives that threaten them.

We call this pattern "negative pluralism," though it certainly involves elements of elite domination as well, for two reasons: (1) it highlights the most critical difference between the great mega-project era, when most constraints were suspended, and the longer periods both before and since; and (2) it is unrealistic to expect ordinary citizens, preoccupied with their private lives and lacking access to institutional resources for mobilization, to initiate or frequently mobilize in support of development policy proposals. The more interesting question is whether they can protect their "use value" interests in the face of threats emanating from the public and business sectors. And we believe this is the only aspect of local development policy that most residents care much about.

The era of minimalist government, until the 1950s, was one in which business itself generally concentrated on the negative: seeking to hold down taxation and spending, to minimize regulation, and to confine the scope of local government to the provision of basic services. This vision was embodied not only in ideology but in the very structure of local government—highly fragmented, subject to strict judicial review, and with a variety of procedural obstacles (such as requirements for voter approval) to increased taxation. Thus efforts to waive the normal constraints, to champion specific proposals that business community leaders might favor, were rare—and even more rarely successful. Business was certainly the most influential group in just about every city, but its capacity—like that of other local interests—was mainly negative. Negative pluralism prevailed in the sense that many could veto, but no one could successfully launch activist initiatives. There were specific exceptions, to be sure, but these were rare and by later standards very modest in scale.

Attitudes shifted dramatically in the wake of World War II, however, and national coalitions mobilized successfully to bring about large-scale programs of federal aid. Within several years the idea of activist government on behalf of local economic development became both fashionable and affordable—because it could be funded without increasing broad-based local taxes. Therefore, the primary lever available to opponents of development initiatives, resistance to taxation, ceased to matter. Virtually no one appreciated, however, how disruptive the new programs would prove to be or their potential to generate a massive public backlash. In the decade and a half, roughly, that it took for this backlash to materialize, the lead role of business in local politics reached its zenith—though numerous scholars found pluralism flourishing (at least in northern cities) outside the development arena.

What is striking in retrospect, however, is how quickly opposition did erupt on a broad scale, and how fragile the arrangements of the great mega-project era proved to be when it did. Business and its public sector allies did not retreat for long, of course. They were now fully committed to the idea of government activism on behalf of local economic development and sensitive to the fact that interlocal (as well as interstate and international) competition for investment was intensifying. But they had to adjust tactically to the reemergence of negative pluralism. One tactic was to de-emphasize large-scale public investment in favor of fiscal and regulatory inducements that could be conferred on developers (so long as their financing was obscure or came from higher-level governments) without attracting much attention from ordinary citizens. This is not to say that business abandoned the theme of direct public investment, however. Quite the contrary. The flow of such projects continued, though in fewer numbers and different configurations than during the great mega-project era. Projects requiring massive clearance—redevelopment in the style of the 1950s, new expressways through residential neighborhoods and public parks, and new airports or runways almost anywhere in urban areas—became extremely rare. The slack was substantially taken up, however, by other types of projects: rail transit lines that could be threaded along existing rights-of-way or placed underground; downtown festival shopping malls, convention centers, and sports arenas that could be built on relatively small sites in low-value industrial or commercial areas; and even some road and airport improvements sited and designed to minimize harmful side effects. These changes did not indicate a displacement of business from its traditional role as the core, indispensable constituency for development policy initiatives. They did indicate a fundamental shift in the direction of negative pluralism, however—which is to say, the capacity of other groups to insist that business-supported public ventures leave them no worse off, and at times to secure positive benefits as the price of their acquiescence.

Which elements of this pattern to emphasize—those of continuity or change, of pluralism or elite dominance—is of course a matter of judgment. Clarence Stone's analysis of Atlanta politics illustrates the problem with particular clarity. In common with nearly all other recent theorists of urban politics, he chooses to stress the themes of continuity and business dominance. At the level of detail, however, he chronicles a far more complicated story. Having sought fruitlessly to preserve white dominance in city government by expanding the city's boundaries, the business leadership had to accommodate to the most urgent demands of a black-majority electorate. Having long championed racial segregation, it helped lead Atlanta peacefully into the era of desegregation when it concluded that the conflicts associated with prolonged resistance would be bad for business. While retaining its primacy in the development arena, it prudently withdrew from most others—including education, the police, and public appointments more generally. It forged strong ties with black professionals, small businesses, and nonprofit institutions, but only by respecting their most critical imperatives and providing a continual flow of jobs, contracts, philanthropic contributions, and honorific benefits to them. Finally, in promoting such projects as the regional airport expansion and new rapid transit system, it accommodated demands for ambitious programs of affirmative action, for route adjustments and bus subsidies, and of course for the avoidance of community disruption. Do these adjustments add up to a fundamental change in the character of Atlanta politics? Stone thinks not. It seems to us, however, that in defining the regime and business dominance so generally that these changes fail to register, he slights the most interesting developments in urban politics of the past half century—developments that have been extremely significant in terms of what ordinary residents care about, the policy options realistically available in various periods, and the balance in local politics among key interests and values.

Conclusion

Each of the theories discussed highlights important, but different, truths about urban politics. The classic pluralists, and particularly Dahl, point out that mega-projects in cities were extremely rare until the enactment of generous programs of federal aid in the 1950s, that local public leadership at times played a vital role in enabling cities to take full advantage of these programs, and that different constituencies tend to focus on, and dominate, different issue areas. Writing at the height of urban renewal, the pluralists were well aware that large institutions, mainly business but also nonprofits such as universities and hospitals, provided the main constituency for redevelopment.[31] They viewed the redevelopment arena as just one among many, however, and so did not extrapolate from this finding to a judgment that such enterprises dominated the whole of local politics.

The distinctive contribution of hard public choice theory has been to explain political regularities as the products of rational choices by narrowly selfish individual actors, including elected officials, responding to generally stable patterns of incentives. It deals far more persuasively with some political phenomena than others: congressional logrolling, most notably, in comparison with the mobilization of social movements and the persistence of institutional arrangements long after their original support base has atrophied. Given the topic of this book, however, its pertinence and power are undeniable, particularly with respect to the following:

—the preference of Congress for decisionmaking by very large majorities, a pattern that maximizes each individual member's chance of inclusion in each winning coalition;

—the tendency of public works proposals to bubble up from below, as expressions of the interests of local development constituencies, rather than to emerge as elements of coherent national plans;

—the desire of members of Congress, before they champion local initiatives in the federal arena, for credible assurances that they will not find themselves embroiled in local controversies;

—the consequent tendency for Congress to mandate extensive studies and public hearings, less as sources of technical information than as forums within which potential conflicts can be identified and resolved.

Hard public choice theorists do not, as far as we know, explore the local effects of these federal requirements. Our own work suggests, however, that they are important contributors to the "do no harm" paradigm in mega-project planning.[32]

---

31. See Banfield (1961, esp. ch. 9).

32. Why, one may ask, was this not the case in the 1950s and early 1960s? One possibility is that members of Congress had little reason to fear then that mega-projects would provoke major local controversies. As neighborhood, minority, environmental, and other "use value" interests mobilized a few years later, however, the risk became highly significant and members of Congress responded accordingly. The implication, of course, is that "do no harm" planning rests on a foundation of "use value" interest mobilization even more fundamentally than on the preference of elected officials for risk-free choices.

Hard public choice theorists also emphasize the obstacles to sustained group mobilization, particularly when groups are large and diffuse. And it was they who (in the mid-1960s) developed the concept of public entrepreneurship to explain how these obstacles are sometimes overcome. Adept individuals, they observed, can at times identify, package, and market "cooperation benefits" for the members of highly diffuse groups and restrict such benefits, largely at least, to those who actually incur membership obligations (such as the payment of dues). Such entrepreneurs, they surmised, reap selective benefits themselves in the same manner as, though typically in different currencies than, business entrepreneurs. The theory is a bit circular, in that any source of human motivation may count as a benefit currency. Its ambiguities matter far more in policy domains where conflict is driven mainly by ideology and group identity (such as abortion, capital punishment, and civil rights), however, than in the domains of public works and economic development. It is, consequently, a highly useful launchpad for thinking about coalition formation and management in the cases here under review.

Paul Peterson's work, which we have labeled soft public choice theory, takes off from the rational actor model as well, but with a critical difference. Whereas hard public choice theorists emphasize conflicts between actor and jurisdictional rationality, Peterson views them as in harmony. Local officials and civic leaders, he maintains, are on the whole motivated to pursue the interests of their jurisdictions rather than merely feather their own nests, and in any event they recognize a congruence between their own direct interests—whether electoral, bureaucratic, or economic—and those of the community at large. We perceive far more narrow rent-seeking than this picture suggests, but Peterson's most important contribution was in any event on a different plane: in recasting urban political theory toward a focus on localities as economic competitors—and competitors, moreover, with negligible market power. Within this framework, he argues, nearly all local interests recognize (quite correctly) that the prime objective of local policy must be to attract investors. They take care, consequently, to insulate development programs from day-to-day politics and to keep redistributive claims—which repel investors—off the public agenda. This is not to say that controversy is absent from local politics; indeed, the media and most local voters are preoccupied with matters in conflict. With rare exceptions, however, these are fundamentally trivial—in the sense that they have negligible bearing on the city's fiscal health or prosperity.

We find this portion of Peterson's argument highly persuasive, but with an important caveat. At least since the late 1960s, the level of conflict about public investment initiatives has been far greater than he indicates. The primary reason is that the details of project development—in particular, siting, financing (insofar as it is local), and mitigation—are largely allocational.[33] Peterson neglects this in his theory as articulated in *City Limits* (1981) and then erects a barrier to its consideration by eliminating his allocational category altogether (absorbing it into his development category) in *The Price of Federalism* (1995).[34]

Both hard and soft public choice theorists start from the premise that observed political patterns reflect current actor interests pursued rationally.[35] Historical-institutional theorists provide a useful balance to this perspective, maintaining that cultural, legal, and institutional factors are often critical in shaping actor behavior, that these express a distinct political history and culture, and that consequently they tend to evolve much more slowly than current interests. Historical-institutional scholars have not, unfortunately, paid a great deal of attention to local politics. We are particularly indebted to David Vogel, however, for his explanation of the ways in which environmental forces managed to "hard wire" their legislative gains of the early 1970s into the processes of urban mega-project decisionmaking, enabling them to defend these gains successfully even as their influence waned in subsequent years.

33. This point has been made previously, though in somewhat different form and without reference to Peterson's allocational category, in Stone and Sanders (1987, pp. 159–81, esp.167–68, 178–79).

34. Even more fundamentally for his theory, this recategorization obfuscates his entire 1981 analysis of overt conflict in local politics. It occurs, however, in the context of a much later book on the federal system and with no explicit reference to his theory of local politics, so it is unclear whether he intended it as applicable to the latter.

35. This is not to say, of course, that public choice theory completely ignores contextual factors. On the contrary, public choice theorists routinely acknowledge framework elements as background for their main arguments. Legislative scholars, for example, assume that members of Congress act within the constitutional system of checks and balances, that they are subject to periodic reelection from single-member districts, and that even in one-party districts they are vulnerable in primaries. And Paul Peterson emphasizes that city governments are embedded in state and national systems, within which they have very limited authority. These sketches, however, are typically very general; they portray very familiar, essentially fixed system elements, and they are not objects of the investigation itself. Within the frameworks portrayed, moreover, public choice theorists tend to assume that cultural, legal, and institutional arrangements are highly malleable, and so can generally be explained in terms of current actor interests.

The distinctive contribution of regime theory, finally, has been to explore the dynamics of local business-government collaboration in detail, emphasizing that business and political leaders can both pursue their aims more effectively in concert than alone. Political leaders need business support if they are to accomplish anything in the development arena, and more generally if they are to enjoy good press and well-funded campaigns. Private growth coalitions need their public officials to secure grants from higher-level governments and to make favorable land use, tax, and infrastructure decisions. In the most prominent statement of regime theory, Clarence Stone adds that stable, effective governance coalitions rest on a foundation of widespread patronage—that is, the wide distribution of selective incentives—and that business groups are far better able to provide such patronage in modern "reformed" cities than local governments. Business groups tend also to have much clearer views than most public officials about developmental strategies and tactics. It is scarcely surprising, therefore, that public-private governing coalitions (regimes) tend to concentrate on the furtherance of business objectives. Logan and Molotch make essentially these points as well.

This is, in one sense, a reformulation of classic urban elite theory. More significantly, however, it focuses attention on the ways in which local groups with widely disparate interests—for example, Atlanta's black political leaders and its white business leaders—can at times forge stable patterns of cooperation and on the mechanisms by which obstacles to local planning, coordination, and resource mobilization may be overcome. We contend that stable regimes, in the sense portrayed by Stone, are rare; even in Atlanta as described by Stone business dominance has been clear only with respect to economic development issues. Even within the development arena, moreover, contemporary growth coalitions must generally be prepared to accommodate numerous other local interests if they realistically hope to prevail.

Nonetheless, regime theory is quite helpful in thinking about the politics of mega-project authorization and financing. Mega-projects are generally nonroutine. They normally require special authorizing, funding, revenue, land acquisition, and regulatory actions by two or more levels of government. They are all at least initially controversial. And they typically proceed so slowly that their political base must hold firm through electoral and business cycles. The stable and overwhelming support required to keep a mega-project on course for many years clearly does involve public-private cooperation of the sort that regime theorists describe.

One need not proceed to the generalization that effective mega-project coalitions are possible only within the framework of general governance regimes. Those discussed in this book were far more specialized and ad hoc, assembled by and for those with the greatest interest in each specific project. The existence of a strong general governance regime is doubtless an additional important asset where it exists. It is probably less important, however, than such factors as the availability of funding from sources unlikely to be perceived as a burden by local voters and the feasibility in specific cases of "do no harm" project implementation.

Logan and Molotch add two further valuable ideas to which we have frequently returned: (1) that the major fault line in urban development politics is between "exchange" and "use" value interests; and (2) that institutions, including business enterprises, vary widely in the degree of their political activism—depending on the strength of their local ties (making exit difficult) and the extent to which their strategies (particularly of land development) hinge on favorable government actions. The mega-project coalitions observed here have, in fact, nearly all been led by major local developers and property owners. (The exceptions were several light rail transit coalitions led by environmental interests.) Their opponents have invariably been mobilized around the protection of use values, notably environmental protection and neighborhood stability.

We are indebted, finally, to Norman and Susan Fainstein, apparently the first to theorize explicitly about local regimes, for their rich, persuasive account of the ways in which local (business-dominated) renewal coalitions adapted to changing circumstances over three decades: from the arrival of new federal aid opportunities in the 1950s, to the emergence of new popular movements in the 1960s, to the waning of these movements and the growing preoccupation with global competitiveness during the 1970s and early 1980s. Better than any of their successors, moreover, they balanced themes of stability and change in their analysis of local development politics—an accomplishment as important, we have come to appreciate, as it is difficult.

Having presented research on just one of its aspects, we stop short of venturing our own general theory of urban politics or, indeed, even a general critique of the theories discussed above. The acid test of any broad theory, however, is its capacity to explain and link specific observations. It is in the accumulation of efforts to use them in this fashion that their power and their deficiencies become known. So it is not presumptuous, we hope, to note that studies like this one are integral parts of the theory-building enterprise, or to suggest that there is a need for much more routine iteration between the tasks of in-depth empirical investigation and general theory refinement.

CHAPTER NINE

What Next?

A plausible argument can be made that the age of urban mega-projects has passed—that such projects have become increasingly marginal as instruments of urban development policy and will become even more so in the near future. Our own prognosis is far more nuanced, but in striving to peer ahead there is no better point of departure than this requiem for mega-projects, which runs more or less as follows.

The imperative to "do no harm," which first took hold in the 1970s, rendered mega-projects of the types most salient during the prior two decades—new expressways and airports and clearance-based redevelopment schemes—entirely out of the question or feasible only at costs far exceeding their benefits. Urban growth coalitions found other types of mega-projects on which to concentrate, from rapid transit systems to stadiums and convention centers, but gradually these too became phenomenally expensive. And from the vantage point of 2002, as this is written, new barriers command attention. State and local tax revenues, after rising rapidly through most of the 1990s, turned sharply downward in 2001 and 2002—reflecting the combined effects of an economic slowdown and burst stock market bubble. At the federal level, where the effects of these economic developments are compounded by a massive tax cut enacted in 2001 (and scheduled to unfold through 2010), the budget outlook has shifted from one of large surpluses toward even larger deficits.

More specifically, airline, airport, and highway user revenues are down substantially from their levels of a year or so ago, and there is little expectation that any of these revenue streams will resume buoyant growth in the near future. Within these sectors, moreover, urgent new security concerns in the wake of September 11 command top priority in the competition for scarce resources, most obviously with respect to aviation but also with respect to protecting bridges and tunnels, monitoring freight, and so on. Tourist-related businesses have also been profoundly affected by recent events. Even before the terrorist attacks there was an oversupply of convention centers, produced by the boom in their construction during the 1990s.[1] With tourism down, moreover, so are revenues from the tourist-based taxes (on hotel rooms and restaurant meals, for example) on which localities have heavily relied to finance sports facilities and convention centers in recent years.

On the other side of the coin, real expenditures for highway, transit, airport, sports facility, and convention center improvements have been at record levels in recent years. At least before September 11, the traditional support coalitions for all these categories of investment appeared highly vigorous. In the nation's capital, furthermore, a new administration leaned strongly toward relaxation of the regulatory constraints that had made large-scale public (and certain types of private) investment so difficult for the previous three decades.[2] This is not to suggest that environmental and community constraints were about to dissolve, but a great debate did seem to be in prospect about their appropriate place in the constellation of government priorities. And so it still may be, as and when buoyant growth resumes. Some particularly notable recent developments merit closer examination.

The Federal Role

Since the late 1980s federal aid for highway, transit, and aviation investment has risen steadily in real terms, as has state and local spending from own-source revenues.[3] The most recent legislation to reauthorize highway and transit programs, for example, the so-called TEA-21 Act of 1998, established record funding levels for both, as did its aviation counterpart, AIR-21,

1. Heywood Sanders, for example, concluded early in 2001 that recent growth in convention center capacity "dwarfs recent demand growth." See Sanders (2001, p. 2).

2. See Margaret Kriz, "Environmentalists Are Howling Again," *National Journal*, January 5, 2002, pp. 50–51; Jim Vandehei and Tom Hamburger, "Business Donors Prepare Another Wish List for Bush: Lobbyists Seek More Tax Breaks, Looser Rules on Workplace and Environment," *Wall Street Journal*, January 18, 2002, p. A20; and "Poor Marks on the Environment," *New York Times*, January 28, 2002.

3. See tables 4-1, 4-2, 5-4, 6-2, 6-4. See also Congressional Budget Office, "Trends in Public Infrastructure Spending" (1999, tables A-7, A-8, A-11).

enacted in 2000. Even before September 11, however, the darkening fiscal outlook and other announced priorities—on the administration side, most notably, new weapons systems and additional tax cuts; on the Democratic side, prescription drug benefits for the elderly—suggested that the recent upswing in federal transportation aid might have run its course. In any event, incentives to concentrate resources on a limited number of mega-projects had been declining for some time.

This was particularly notable in the highway arena, where the Interstate Highway Program had for decades been the federal government's main priority, providing 90 percent funding for approved projects over and above all formula aid and regardless of their ultimate cost. With its completion, states considering potential successors to the artery/tunnel and Century Freeway projects have had to confront the daunting prospect of raising most of their cost at home (or diverting a very large share of their federal formula aid from other popular projects).[4] Offsetting this in part, Congress has become progressively more disposed since the early 1980s to include ad hoc project earmarks in omnibus transportation bills. It has generally done so in accord with its historic norm of distributing funds very widely across congressional districts, however—with the largest prizes for particularly influential members—rather than in large doses for specific projects.

The increased disposition of Congress to focus on jurisdictional shares, as opposed to major projects or national purposes, has been even more apparent in the allocation of formula grant money. Responding to an intense campaign by "donor" states, for example, TEA-21 guaranteed each state a share of federal highway aid closely corresponding to its share of motor vehicle tax contributions.[5] Demands for a more even distribution of transit grants are expected to be a major issue when surface transportation pro-

4. The artery/tunnel may stand as an object lesson to states that are tempted. Congress effectively ended the Interstate Highway Program in 1991, capping the future amount of inter-state assistance that states with remaining projects (most notably Massachusetts) would receive for them on the basis of then-current cost estimates. As a result of subsequent escala-tion it now appears that the direct state share of the artery/tunnel cost will exceed $6 billion, in comparison with the $700 million (in 2002 dollars) estimated in 1987, when Congress was persuaded to place the project on the interstate system, and with estimates still below $1 bil-lion in 1991. The state has also been compelled, in making up the fiscal shortfall, to allocate $4.2 billion in federal formula highway aid that would otherwise have been available for other highway or transit projects in the state. See table 4-3.
5. The law guaranteed that highway grants provided to each state would equal at least 90.5 percent of the federal motor vehicle–related excise taxes used for highways paid in that state. (The provision does not apply, however, to the proportion of highway user taxes used in support of mass transit.) See Department of Transportation, "A Summary: Transportation Equity Act for the 21st Century" (1998).

grams again come up for authorization in 2003. Similarly, AIR-21 accentuated the historic pattern of favoring small commercial and general aviation airports in the distribution of federal airport aid.[6]

In November 2001, on the other hand, Congress enacted and President Bush signed the Aviation and Transportation Security Act, which directly federalized most airport security responsibilities. The great majority of expenditures pursuant to this act will be direct rather than in the form of grants-in-aid, but they will—in calibration with the perceived threat—be heavily concentrated at major airports. Only a public safety crisis could have brought this about, but it does represent a conspicuous exception to the general trend toward diffusion of federal infrastructure-related expenditures.

Growing Pressure for New Road and Runway Construction

During the latter three decades of the twentieth century demands for new urban highway and runway capacity were, for the most part, trumped by environmental and neighborhood resistance. Throughout most of this period, moreover, levels of congestion were stable or declining. That is, Americans were able to travel farther and more frequently, at constant or rising speeds, even as they blocked the great majority of proposals for new expressway and runway construction. How was this possible?

On the highway side, the primary explanation is that motorists exploited spare capacity already in existence or under construction by 1970. They were moving from cities to suburbs, and from older (more concentrated) to newer (more dispersed) regions, where they were able to use roads less congested than those they were leaving behind.[7] Secondarily, of course, some new capacity was built, particularly on the fringes of fast-growing regions, and more flexible work schedules may have facilitated the spread of travel demand peaks over a greater number of hours each day. In consequence of these factors in combination, while urban residents traveled greater distances

6. As of 1996 the nation's 71 major commercial airports, which served 90 percent of air travelers, received 41 percent of federal airport grant money, slightly less than its 3,203 nonhub and general aviation airports, which served 3.4 percent of air travelers (see table 5-5). AIR-21 seemed likely to exacerbate this pattern, as it raised the federal aid penalty for airports using passenger facility charges (PFCs). Whereas previously they lost 50 cents from their formula airport grant entitlement for each PFC dollar they raised (up to a maximum of 50 percent of their total entitlement), they were now to lose 75 cents. Kirk (2000, pp. 9–10).

7. The continuing shift from transit to automotive commutation was also a factor, though a very minor one. Urban travel by transit is only about half as fast, on average, as by automobile. Even in 1970, however, transit accounted for less than 4 percent of urban passenger mileage. (See table 6-5.)

in their new dispersed environments, they did so at sufficiently higher speeds that average commute times actually declined from the late 1960s until the early 1980s.[8] Beginning in the mid-1980s, however, slack road capacity was increasingly exhausted and travel times began rising—to an extent that became increasingly apparent during the 1990s. By 2000, according to the U.S. census, the average one-way commute trip took nearly two minutes (8 percent) longer than in 1990.[9]

The air travel system had a larger repertoire of adjustment techniques, including the use of larger aircraft, yield management pricing to balance loads (by season, day of the week, and time of day), some flexibility in the location of hub operations, and air traffic control improvements. As travel surged during the boom of the 1990s, though, delays became endemic—in part because most of the potential gains from yield management and from channeling travelers through hub airports had already been realized, and in part because commuter services, which used small aircraft, were expanding very rapidly. Aviation and business groups responded with vigorous campaigns, both national and local, to encourage the development of new runways, and toward this end to streamline environmental reviews.[10] The

8. According to the National Personal Transportation Survey, average commute times dropped from 22 minutes in 1969 to 19.7 minutes in 1977 and to 18.2 minutes in 1983 before rising to 19.6 minutes in 1990. See Federal Highway Administration, "National Personal Transportation Study, 1969: Home to Work Trips and Travel" (1973, tables A-20, A-21), "National Personal Transportation Study, 1973: Home to Work Trips and Travel" (1980, tables A-12, A-14), "National Personal Transportation Survey, 1995: Summary of Travel Trends" (1999, table 25). These figures are slightly lower than those reported by the U.S. Census, which first asked about commuting in 1980. It recorded an average commute time of 21.7 minutes in 1980 and 22.4 minutes in 1990. Federal Highway Administration, "Journey to Work Trends in the United States and Its Major Metropolitan Areas, 1960–1990" (1993, table 2-1, p. 2-2).

9. The increase was from 22.4 to 24.3 minutes. Bureau of the Census, "Census 2000 Supplementary Survey Profile, Table 3: Profile of Selected Economic Characteristics" (www.census.gov/acs/www/ [October 2002]); and Federal Highway Administration, "Journey to Work Trends in the United States and Its Major Metropolitan Areas, 1960–1990" (1993, table 2-1, p. 2-2). A portion of this increase—Alan Pisarski estimates one-fifth to one-fourth—may have been due to changes in the wording of the question. Pisarski (2001).

10. Advocates for improved rail service pressed their case as well, arguing that airport congestion could be relieved by a multibillion-dollar federal program (approximately $3.5 billion a year for 20 years) to support the construction of high-speed rail in many congested corridors. Most analysts doubt, however, that such an investment outside the Boston–Washington, D.C., corridor would have a substantial impact on air travel volumes, and there is no likelihood of congressional action in the near future. Indeed, at this writing Amtrak is in the midst of a major fiscal crisis and there is serious discussion of privatizing its operations. See Transportation Research Board and National Research Council (1991b); Dunn (1998, ch. 5); and Amtrak Reform Council (2002).

term *streamline* implied that their aims were merely to increase efficiency and reduce delays. In practice, however, the goal was substantive and clear—in the words of one industry leader: "to reduce statutory and regulatory impediments that make it difficult for airports to . . . expand runway capacity."[11]

Prohighway forces engaged in a similar, though more muted, campaign. Both these initiatives were consistent with other business-led efforts to relax regulatory constraints—on energy exploration, for example, and power plant siting—and with the priorities of the new Bush administration beginning in 2001. The federal judiciary, moreover, was sharply curtailing the ability of environmental and community groups to litigate against government plans—notably by retreating from its permissive standards of the 1970s on who has standing to sue.[12]

In short, the factors that gave rise to the "do no harm" planning paradigm were now themselves under siege. The evidence of recent history, though, was that the paradigm had extraordinary resilience. Two prior attacks, in President Reagan's first term and during the mid-1990s (when conservative Republicans gained control of Congress), had come to surprisingly little. The statute books remained essentially unchanged, and environmental organizations were reinvigorated. The controversies surrounding these efforts, moreover, proved damaging to those perceived as antienvironment. Reading the polls and subsequent election results, Republican leaders in both cases retreated from their direct assaults on environmental laws and regulations, though they continued to employ less visible tactics such as cutting back enforcement budgets, prohibiting the adoption of new regulations, and preventing the enactment of new environmental laws.[13]

Similarly, the Bush administration provoked a whirlwind of criticism with its early efforts to roll back some environmental regulations issued in the final days of the Clinton administration, its proposal to authorize drilling for oil in the Arctic National Wildlife Refuge, and its rejection of the Kyoto Treaty on global warming. The administration, taking note, quickly muted its rhetoric and took a few steps favored by environmentalists (ordering General Electric, for example, to carry out a $500-million cleanup of PCBs

11. The quotation is from remarks by David Plavin, president of the Airports Council International–North America, at an aviation industry summit meeting, Washington, D.C., February 2, 2001. See Airports Council International–North America, "Building More Runways: The Biggest Piece of the Capacity Pie," February 2, 2001, press release (www.aci-na.org [February 2002]).

12. For an overview, see Duke Environmental Law Symposium (2001).

13. Kraft (2000); and Bosso (2000).

in the Hudson River). Its orientation was still toward less stringent regulation of development activity, but there was clearly no prospect of congressional action to significantly weaken environmental statutes.

These patterns survived September 11 but, as noted above, it was less clear how the campaigns for highway and airport expansion might be affected by the downturn in public tax collections and public fears of air terrorism. Let us turn briefly to early evidence bearing on these questions, and then to the outlook for rail transit as well.

Highways

Aggregate highway spending by all levels of government, adjusted for inflation, reached an all-time high in 1999 (the last year for which complete data are available at this writing). But economic trends turned negative in 2002 and highway user tax receipts, which are highly sensitive to economic conditions, declined sharply in 2001–2. Because of a key provision of TEA-21 this revenue contraction generated an intense political struggle.

TEA-21, which authorizes federal highway and transit programs for fiscal years 1998 through 2003, provides for highway expenditures to vary in response to the level of Highway Trust Fund receipts (averaged over several years, including future projections by the Treasury Department). This provision, sought by highway advocates to prevent a buildup of unspent revenue in the Highway Trust Fund, generated a windfall during fiscal years 2000 through 2002, including a $4.5-billion adjustment in 2002 over and above the level originally projected in TEA-21. In January 2002, however, the Treasury reported that receipts for fiscal year 2001 had come in 11 percent lower than anticipated a year earlier, and it projected only a very modest recovery during fiscal years 2002 and 2003. In this situation, the law called for a double adjustment in fiscal 2003—to offset overspending in fiscal years 2001 and 2002 and to stay within the new, revised estimates of future revenue. The result would have been a 27 percent ($8.6 billion) spending cut in the federal aid highway program from fiscal 2002 to 2003, and the president did in fact call for a reduction of this magnitude in his fiscal year 2003 budget.[14] Highway interests were aghast, of course, and at this writing it appears Congress will accept less than half the president's proposed cut. With the overall budget in deficit and the president focused on other priorities, however, little real growth in highway spending appears likely during the next few years.

---

14. Department of Transportation, "Fiscal Year 2003 Budget in Brief" (2002, pp. 18–19).

Quite aside from spending constraints, moreover, the barriers to new urban expressway construction remain highly formidable. In California, illustratively, even as he dedicated a new urban freeway (first planned in the 1960s) in August 2001, Governor Gray Davis observed that the state had no others in its pipeline and that he doubted it ever would again.[15] Some other states are building expressways in metropolitan areas, but almost exclusively in fringe locations, where little or no urbanized development has yet occurred. Notably, a 58-mile beltway encircling about 80 percent of Denver is in construction, and plans are well advanced for both a 170-mile beltway around Houston and a major connector across the northern tier of the Atlanta region.[16] Such projects are increasingly subject to criticism, however, on the grounds that they induce more traffic, contribute to urban sprawl, and thereby impede compliance with air quality regulations. Both the Houston and Atlanta beltway projects have been delayed and scaled back as a result of such criticism, though they continue to move forward.[17]

A few large projects are also proceeding closer in, but these are virtually all replacements of older facilities. The federal government, Virginia, and Maryland are spending more than $2 billion to replace and expand the Woodrow Wilson Bridge and its approach roads just south of Washington, D.C. (The bridge itself is federally owned.) This project, significantly, involves the displacement of about 300 residential apartments, a violation of the norm to "do no harm." Vast numbers of people and companies have come to depend on the Wilson Bridge over the years, however, and it was threatened with closure for safety reasons unless major improvements were undertaken. The project includes extensive mitigation, moreover: wetland replacement, decking over approach roads, nearby parkland improvements, and generous relocation benefits for those displaced.[18]

15. James Sterngold, "California Governor Sees an End to Freeway Building," *New York Times*, August 21, 2001, p. A10.

16. The Denver beltway will include two separate road designations (E-470 and the Northern Parkway). See www.e-470.com and www.northwestparkway.org. For information on the Houston and Atlanta projects, respectively, see www.grandpky.com and www.northernarc.com.

17. It is doubtful, however, that federal regulators will block any projects outright. They have not in the past, and the current (George W. Bush) administration is clearly less disposed than some of its predecessors toward allowing environmental concerns to impede development initiatives. Federal environmental statutes can provide a basis for private lawsuits, however, as well as actions by state environmental regulators and political controversy. For an overview of the record thus far, see Howitt and Altshuler (1999); and Garrett and Wachs (1996).

18. For an overview of the project, see www.wilsonbridge.com; and Fredrick Kunkle, "New Wilson Bridge Construction Leaves Residents Divided: Good or Bad, Alexandrians Feel Project's Impact," *Washington Post*, July 19, 2001, p. B10.

On a much smaller scale, the state of Ohio recently rebuilt an existing waterfront expressway in Cincinnati as a depressed and partially decked facility.[19] The state of Wisconsin will shortly replace a mile-long elevated freeway spur in Milwaukee with a surface boulevard and mixed-use development. The Washington State DOT has proposed replacing the Alaskan Way viaduct with a depressed and covered facility, and a New York State DOT planning study is examining a similar option for the Gowanus Expressway in Brooklyn.[20] Several urban areas are also embarked at this writing on major projects to improve the flow of traffic near busy ports. The state of Washington, for example, in cooperation with the port authorities of Seattle and Tacoma (and drawing on its federal highway aid), plans to expend about $400 million to eliminate grade crossings on approaches to these ports. The state of New Jersey is moving forward with a plan (costing three quarters of a billion dollars) for a truck-only route between its port facilities and nearby rail yards and highways.

In a related vein, a consortium of state and local agencies recently opened a 20-mile rail connector (roughly half depressed, in a 30-foot-deep open trench) known as the Alameda Corridor, from the seaports of Los Angeles and Long Beach to the Los Angeles area's main rail and truck marshalling yards. The primary aims of this project—in gestation for more than two decades—are, by eliminating at-grade rail crossings of streets and highways, to reduce the very high cost of moving freight to and from the seaports, and thereby to enhance the competitiveness of both the seaports and the region as a whole. More generally, it will ameliorate some of the most severe road congestion in the Los Angeles area and significantly improve conditions in neighborhoods along the corridor. Its major sources of financing include revenue bonds and a federal loan (both secured by projected fee revenue from railroads using the corridor), local port authority grants from their surplus earnings, federal and state highway and transit grants, and local sales tax revenues earmarked for regional transit improvements.[21]

19. This $314 million project, completed in August 2000, was designed to support an ambitious waterfront redevelopment program, costing in excess of $1 billion, that included two new stadiums and a new museum. See Aileen Cho, "Where There's a Will, There's a New Fort Washington Way in 34 Months: 'Impossible' Fast Track Job Spurs Cincinnati Urban Revival," *Engineering News-Record,* April 3, 2000, pp. 36–39.

20. See Washington State Department of Transportation, "SR 99 Alaskan Way Viaduct and Seawall Project" (www.wsdot.wa.gov/projects/Viaduct/plans.htm [September 2002]); and New York State Department of Transportation, "The Gowanus Project" (www.dot.state.ny.us/reg/r11/gowanus/index.html [March 2002]).

21. Alameda Corridor Transportation Authority (1999, pp. 24–26).

Airports

As discussed in chapter 5, the situation just before September 11, 2001, was thus. Among major metropolitan areas, only Denver had managed to build a new passenger airport since the early 1970s, and while several ideas for the next had attracted significant support, none appeared close to approval. On the other hand, a boom in the expansion and modernization of existing airports had gathered force in recent years, with the largest efforts carrying price tags as large as $12 billion (Los Angeles) and $6 billion (Chicago). As of late 2002 the great questions are whether long-term estimates of air travel growth need to be scaled back, whether airports will have adequate revenue bases for the ambitious plans they developed in the 1990s, and, even if so, whether security needs will crowd out many of their expansion and amenity-enhancing priorities.

In the short run at least, these concerns loom very large. Though airline patronage has rebounded substantially from its trough right after September 11, from January through August 2002 airline patronage was 11 percent below year-earlier figures and, because the airlines had cut fares as well, their revenues were down about 16 percent.[22] If years pass without new acts of air terrorism, the historic trajectory of air travel growth will doubtless resume (while varying from year to year in response to economic conditions). But this is a very big "if."

Meanwhile, the patronage decline and new security costs have left the federal government, airports, and airlines with unprecedented revenue shortfalls, calling into question their capacity to finance major improvements. At the federal level, the new Transportation Security Administration (TSA) estimated in March 2002 that it would need $6.8 billion by the end of fiscal year 2002, more than three times the actual revenue projected from the airline ticket surcharge and mandated airline payments earmarked for its needs in the Aviation and Transportation Security Act of 2001, in order to fulfill its responsibilities under the act. It anticipated that this shortfall would ease only slightly in fiscal year 2003, moreover.[23] These estimates exclude,

22. After declining 40–45 percent during the period September 11–30, 2001, monthly enplanements were down 23 percent from figures of the previous year in October, 20 percent in November, and 14 percent in December. From January through August 2002 they were down 11.1 percent. January to August 2002 revenues were down 16 percent from the same period in 2001, and were 24 percent lower than in the similar period in 2000, before the current economic downturn began. See Air Transport Association, "ATA Monthly Passenger Report" (www.airlines.org/public/industry/display1.asp?nid=1037 [October 2002]); and John Heimlich, "U.S. Airlines: The Road to Resuscitation," Air Transport Association, September 27, 2002, pp. 16–17 (www.airlines.org/public/industry/bin/Econ102.pdf [October 2002]).

23. See Mead (2002b).

furthermore, the estimated cost of $2.3 billion for airport building retrofits to accommodate new baggage screening machines, their operators, and the projected lines of people waiting for their baggage to be screened.[24] Airport executives have called on the federal government not only to shoulder these costs but also to provide reimbursement for the increased security procedures that they implemented at federal direction immediately after September 11, before the federal government assumed formal responsibility for airport security.[25] The airlines, finally, have warned that they are unable to bear any increased security costs because they lost more than $7 billion in 2001—even after taking into account a $5-billion bailout by the federal government—and an estimated $10 billion in 2002.[26]

Not surprisingly in this context, most airport operators moved aggressively to curtail their discretionary—including capital—spending in late 2001 and early 2002. Fitch Ratings, for example, found in a review of 64 large- and medium-size U.S. airports that the great majority had imposed hiring freezes (except in their security units), reduced operating budgets, and postponed capital improvements that were not yet under way while indefinitely delaying many long-term projects. San Francisco, for example, cancelled a $54-million renovation of its former central terminal and delayed more than half the elements in its four-year, $800-million capital spending plan. Denver indefinitely delayed one-third of the projects in a $1.5-billion, five-year capital plan, including a regional jet facility for United Airlines and a new parking structure. Las Vegas put about one quarter of its 10-year $1.5-billion capital plan on hold, including a gate expansion and a new parking facility, while the Massachusetts Port Authority deferred one-third of the capital spending it had planned to undertake at Logan Airport over the next two years. And the new mayor of Los Angeles, James Hahn, ordered the preparation of a thoroughly revised master plan for LAX, emphasizing improved security and greater reliance

24. For the $2.3 billion estimate, see Mead (2002b); for higher estimates, see D. Z. Plavin and C. Barclay, of American Association of Airport Executives and Airports Council International, letter to Senator Robert C. Byrd, April 23, 2002; and James S. Gilliland and others, "U.S. Airports in the 21st Century: Secure at What Cost?" Fitch ICBA, April 10, 2002, p. 4 (www.fitchratings.com [July 2002]).

25. In late 2001 Congress appropriated $175 million to reimburse airports for the cost of mandated security changes. The airports, however, submitted $444 million in eligible claims, which has led airport operators to seek an additional $270 million. See Plavin and Barclay to Byrd.

26. Heimlich, "U.S. Airlines," p. 4; and James C. May, president and CEO, Air Transport Association, "Government Imposed Security Costs," testimony before the Subcommittee on Aviation, Senate Commerce Committee, U.S. House of Representatives, February 5, 2003.

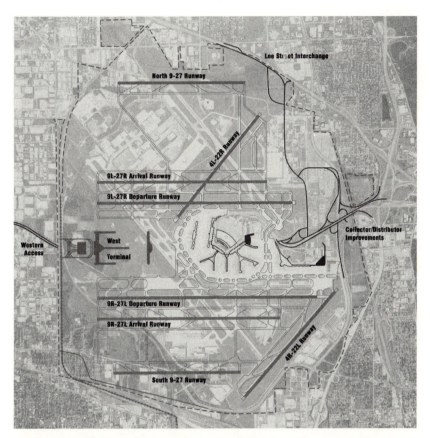

The O'Hare International Airport plan that was unveiled in late 2001 would require the clearance of more than 500 housing units on more than 400 acres of land. The plan calls for five new full-length runways, a new western terminal complex, and substantial new road and transit construction, as well as the decommissioning of three existing full-length runways and one shorter runway. Credit: Courtesy of Landrum & Brown.

on secondary airports rather than the massive LAX expansion plan favored by his predecessor.[27]

Not all were pausing, however. Atlanta and Chicago, notably, were proceeding apace with very large investment programs—a $5.4-billion expansion of Hartsfield in the former case, including a $1.3-billion new

27. See James S. Gilliland and others, "U.S. Airport Debt 2002–2006: A Post Sept. 11 Survey," Fitch ICBA, April 11, 2002 (www.fitchratings.com [April 2002]); Peter Stettler and others, "Unexpected Turbulence: U.S. Airports Respond to a Changing Economic Environment," Fitch and Fitch Ratings, January 29, 2002, p. 4 (www.fitchratings.com [February 2002]); and Jennifer Oldham, "Mayor Subs Security for LAX Growth," *Los Angeles Times*, October 8, 2001, p. 1.

runway, and a $2-billion set of improvements at O'Hare. In December 2001 Chicago mayor Richard Daley and Illinois governor George Ryan, each previously a champion of his own plan and an opponent of the other's, agreed to combine forces in support of both Daley's $6-billion longer-term program for expansion of O'Hare and Ryan's plan for at least initial development of a new airport in suburban Peotone. More generally, not one of the nine runways under construction at major airports as of September 11 was cancelled in its wake, two others received final FAA approval during the fall of 2001, and key officials reaffirmed their commitments to nearly all of the other runway proposals in their planning pipelines.[28]

Overall, though, it seems clearer for airports than any other category of urban mega-project that a new era began September 11, 2001. At the very least, the near-term outlook is for sharply lower investment in projects to expand capacity and amenity, offset in part by substantial investments to improve security. Beyond that, the outlook is highly uncertain. As and when buoyant traffic growth resumes, the campaign for capacity-expanding airport investment will doubtless revive as well. But this scenario presumes strong economic growth and a continuing revival of public confidence in aviation safety. Looking out several years, the former seems a very good bet, but the latter hinges on a great uncertainty: the avoidance of new acts of terrorism.

Rail Transit

As of mid-2001 despite widespread criticism that the new rail systems and lines constructed in recent decades had (with rare exceptions) attracted far too little patronage to justify their costs, the boom in rail transit investment showed no signs of abating. Federal aid was at an all-time high. Roughly two dozen major projects—new lines and extensions—were in construction or about to be, and detailed planning was under way for about three dozen more. A year later this pattern appears remarkably robust. Having not received any windfalls (as the highway program did) when federal Highway Trust Fund revenues exceeded projections in fiscal 2000 and 2001, transit has not been threatened with cutbacks as a result of their subsequent decline. Indeed, the president's budget for fiscal 2003 provided for slightly increased transit funding, in accord with the TEA-21 authorized schedule.[29] Of at least equal significance, although most states and localities

28. The nine airports with runway projects under way as of September 11, 2001, were Charlotte, Denver, Detroit, Houston (Bush), Minneapolis/St. Paul, Miami, Orlando, St. Louis (Lambert), and Seattle/Tacoma. See Mead (2002c, pp. 12–14).

29. Department of Transportation, "Fiscal Year 2003 Budget in Brief" (2002, pp. 24–27).

are themselves grappling with severe revenue downturns, not one appears to have significantly curtailed its capital commitments for mass transit.

Even with federal resources flowing at record levels in recent years, however, competition for the limited local supply has sharply intensified. Constraints on rail transit expansion (unlike proposals for major highway additions, which are more limited by siting and environmental considerations) are mainly fiscal, and the demand for transit capital grants has escalated a good deal faster than available resources. TEA-21, for example, both modestly increased the level of transit capital assistance and added 190 new projects (rail and bus combined) to the list of those approved to receive it. The spending levels authorized were far from adequate to finance all these projects, however, along with those still in the pipeline from earlier surface transportation acts. In 2000 the Federal Transit Administration (FTA) indicated that it would probably be able to fund just 29, leaving the other 161 to await future authorization cycles.[30]

In order to fund as many projects as possible, moreover, the FTA was generally committing to federal shares in the range of 50 percent rather than the 80 percent maximum permitted by law, with liability for overruns on the applicant. Not surprisingly, this translated into closer scrutiny of, and intensified controversy about, project costs at the local level. Since the late 1980s, when this shift occurred, about three quarters of local ballot propositions to raise taxes for transit, particularly for ambitious downtown-oriented rail systems, have failed. This pattern has continued in very recent years. From 1998 through 2001 voters rejected 12 proposed tax hikes for transit—in Kansas City (twice), Austin, San Antonio, Miami, Portland, Aspen, Columbus (Ohio), Virginia Beach, Birmingham, and California's Marin and Sonoma Counties—while approving just four such measures (in Phoenix, Salt Lake City, Denver, and Charlotte).[31]

The rejection of a specific plan, however, was often just a temporary setback for project advocates—who adapted successfully by amending their plans or by identifying revenue sources that did not require voter approval.

30. See General Accounting Office, "Implementation of FTA's New Starts Evaluation Process and FT 2001 Funding Proposals" (2001). The FTA commits to a project by entering into a "full funding agreement" with the local applicant, specifying anticipated flows of federal aid over the project's life, subject to congressional appropriations.

31. See Wendell Cox Consultancy, "U.S. Urban Rail Referendum Results to November 2000," *Public Purpose Urban Transport Fact Book* (www.publicpurpose.com/ ut-railv.htm [February 2002]); Kenneth Orski, "The Uncertain Future of Urban Rail," *Innovations Briefs*, March–April 2001; and Yvette Shields, "Kansas City Voters Soundly Reject Light Rail Plan; Supporters Look to Next Year," *Bond Buyer*, August 9, 2001, p. 40.

Denver and Seattle voters, for example, approved transit plans on a second go-round after the rail components were cut back and projects intended to attract suburban voters were added, while Portland found alternative revenue sources for its line to the airport (transit and redevelopment agency contributions, an airline ticket surcharge, and lease income from 120 acres of airport-owned land).

More generally, the interest group support base for rail transit has continued to grow in recent years, with advocates of "smart growth," who view it as an antidote to urban sprawl, joining the traditional constituencies of downtown business, transit labor, and environmental organizations.[32] Whereas only five urban areas had functioning rail systems in the 1960s, more than 30 have such systems in place, under construction, or in advanced planning in 2002. The consequence is a vastly enlarged national constituency (even if not user base) for transit investment, firmly allied with the national highway coalition and likely to share in its political victories for a good many years to come.

Continuity and Change

In short, the era of urban mega-projects is not over. Indeed, the current sources of policy turbulence seem minor by comparison with those of the late 1960s and early 1970s. Central cities and states, spurred by private producer interests, remain centrally focused on the pursuit of growth, and the political climate seems favorable except as constrained by fiscal shortfalls and new security imperatives.

By comparison, what mega-project advocates faced three decades ago was a broad-gauge backlash against their most favored programs and standard operating procedures. Responding to that challenge, local growth coalitions made important adjustments, including a shift toward greater reliance on financial and regulatory inducements to major investors. But they never lost faith in direct investment as a key instrument of development policy—as witness the recent record levels of investment in urban transportation, sports facilities, and convention centers—and there is no indication that they are about to do so. Though additional spending growth

32. There is little evidence in fact that new transit investments have retarded sprawl in recent decades, and there is little reason to expect that they will unless implemented in concert with strong land use policies—as in Portland, Oregon—to promote compact development. See Cervero and Landis (1997); and A. C. Nelson (1999). Politically, however, the critical fact is popular belief that rail transit can strengthen core areas and reduce sprawl without constraining any particular residents' freedom of action.

will be difficult in the near term, mega-project advocates—promising economic stimulus and proposing to draw on revenue sources that most voters are unlikely to notice (such as development tax increments, passenger facility charges, and hotel taxes)—have often in the past achieved conspicuous victories even in circumstances of austerity for other local services.

Within this enduring framework change has been endemic—occasionally abrupt (as during the expansion of renewal, highway, and airport activities during the 1950s and the mass campaigns against them 10 to 15 years later), but quite striking even through less turbulent periods. The sources of change have in part been technical, such as the need to accommodate jumbo jets at airports and, at least arguably, the declining marginal value of new highway mileage. Far more significantly, though, they appear to have been political and competitive: political in the sense of changing constraints, competitive in the sense of pressure to keep up with other cities.

Key constraints varied during the half century time frame of this study, from powerful norms and procedural barriers (such as referendum requirements for the issuance of long-term bonds) restricting local government activism at mid-century, to environmental and neighborhood mobilization, strongly reinforced by new environmental statutes and judicial doctrines in the decades after 1970, to intensified voter resistance to increases in broad-based taxes starting in the late 1970s. In each period such constraints seemed impermeable—but they frequently later proved vulnerable to end runs or erosion over time.

For example, local growth interests gained leverage in national politics during the late 1940s and the 1950s by joining national industry-based coalitions with much broader agendas. The products of these alliances, major new aid programs for central area redevelopment and urban expressway construction, stimulated more general shifts in most cities toward proactive development policy. Two decades later, frustrated by voter resistance to bond issues and to broad-based tax increases for capital projects, local growth coalitions forged pathways exempt from direct voter approval.[33] They induced state governments to authorize certain projects (including their funding packages) directly, for example, and to establish special authorities exempt from referendum requirements. Toward the end of the century, finally, and into the twenty-first, business-led campaigns at all levels of government generated substantial increases in public capital

33. The proportion of local tax-exempt bonds approved directly by voters declined from more than half in 1968 to less than 15 percent in the mid-1970s. See G. E. Peterson (1978, p. 59); and also Sanders (1995, pp. 191–96).

spending and some relaxation (still modest) of the imperative to "do no harm" when carrying out developmental projects.

The competitive terrain has also shifted over time. Through most of the 1950s and 1960s, cities were preoccupied with completing their interstate highway networks, carrying out slum clearance and central area development programs, and building new airports or vastly expanding existing ones. After 1970, mainly blocked on these fronts, they shifted in part toward development strategies other than direct public investment but also toward less disruptive categories of investment such as rail transit, festival retail markets, convention centers, and sports facilities. In the transit case this shift required intermunicipal collaboration as well as competition, to spearhead a national coalition for increased federal aid. In the retail, convention center, and sports facility cases, on the other hand, cities were basically on their own, scrambling to satisfy national corporate interests. The major sports leagues, in particular, were highly organized entities that became increasingly adept at stimulating and profiting from intermunicipal competition. Further, airport expansion reemerged as a priority during the 1990s—due primarily to alarming trends in air traffic congestion and the conviction of business leaders that high-quality air service is essential to local competitiveness, but also to a widespread perception that some of the constraints so binding over the previous two decades should now be subject to at least modest relaxation.

These have also been decades of profound change with reference to the land use effects of urban mega-project development and to the balance in mega-project politics between growth interests and those potentially in their way. During the 1950s and 1960s mega-project advocates were as eager to throw out the old as to bring in the new. Low-income neighborhoods and employment districts, public parks, and historic sites were obliterated on a grand scale. With rare exceptions, environmental impacts were disregarded. The mega-projects themselves—particularly new expressways and airports—were powerful if largely unintended stimuli to urban sprawl. Urban renewal, exceptionally, was intended to reinforce the core, but at the cost of transforming it and forcing out large numbers of its people. By comparison, most recent mega-projects strive to reinforce existing land uses and to avoid both neighborhood and environmental disruption. On the subject of sprawl, to be sure, the record is mixed. Such projects as the new Denver airport, the numerous expressways still being built on the fringes of metropolitan areas, and commuter rail lines extending out to distant suburbs almost surely accelerate it. The dominant mega-project types of recent decades, though—

rail rapid transit, festival retail markets, convention centers, and sports facilities (with the conspicuous exception of football stadiums)—are by and large oriented toward reinforcing downtowns.

Far more significant, at least from the standpoint of this study, has been the long-term shift in balance between development interests and those fighting to preserve their homes, neighborhoods, and natural amenities. Whereas the former were able to victimize the latter on a grand scale during the 1950s and 1960s, and to proceed with a blithe disregard for environmental consequences, they subsequently had to find ways to pursue their objectives without (or with very minimal) disruption. And while the constraints have recently lifted a bit, contemporary mega-projects still rarely involve substantial neighborhood or environmental harm. Even those in urban core locations are generally sited in obsolete factory or warehouse districts, or underground, or in existing transportation corridors; and some replace long-disliked facilities such as elevated roads with more attractive uses (above ground, at least) such as parks and boulevards.

It is easy to scant this shift—as, indeed, nearly all theorists of urban politics have—because all but a few central cities continue to treat growth and competitiveness as top priorities, and because the primary constituencies for their development activities continue to be producer interests. Indeed, while observing that public officials often initiate mega-projects and play critical roles in driving them forward politically, this study itself has emphasized that, except in very rare instances, an indispensable requisite for their success is active business support. The pattern of government-business interaction in such cases resembles that between entrepreneurs and sources of capital in the private sector: the former generate many ideas; the latter select few. Because their support is essential, though, virtually all proposals that eventually succeed are crafted from the outset to attract them.

Striking the Right Balance

Be that as it may, the shift in balance between development interests and those potentially in their way has been profound. The enhanced influence of nonproducer groups—ordinary residents above all—has with rare exceptions been passive rather than active.[34] What they have gained is "merely" far greater capacity to protect their homes, their neighborhoods, and their ecological surroundings against the initiatives of others. But that, as nearly

34. The exceptions, discussed in chapter 6, have been in the arena of mass transit.

as one can tell, is all they have ever cared to achieve. If power is the capacity to realize objectives, they have clearly made important gains, and their historic adversaries have had to adapt.

Did the pendulum swing too far? Or, even if not in the circumstances of the 1970s, has the time now come for a swing back toward development priorities? There are certainly many who think so, and their arguments are in part persuasive. It does seem clear that some valuable projects have been blocked in recent decades, while the costs of others have been driven to outrageous levels by "do no harm" and mitigation requirements. Before September 11, moreover, air and highway congestion were reaching unprecedented levels. Slack capacity available in the early years of "do no harm" politics had been virtually exhausted, and all projections were for indefinitely continuing traffic growth. Since the terrorist attacks most near-term forecasts of travel demand growth, particularly in aviation, have been revised downward, but the expectation remains that substantial additional capacity will be needed in years to come.

Roads and airports are essential elements of the modern economy, so sustained imbalances between travel and capacity growth are inevitably products of broad public concern. No comparable arguments can be made, however, about the mega-project types that have most thrived since the 1970s: for example, new rail transit systems, sports facilities, and convention centers. All provide benefits, to be sure, but none can be portrayed as responses to urgent local needs. Nor, more generally, do lists of the benefits of mega-projects provide much help in determining just how to weigh them against project costs and alternative priorities.

Our own view is that on balance the constraints placed on mega-project development since about 1970 have been beneficial, and that future adjustments should be guided at least as much by concerns about the pressures for excessive mega-project investment as the barriers to enough. Project merits have not been a central concern of this book, but it seems clear that a large proportion of recent mega-projects fail any reasonable benefit-cost test. And why should it be otherwise, with rent-seeking constituencies in the vanguard, able to tap sources of revenue (from federal grants to hotel taxes) that are all but invisible to most local voters?

The problem of balancing multiple values has no solution, of course, that will command universal assent. Nor is it realistic to believe that most policymakers will ever care more about the achievement of balance than the views of key constituencies with the potential to further or derail their careers. It is useful to pose and ponder the problem, however, because the general climate of opinion often shapes perceptions of self-interest, because actors without strong interests at times hold the balance of power, and because process design can profoundly affect the character of public scrutiny and deliberation.

In principle, at least, we believe there is wide agreement in American society on several criteria for evaluating major public investment proposals. These are admittedly very general and partially in tension with one another, so they do not by themselves constitute a solution. But they are an essential starting point for deliberation about more operational rules and procedures. The most significant of these criteria are as follows:

—Public investments should generate net benefits for society as a whole rather than just, or even primarily, a narrow but mobilized group of claimants (rent-seekers).

—Where specific beneficiaries, and particularly corporations, do seem likely to reap large benefits, they should bear a proportionate share of project costs and risks.

—Projects should not significantly harm individuals, communities, or the natural environment—at least not when viewed in combination with efforts to mitigate and compensate for such harm as may be unavoidable.

—Decisions to proceed should be arrived at democratically, following full and open public debate.

—Access to the courts for review of significant issues of statutory interpretation and compliance should be relatively liberal, but the judicial process should not be available to project critics merely engaged in delaying actions or seeking to extract costly benefits having little to do with the project at hand.

For many development interests, the priorities at present are to relax environmental rules and tightly restrict project critics' access to the courts. We disagree. This is not to say that we reject adjustments out of hand. Certainly some of the projects blocked—for example, New York's Westway— would have been highly beneficial; the costs of others have been driven up excessively; and doubtless many useful projects have never left the drawing board because their realization has seemed so unlikely. There is no reason to believe, however, that overall the nation would be more prosperous if development forces had continued to reign unchallenged over the past several decades, as they did through the 1950s and most of the 1960s—and vast numbers of people have reason to be grateful that the devastation of valued urban places was averted.

Some modest adjustments to streamline project approval processes have in fact occurred in recent years, and the courts have become less receptive to citizen and class action suits. Overall, these strike us as reasonable reactions to regulatory and litigation excesses of the 1970s. But we do not anticipate rapid progress toward a new political settlement in the near term. The forces in contention are too polarized, the detailed agreements required too difficult.

We are particularly skeptical of proposals for substantial change unless they are accompanied by political reforms to democratize project decision-making. The current system is highly imperfect, but it does enable project victims to negotiate with project managers on a more or less equal basis. This is quite different from saying that they can routinely block projects. Except where the impacts are truly extraordinary, as in the case of new airports and in-town expressways, they generally cannot. But they can effectively insist on aggressive mitigation and, where mitigation cannot fully offset harms, on compensation. This is as it should be. We are struck especially by agreements that have recently accompanied the construction of new runways in Atlanta, Cleveland, and Minneapolis. Airport operators in these locales have engaged in active programs of soundproofing and land purchases for aviation easements. At times they have also paid generous prices to purchase severely impacted homes and given affected communities a share of the economic benefits likely to accrue from runway construction. Cleveland's agreement is particularly notable in that it was put to voters in the affected community (an adjacent suburb), who approved it by a narrow margin.

In addition to reducing critics' access to the courts, development interests have frequently sought—from the earliest days of urban renewal—to insulate policymaking and implementation from the normal give-and-take of local politics. One approach is to reduce or eliminate local cost-consciousness by arranging for nonresidents to pay all or the great majority of project costs. Federal and state aid programs have long filled this role, particularly when the money is earmarked for specific projects and required local contributions are zero or negligible. In recent years local tourist taxes have often served this function as well, particularly for projects ineligible for federal aid. Another tactic is to assign responsibility, including authorization to levy fees and issue bonds, to independent authorities. Still another is to obtain state waivers of referendum requirements (in localities where they normally apply) for the imposition of taxes earmarked for development projects.

Each of these approaches has a legitimate place in the public policy arsenal but should be employed with great caution. This, of course, reflects our view that it is as important to screen out projects with weak public interest justifications as to enhance the prospects of meritorious projects, and that the best safeguard against dominance by rent-seeking project promoters is a vigorous pluralism.

We are not, for example, opposed to grant-in-aid financing for major public investments. Given the limitations on local fiscal capacity and the fact that many projects have benefits extending well beyond local boundaries, such aid is often a prerequisite to the serious consideration of meritorious proposals. We favor flexibility in federal and state aid programs, however, to ensure that each proposal must compete with many others in local policy deliberations, and requirements for substantial local contributions to confront local voters sharply with the issue of whether a project's benefits are actually worth its costs.

As it happens, federal policy has actually trended in the directions we favor over the past several decades. The Interstate Highway Program, for example, which accounted for most federal highway spending through the 1960s and 1970s, earmarked its grants very tightly for specific projects (nearly all of which had been planned decades earlier) and required just a 10 percent nonfederal contribution (all paid by states rather than localities). It acquired a significant element of flexibility in 1973, however, with the enactment of Interstate Transfer, and the program ended in the 1990s. Congress has, it is true, increasingly earmarked funds over the past two decades for so-called "demonstration projects" favored by key members, but such projects have never accounted for more than 6 percent of total federal highway spending, and the overall highway program trend has been toward vastly greater flexibility. Localities are still not required to contribute toward the cost of federally aided highway projects, but since 1991 they have had a major role in urban areas with populations of 200,000 or more in determining investment priorities.

Congress still earmarks federal transit grants on a project-by-project basis, but as local demand for aid has raced ahead of available funding the typical federal matching ratio has declined from a peak of 80 percent to the range of 50 percent. Almost invariably, moreover, local taxpayers are called upon to finance part of the nonfederal share. Meanwhile, federal aid was effectively terminated in the 1980s as a source of assistance for downtown revitalization efforts and declined sharply as a prime source of funding for improvements at major airports in the 1990s.

With the decline of federal aid as a source of insulation from local democracy, development interests have turned increasingly toward state aid, state creation of independent authorities (with broad authority to raise revenue, issue bonds, and carry out projects), and reliance at the local level on visitor taxes. Again, all of these are reasonable methods in some circumstances, but not nearly as many as those in which they have been used. In particular, we judge, state intervention to bypass requirements for explicit local approval of major project decisions is a recipe for the triumph of development rent-seekers. Whatever the local fiscal contribution, major projects have important land use, traffic, public safety, and other impacts within host localities, and those with objections should have democratic and authoritative forums in which to press their views. It may be appropriate for state governments at times to countermand local objections, including those adopted formally by local governments or in local referendums, but such overrides should only be to satisfy urgent regional needs—for example, to ensure adequate airport or waste treatment capacity—and they should be made by legislatures rather than executive branch or independent authority officials. Overrides are very rarely justified, moreover, to authorize convention center, sports facility, or public-private partnerships for commercial development, because there is almost never a compelling case that they represent urgent regional needs.

Our views are similar with respect to local visitor taxes. They are so attractive politically that one cannot imagine local governments forgoing them. They are a limited resource, however, and properly viewed as part of a locality's general tax base. That is, they cannot be raised significantly above the levels imposed by competitor localities without driving business away, and they can in principle be imposed to finance any local services. Given the potential for visitor taxes to harm tourist businesses, it is certainly appropriate for their views to receive considerable deference in debates about whether and for what purposes to impose such levies. But we see little justification for insulating decisions about them, and particularly their long-term commitment in support of project revenue bonds, from the normal workings of local democracy.

These "normal workings" vary widely, of course, in some cases placing final authority in the hands of elected boards or councils, in others requiring—or enabling citizens to initiate—referendums on major local decisions. We do not have a strong position on precisely which model is best, but a word on referendums may be pertinent. In the best of circumstances, referendums provide a mechanism for ordinary voters to make their views heard when representative institutions, in thrall to vested interests, have become unresponsive. There is some evidence, moreover, that in the specific arena of local capital investment public amenities tend to increase and—where public-private partnerships are involved—public subsidies to diminish when direct voter approval is required.[35] Referendum democracy is itself highly vulnerable to dominance by narrow interests, however; it tends to pose rigid choices in simplistic campaigns, and it may significantly undermine representative democracy.[36]

Bearing in mind both these pros and cons, we lean in favor of enabling critics to initiate referendums on urban mega-projects—but with three very important caveats: (1) such votes should be restricted to up or down expressions of opinion on projects already approved by the locality's duly constituted representative institution(s); (2) the requirements for ballot access should be relatively formidable (to discourage frivolous challenges); and (3) the elected representatives should be free to reaffirm their original decision, even in the face of a referendum defeat, if they can stand the political heat.

This specific judgment reflects, but is also subsidiary to, the more general conclusion that we take away from this study: while private rent-seekers and public entrepreneurs are invaluable sources of energy and ingenuity in the evolution of urban mega-projects, local champions of environmental protection, of neighborhood preservation, and of fiscal sobriety have no less valuable roles to play. Further, in seeking the wisest balance among these multiple perspectives, there are no good substitutes for representative democracy, empowered and required to approve all major projects, and a vibrant local pluralism.

35. See Sanders (1992b); Agostini, Quigley, and Smolensky (1997); and Plott (1968).

36. There is an extensive literature on referendums, though little of it focuses on the local level—something of a surprise in that the great majority of referendums are in fact local. On local referendums specifically, see Fort (1997); Steunenberg (1992); and Stone (1965). For valuable works on referendums more generally, see Cronin (1989); Ellis (2002); and Gerber (1999).

References

Adler, Sy. 1993. "The Evolution of Federal Transit Policy." In *Urban Public Policy*, edited by Martin Melosi. Pennsylvania University Press.

Adler, Sy, and Sheldon Edner. 1990. "Governing and Managing Multimodal Regional Transit Agencies in a Multicentric Era." In *Public Policy and Transit System Management*, edited by George Guess. Greenwood Press.

Agostini, Stephen J., John M. Quigley, and Eugene Smolensky. 1997. "Stickball in San Francisco." In *Sports, Jobs, and Taxes: The Economic Impact of Sports Teams and Stadiums*, edited by Roger Noll and Andrew Zimbalist. Brookings.

Alameda Corridor Transportation Authority. 1999. "Official Statement, Alameda Corridor Transportation Authority, $494,893,616.80 Tax-Exempt Senior Lien Revenue Bonds, Series 1999A: $25,165,000 Tax-Exempt Subordinate Lien Revenue Bonds, Series 1999B." Carson, Calif.

Aldrich, Mark. 1980. *A History of Public Works in America, 1790–1970*. Government Printing Office.

Allen, Frederick. 1996. *Atlanta Rising: The Invention of an International City, 1946–1996*. Longstreet Press.

Almy, Timothy, William Hildreth, and Robert Golembiewski. 1981. "Assessing Electoral Defeat: New Directions and Values for MARTA." In "Mass Transit Management: Case Studies of the Metropolitan Atlanta Rapid Transit Authority." Report prepared for the Urban Mass Transportation Administration. Washington.

Altshuler, Alan A. 1963. "The Politics of Urban Mass Transportation." Paper prepared for the Annual Meeting of the American Political Science Association, New York, September 4–7.

———. 1965. *The City Planning Process: A Political Analysis*. Cornell University Press.

———. 1979. *The Urban Transportation System: Politics and Policy Innovation*. MIT Press.

———. 1989. "Massachusetts Gov. Sargent: Sarge in Charge." *Journal of State Government* 62 (4): 153–60.

Altshuler, Alan A., and Robert Curry. 1975. "The Changing Environment of Urban Development Policy: Shared Power or Shared Impotence?" *Urban Law Annual* 10 (3): 3–41.

Altshuler, Alan A., and José Gómez-Ibáñez. 1993. *Regulation for Revenue: The Political Economy of Land Use Exactions*. Brookings and Lincoln Institute of Land Policy.

Altshuler, Alan A., and Roger Teal. 1979. "The Political Economy of Airline Deregulation." In *Current Issues in Transportation Policy*, edited by Alan A. Altshuler. Lexington Books.

Altshuler, Alan A., and Norman C. Thomas, eds. 1977. *The Politics of the Federal Bureaucracy*. Harper and Row.

American Public Transit Association. 1978. *Transit Fact Book: 1977–78*. Washington.

———. 1987. *Transit Fact Book: 1987*. Washington.

———. 2000. *Transit Fact Book: 2000*. Washington.

Amtrak Reform Council. 2002. "An Action Plan for Restructuring and Rationalizing the National Intercity Rail Passenger System: A Report to the United States Congress." Washington.

Anderson, Martin. 1964. *The Federal Bulldozer: A Critical Analysis of Urban Renewal, 1949–1962*. MIT Press.

Arrington, G. B. 1995. "Beyond the Field of Dreams: Light Rail and Growth Management in Portland." In *Seventh National Conference on Light Rail Transit*, vol. 1. National Academy Press.

Arthur, W. Brian. 1994. *Increasing Returns and Path Dependence in the Economy*. University of Michigan Press.

Baade, Robert, and Allen Sanderson. 1997. "The Employment Effects of Teams and Sports Facilities." In *Sports, Jobs, and Taxes: The Economic Impact of Sports Teams and Stadiums*, edited by Roger Noll and Andrew Zimbalist. Brookings.

Bachelor, Lynn W. 1994. "Regime Maintenance, Solution Sets, and Urban Economic Development." *Urban Affairs Quarterly* 29 (4): 596–616.

Bachrach, Peter, and Morton S. Baratz. 1962. "Two Faces of Power." *American Political Science Review* 56 (4): 947–52.

———. 1970. *Power and Poverty.* Oxford University Press.

Bae, Christine Chang-Hee. 1993. "Air Quality and Travel Behavior: Untying the Knot." *Journal of the American Planning Association* 59 (1): 65–74.

Baily, Elizabeth E., David R. Graham, and Daniel P. Kaplan. 1985. *Deregulating the Airlines.* MIT Press.

Banfield, Edward C. 1961. *Political Influence.* Free Press.

Barrett, Paul. 1983. *The Automobile and Urban Transit: The Formation of Public Policy in Chicago, 1900–1930.* Temple University Press.

Barry, John M. 1989. *The Ambition and the Power.* Viking.

Behrman, Bradley. 1980. "Civil Aeronautics Board." In *Politics of Regulation,* edited by James Q. Wilson. Basic Books.

Bennett, Ricarda. 1982. "Airport Noise Litigation: Case Law Review." *Journal of Air Law and Commerce* 47 (3): 449–94.

Bianco, Martha Janet. 1994. "Private Profit versus Public Service: Competing Demands in Urban Transportation History and Policy; Portland, Oregon, 1872–1970." Ph.D. dissertation, Portland State University.

Blackman, Lee, and Roger Freeman. 1987. "The Environmental Consequences of Municipal Airports: A Subject of Federal Mandate?" *Journal of Air Law and Commerce* 53 (1): 375–99.

Bosso, Christopher J. 2000. "Environmental Groups and the New Political Landscape." In *Environmental Policy: New Directions for the Twenty-First Century,* edited by Norman J. Vig and Michael E. Kraft. Congressional Quarterly Press.

Boston Redevelopment Authority. 1975. "Central Artery Feasibility Study."

Bottles, Scott L. 1987. *Los Angeles and the Automobile: The Making of the Modern City.* University of California Press.

Boyer, Christine M. 1983. *Dreaming the Rational City: The Myth of American City Planning.* MIT Press.

Braden, Betsy, and Paul Hagan. 1989. *A Dream Takes Flight: Hartsfield Atlanta International Airport and Aviation in Atlanta.* Atlanta Historical Society. University of Georgia Press.

Brown, Anthony E. 1987. *The Politics of Airline Deregulation.* University of Tennessee Press.

Buchanan, James M. 1962. *The Calculus of Consent: Logical Foundations of Constitutional Democracy.* University of Michigan Press.

Button, James. 1978. *Black Violence: Political Impact of the 1960s Riots.* Princeton University Press.

Caldwell, Lynton, Lynton R. Hayes, and Isabel MacWhirter. 1976. *Citizens and the Environment: Case Studies in Popular Action.* Indiana University Press.

Carlson, Daniel, Lisa Wormser, and Cy Ulberg. 1995. *At Road's End: Transportation and Land Use Choices for Communities.* Island Press.

Caro, Robert A. 1974. *The Power Broker: Robert Moses and the Fall of New York.* Alfred A. Knopf.

Castells, Manuel. 1978. *City, Class, and Power.* St. Martin's Press.

Cavanaugh, Cam. 1978. *Saving the Great Swamp: The People, The Power Brokers, and an Urban Wilderness.* Columbia Publishing.

Cervero, Robert. 1984. "Light Rail Transit and Urban Development." *Journal of the American Planning Association* 50 (2): 133–47.

Cervero, Robert, and John Landis. 1997. "Twenty Years of BART: Land Use and Development Impacts." *Transportation Research, Part A—Policy and Practice* 31 (4): 309–33.

Choate, Pat, and Susan Walter. 1981. *America in Ruins: Beyond the Public Works Pork Barrel.* Washington: Council of State Planning Agencies.

Chubb, John E., and Terry M. Moe. 1990. *Politics, Markets, and American Schools.* Brookings.

Cidell, Julie L., and John S. Adams. 2001. "The Groundside Effects of Air Transportation." University of Minnesota, Center for Transportation Studies.

City and County of Denver. 1989. "Final Environmental Impact Statement for New Denver Airport."

Clavel, Pierre, and Nancy Klniewski. 1990. "Space for Progressive Local Policy: Examples from the United States and the United Kingdom." In *Beyond the City Limits: Urban Policy and Economic Restructuring in Comparative Perspective,* edited by John R. Logan and Todd Swanstrom. Temple University Press.

Conlan, Timothy. 1988. *New Federalism: Intergovernmental Reform from Nixon to Reagan.* Brookings.

Coogan, Matthew A., and others. 1970. "Transportation Politics in Atlanta: The Mass Transit Bond Referendum of November 1968." Harvard University, Harvard Law School.

Couch, Jim F., and William F. Shughart. 1998. *The Political Economy of the New Deal*. Edward Elgar.

Creager, Steven. 1983. "Airline Deregulation and Airport Regulation." *Yale Law Journal* 93 (2): 319–39.

Creswell, Lyn Lloyd. 1990. "Airport Policy in the United States: The Need for Accountability, Planning, and Leadership." *Transportation Law Journal* 19 (1): 1–111.

Cronin, Thomas E. 1989. *Direct Democracy: The Politics of Initiative, Referendum, and Recall*. Harvard University Press.

Czaplicki, Michael. 1998. "Constructing the Natural Center: Airport Planning and the Failure of Liberalism in Chicago." Master's thesis, Michigan State University.

Dahl, Robert A. 1961. *Who Governs? Democracy and Power in an American City*. Yale University Press.

Danielson, Michael. 1965. *Federal-Metropolitan Politics and the Commuter Crisis*. Columbia University Press.

———. 1997. *Home Team: Professional Sports and the American Metropolis*. Princeton University Press.

Danielson, Michael, and Jameson W. Doig. 1982. *New York: The Politics of Urban Regional Development*. University of California Press.

David, Paul A. 1985. "Clio and the Economics of QWERTY." *American Economic Review* 75 (2): 332–37.

Davies, R. E. G., and I. E. Quastler. 1995. *Commuter Airlines of the United States*. Smithsonian Institution Press.

Dawson, Michael, Leslie M. Dean, and John R. Meyer. 1995. "Does New England Need Another Major Airport?" Harvard University, A. Alfred Taubman Center for State and Local Government, Kennedy School of Government.

DeLeon, Richard Edward. 1992. *Left Coast City: Progressive Politics in San Francisco, 1975–1991*. University Press of Kansas.

Dempsey, Paul Stephen, Andrew R. Goetz, and Joseph S. Szyliowicz. 1997. *Denver International Airport: Lessons Learned*. McGraw-Hill.

De Neufville, Richard. 1976. *Airport Systems Planning: A Critical Look at the Methods and Experience*. MIT Press.

Denver Regional Council of Government. 1983. "Metro Airport Study: Final Report."

Denzau, Arthur T., and Barry R. Weingast. 1982. "The Political Economy of Land Use Regulation." *Urban Law Annual* 23: 385–405.

Derthick, Martha, and Paul J. Quirk. 1985. *The Politics of Deregulation.* Brookings.

DiGaetano, Alan, and John S. Klemanski. 1999. *Power and City Governance: Comparative Perspectives on Urban Development.* University of Minnesota Press.

DiMento, Joseph, and others. 1991. "Court Intervention: The Consent Decree and the Century Freeway." University of California, Irvine, Public Policy Research Organization.

Doherty, Richard. 1970. "The Origin and Development of Chicago-O'Hare International Airport." Ph.D. dissertation, Ball State University.

Doig, Jameson W. 1966. *Metropolitan Transportation Politics and the New York Region.* Columbia University Press.

———. 2001. *Empire on the Hudson: Entrepreneurial Vision and Political Power at the Port of New York Authority.* Columbia University Press.

Domhoff, G. William. 1978. *Who Really Rules: New Haven and Community Power Re-examined.* Transaction Books.

Downs, Anthony. 1957. *An Economic Theory of Democracy.* Harper.

———. 1992. *Stuck in Traffic: Coping with Peak Hour Traffic Congestion.* Brookings and Lincoln Institute of Land Policy.

Dreiser, Theodore. 1914. *The Titan.* John Lane.

Duke Environmental Law Symposium. 2001. "Citizen Suits and the Future of Spending in the 21st Century: From Lujan to Laidlaw and Beyond." *Duke Environmental Law and Policy Forum* 12 (Fall).

Dunn, James A. 1998. *Driving Forces: The Automobile, Its Enemies, and the Politics of Mobility.* Brookings.

Dupuy, Gabriel, and Joel A. Tarr. 1982. "Sewers and Cities: France and the United States Compared." *Journal of the Environmental Engineering Division* 108 (April): 327–37.

Dye, Thomas R. 1990. *American Federalism: Competition among Governments.* Lexington Books.

Edner, Sheldon, and G. B. Arrington. 1985. "Urban Decision Making for Transportation Investments: Portland's Light Rail Transit System." Report prepared for the Urban Mass Transportation Administration. Washington.

Eisinger, Peter. 2000. "The Politics of Bread and Circuses: Building the City for the Visitor Class." *Urban Affairs Review* 35 (3): 316–33.

Elkin, Stephen. 1985. "Twentieth Century Urban Regimes." *Journal of Urban Affairs* 7 (2): 11–28.

———. 1987. *City and Regime in the American Republic.* University of Chicago Press.

Ellett, E. Tazewell. 1987. "The National Air Transportation System: Design by City Hall?" *Journal of Air Law and Commerce* 53 (1): 1–30.

Ellis, Richard J. 2002. *Democratic Delusions: The Initiative Process in America.* University Press of Kansas.

Euchner, Charles C. 1993. *Playing the Field: Why Sports Teams Move and Cities Fight to Keep Them.* Johns Hopkins University Press.

Evans, Diana. 1994. "Policy and Pork: The Use of Pork Barrel Projects to Build Policy Coalitions in the House of Representatives." *American Journal of Political Science* 38 (4): 894–917.

Fainstein, Norman I., and Susan S. Fainstein. 1983. "Regime Strategies, Communal Resistance, and Economic Forces." In *Restructuring the City: The Political Economy of Urban Development,* edited by Susan S. Fainstein and others. Longman.

Fainstein, Susan S., and Dennis Judd. 1999. "Cities as Places to Play." In *The Tourist City,* edited by Dennis Judd and Susan S. Fainstein. Yale University Press.

Fainstein, Susan S., and others, eds. 1983. *Restructuring the City: The Political Economy of Urban Redevelopment.* Longman.

Fairbanks, Robert. 1992. "A Clash of Priorities: The Federal Government and Dallas Airport Development, 1917–1964." In *American Cities and Towns: Historical Perspectives,* edited by Joseph Rishel. Duquesne University Press.

———. 1998. *For the City as a Whole: Planning, Politics and the Public Interest in Dallas, Texas, 1900–1965.* Ohio State University Press.

Falzone, Kristin L. 1999. "Airport Noise Pollution: Is There a Solution in Sight?" *Boston College Environmental Affairs Law Review* 26 (Summer): 769–807.

Feldman, Elliot J., and Jerome Milch. 1980. "Options on the Metropolitan Fringe: Strategies of Airport Development." In *National Resources and Urban Policy,* edited by Douglas Ashford. Methuen.

———. 1982. *Technocracy versus Democracy: The Comparative Politics of International Airports.* Auburn House.

Ferejohn, John. 1974. *Pork Barrel Politics: Rivers and Harbors Legislation, 1947–68.* Stanford University Press.

Fiorina, Morris P. 1981. "Universalism, Reciprocity, and Distributive Policy Making in Majority Rule Institutions." In *Research in Public Policy Analysis and Management,* edited by John Crecine. JAI.

Fischel, William A. 2001. *The Homevoter Hypothesis: How Home Values Influence Local Government Taxation, School Finance, and Land Use Policy.* Harvard University Press.

Flyvbjerg, Bent, Nils Bruzelius, and Werner Rothengatter. 2003. *Megaprojects and Risk: An Anatomy of Ambition.* Cambridge University Press.

Foard, Ashley A., and Hilbert Fefferman. 1966. "Federal Urban Renewal Legislation." In *Urban Renewal: The Record and the Controversy,* edited by James Q. Wilson. MIT Press.

Fogelson, Robert M. 1967. *The Fragmented Metropolis: Los Angeles, 1850–1930.* Harvard University Press.

Fogleman, Valerie M. 1990. *Guide to the National Environmental Policy Act: Interpretations, Applications, and Compliance.* Quorum Books.

Fort, Rodney. 1997. "Direct Democracy and the Stadium Mess." In *Sports, Jobs, and Taxes: The Economic Impact of Sports Teams and Stadiums,* edited by Roger Noll and Andrew Zimbalist. Brookings.

Foster, Kathryn. 1997. *The Political Economy of Special Purpose Government.* Georgetown University Press.

Frieden, Bernard, and Lynne Sagalyn. 1989. *Downtown, Inc.: How America Rebuilds Cities.* MIT Press.

Friedland, Roger, Frances Fox Piven, and Robert A. Alford. 1977. "Political Conflict, Urban Structure, and the Fiscal Crisis." *International Journal of Urban and Regional Research* 1 (3): 447–71.

Friedman, Paul David. 1978. "Fear of Flying: The Development of Los Angeles International Airport and the Rise of Public Protest over Jet Aircraft Noise." Master's thesis, University of California, Santa Barbara.

Fulton, William. 1997. *The Reluctant Metropolis: The Politics of Urban Growth in Los Angeles.* Solano Press Books.

Gakenheimer, Ralph. 1976. *Transportation Planning as a Response to Controversy: The Boston Case.* MIT Press.

Gans, Herbert J. 1962. *The Urban Villagers: Group and Class in the Life of Italian-Americans.* Free Press.

Garrett, Mark, and Martin Wachs. 1996. *Transportation Planning on Trial: The Clean Air Act and Travel Forecasting.* Sage Publications.

Gates, Paul W., and Robert Swenson. 1968. *History of Public Law Land Development.* Government Printing Office.

Geiser, Kenneth, Jr. 1970. "Urban Transportation Decision Making: Political Processes of Urban Freeway Controversies." Massachusetts Institute of Technology, Department of Urban Studies and Planning.

Gelfand, Mark I. 1975. *A Nation of Cities: The Federal Government and Urban America, 1933–1965.* Oxford University Press.

Gentry, Daniel, Jack D. Howell, and Nawal Taneja. 1977. "Report on Airport Capacity: Large Hub Airports in the United States." Report prepared for the Federal Aviation Administration. Springfield, Va.: National Technical Information Service.

Gerber, Elizabeth R. 1999. *The Populist Paradox: Interest Group Influence and the Promise of Direct Election.* Princeton University Press.

Gilmour, Robert S., and John A. McCauley. 1976. "Environmental Preservation and Politics: The Significance of 'Everglades Jetport.'" *Political Science Quarterly* 90 (4): 719–38.

Gist, John R. 1980. "Urban Development Action Grants: Design and Implementation." In *Urban Revitalization,* edited by Donald B. Rosenthal. Sage Publications.

Gómez-Ibáñez, José. 1985. "A Dark Side to Light Rail? The Experience of Three New Transit Systems." *Journal of the American Planning Association* 51 (3): 337–52.

———. 1994. "Boston's Transit Future: The Dilemma of Maintaining Ridership While Controlling the MBTA Deficit." Harvard University, A. Alfred Taubman Center for State and Local Government, Kennedy School of Government.

Gómez-Ibáñez, José, and Mary O'Keeffe. 1985. "The Benefits from Improved Investment Rules: A Case Study of the Interstate Highway System." Report prepared for the Federal Highway Administration.

Gómez-Ibáñez, José, and others. 1994. "Hard Choices: Boston's Transit Deficits and Ridership." Harvard University, A. Alfred Taubman Center for State and Local Government, Kennedy School of Government.

Goodrich, Carter. 1965. *Government Promotion of American Canals and Railroads, 1800–1890.* Columbia University Press.

Goodwin, Doris Kearns. 1994. *No Ordinary Time: Franklin and Eleanor Roosevelt: The Home Front in World War II.* Simon and Schuster.

Goodwin, P. B. 1992. "A Review of New Demand Elasticities with Special Reference to Short and Long Run Effects of Price Changes." *Journal of Transport Economics and Policy* 26 (2): 155–69.

Gordon, David. 1976. "Capitalism and the Roots of the Urban Crisis." In *The Fiscal Crisis of American Cities,* edited by Roger Alcaly and David Mermelstein. Vintage Books.

Governor's Task Force on Intercity Transportation. 1971. Report prepared for Governor Sargent. Boston.

Green, Anthony David. 1979. "Planning the Central Artery: Constraints on Planners and the Limits of Planning in Boston, 1909–1979." Bachelor's thesis, Harvard University.

Greer, Scott A. 1963. *Metropolitics: A Study of Political Culture*. Wiley.

Greve, Michael. 1996. *The Demise of Environmentalism in American Law*. American Enterprise Institute Press.

Gryszkowiec, Michael. 1995. "Denver International Airport." Testimony before the Subcommittee on Aviation, Committee on Transportation and Infrastructure, U.S. House. May 14. General Accounting Office.

Hahn, Robert W., and Randall S. Kroszner. 1989. "The Mismanagement of Air Transport: A Supply Side Analysis." *Public Interest*, no. 95 (Spring): 100–11.

Hall, Peter A., and Rosemary C. R. Taylor. 1996. "Political Science and the Three New Institutionalisms." *Political Studies* 44 (5): 936–57.

Hall, Peter Geoffrey. 1982. *Great Planning Disasters*. University of California Press.

Hamer, Andrew Marshall. 1976. *The Selling of Rail Rapid Transit: A Critical Look at Urban Transportation Planning*. Lexington Books.

Hardaway, Robert. 1991. "Economics of Airport Regulation." *Transportation Law Journal* 20 (1): 47–75.

Harper, Donald. 1988. "Regulation of Airport Noise at Major Airports: Past, Present, and Future." *Transportation Law Journal* 17 (1): 117–66.

Harrison, David, Jr. 1983. "The Regulation of Airport Noise." In *Incentives for Environmental Protection*, edited by Thomas Schelling. MIT Press.

Hebert, Richard. 1972. *Highways to Nowhere: The Politics of City Transportation*. Bobbs-Merrill.

Heppenheimer, T. A. 1995. *Turbulent Skies: The History of Commercial Aviation*. Wiley.

Herman, Shelby. 2000. "Fixed Assets and Consumer Durable Goods." *Survey of Current Business* 80 (4): 17–30.

Herson, Lawrence J. R. 1957. "The Lost World of Municipal Government." *American Political Science Review* 51 (2): 330–45.

Herzlinger, Regina. 1979. "Costs, Benefits, and the West Side Highway." *Public Interest*, no. 55 (Spring): 77–98.

Hestermann, Dean, and others. 1993. "Effects of a Consent Decree on the 'Last Urban Freeway': Interstate 105 in Los Angeles County." *Transportation Research, Part A—Policy and Practice* 27 (4): 299–313.

Heying, Charles H. 1997. "Civic Elites and Corporate Delocalization: An Alternative Explanation for Declining Civic Engagement." *American Behavioral Scientist* 40 (5): 657–68.

Hill, Richard Child. 1978. "Fiscal Collapse and Political Struggle in Decaying Central Cities in the United States." In *Marxism and Metropolis: New Perspectives on Urban Political Economy,* edited by William K. Tabb and Larry Sawers. Oxford University Press.

Hilton, George W. 1974. *Federal Transit Subsidies: The Urban Mass Transportation Assistance Program.* American Enterprise Institute Press.

Hood, Clifton. 1993. *722 Miles: The Building of the Subways and How They Transformed New York.* Simon and Schuster.

Howitt, Arnold M., and Alan Altshuler. 1999. "The Politics of Controlling Auto Air Pollution." In *Essays in Transportation Economics and Policy,* edited by José Gómez-Ibáñez and others. Brookings.

Howitt, Arnold, and Elizabeth Moore. 1999. "Linking Transportation and Air Quality Planning: Implementation of the Transportation Conformity Regulations in 15 Nonattainment Areas." Harvard University, A. Alfred Taubman Center for State and Local Government, Kennedy School of Government.

Hunter, Floyd. 1953. *Community Power Structure: A Study of Decision Makers.* University of North Carolina Press.

Immergut, Ellen M. 1998. "The Theoretical Core of the New Institutionalism." *Politics and Society* 26 (1): 5–34.

Jackson, Kenneth. 1985. *Crabgrass Frontier: The Suburbanization of the United States.* Oxford University Press.

Jacobs, Jane. 1961. *The Death and Life of Great American Cities.* Random House.

Jacobs, Susan S., and Elizabeth A. Roistacher. 1980. "The Urban Impacts of HUD's Urban Development Action Grant Program." In *The Urban Impacts of Federal Policies,* edited by Norman Glickman. Johns Hopkins University Press.

Jamaica Bay Environmental Study Group. 1971. *Jamaica Bay and Kennedy Airport: A Multidisciplinary Environmental Study.* Washington: National Academy of Sciences, National Academy of Engineering.

Jaret, Charles. 1983. "Recent Neo-Marxist Urban Analysis." *Annual Review of Sociology* 9: 499–525.

Jenkins, John J. 1994. "The Airport Noise and Capacity Act of 1990: Has Congress Finally Solved the Aircraft Noise Problem?" *Journal of Air Law and Commerce* 59 (May–June): 1023–55.

Jonas, Andrew E. G., and David Wilson, eds. 1999. *The Urban Growth Machine: Critical Perspectives Two Decades Later.* State University of New York Press.

Jones, Bryan D., and Lynn W. Bachelor. 1993. *The Sustaining Hand: Community Leadership and Corporate Power.* University of Kansas Press.

Kahn, Ronald. 1982. "Political Change in America: Highway Politics and Reactive Policymaking." In *Public Values and Private Power in American Politics,* edited by J. David Greenstone. University of Chicago Press.

Kain, John F. 1990. "Deception in Dallas: Strategic Misrepresentation in Rail Transit Promotion and Evaluation." *Journal of the American Planning Association* 56 (2): 184–96.

Kain, John F., and Zhi Lui. 1995. "Secrets of Success: How Houston and San Diego Transit Providers Achieved Large Increases in Transit Ridership." Report prepared for the Federal Transit Administration.

Kaplan, Harold. 1963. *Urban Renewal Politics: Slum Clearance in Newark.* Columbia University Press.

Kaplan, Marshall. 1984. "Hard Choices: A Report on the Increasing Gap between America's Infrastructure Needs and Our Ability to Pay for Them." Report prepared for the Subcommittee on Economic Goals and Intergovernmental Policy of the Joint Economic Committee. Government Printing Office.

Kaplan, Morton. 1957. *System and Process in International Politics.* Wiley.

Karsner, Douglas George. 1993. "Leaving on a Jet Plane: Commercial Aviation, Airports, and Post-Industrial American Society, 1933–1970." Ph.D. dissertation, Temple University.

Katznelson, Ira. 1976. "The Crisis of the Capitalist City: Urban Politics and Social Control." In *Theoretical Perspectives on Urban Politics,* edited by Willis D. Hawley. Prentice-Hall.

———. 1981. *City Trenches: Urban Politics and the Patterning of Class in the United States.* Pantheon Books.

Kaufman, Herbert. 1952. "Gotham in the Air Age." In *Public Administration and Policy Development,* edited by Harold Stein. Harcourt, Brace.

Keating, Larry. 2001. *Atlanta: Race, Class, and Urban Expansion.* Temple University Press.

Kennedy, David. 1984. "UMTA and the New Rail Start Policy." Harvard University, Kennedy School of Government Case Program.

Kent, Richard J., Jr. 1980. *Safe, Separated, and Soaring: A History of Federal Civil Aviation Policy, 1961–1972.* Government Printing Office.

Keohane, Robert, and Joseph Nye. 1977. *Power and Independence: World Politics in Transition.* Little, Brown.

Kerner Commission. 1968. "Report of the National Advisory Commission on Civil Disorders." Government Printing Office.

Key, V. O., Jr. 1942. *Politics, Parties, and Pressure Groups.* Thomas Y. Crowell.

Keyes, Langley C., Jr. 1969. *The Rehabilitation Planning Game: A Study in the Diversity of Neighborhood.* MIT Press.

King, Desmond. 1992. "The Establishment of Work-Welfare Programs in the United States and Britain: Politics, Ideas, and Institutions." In *Structuring Politics: Historical Institutionalism in Comparative Analysis,* edited by Sven Steinmo and others. Cambridge University Press.

Kirk, Robert. 2000. "Airport Improvement Program." Washington: Congressional Research Service.

Knowles, Elizabeth, ed. 1999. *Oxford Dictionary of Quotations.* Oxford University Press.

Komons, Nick A. 1978. *Bonfires to Beacons: Federal Civil Aviation Policy under the Air Commerce Act, 1926–1938.* Government Printing Office.

Kraft, Michael E. 2000. "Environmental Policy in Congress." In *Environmental Policy: New Directions for the Twenty-First Century,* edited by Norman J. Vig and Michael E. Kraft. Congressional Quarterly Press.

Krasner, Stephen D. 1983a. "Regimes and the Limits of Realism: Regimes as Autonomous Variables." In *International Regimes,* edited by Stephen D. Krasner. Cornell University Press.

———. 1983b. "Structural Causes and Regime Consequences: Regimes as Intervening Variables." In *International Regimes,* edited by Stephen D. Krasner. Cornell University Press.

Krueger, Anne O. 1974. "The Political Economy of the Rent-Seeking Society." *American Economic Review* 64 (3): 291–303.

Laird, Nick. 1990. "Successful Consensus Building for Public-Political-Financial Support: Case Study of the Houston Metro Experience." Report prepared for the Urban Mass Transportation Administration. Springfield, Va.: National Technical Information Service.

Laslo, David. 1998. "Proliferating Convention Centers: Issues in Community, Equity, and Efficiency and the Case of St. Louis' Convention Center Expansion." Paper prepared for the Annual Meeting of the American Political Science Association, Boston, September 3.

Latham, Earl. 1952. *The Group Basis of Politics: A Study in Basing Point Legislation.* Cornell University Press.

Lave, Charles A. 1981. "Dealing with the Transit Deficit." *Journal of Contemporary Studies* 4 (2): 53–60.

Leavitt, Helen. 1970. *Superhighway-Superhoax*. Doubleday.

Liebman, Jeffrey B. 2002. "Redistribution in the Current U.S. Social Security System." In *The Distributional Aspects of Social Security and Social Security Reform,* edited by Martin Feldstein and Jeffrey B. Liebman. University of Chicago Press.

Logan, John R., and Harvey Molotch. 1987. *Urban Fortunes*. University of California Press.

Long, Judith Grant. 2002. "Full Count: The Real Cost of Public Funding for Major League Sports Facilities and Why Some Cities Pay More to Play." Ph.D. dissertation, Harvard University.

Long, Norton E. 1958. "The Local Community as an Ecology of Games." *American Journal of Sociology* 64 (3): 251–61.

Lowi, Theodore J. 1964. *At the Pleasure of the Mayor: Patronage and Power in New York City, 1898–1958*. Free Press.

———. 1968. "Gosnell's Chicago Revisited via Lindsay's New York." Foreword in *Machine Politics: Chicago Model,* 2d ed., by Harold Gosnell. University of Chicago Press.

Luberoff, David, and Alan Altshuler. 1996. "Mega-Project: A Political History of Boston's Multibillion Dollar Artery/Tunnel Project." Harvard University, A. Alfred Taubman Center for State and Local Government, Kennedy School of Government.

Luberoff, David, and Jay Walder. 2000. "U.S. Ports and the Funding of Intermodal Facilities: An Overview of Key Issues." *Transportation Quarterly* 54 (4): 23–45.

Lubove, Roy. 1996. *Twentieth Century Pittsburgh: The Post Steel Era*. University of Pittsburgh Press.

Lupo, Alan, Frank Colcord, and Edmund P. Fowler. 1971. *Rites of Way: The Politics of Transportation in Boston and the U.S. City*. Little, Brown.

March, James G., and Johan P. Olsen. 1984. "The New Institutionalism: Organizational Factors in Political Life." *American Political Science Review* 78 (3): 734–49.

———. 1989. *Rediscovering Institutions: The Organizational Basis of Politics*. Free Press.

Martin, Roscoe C. 1965. *The Cities and the Federal System*. Atherton Press.

Massachusetts Department of Public Works. 1985. "Massachusetts Report to the Federal Highway Administration." Boston.

Massachusetts Highway Department. 1994. "Finance Plan: Central Artery/Tunnel Project." Boston.

———. 1996a. "Finance Plan: Central Artery/Tunnel Project, August 1995, as Amended January 1996." Boston.

———. 1996b. "Finance Plan: Central Artery/Tunnel Project, August 1995, as Amended February 1996." Boston.

Massachusetts Office of Inspector General. 2001. "A History of Central Artery/Tunnel Project Finances, 1994–2001." Boston.

Massachusetts State Secretary, Environmental Affairs. 2001. "Certificate of the Secretary of Environmental Affairs, Logan Airside Improvements Planning." EOEA number 10458. Boston.

Massachusetts Taxpayers Foundation. 1999. "Reaching the Breaking Point: The Commonwealth's Capital Dilemma." Boston.

Massachusetts Turnpike Authority. 1999. "Central Artery/Tunnel Project Finance Plan." Boston.

———. 2000. "Central Artery/Tunnel Project Finance Plan." Boston.

———. 2001. "Central Artery/Tunnel Project Finance Plan." Boston.

McCool, Daniel. 1992. "Water Welfare and the New Politics of Water." *Halcyon* 14: 85–102.

McCubbins, M. D., and Thomas Schwartz. 1984. "Congressional Oversight Overlooked: Police Patrols vs. Fire Alarms." *American Journal of Political Science* 28 (1): 165–79.

McLaughlin, Joseph Paul, Jr. 1999. "The Invisible Politics of Regional Cooperation: Philadelphia and Suburban Parties in the Legislature, 1985–1996." Ph.D. dissertation, Temple University.

McShane, Clay. 1988. "Urban Pathways: The Street and Highway, 1900–1940." In *Technology and the Rise of the Networked City in Europe and America,* edited by Joel A. Tarr and Gabriel Dupuy. Temple University Press.

———. 1994. *Down the Asphalt Path: The Automobile and the American City.* Columbia University Press.

McSpadden, Lettie. 1995. "The Courts and Environmental Policy." In *Environmental Politics and Policy: Theories and Evidence,* edited by James P. Lester. Duke University Press.

———. 2000. "Environmental Policy in the Courts." In *Environmental Policy: New Directions for the Twenty-First Century,* edited by Norman J. Vig and Michael E. Kraft. Congressional Quarterly Press.

Mead, Kenneth. 2002a. "Department of Transportation Budget for Fiscal Year 2003." Testimony before the Subcommittee on Transportation and

Related Agencies, Appropriations Committee, U.S. House. February 13. U.S. Department of Transportation.

———. 2002b. "Key Challenges Facing the Transportation Security Administration." Testimony before the Subcommittee on Transportation, Appropriations Committee, U.S. House. June 20. Office of Inspector General, U.S. Department of Transportation.

———. 2002c. "Key Issues concerning Implementation of the Aviation and Transportation Security Act." Testimony before the Committee on Commerce, Science, and Transportation, U.S. Senate. February 5. Office of Inspector General, U.S. Department of Transportation.

Melosi, Martin. 2000. *The Sanitary City: Urban Infrastructure in America from Colonial Times to the Present*. Johns Hopkins University Press.

Merewitz, Leonard. 1973. "Cost Overruns in Public Works." In *Benefit-Cost and Policy Analysis Annual 1972*, edited by William Niskanen. Aldine.

Merrow, Edward W. 1988. *Understanding the Outcomes of Megaprojects: A Quantitative Analysis of Very Large Civilian Projects*. Santa Monica, Calif.: Rand Corporation.

Merton, Robert K. 1973. "Latent Functions of the Machine." In *American Urban History: An Interpretive Reader with Commentaries*, edited by Alexender B. Callow Jr. Oxford University Press.

Meyer, John R., and José Gómez-Ibáñez. 1981. *Autos, Transit, and Cities*. Harvard University Press.

Meyer, John R., John F. Kain, and Martin Wohl. 1965. *The Urban Transportation Problem*. Harvard University Press.

Mietus, John, Jr. 2001. "Recent Developments in Aviation." *Transportation Law Journal* 28 (Spring): 229–38.

Miller, Donald L. 1996. *City of the Century: The Epic of Chicago and the Making of America*. Simon and Schuster.

Miller, Jeffrey. 1983. *Stapleton International Airport: The First Fifty Years*. Pruett.

Mills, C. Wright. 1956. *The Power Elite*. Oxford University Press.

Mills, Edwin S. 1991. "Should Governments Own Convention Centers?" Chicago: Heartland Institute.

Mohl, Raymond. 1993. "Race and Space in the Modern City: Interstate 95 and the Black Community in Miami." In *Urban Policy in Twentieth Century America*, edited by Arnold R. Hirsch and Raymond A. Mohl. Rutgers University Press.

Mollenkopf, John Hull. 1975. "The Post-War Politics of Urban Development." *Politics and Society* 5 (3): 247–95.

Molotch, Harvey. 1976. "The City as Growth Machine: Toward a Political Economy of Place." *American Journal of Sociology* 82 (2): 309–32.

Montealegre, Ramiro, and others. 1996. "BAE Automated Systems." Harvard Business School Publishing.

Moore, Scott. 1989. "Growth Politics in the Denver Region: The 1988 Adams County Airport Annexation Election." Paper prepared for the Thirty-First Annual Conference of the Western Social Science Association, Albuquerque, April 26–29.

Moses, Leon N., and Harold F. Williamson. 1963. "Value of Time, Choice of Mode, and the Subsidy Issue in Urban Transportation." *Journal of Political Economy* 71 (3): 247–64.

Moses, Robert. 1970. *Public Works: A Dangerous Trade*. McGraw-Hill.

Mowbry, A. Q. 1969. *Road to Ruin*. Lippincott.

Mumford, Lewis. [1963] 1981. *The Highway and the City*. Greenwood Press.

National Council on Public Works Improvement. 1988. *Fragile Foundations: A Report on America's Public Works*. Washington.

Nelkin, Dorothy. 1974. *Jetport: The Boston Airport Controversy*. Transaction Books.

Nelson, Arthur C. 1999. "Urban Containment: Central City Vitality and Quality of Life." Paper prepared for Bridging the Divide, Department of Housing and Urban Development, Washington, December 31.

Nelson, Robert H. 1977. *Zoning and Property Rights: An Analysis of the American System of Land-Use Regulation*. MIT Press.

New Jersey Governor's Select Commission on Civil Disorder. 1972. *Report for Action: An Investigation into the Causes and Events of the 1967 Newark Race Riots*. Lemma.

Niskanen, William. 1988. *Reaganomics: An Insider's Account of the Policies and the People*. Oxford University Press.

Oakerson, Ronald. 1999. *Governing Local Political Economies: Creating the Civic Metropolis*. ICS Press.

O'Connor, James. 1976. *The Fiscal Crisis of the State*. St. Martin's Press.

O'Connor, Thomas H. 1973. *Building a New Boston: Politics and Urban Renewal*. Northeastern University Press.

Olson, Mancur, Jr. 1965. *The Logic of Collective Action: Public Goods and the Theory of Groups*. Harvard University Press.

Ostrom, Vincent, Robert Bish, and Elinor Ostrom. 1988. *Local Government in the United States*. ICS Press.

Ostrom, Vincent, Charles M. Tiebout, and Robert Warren. 1961. "The Organization of Government in Metropolitan Areas: A Theoretical Inquiry." *American Political Science Review* 55 (4): 831–42.

Owen, Wilfred. 1966. *The Metropolitan Transportation Problem*. Brookings.

Paaswell, Robert, and Joseph Berechman. 1982. "Light Rail Development: Constraints and Conditions." In *Light Rail Transit: Planning Design and Implementation*. Washington: National Academy of Sciences.

Perry, David C. 1995. "Building the City through the Back Door: The Politics of Debt, Law, and Infrastructure." In *Building the Public City: The Politics, Governance, and Finance of Public Infrastructure*, edited by David C. Perry. Sage Publications.

Pescatello, Paul. 1985. "Westway: The Road from New Deal to New Politics." Ph.D. dissertation, Cornell University.

Peterson, David C. 1996. *Sports, Convention, and Entertainment Facilities*. Washington: Urban Land Institute.

Peterson, George E. 1978. "Capital Spending and Capital Obsolescence." In *Fiscal Outlook for Cities: Implications of a National Urban Policy*, edited by Roy Bahl. Syracuse University Press.

———. 1990. "Is Public Infrastructure Being Undersupplied?" In *Is There a Shortfall in Public Capital Investment?* edited by Alicia H. Munnell. Federal Reserve Bank of Boston.

Peterson, Paul E. 1981. *City Limits*. University of Chicago Press.

———. 1995. *The Price of Federalism*. Brookings.

Peterson, Paul E., Barry G. Rabe, and Kenneth K. Wong. 1986. *When Federalism Works*. Brookings.

Pickrell, Don. 1984. "Airport Congestion and New Entrant Access." In *Deregulation and the New Airline Entrepreneurs*, edited by John R. Meyer and Clinton Oster Jr. MIT Press.

———. 1990. "Urban Rail Transit Projects: Forecast vs. Actual Ridership and Costs." Report prepared for the Urban Mass Transportation Administration. Washington.

———. 1992. "A Desire Named Streetcar: Fantasy and Fact in Rail Transit Planning." *Journal of the American Planning Association* 58 (2): 158–76.

Pickvance, Christopher. 1995. "Marxist Theories of Urban Politics." In *Theories of Urban Politics*, edited by David Judge and others. Sage Publications.

Pierson, Paul. 2000. "Increasing Returns, Path Dependence, and the Study of Politics." *American Political Science Review* 94 (2): 251–67.

Pilgrim, Richard. 2000. "Are We Pricing Light Rail Transit Systems out of Reach?" In *Light Rail: Investment for the Future—8th Joint Conference on Light Rail Transit*. Washington: National Research Council.

Pisarski, Alan. 2001. "A Review of the Journey to Work Data Findings from the 2000 Census Supplementary Survey." Report prepared for the Subcommittee on Highways and Transit, Committee on Transportation and Infrastructure, U.S. House.

Piven, Frances Fox, and Richard A. Cloward. 1977. *Poor People's Movements: Why They Succeed, How They Fail*. Pantheon Books.

Piven, Frances Fox, and Roger Friedland. 1984. "Public Choice and Private Power: A Theory of Fiscal Crisis." In *Public Service Provision and Urban Development*, edited by Andrew Kirby and others. St. Martin's Press.

Plott, Charles. 1968. "Some Organizational Influences on Urban Renewal Decisions." *American Economic Review* 58 (2): 302–21.

Polsby, Nelson W. [1960] 1980. *Community Power and Political Theory: A Further Look at Problems of Evidence and Inference*. Yale University Press.

Popper, Frank J. 1991. "LULUs and Their Blockage." In *Confronting Regional Challenges*, edited by Joseph Dimento and LeRoy Graymer. Cambridge, Mass.: Lincoln Institute of Land Policy.

Pratt, Joseph A., and Christopher J. Castaneda. 1999. *Builders: Herman and George R. Brown*. Texas A & M University Press.

Pucher, John R. 1981. "Equity in Transit Finance: Distribution of Transit Subsidy Benefits and Costs among Income Classes." *Journal of the American Planning Association* 47 (4): 387–407.

Putnam, Robert D. 2000. *Bowling Alone: The Collapse and Revival of American Community*. Simon and Schuster.

Rae, John Bell. 1971. *The Road and the Car in American Life*. MIT Press.

Reagan, Ronald. 1989. "Message to the House of Representatives, Returning without Approval the Surface Transportation and Uniform Relocation Assistance Act of 1987." In *Public Papers of the Presidents of the United States*. Government Printing Office.

Reed, Adolph, Jr. 1987. "A Critique of Neo Progressivism in Theorizing about Local Development Policy: A Case from Atlanta." In *The Politics of Urban Development*, edited by Clarence N. Stone and Heywood T. Sanders. University of Kansas Press.

Rhoads, Steven. 1974. *Policy Analysis in the Federal Aviation Administration*. Lexington, Mass.: Lexington Books.

Richmond, Jonathan. 2001a. *The Private Provision of Public Transport*. Harvard University, A. Alfred Taubman Center for State and Local Government, Kennedy School of Government.

———. 2001b. "A Whole-System Approach to Evaluating Urban Transit Investments. *Transport Reviews* 21 (2): 141–79.

———. 2003. "Transport of Delight: The Mythical Conception of Rail Transit in Los Angeles." University of Akron Press.

Ripley, Randall. 1969. "Congress Champions Aid to Airports, 1958–59." In *Congress and Urban Problems: A Casebook on the Legislative Process*, edited by Frederic Cleaveland and others. Brookings.

Rochester, Stuart J. 1976. *Takeoff at Mid-Century: Federal Civil Aviation in the Eisenhower Years, 1953–1961*. Government Printing Office.

Rose, Mark H. 1979. *Interstate: Express Highway Politics, 1941–1956*. Lawrence: Regents Press of Kansas.

Rosegrant, Susan. 2001. "Sound Move: The Debate over Seattle's Regional Transit System." Harvard University, Kennedy School of Government Case Program.

Rosenbaum, Walter. 1995. "Bureaucracy and Environmental Policy." In *Environmental Politics and Policy*, edited by James P. Lester. Duke University Press.

Sanders, Heywood T. 1980. "Urban Renewal and the Revitalized City." In *Urban Revitalization*, edited by Donald B. Rosenthal. Sage Publications.

———. 1992a. "Building the Convention City: Politics, Finance, and Public Investment in Urban America." *Journal of Urban Affairs* 14 (2): 135–59.

———. 1992b. "Urban Political Economy and the Evolution of the Public Fisc: A Comparative Framework." Paper prepared for the Annual Meeting of the American Political Science Association, Chicago, September 3–6.

———. 1995. "Public Works and Public Dollars: Federal Infrastructure Aid and Local Investment Policy." In *Building the Public City*, edited by David C. Perry. Sage Publications.

———. 1997. "If We Build It Will They Come? And Other Questions about the Proposed Boston Convention Center." Boston: Pioneer Institute for Public Policy Research.

———. 1998. "Convention Center Follies." *Public Interest*, no. 132 (Summer): 58–72.

———. 1999. "Flawed Forecasts: A Critical Look at Convention Center Feasibility Studies." Boston: Pioneer Institute for Public Policy Research.

———. 2001. "Convention Wisdom Revisited: Boston Convention Center Projections." Boston: Pioneer Institute for Public Policy Research.

Savitch, H. V., and John Clayton Thomas, eds. 1991. *Big City Politics in Transition*. Sage Publications.

Sayre, Wallace, and Herbert Kaufman. 1960. *Governing New York City: Politics in the Metropolis*. New York: Russell Sage Foundation.

Sbragia, Alberta M. 1996. *Debt Wish: Entrepreneurial Cities, U.S. Federalism*. University of Pittsburgh Press.

Schattschneider, E. E. 1960. *Semi-Sovereign People*. Holt, Rinehart and Winston.

Schelling, Thomas. 1960. *The Strategy of Conflict*. Harvard University Press.

Schneider, Mark. 1989. *The Competitive City: The Political Economy of Suburbia*. University of Pittsburgh Press.

Schneider, Mark, and Paul Teske. 1995. *Public Entrepreneurs: Agents for Change in American Government*. Princeton University Press.

Schoen, Jeffrey. 1986. "Airport Noise: How State and Local Governments Can Protect Airports from Urban Encroachment." *Arizona State Law Journal*: 309–36.

Schoenbaum, Thomas J., and Richard B. Stewart. 2000. "The Role of Mitigation and Conservation Measures in Achieving Compliance with the Environmental Regulatory Statutes: Lessons from Section 316 of the Clean Water Act." *New York University Environmental Law Journal* 8 (2): 237–331.

Schwartz, Gary T. 1976. "Urban Freeways and the Interstate System." *Southern California Law Review* 49 (3): 406–513.

Scott, Esther. 1993. "Cleaner Air and Clearer Roads: A Plan for the Los Angeles Region." Harvard University, Kennedy School of Government Case Program.

Scott, Stanley, and Levi Davis. 1974. *A Giant in Texas: A History of the Dallas-Fort Worth Regional Airport Controversy*. Nortex Press.

Seely, Bruce Edsall. 1987. *Building the American Highway System: Engineers as Policy Makers*. Temple University Press.

Shapiro, Sidney. 1992. "Lessons from a Public Policy Failure: EPA and Noise Abatement." *Ecology Law Quarterly* 19 (1): 1–61.

Shefter, Martin. 1976. "The Emergence of the Political Machine: An Alternative View." In *Theoretical Perspectives on Urban Politics,* edited by Willis D. Hawley. Prentice-Hall.

Shepsle, Kenneth, and Mark S. Bonchek. 1997. *Analyzing Politics: Rationality, Behavior, and Institutions.* Norton.

Shepsle, Kenneth, and Barry R. Weingast. 1981. "Political Preferences for the Pork-Barrel: A Generalization." *American Journal of Political Science* 25 (1): 96–111.

Siegfried, John, and Andrew Zimbalist. 2000. "The Economics of Sports Facilities and Their Communities." *Journal of Economic Perspectives* 14 (3): 95–114.

Smerk, George M. 1991. *The Federal Role in Urban Mass Transportation.* Indiana University Press.

Smith, Michael Peter, and Marlene Keller. 1983. "Managed Growth and the Politics of Uneven Development in New Orleans." In *Restructuring the City: The Political Economy of Urban Redevelopment,* edited by Susan S. Fainstein and others. Longman.

Sogg, Wilton, and Warren Wertheimer. 1966. "Legal and Governmental Issues in Urban Renewal." In *Urban Renewal: The Record and the Controversy,* edited by James Q. Wilson. MIT Press.

Steinmo, Sven. 1993. *Taxation and Democracy: Swedish, British, and American Approaches to Financing the Modern State.* Yale University Press.

Steinmo, Sven, Kathleen Thelen, and Frank Longstreth, eds. 1992. *Structuring Politics: Historical Institutionalism in Comparative Analysis.* Cambridge University Press.

Steunenberg, Bernard. 1992. "Referendum, Initiative, and Veto Power: Budgetary Decision Making in Local Government." *Kyklos* 45 (4): 501–29.

Stewart, John Patrick. 1995. "The Powertics of Public Policy." Ph.D. dissertation, Pennsylvania State University.

Stockman, David. 1975. "The Social Pork Barrel." *Public Interest*, no. 39 (Spring): 3–30.

———. 1987. *The Triumph of Politics: How the Reagan Revolution Failed.* Avon Books.

Stone, Clarence N. 1965. "Local Referendums: An Alternative to the Alienated Voter Model." *Public Opinion Quarterly* 29 (2): 213–22.

———. 1987. "Summing Up: Urban Regimes, Development Policy, and Political Arrangements." In *The Politics of Urban Development,* edited by Clarence N. Stone and Heywood T. Sanders. University Press of Kansas.

———. 1989. *Regime Politics: Governing Atlanta, 1946–1988.* University Press of Kansas.

———. 1993. "Urban Regimes and the Capacity to Govern: A Political Economy Approach." *Journal of Urban Affairs* 15 (1): 1–28.

Stone, Clarence N., and Heywood T. Sanders. 1987. "Reexamining a Classic Case of Development Politics: New Haven, Connecticut." In *The Politics of Urban Development,* edited by Clarence N. Stone and Heywood T. Sanders. University Press of Kansas.

Stroud, John. 1956. *Famous Airports of the World.* F. Muller.

Talbot, Allan R. 1983. *Settling Things: Six Case Studies in Environmental Mediation.* Washington: Conservation Foundation and New York: Ford Foundation.

Tarr, Joel. 1984. "The Evolution of the Urban Infrastructure in the Nineteenth and Twentieth Centuries." In *Perspectives on Urban Infrastructure,* edited by Royce Hanson. Washington: National Academy Press.

Taylor, Brian. 1995. "Public Perceptions, Fiscal Realities, and Freeway Planning: The California Case." *Journal of the American Planning Association* 61 (1): 43–56.

———. 2000. "When Finance Leads Planning: Urban Planning, Highway Planning, and Metropolitan Freeways in California." *Journal of Planning, Education, and Research* 20 (2): 196–214.

Taylor, Brian, and Eugene Kim. 1999. "The Politics of Rail Transit Planning: A Case Study of the Wilshire Red Line in Los Angeles." University of California, Los Angeles, Department of Urban Planning.

Teaford, Jon C. 1984. *The Unheralded Triumph: City Government in America, 1870–1900.* Johns Hopkins University Press.

———. 1990. *The Rough Road to Renaissance: Urban Revitalization in America, 1940–1985.* Johns Hopkins University Press.

Thelen, Kathleen, and Sven Steinmo. 1992. "Historical Institutionalism in Comparative Perspective." In *Structuring Politics: Historical Institutionalism in Comparative Analysis,* edited by Sven Steinmo and others. Cambridge University Press.

Thomas, Robert D., and Richard W. Murray. 1991. *Progrowth Politics: Change and Governance in Houston.* University of California Press.

Tiebout, Charles M. 1956. "A Pure Theory of Local Expenditures." *Journal of Political Economy* 64 (5): 416–24.

Transportation Research Board and National Research Council. 1991a. *In Pursuit of Speed: New Options for Intercity Passenger Transport.* Washington.

———. 1991b. *Winds of Change: Domestic Air Transport since Deregulation*. Washington.

———. 1995. *Expanding Metropolitan Highways: Implications for Air Quality and Energy Use*. Washington.

Truman, David B. 1951. *The Governmental Process*. Knopf.

Tuegel, Donald. 1998. "Airport Expansions: The Need for a Greater Federal Role." *Washington University Journal of Urban and Contemporary Law* 54 (Summer): 291–318.

Uhl, Raymond T. 1972. "An Evaluation Study of the Airport Development Aid Program FY 1971–72." Report prepared for the U.S. Department of Transportation.

United Kingdom Ministry of Transportation. 1963. *Traffic in Towns: A Study of the Long Term Problems of Traffic in Urban Areas*. London: Her Majesty's Stationery Office.

U.S. Aviation Advisory Commission. 1973. *The Long Range Needs of Aviation: Report of the Aviation Advisory Commission*. Government Printing Office.

U.S. Public Roads Administration. 1939. "Toll Roads and Free Roads." Government Printing Office.

U.S. Senate. 1962. "Hearings on Urban Mass Transit Aid Programs within Housing and Home Finance Agency: Senate Subcommittee on Housing, Committee on Banking and Currency." April 24–27. Government Printing Office.

Vaughan, Roger J. 1983. *Rebuilding America: Financing Public Works in the 1980s*. Washington: Council of State Planning Agencies.

Vaughan, Roger J., and Robert Pollard. 1984. *Rebuilding America: Planning and Managing Public Works in the 1980s*. Washington: Council of State Planning Agencies.

Vig, Norman J., and Michael E. Kraft, eds. 2000. *Environmental Policy: New Directions for the Twenty-First Century*. Congressional Quarterly Press.

Vogel, David. 1993. "Representing Diffuse Interests in Environmental Policymaking." In *Do Institutions Matter? Government Capabilities in the United States and Abroad*, edited by R. Kent Weaver and Bert A. Rockman. Brookings.

Von Hoffman, Alexander. 2000. "A Study in Contradictions: The Origins and Legacy of the Housing Act of 1949." *Housing Policy Debate* 11 (2): 299–326.

Wachs, Martin. 1986. "Technique v. Advocacy in Forecasting: A Study of Rail Rapid Transit." *Urban Resources* 4 (1): 23–30.

———. 1989. "When Planners Lie with Numbers." *Journal of the American Planning Association* 55 (4): 476–79.

———. 1990. "Ethics and Advocacy in Forecasting for Public Policy." *Business and Professional Ethics Journal* 9 (1–2): 144.

———. 1996. "The Evolution of Transportation Policy in Los Angeles: Images of Past Policies and Future Prospects." In *The City: Los Angeles and Urban Theory at the End of the Twentieth Century,* edited by Alan J. Scott and Edward Soja. University of California Press.

Wallis, Allan. 1992a. "Denver's International Airport: A Case Study in Large Scale Infrastructure Development, Part 1." *Municipal Finance Journal* 13 (2): 60–79.

———. 1992b. "Denver's International Airport, Part 2." *Municipal Finance Journal* 13 (3): 62–79.

Warner, Sam Bass, Jr. 1978. *Streetcar Suburbs: The Process of Growth in Boston, 1870–1900.* Harvard University Press.

Webber, Melvin M. 1979. "The BART Experience: What Have We Learned?" In *Current Issues in Transportation Policy,* edited by Alan A. Altshuler. Lexington Books.

Weiner, Andrew. 1975. "Aviation." In *The Commerce Committee,* edited by David Price. Grossman.

Weiss, Marc A. 1985. "The Origins and Legacy of Urban Renewal." In *Federal Housing Policy and Programs: Past and Present,* edited by J. Paul Mitchell. Rutgers University Press.

Wenner, Lettie McSpadden. 1982. *The Environmental Decade in Court.* Indiana University Press.

Whitt, J. Allen. 1982. *Urban Elites and Mass Transportation: The Dialectics of Power.* Princeton University Press.

Whitten, Robert. 1930. "Report on a Thoroughfare Plan for Boston." Report prepared for the Boston City Planning Board.

Wildavsky, Aaron B. 1964. *Leadership in a Small Town.* Bedminster Press.

Wilmsen, Steven K. 1991. *Silverado: Neil Bush and the Savings and Loan Scandal.* National Press Books.

Wilson, James Q. 1973. *Political Organizations.* Basic Books.

———. 1995. *Political Organizations.* 2d ed. Princeton University Press.

———, ed. 1966. *Urban Renewal: The Record and the Controversy.* MIT Press.

Wilson, John R. M. 1979. *Turbulence Aloft: The Civil Aeronautics Administration amid Wars and Rumors of Wars, 1938–1953*. Government Printing Office.

Wirt, Frederick M. 1974. *Power in the City: Decision Making in San Francisco*. University of California Press.

Wohlstetter, Albert C. 1959. "The Delicate Balance of Terror." *Foreign Affairs* 37 (2): 211–34.

Wolfinger, Raymond E. 1971. "Nondecisions and the Study of Local Politics." *American Political Science Review* 65 (4): 1063–80.

Wood, Robert C. 1961. *1400 Governments: The Political Economy of the New York Metropolitan Region*. Harvard University Press.

Woodman, G. Kent, Jane Sutter Starke, and Leslie D. Schwartz. 1995. "Transit Labor Protection—A Guide to Section 13(c)." *Legal Research Digest*, no. 4 (June): 1–32.

Yates, Douglas. 1977. *The Ungovernable City*. MIT Press.

Yuhnke, Robert. 1991. "The Amendments to Reform Transportation Planning in the Clean Air Act Amendments of 1990." *Tulane Environmental Law Journal* 5 (1): 239–53.

Zamora, Anthony N. R. 1989. "The Century Freeway Consent Decree." *Southern California Law Review* 62 (6): 1805–44.

Zeigler, Harmon. 1964. *Interest Groups in American Society*. Prentice-Hall.

Zipp, John. 1996. "Economic Impact of the Baseball Strike of 1994." *Urban Affairs Review* 32 (2): 157–85.

Zwerling, Stephen. 1974. *Mass Transit and the Politics of Technology: A Study of BART and the San Francisco Bay Area*. Praeger.

Index

ABC. *See* Artery Business Committee

ACT. *See* Southeastern Pennsylvania Area Coalition for Transportation

Adams County (Colorado): Denver Airport agreements, 159, 162–63, 226; noise impact of airport, 161; opposition to Stapleton International Airport expansion, 137, 158; referendum on new airport, 163

AFL-CIO, 182, 192

African Americans: Atlanta leaders, 69, 70, 71, 147–49, 183, 189, 267; civil rights movement, 22; desegregation, 263; displaced by highway construction, 88; effects of urban renewal, 22; in Houston, 208; middle class, 70, 71; poor, 22, 88; urban riots, 24–25, 66, 235, 252

AIR-*21*. *See* Wendell H. Ford Aviation Investment and Reform Act for the 21st Century

Airlines: deregulation, 142–44; financial problems, 280; hub-and-spoke route structures, 143, 146, 150; jets, 132–33, 144; leases at Denver airport, 166–67; number of flights, 168; regional, 143–44; use taxes, 141; view of passenger facility charges, 239; yield management pricing, 143, 168. *See also* Air travel

Airmail contracts, 124

Airport improvements: business support, 124, 129, 131, 137, 139–40, 160–61, 163–64, 165, 168–69; capital spending, 133–34, 144; construction sites, 124–25, 129, 135–36, 147, 229; controversies, 26, 133–41; costs, 279; decline in construction, 5, 252; displacement of residents from construction, 136, 152; during Depression, 12, 130; environmental issues, 26–27, 151, 161, 173; expansion opponents, 123, 129, 138, 151, 168; expansions, 124–25, 229; expenditures on, 271; federal aid, 124, 125, 128, 134, 165–66; financing, 16–17, 21, 131, 132, 146–47, 159–60, 166–67, 240–41; funding with passenger facility charges, 152–53, 169, 236, 237, 239, 241; future of, 44, 175, 282; noise mitigation, 150, 229; obstacles and opposition to, 26–27, 123–24, 135–36, 252; passenger capacity increases, 143, 144, 145; in postwar period, 128–33; pressures for, 132–33, 140–41, 168–69,

321

Brookings Institution

The Brookings Institution is an independent organization devoted to non-partisan research, education, and publication in economics, governance, foreign policy, and the social sciences generally. Its principal purposes are to aid in the development of sound public policies and to promote public understanding of issues of national importance. The Institution was founded on December 8, 1927, to merge the activities of the Institute for Government Research, founded in 1916, the Institute of Economics, founded in 1922, and the Robert Brookings Graduate School of Economics and Government, founded in 1924. The Institution maintains a position of neutrality on issues of public policy. Interpretations or conclusions in Brookings publications should be understood to be solely those of the authors.

Lincoln Institute of Land Policy

The Lincoln Institute of Land Policy is a nonprofit and tax-exempt educational institution established in 1974. Its mission as a school is to study and teach land policy, including land economics and land taxation. The Institute is supported primarily by the Lincoln Foundation, which was established in 1947 by Cleveland industrialist John C. Lincoln, who drew inspiration from the ideas of Henry George, the nineteenth-century American political economist and social philosopher.

The Institute's goals are to integrate theory and practice to better shape land policy and to share understanding about the multidisciplinary forces that influence public policy. The Institute seeks to improve the quality of debate and disseminate knowledge of critical issues in land policy by bringing together scholars, policymakers, practitioners, and citizens with diverse backgrounds and experience in planning, development, and property taxation.